Tell the Court I Love My Wife

Race, Marriage, and Law—An American History

Peter Wallenstein

"Indian Foremothers" by Peter Wallenstein, from *The Devil's Lane: Sex and Race in the Early South,* edited by Catherine Clinton and Michele Gillespie, © 1996 by Catherine Clinton and Michele Gillespie. Used by permission of Oxford University Press, Inc.

First published 2002 by
PALGRAVE MACMILLAN™
175 Fifth Avenue, New York, N.Y. 10010 and
Houndmills, Basingstoke, Hampshire, England RG21 6XS.
Companies and representatives throughout the world.

PALGRAVE MACMILLAN IS THE GLOBAL ACADEMIC IMPRINT OF THE PALGRAVE MACMILLAN division of St. Martin's Press, LLC and of Palgrave Macmillan Ltd. Macmillan® is a registered trademark in the United States, United Kingdom and other countries. Palgrave is a registered trademark in the European Union and other countries.

ISBN 0-312-29474-3 hardback

Library of Congress Cataloging-in-Publication Data
Wallenstein, Peter.
Tell the court I love my wife : race, marriage, and law : an American history / by Peter Wallenstein.
p.   cm.
Includes index.
ISBN 0-312-29474-3 (cl)
1. Interracial marriage—Law and legislation—United States—History.   I. Title.
KF 511.W35   2002
346.7301'6—dc21

2002072510

A catalogue record for this book is available from the British Library.

Design by Letra Libre.

First edition: November 2002
10   9   8   7   6   5   4   3   2   1

Printed in the United States of America.

For my miracle,
Sookhan

C ONTENTS

List of Illustrations   ix
Preface   xi

Introduction: "That's No Good Here"   1

PART ONE
Abominable Mixture and Spurious Issue

1. Sex, Marriage, Race, and Freedom in the Early Chesapeake   13

2. Indian Foremothers and Freedom Suits in Revolutionary Virginia   27

3. From the Chesapeake Colonies to the State of California   39

4. Race, Marriage, and the Crisis of the Union   51

PART TWO
Equal Protection of the Laws

5. Post–Civil War Alabama   69

6. Reconstruction and the Law of Interracial Marriage   81

7. Accommodating the Law of Freedom to the Law of Race   95

8. Interracial Marriage and the Federal Courts, 1857–1917   107

Interlude: Polygamy, Incest, Fornication, Cohabitation—
and Interracial Marriage   123

PART THREE
Problem of the Color Line

9. Drawing and Redrawing the Color Line   133

10. Boundaries—Race and Place in the Law of Marriage   147

11. Racial Identity and Family Property   161

12. Miscegenation Laws, the NAACP, and the Federal Courts, 1941–1963   173

PART FOUR
If the Right to Marry Is a Fundamental Right

13. A Breakthrough Case in California 189

14. Contesting the Antimiscegenation Regime—the 1960s 201

15. Virginia versus the Lovings—and the Lovings versus Virginia 215

16. America after *Loving* v. *Virginia* 231

Epilogue: The Color of Love after *Loving* 247

APPENDICES

1. Permanent Repeal of State Miscegenation Laws, 1780–1967 253

2. Intermarriage in Nazi Germany and Apartheid South Africa 255

3. Identity and Authority: An Interfaith Couple in Israel 257

4. Transsexuals, Gender Identity, and the Law of Marriage 259

Notes 261
Index 297

8 pages of illustrations appear between pages 160 and 161.

LIST OF ILLUSTRATIONS

Figure 1. Pocahontas

Figure 2. Chief Justice Roger B. Taney

Figure 3. Abraham Lincoln in 1857

Figure 4. *What Miscegenation Is!* (1865)

Figure 5. Justice John Marshall Harlan

Figure 6. States with miscegenation laws, 1866

Figure 7. States with miscegenation laws, 1874

Figure 8. States with miscegenation laws, 1913–1948

Figure 9. States with miscegenation laws, 1958

Figure 10. States with miscegenation laws, 1966

Figure 11. An extended family—all "white"—in early Oklahoma

Figure 12. Judge Leon F. Bazile, Caroline County (Va.) Circuit Court

Figure 13. The three Loving children

Figure 14. An interracial wedding, 1967

Perhaps this book originated with my discovery, some twenty years ago while writing my first book, of a case in Georgia in the 1850s in which Joseph Nunez's legal right to sell his slaves hinged on his racial identity as a white man—on which there was no agreement. By the early 1990s, I was teaching a course every spring semester on Virginia history, and my research had begun to emphasize Virginia. So in 1990, when Charles D. Lowery and John F. Marszalek invited me to contribute some 200-word entries to a reference work they were editing, *Encyclopedia of African-American Civil Rights* (1992), I picked a number of Virginia items, among them a 1967 Supreme Court case, *Loving* v. *Virginia*. That got me started—and hooked.

Virginia Polytechnic Institute and State University awarded me a Humanities Summer Stipend for work in 1993 on "*Loving* v. *Virginia*: Interracial Marriage, the ACLU, and the Supreme Court." Also in 1993, Paul Finkelman, my colleague at Virginia Tech at the time, urged me to write an essay for a special *Chicago-Kent Law Review* volume (1994) he was editing on "The Law of Freedom," and I chose to develop the Lovings' story and place it in a larger historical context. That essay compared the stories of miscegenation legislation and litigation in Alabama and Virginia across a hundred-year period, from the Civil War to the Civil Rights Movement, and it far exceeded the targeted length. Along the way, I spoke with Bernard S. Cohen, a lawyer who had taken the Lovings' case and had remained close to the family, and he introduced me to Mrs. Loving, who told me more.

I soon conceived this book, and—though often interrupted by other tasks—I continued to work on it, supported in part by the Virginia Tech history department's Frank L. Curtis Research Fund. Meanwhile, other scholars were working up parts of the larger story of sex, marriage, and race in American history. A conversation with Catherine Clinton, who was co-editing *The Devil's Lane: Sex and Race in the Early South* (1997), led me to convert a 1992 conference paper into an essay on "Indian Foremothers" that occasioned my further developing parts of the story, a story that grew ever more complex and compelling. Melvin I. Urofsky, by inviting me to contribute an essay to the *Journal of Supreme Court History* (1998), led me to refine some of my earlier work and push forward on the broader project. Along the way, other papers and publications also contributed to the book. A presentation in 1999 at the University of Akron College of Law occasioned an insistent question by a law student—how, he demanded to know, could states refuse to recognize a valid out-of-state marriage, solely because it was interracial?—to which I eventually found a better answer than I could offer at that time.

To each of these people, and to others as well—among them friends, scholars, and archivists—who have nurtured this book, I am grateful. In particular, Jane Dailey offered astute comments on substantial portions of it. Comments from the anonymous outside readers for St. Martin's Press helped shape the final product, and Deborah Gershenowitz, my magnificent editor at Palgrave, helped me sharpen the focus and trim the book down to size. In the closing stages, John Boyer, in the Virginia Tech geography department, produced the maps, and people from various institutions helped me obtain the illustrations.

Contributing in special ways over the years has been the perception by Sookhan Ho that, twenty years before we had our own wedding in Virginia, we could not have done so. The Lovings' trip to the Supreme Court, she understands, made our shared lives in Virginia fully possible. Sookhan supports my other projects, too, but this one has sustained her special interest, and this book, an anniversary present, is dedicated to her.

It is also dedicated to Mrs. Loving and the memory of Mr. Loving, as well as to the two Kinney families in nineteenth-century Virginia and the many other couples who found themselves entangled in miscegenation laws, who contested the authority of those laws, and whose stories I have tried to tell.

Blacksburg, Virginia
October 5, 2001

"That's No Good Here"

One night in July 1958, two newlyweds suddenly awoke at their home in Caroline County, Virginia, startled by the sound of men in their room and the glare of flashlights on their faces. One of the three intruders demanded to know who they were and what they were doing in bed together. Mildred Loving murmured, "I'm his wife," and Richard Loving pointed to a marriage certificate hanging on the wall. "That's no good here," retorted the trio's leader, Sheriff R. Garnett Brooks. The young couple were arrested and hauled off to the county jail.[1]

Mildred Jeter and Richard Loving had been seeing each other for several years, and during the spring of 1958 they determined that the time had come for them to marry. They had the impression that they could not have their wedding in Virginia, but he thought they would be all right if they went to the District of Columbia. They drove the hundred miles north to the nation's capital, had their ceremony, returned to the community where they had lived all their lives, and moved in with Mrs. Loving's parents.

The issue that had given him pause and led to their trip to the big city—and the problem that led to their arrest that summer night—was that, while Richard Loving was Caucasian, Mildred Jeter was not. It was no crime in Virginia to be white or black, male or female. But it was a crime for two people to marry if one of them was white and the other not. It was a serious crime. Marrying in violation of Virginia's law against interracial marriage could bring a term in the state penitentiary—for at least one year and for as long as five years.

The Lovings were terrified at the prospect of years in prison. They were free while awaiting their trial, but a trial nonetheless loomed. Not only was there no way to turn the clock back to May; they would not have wanted to. They wanted to marry, and they wanted to live together in peace in their rural community. Richard Loving had thought they could do both if they went out of state to marry, but they discovered that the same law banning their getting married in Virginia also outlawed their living together there as an interracial married couple—expressly so, if they had briefly left the state to evade the law that prevented their marrying each other in Virginia.

An Antimiscegenation Regime in a Land of Liberty

The man and woman who wanted to be Mr. and Mrs. Loving were by no means unique in having their freedom threatened because of their racial identities under the law. For generations, other Virginians had encountered similar threats to their happiness, although the specific provisions of Virginia law had changed since the colonial era. A 1691 law had mandated the banishment of white people like Mr. Loving who crossed racial boundaries when they married. Virginia's five-year prison sentence for both parties to an interracial marriage had been enacted in 1878.

Nor was Virginia remotely unique, even as late as 1958. Most of the states in the United States, in the North and the West as well as in the South, had, at one time or another, banned interracial marriages. The term "miscegenation"—the term that was applied to laws that restricted interracial marriage—originated in the North during the Civil War, when Democrats tried to worry voters there that the party of Abraham Lincoln favored interracial marriage. Massachusetts maintained such a law until 1843, shortly before the Civil War, and California did so until 1948, only 10 years before the Lovings' marriage and arrest. At the time of the Lovings' arrest, state laws continued to ban interracial marriages in exactly half of the 48 states—everywhere in the South (17 states extending from Delaware to Texas) and in 7 other states as well.

The threat of imprisonment was less universal than the restrictive laws themselves, and the laws did not all specify the same racial boundaries between the groups that were barred from intermarrying. For many years, California banned marriages between whites and either blacks or Asians; Oklahoma, which classified American Indians—indeed, anyone who had no African ancestry—as "white," outlawed marriages between people who were "of African descent" and people who were "not of African descent." In California, interracial couples were for many years unable to get a marriage license, but such people sometimes went out of state and, unlike the Lovings, moved back home with impunity. Oklahoma had rarely prosecuted anyone for the crime of interracial marriage, but inheritance of property had been tangled up in that state's miscegenation laws many times since statehood in 1907.

These various considerations point up that the law of miscegenation could be both variable and unyielding. Federal authority, generally viewed as inapplicable to the law of marriage, left states with sole jurisdiction in virtually every respect, in much the way that, before the American Revolution, colonies had worked up their own legal environments regarding family matters. In the absence of uniform laws, how individuals and their behavior were classified and treated varied across time and territory. Laws against interracial marriage were enacted as early as Maryland's in 1664, even before some of the 13 colonies had been established; repealed as early as Pennsylvania's action in 1780, during the American Revolution; and elaborated as late as the 1930s, when California, Arizona, Maryland, and Utah all acted to bar men from the Philippines from marrying white women.

According to anthropologist Kingsley Davis—writing in 1941, at the height of the antimiscegenation regime's power—"either intermarriage must be strictly forbidden or racial caste abandoned."[2] Long related to the system of caste in the United States, with cultural forces generally reinforced through public policy, were such important matters as individual identity and group identity, social relationships and family formation, property inheritance and political power.

The long history of the antimiscegenation regime reveals that white privilege did not extend to upholding a white man's right to marry a black woman. The 1691 law—calling for the banishment of a white person who married a nonwhite—supplies an early clue. The greatest taboo was generally attached to a black man marrying a white woman. Yet no white person, whether a man or a woman, should make a formal display of racial equality through a marriage to someone with a nonwhite identity. Better that they carry on a sexual relationship outside marriage than that they formalize their relationship.

Before the 1960s, the U.S. Supreme Court treated miscegenation laws as constitutionally permissible. The Court upheld a miscegenation law in *Pace* v. *Alabama* (1883). The decision in *Plessy* v. *Ferguson* (1896), which for half a century validated the concept of "separate but equal" in American life and law, dealt with segregated transportation but also spoke of laws requiring school segregation and laws against interracial marriage, both of which, it said, had been "universally recognized as within the police power of the state."[3] In *Buchanan* v. *Warley* (1917), both sides agreed that the constitutional issue was closed in transportation, education, and marriage, and that segregation was permissible in each of those areas, but they differed as to whether property rights were violated by city ordinances requiring segregated housing.

What Is a White Man?

In a brief essay published in the late nineteenth century, the mixed-race novelist and short story writer Charles W. Chesnutt asked "What Is a White Man?" Surveying the heterogeneous legal definitions of white and black among the various states in the 1880s, Chesnutt noted wryly that, in a nation, state, or region that trumpeted notions of white supremacy, it was presumably important to know just who belonged to the superior race and who did not. Yet at the time of his writing, "reputation," he said, seemed as important as "admixture" in South Carolina in determining the assignment of racial identity, and racial segregation was widely imposed under the law only "in schools and in the marriage relation."[4]

Soon after Chesnutt wrote, legally mandated segregation spread more thoroughly to public transportation. In the years that followed, states continued to tinker with racial definitions and with their application, and many people found that they were being assigned new racial identities depending on when and where the question arose. The proportion "black" or "white" that defined blackness or whiteness changed. Virginia, for example—abandoning its traditional one-fourth fraction (people were black if as much as one-fourth black)—adopted the fraction one-sixteenth in 1910, and then, in 1924, went all the way to the "one-drop" approach (the idea that one drop of "African blood"—any black African ancestry—made one "black"). In various states, whiteness was a far more exclusive property by 1930 than it had been half a century before. People who had at one time been legally white, and therefore had to marry other whites, could find themselves—whether through the passage of time or by crossing a state line—newly black. Moreover, such states as Virginia, Maryland, and Tennessee made it emphatically clear in the late nineteenth century that valid marriages contracted in one state, if interracial, might not necessarily be imported into another state.

By no means could people be certain when they might face arrest or what might occasion it. Laws might be enforced, or they might not be; they might be applied to a given family, or they might not. Authorities might leave an interracial family unmolested for a long time and yet suddenly bring charges, or they might prosecute and even convict—and then leave the family in peace again. Laws might change—or fail to change—in ways that had profound consequences for entire families. All was contingent, all was contested—miscegenation laws' details, their application, as well as their constitutionality.

Providing weapons that could be deployed at any time, miscegenation laws supplied standby powers that could be brought to bear as changing circumstances, or individual whim, seemed to require. Such standby authority could be used to pursue grudges, challenge status, deny personal freedom, impose incarceration, terminate custody, forfeit property, and, above all, enforce a system of caste.

Power Imposed, Power Resisted

In January 1959, the Lovings went on trial for their crime of marrying each other, just as many interracial couples had before them, first in the American colonies and then in the American states. In those many times and places in U.S. history, partners to a marriage were indicted for a crime that arose for the sole reason that somebody with one racial identity was alleged to have married someone of another racial identity. For the nine years between 1958 and 1967, Mr. and Mrs. Loving lived with the consequences of the Virginia law, challenged that law, and eventually changed it, not only for Virginians but for all Americans.

This book operates at the intersections of race and sex, law and culture, marriage and property, identity and power.[5] It emphasizes the connections between family and state, society and politics. Where the state defined race and regulated marriage, the public sphere sought to govern the most private dimensions of people's lives. In turn, when people challenged the law as it was applied to them, private relationships could shape public policy. *Tell the Court* examines ways in which individuals or groups used—or at least attempted to use—the power of public authority to enhance their private positions, to privilege themselves at the expense of others. It is, in particular, a study of marriage, an exploration of love and pain—pain, penalty, and prejudice inflicted through public authority's threat of separation and imprisonment; longing, love, and loyalty that impelled resistance to all obstacles. It is, finally, a study of power—power imposed, power resisted.

Four chapters on the two centuries from the 1660s to the 1860s provide background, but this book focuses on the period between the 1860s and the 1960s, from the Civil War to the Civil Rights Movement. During that time, miscegenation laws in the United States grew more universal; imposed more severe penalties than had often been applied in the past; and moved the boundary between "white" and "nonwhite" racial identities to make the definition of "white" ever more exclusive, thereby altering the meaning of "interracial." Beginning in the 1940s, the laws came under increasingly successful attack. When the racial barrier in the law of marriage came down with the Lovings' victory in 1967, the last of the segregation laws—the last formal vestige of Jim Crow—had been brought down. In that sense, the Civil Rights Movement had triumphed.

Tell the Court reconstructs the changing law of race and marriage not just by highlighting the findings of various courts but by telling the stories behind a number of court cases. Although the emphasis here is on the South, episodes from throughout the nation reveal the pervasiveness of miscegenation laws and the manifold ways in which they operated to shape individuals' lives and opportunities. These stories reveal not only the law as it was articulated and applied, but the social history and individual experiences that lay behind the court decisions. Tales about changing definitions and contested identities reveal the contingent nature of the law and the chronic uncertainty regarding what it was and how it might be applied to any particular family.

After the Lovings won their Supreme Court case in 1967, their story lived on. Their victory led, more or less immediately, to an end to the enforcement of miscegenation laws not only in Virginia but also in fifteen other states. For the first time, an American man and an American woman could, regardless of their racial identities, marry in any state in the Union and move to any other state. Even when interracial couples no longer ran into legal obstacles to marrying, however, racial considerations could affect the law of marriage, as when a married Caucasian couple broke up, and the parent who won custody of their child subsequently married an African American.

In the 1990s, many articles in law reviews referred to the *Loving* decision, but by then, the great question in many minds was no longer whether two people with different racial identities could marry but, rather, whether two people of the same sex could. The nation's long experience with miscegenation laws provided a history analogous to the emerging controversy over same-sex marriages. On election day 1998, when voters in South Carolina removed a provision in their state constitution against interracial marriage, their counterparts in Hawaii and Alaska put provisions against same-sex marriages into their constitutions. In November 2000, voters in Alabama echoed South Carolina, taking out the last remnant of the pre-*Loving* past, while their counterparts in Nebraska and Nevada emulated Hawaii and Alaska.

But this book is about the law of marriage as it has related to race in American history, and the law of race as it has related to marriage. Richard Loving's plea to his attorneys in 1967, to "tell the court I love my wife," proved timely.[6] For most of the untold numbers of people who came before, such pleas brought no relief from judges or juries. After the Supreme Court ruled in the Lovings' case, couples no longer had to worry about the law of interracial marriage. That law had vanished, vanished so completely that people growing up a generation later typically had no understanding that such laws—which had lasted so long, been so widespread, and affected so many Americans, "white" and "nonwhite"—had ever been in place.

King Color—Race Rules—the Antimiscegenation Regime

Most physical anthropologists have long come to the conclusion that "race" is a myth, that its biological basis is far less evident or significant than its social, cultural, psychological, or legal consequences.[7] Yet those consequences are very real. In many places and at many times, race has governed, with extraordinary power, all kinds of human relations. If it has been a myth, then, "race" has certainly not been a myth powerless to shape and reshape the world people live in. Its impact on the law of marriage, a core institution in society and in many—even most—individuals' lives, is the subject of this book.

Because racial considerations—racial identity, racial politics—have bewitched so many Americans for so many years, scholars are necessarily drawn to study the history of "race" and bring its workings a bit further into the light. In this enterprise, the terms "black" and "white," whatever they may have meant in the twentieth century, must not automatically be assumed to categorize all individuals in the deeper past in the same ways. The preponderance of evidence undermines any notion that a "one-drop rule" prevailed in all times and places. Nor can it be assumed that, at any time or place, all parties agreed on the definition or the significance of racial identity—or that, whatever its general meaning, its application in any particular case automatically followed. The presence of racial categories and terms in the American past is undisputed; their meaning is not. I prefer the term "racial identity"—whether adopted by or imposed upon an individual—to "race."

I have termed "the antimiscegenation regime" the complex of power and policies that long supported legal restrictions on what marital partners people with various racial identities were allowed to choose from—and what groups were forbidden. The antimiscegenation regime—a racial regime specifically targeting matters of marriage—lasted from the 1660s to the 1960s. It grew with the nation and once covered much of the North American continent. Subsequently, however, as one American state after another abandoned it, the antimiscegenation regime grew smaller in space and power. Tracking the system's rise and fall, *Tell the Court* explores first the ramifications of its long hold on power and then the process by which it shrank and then was toppled.

The degree of formal equality in suffrage and marriage in American history—the presence or absence of racial barriers to voting and marrying—tended to rise and fall together. In the northern states before the Civil War, the two issues often appeared as twin concerns. In the *Dred Scott* decision in 1857, Chief Justice Roger B. Taney made the linkage when he pressed his thesis that, even after slavery, black northerners were denied anything approaching complete freedom under the law—that, slave or free, surely they were not widely perceived by whites as citizens. Taney's best evidence that white Americans had not meant African Americans to be citizens came from a combination of miscegenation laws and disfranchisement provisions in northern states in the first generation after U.S. independence.

In the century between the Civil War and the Civil Rights Movement, developments in those two dimensions of liberty and empowerment—marriage rights across racial lines and voting rights among African Americans—moved more or less in tandem. In the 1860s, when the Civil War brought slavery to an end as a formal means of dominating black southerners, white southerners swiftly put new power behind miscegenation laws to govern race relations. From the late 1860s through the mid-1870s, when black men shared power with whites in the 11 states of the former Confederacy, the miscegenation laws were lifted in 7 of those states. But by the late 1870s, black political power was sharply curtailed across much of the South, and the miscegenation laws were soon restored there. At about the same time, by contrast, heightened black political power in such northern states as Illinois and Ohio led to the repeal of miscegenation laws there. The renewed divergence of the North from the South in the 1880s pointed the way, even at the dawn of the Age of Segregation, toward a new struggle that eventually brought an end to that era.

Between the 1850s and the 1960s, a transformation took place in voting rights and miscegenation laws. In 1965, after a long interlude, the Voting Rights Act signaled a far greater role for black southerners in state and national politics. Two years later, the antimiscegenation regime was toppled from power across the South—in the last 17 states where it had held on. With *Loving* v. *Virginia* in 1967, the inverse of the *Dred Scott* decision had been brought to life. The U.S. Constitution, American citizenship, and the law of marriage had been brought once again into consistency—this time with a very different resolution.

An American History

The subject of race, marriage, and the law reaches out and affects a universe of matters, from the inheritance of property to the history of segregation, each of which looks different when seen in the light of the history of miscegenation laws. Many books on such matters as marriage, family, race, law, property, privacy, civil rights, and immigration do not bring in the subject of this book at all, and few of them give it much prominence. Perhaps it should be otherwise. Surely the notion of an almost stateless society of free individuals freely constructing their lives, freely choosing their life partners, entirely misses the stories of the people whose lives, in part, I have tried to recount.

Fiction writers and academic scholars have explored various dimensions of the history of race, sex, identity, and marriage in U.S. history. Yet sustained work on the broad subject of the legal history of interracial marriage has remained scant into the twenty-first century. Portions of the terrain have been mapped out, yet much of the topography remains largely uncharted.[8] This book—a social, political, and legal history—is offered as a contribution toward a more complete exploration of that strange land. By no means does it seek to be encyclopedic, but, by examining various facets of the larger story, it seeks to supply a historical context and outline a reliable interpretive structure within which to understand those aspects.

Tell the Court is an American history. It is not only about people identified as African Americans (though they appear in every chapter), or Native Americans (who dominate the story line in at least one chapter), or Asian Americans (who are at the center of change in the mid-twentieth century), or European Americans (who are ubiquitous in the story of marriage, race, and law). It is about all Americans—those who did marry across some line that separated racial identities; those who might have so married had the law been different; and also those who could not accept the notion that they or their relatives might do so or that anyone should. The subject of race, marriage, and the law has vital connections across the sweep of U.S. history, through the eras of the American Revolution and the Constitution, the Civil War and Reconstruction, and the Cold War and the Great Society, and from slavery to emancipation to the Civil Rights Movement.

Notes on Language

"Miscegenation"—a noun that refers to marriage or sexual relations between a man of one racial identity and a woman of another—is typically used in this book as an adjective referring to laws that regulated interracial marriage. Those laws were intended, of course, to curtail such marriage—they were "antimiscegenation" laws. But I have generally limited the use of the prefix to the term "antimiscegenation regime." States exhibiting allegiance to the antimiscegenation regime each supported a system of laws that in some manner defined racial identity and regulated behavior according to that identity, but the term "antimiscegenation regime" has specific application to restrictions on interracial marriage.

This book retains the original spelling when documents are quoted, even if that spelling is archaic (as it often is in the laws of early Virginia and Maryland) or idiosyncratic.

PART ONE

ABOMINABLE MIXTURE AND SPURIOUS ISSUE

SEX, MARRIAGE, RACE, AND
FREEDOM IN THE EARLY CHESAPEAKE

"For prevention of that abominable mixture and spurious issue which hereafter may encrease in this dominion, as well by negroes, mulattoes, and Indians intermarrying with English, or other white woman, as by their unlawfull accompanying with one another"

—Law of Virginia (1691)

No wedding photos, no baby pictures, commemorate the events. John Rolfe and Pocahontas married in 1614, and their son Thomas was born in 1615, when the English colony that was planted in 1607 at Jamestown, Virginia, was still very new. Multiracial Virginians originated as early as that time, and many people—sojourners and residents, English and Native Americans alike—welcomed the interracial marriage that enhanced the likelihood of peace in the Chesapeake region of North America.[1]

No law at that time specifically governed interracial sex, interracial marriage, or multiracial children. Law or no law, few whites married Native Americans in colonial Virginia, so the union of John Rolfe and Pocahontas proved a notable exception. Restrictive laws, when they emerged, reflected lawmakers' overriding concerns regarding Virginians of African ancestry, but they affected people in all other groups, too. At about the same time that Virginia began to legislate on the identity and status of mixed-race people, Maryland did as well.

When slavery supplanted servitude in supplying a labor force for the Chesapeake colonies, more African Americans lived in Virginia and Maryland combined than in all the other British North American colonies put together. For some years after the American Revolution, the two states on the Chesapeake Bay continued to contain a majority of all people with African ancestry living in the new nation. Thus the Chesapeake region generated the dominant experience of black and multiracial people in the settler societies of British North America and the early American republic.

Race, sex, slavery, and freedom commingled with society, economics, politics, and law in Virginia and Maryland in various and changing ways. In 1607—just before men on three ships from England made their way up what they named the James River, arrived at a place they called Jamestown, and established a colony there—the many residents of the Chesapeake region were all Native Americans. Over the next two centuries, newcomers and their progeny from both Europe and Africa soared in numbers while Indians seemed to vanish.

If the patterns had been more simple than they were, it might be possible to speak as though everyone was either white or black, and as though all blacks were slaves, whether in 1750 or 1850. But such was not the case, and boundaries were not so clear. Some black residents were free; Indians refused to vanish; and many people in Maryland and Virginia were multiracial. Some mixed-race people, though born unfree, were designated to remain so only for specific (though lengthy) periods—18, 21, 30, or 31 years. Some people, moreover, though born into lifelong slavery, gained their freedom.

Within marriage or outside it, people of European origin had children with Native Americans or people of African ancestry. This chapter and the next explore each of those complicating features of the social landscape, emphasizing two groups, those descended from white mothers and black (or mixed-race) fathers and those claiming Indian foremothers. Both chapters focus on a region— where most Virginians lived, east of the Blue Ridge mountains—whose population, in the years between 1760 and 1860, was roughly half white and half nonwhite, half free and half slave. In many times and places, only a minority was white, yet only a minority was slave. Tilting the balance was a middle group of people who were considered free but not white. This chapter takes a fresh look at their origins. In particular, it offers a history of the beginnings of legal restrictions on marriage between colonists who were defined as white and people who were defined as nonwhite.

Like Mother, Like Child

Before a law of race could fully develop, definitions of racial categories had to be put in place. In seventeenth-century Virginia and Maryland, these took a while to develop, although some kind of line separating white from nonwhite was ever-present. When, for example, the Virginia House of Burgesses wanted to refer to people of various groups, Europeans might variously be termed "Christians," "English," and "English or other white" persons. Race or color, religion, language or nation of origin—any category might do. Other people tended to get lumped under such categories as "negroes, mulattoes, and other slaves"; "negroe slaves"; "Indians or negroes manumitted, or otherwise free"; and any "negroe, mulatto, or Indian man or woman bond or free."[2]

In 1662, Virginia's colonial assembly first addressed the question of the status of the children of interracial couples. The question before the legislators was whether "children got by any Englishman upon a negro woman should be slave or ffree." The new law supplied a formula: "all children borne in this country [shall be] held bond or free only according to the condition of the mother."[3]

According to the 1662 law, children would follow the status of their mothers. Slave women would have slave children, regardless of who the father was; if she were a slave, then any child she had, even with a white father, would be a slave. Free women, whether white or not, would have free children, again no matter who the father was; if the woman was free, her child—black, white, or mixed-race—would be free too. All depended on whether the woman—whatever her racial identity—was slave or free. The father's identity did not matter, so neither could his race or his status. Moreover, the 1662 law assumed that the mixed-race child was born to a couple who were not married to each other—in many cases, a slave woman and the white man who owned her. It did not address the question of interracial marriage itself.

Marriage, Children, and the Racial Identity of the Father

A successor act in 1691 took on the matter of marriage. That year, the Virginia assembly took action against sexual relations between free whites and nonwhites, at least in certain circumstances, regardless of whether the couple were single or had married. As a rule, colonial governments and churches fostered marriages between adults, but—reflecting a widespread pattern in colonial America—the Virginia assembly was not necessarily going to do any such thing regarding interracial unions. Slaves could contract no marriages that the law recognized. Free people could, but, after 1691, white people were not free to marry across racial lines. Prior to this time, some white women had married nonwhite men; the assembly tried to curtail the practice, punish infractions, and contain the consequences.[4]

The 1691 act, couched in the language of hysteria rather than legalese, was designed "for prevention of that abominable mixture and spurious issue which hereafter may encrease in this dominion, as well by negroes, mulattoes, and Indians intermarrying with English, or other white woman, as by their unlawfull accompanying with one another." In the cultural world that these legislators inhabited, it was anathema for white women to have sexual relations with nonwhite men. For the relationship to be sanctified in marriage was no better—if anything, it was worse—than if the couple remained unwed.[5]

The 1691 statute targeted sexual relations between white women and black men (the "abominable mixture") and the children of such relationships (the "spurious issue"). The first thing the new law did was to outlaw interracial marriage for white men and white women alike. Actually, it did not ban the marriage but, rather, mandated the banishment of the white party to any interracial marriage that occurred, if that person was free and thus owed labor to no planter: "Whatsoever English or other white man or women being free shall intermarry with a negroe, mulatto, or Indian man or woman bond or free, shall within three months after such marriage be banished and removed from this dominion forever."[6] If the bride in the interracial couple was white, then she would vanish from Virginia, and her mixed-race child would be born and raised outside Virginia.

The law began by condemning all marriages between whites and nonwhites, but its main intent was to target white women who strayed across racial lines, whether they actually married nonwhite men or not. An occasional white woman, even though unmarried, would have a child whose father was "negro or mulatto" (here lawmakers did not include Indians). Concerned about that contingency, legislators targeted the white mothers of interracial children—"if any English woman being free shall have a bastard child by any negro or mulatto," she must, within a month of the birth, pay a fine of 15 pounds sterling to the church wardens in her parish. Her crime, such as it was, entailed a sexual relationship with a nonwhite man—in particular, a relationship that resulted in a mixed-race child.[7]

If the white mother of a multiracial child was free but could not pay the fine, the church wardens were to auction off her services for five years. The penalty called for her to pay in either money or time, property or liberty. But if she was an indentured servant, the law did not mean to punish her owner by denying him her labor (and thus his property). If she was a servant and thus not the owner of her own labor at the time of the offense, her sale for five years would take place after she had completed her current indenture.

In view of the provision for banishment, few white Virginians involved in interracial marriages would still be in the colony when their children came along. But this addressed only the question of the children—the "spurious issue"—of white women who actually went through a wedding ceremony, whose relationship would have been, before 1691, lawful. What about children whose parents' "accompanying with one another" was "unlawful"—that is, the couple was unmarried? Any "such bastard child," mixed-race and born in Virginia, was to be taken by the wardens of the church in the parish where the child was born and "bound out as a servant . . . untill he or she shall attaine the age of thirty yeares."[8]

If the mother stayed in Virginia and retained her freedom, therefore, she lost her child, who would be bound out as a servant until the age of 30. As is evident from this act, mixed-race children troubled the Virginia assembly if their mothers were white, not if they were black. The old rule continued to operate for the mixed-race children of white fathers, but a new rule targeted the problem of mixed-race children of white mothers. The law said nothing, however, about the nonwhite father of a white woman's child. It imposed no penalty of loss of labor or liberty, though it surely broke up any family there might have been. The father was important to the law because, regardless of whether he was free or slave, he was nonwhite and had fathered a child by a white woman. But the penalties were imposed on the woman and the child.

The status, slave or free, of the child of a white man and a black woman continued, under the 1662 law, to depend on the status of the mother. The 1691 legislature worried about other questions, and it devised a new rule to address them. The new rule meant that the father's identity could be as important as the mother's. By 1691, the central question regarding the status of a child in Virginia had to do with whether the mother was white or black as much as whether she was free or slave. Most black women were slaves, so most children of black women would be slaves, although nonslave, nonwhite mothers would still bear nonslave children. If the mother was white, the answer depended on the racial identity of the father.

The legislature had, as its primary object, seeing that white men retained exclusive sexual access to scarce white women. It also had, as a significant secondary object, propelling the mixed-race children of a white mother out of the privileged white category and into a racial category that carried fewer rights, and out of the group born free and into long-term servitude to a white person.[9]

Eighteenth-Century Amendments

Legislation in 1705 modified the 1691 statute in several significant ways. In framing an act "declaring who shall not bear office in this country" that excluded "any negro, mulatto, or Indian," the Virginia legislature defined "mulatto"—for the purpose of "clearing up all manner of doubts" that might develop regarding "the construction of this act, or any other act"—as "the child, grand child, or great grand child, of a negro."[10] It thereby defined as "mulatto" any mixed-race Virginian with at least one-eighth African ancestry. The statute probably sufficed at the time to exclude virtually all Virginians with any traceable African ancestry. In 1705, only some 86 years after the arrival in 1619 of the first black immigrants to the Virginia colony, probably few great-great-grandchildren of a black Virginian had yet been born, let alone grown old enough to marry or hold public office.

Under another new provision enacted in 1705—designed "for a further prevention of that abominable mixture and spurious issue"—a white Virginian would face six months in prison and a fine, rather than suffer exile, for entering into a marriage with a nonwhite partner, defined as "a negro or mulatto man or woman, bond or free."[11] The 1705 legislation therefore did two main things. It expressly banned marriages between whites and nonwhites, upon penalty of a fine and imprisonment for the white offender, and it defined "mulatto" and equated it, for various legal purposes including the regulation of marriage, with "negro."

Moreover, the 1705 bill set a fine of 10,000 pounds of tobacco for any preacher who officiated at a marriage between a white and a nonwhite; half that amount would go to the colony and half to the informer. In view of this penalty, preachers would not likely get involved in ceremonies that violated the law, so the law was, in that sense, self-enforcing. According to the 1705 law, in addition, any child that might result from a sexual relationship, outside of wedlock, between a white woman and a nonwhite man would be bound as a servant until the age of 31, rather than 30. What continued to matter—little had changed since 1691—was that the mother was white and the father black, not whether the woman was a servant or free.[12]

A 1723 law extended to the next generation the time of servitude established for mixed-race Virginians born under the laws of 1691 and 1705—the mixed-race, nonslave grandchildren of white women through their mixed-race daughters. Hereafter, "where any female mullatto, or indian, by law obliged to serve 'till the age of thirty or thirty-one years, shall during the time of her servitude, have any child born of her body, every such child shall serve the master or mistress of such mullatto or indian, until it shall attain the same age the mother of such child was by law obliged to serve unto."[13] The terms of 30 or 31 years were to be inherited, from mother to child. In effect, a third category had been established with reference to the 1662 law, and just as slave women bore slave children, and free women bore free children, these mixed-race long-term servants bore mixed-race long-term servants.

The 1723 act went far to perfect Virginia's laws of race and slavery. The same statute barred slave owners from freeing any of their "negro, mullatto, or indian slaves." Perfecting the 1705 law against nonwhites holding public office, it declared, too, that "no free negro, mullatto, or indian" would vote in any subsequent election.[14]

The rules changed again in 1765, when the Virginia assembly relaxed the terms of its 1691, 1705, and 1723 legislation in one important respect. Declaring the terms of 30 or 31 years for mixed-race descendants of black men and either free white mothers or women servants—whether the first or subsequent generations—to be "an unreasonable severity to such children," the legislature reduced the terms to 18 years for females and 21 years for males. These were the same numbers the legislature applied when unmarried white women, whether servants or free, had white children who would otherwise become public charges.[15]

Virginia acted as early as 1691 and 1705 to outlaw marriage between whites and nonwhites. After 1691, the broad contours of Virginia's laws on race, sex, and marriage persisted through the colonial era, the American Revolution, and even the Civil War. One significant change, in 1785, redefined a "white" person as someone with less than one-quarter, rather than one-eighth, African ancestry. Another, after the Civil War, provided prison terms for both parties, black and white, in an interracial marriage.[16] Under Virginia law, there never was a time—from the 1690s to the 1960s—that a marriage across racial lines involving someone defined as a white person did not carry severe penalties.

"Bond or Free Only According to the Condition of the Mother"

By the eighteenth century, two major rules had come into play to determine the destinies of mixed-race children. If the mother was black and the father white, the law wanted only to know the status of the mother; the child's status, slave or free, would follow the mother's. But if the mother was white, then the law inquired into the identity of the father. If the father was black, then the mother was penalized—fined or sold into five years of servitude—and the child entered a very long period of unfreedom as a servant.

Individual stories help illustrate the complexity of these laws. An unnamed "Christian white woman" had a daughter, Betty Bugg, whose father was black. Under the 1705 Virginia law, Betty Bugg was to be a servant to the age of 31. During her servitude, she had a son, who in 1769, while in his twenties, brought suit for his freedom. His master's lawyer thwarted the effort. He conceded that the 1705 statute required mixed-race children like Betty Bugg (whose mothers were not slaves) to be bound out for 31 years but, silent on the status of their children, presumably left them free. The 1723 act, however, required children of that next generation, too, to live as servants to age 31.[17]

Bugg's son was born after 1723, so he was subject to that law, not its 1705 predecessor. Born after 1723 but before 1765, he was born too late to gain his freedom at birth and too soon to obtain it at age 21. Yet his bondage was not for life; he, like his mother, would become free at age 31.

Sarah Madden and her family demonstrate a variant version of the Virginia laws of race and sex at work. Her mother, Mary Madden, who probably came to Virginia from Ireland in the 1750s as an indentured servant, gave birth to a mulatto daughter, Sarah, on August 4, 1758. Sarah Madden, bound out until the age of 31, finally gained her freedom in 1789 (the year a new national government began operations under the U.S. Constitution). In the meantime, she had children of her own, beginning with Rachel in 1776 (the year of the Declaration of Independence), who presumably gained her own freedom at the age of 18 in 1794. Another child, David, born in 1780, likely gained his freedom at the age of 21 in 1801, soon after his sister Betty, born in 1782, reached the age of 18 and shortly before Polly, born in 1785, did so.[18]

Sarah Madden's seventh child, Fanny, came along on July 6, 1789, just weeks before Madden turned 31. Had Fanny been born a month later—after Sarah Madden turned 31—she would have gained her freedom at birth, instead of having to wait until 1807. Nelly, by contrast, was born in 1793, and Nancy in 1796, so they were born free, as was Willis, born in 1799. As for Sarah Madden's daughters, they appear to have waited until at least the age of 18 before having any children of their own. Sarah Madden's grandchildren (more precisely, her daughters' children) were therefore born free. So were her own children who were born in the 1790s—but not she herself and not the children she bore between the Declaration of Independence and the ratification of the U.S. Constitution.[19] Sarah Madden's children exemplified how, even after the American Revolution—under the series of laws that began in 1691 and continued through 1705, 1723, and 1765—long-term, mixed-race servants continued to be born to long-term, mixed-race, women servants.

Regardless of Sarah Madden's experience, the decade between the Declaration of Independence and the Constitutional Convention of 1787 brought important changes to the law of race and slavery in Virginia. In 1778, during the American Revolution, the legislature of the new state of Virginia passed a law declaring that "no slave or slaves shall hereafter be imported into this commonwealth by sea or land"—that is, brought in for sale, whether from outside the United States or even from another state—and "every slave imported into this commonwealth, contrary to . . . this act, shall upon such importation become free." The children of slave women would continue to be born into lifelong slavery, but the only other way for new slaves to come to inhabit Virginia would be if their owners moved with them from another state.[20]

A Legislated Path from Black Slavery to Black Freedom

In 1782, the Virginia legislature went beyond curtailing the growth of slavery through commerce and provided authority for slave owners to free their slaves. Owners could, without restriction, emancipate slave women between the ages of

18 and 45 and slave men between the ages of 21 and 45, provided the new freedpeople were "of sound mind and body." Otherwise, the new right carried significant restrictions. Slaves younger than 18 or 21 and older than 45, as well as slaves between those ages who were not "of sound mind and body," could be freed only if the former owners "supported" them, that is, saw that the people newly freed did not become charges upon the county. George Washington, for one, provided for the freedom of all his many slaves.[21]

The manumission law of 1782 held without material change until 1806, when the legislature mandated that, in the future, slaves who gained their freedom must leave the state within a year or forfeit their freedom.[22] County officials could still permit newly freed people to stay, but the privilege of staying could be denied, and by that time the willingness of slave-owning Virginians to manumit some of their human property had receded.

Beginning in 1782, therefore, slavery in Virginia was, in effect, redefined. Enslavement was still defined as lifelong, and it was still inherited from a slave mother, but owners could now (more readily than before) free their slaves. As had been the case ever since the 1662 law clarified matters, nonwhite women, if free, would bear free children. In all those years, because there had never been many free nonwhite women, few nonwhite children had been born free. Beginning in 1782, through manumission, the number of people in Virginia who though nonwhite were free began rapidly to grow. Whether slavery proved to be lifelong had become contingent—it now depended on how the new legal environment in Virginia affected that individual. After growing rapidly in the 24 years beginning in 1782, Virginia's free nonwhite population continued to increase each decade from the 1810s through the 1850s, though it did so at a much more modest pace.

During the last half century of Virginia slavery, approximately one in ten nonwhite Virginians were free. The number of free nonwhites grew by more than half in the 1790s, to 20,124, and then to 30,570 by 1810. The number of counties increased in which that group's presence made it possible for a majority of residents to be free even though only a minority of residents were white. By 1830, the Tidewater region as a whole displayed that pattern—48.6 percent of all residents were slaves and 7.6 percent were free nonwhites—as did the cities of Richmond and Petersburg and such counties as Southampton and Surry.[23]

Race, Sex, and Suits for Freedom

There were three main ways, not just two, in which the population of free nonwhite Virginians grew in the late eighteenth century. Certainly some people were born to free mothers who were classified as nonwhite, whether they were black, Indian, or mixed-race. Far more Virginians gained their freedom from owners who, whatever their motivation, determined to manumit one or more of their slaves. But a third group consisted of people who went to court to force the question and in that manner, if successful, won their freedom. Although held as slaves, they contested the matter with people who had every intention of remaining, if they could, in the slave-owning business.

In one case, Nanny Pagee, who was held as a slave, along with her children, sued for her freedom on the grounds that she had been brought illegally into Virginia from North Carolina as a slave after passage of the 1778 act and thus should be free—and, moreover, that she was a white woman. At the trial, she was inspected—her hair, for example, was examined, and her fingertips—in an effort to determine whether she was indeed white. The court, determining that she appeared to be white, and with no evidence introduced to show her to be the daughter of a slave woman, declared her free—she had been held as a slave for over 30 years—and thus her children (though perhaps the mixed-race offspring of a slave father) were free as well. The appeals court upheld the trial court's reasoning and conclusion, so she "(and of course her children)" gained their freedom.[24]

The courts were solicitous of freedom suits. They demonstrated a willingness to consider the freedom claims of Virginians and, with some frequency, to come down on the side of freedom. Perhaps the relative prevalence of a long-term, but finite, status of unfreedom—an intermediate station between slave and free—helps explain why the courts felt obligated to scrutinize freedom suits as possibly meritorious. The possibility that white people might get caught up in slavery offers another explanation. Still another reason for their willingness often to side with the plaintiffs relates to ideas of human liberty that came out of the American Revolution.

The American Revolution related to American slavery in powerful, but contradictory, ways. The presence of slaves at Monticello, Mount Vernon, and elsewhere in eighteenth-century Virginia symbolized—in the most graphic of ways—what a loss of freedom could mean; in that sense, slavery by itself energized free colonists to become rebels and fight to safeguard their own freedom. Fighting for their own freedom, but not necessarily for freedom as a universal right, the rebels created a nation that provided a haven for black slavery to grow and prosper. Along the way, nonetheless, even in the South, the Revolution's ideas could relax the hold that slavery had on individual Americans who had some African ancestry.

Race, Marriage, Slavery, and Freedom in Early Maryland

Virginia was not the first of the British North American colonies to enact laws restricting interracial marriage, and it surely was not the last. In Maryland as in Virginia, whites dominated, but three races mingled. Maryland—Virginia's twin, across the Potomac River and the Chesapeake Bay—also imported slaves, exported tobacco, and regulated its labor supply and its multiracial society. Regarding interracial marriage, Maryland acted first.

In 1681, when Lord Baltimore returned to Maryland after four years away in England, he brought with him "Irish Nell," a servant who had been born a free white female named Eleanor Butler. In August of that year, Irish Nell married a slave known as Negro Charles.

The Catholic Church blessed the marriage; the Maryland legislature condemned it. Nell immediately fell under a 1664 Maryland law that had been designed, it declared, "for deterring such freeborne women from such shamefull Matches." That law intoned that "whatsoever free borne woman shall inter marry with any slave . . . shall serve the master of such slave dureing the life of her husband," and "all the Issue of such freeborne women soe marryed, shall be slaves as their fathers were." Negro Charles lived a long life—he was still living in 1730—and Irish Nell evidently remained a servant all those years. Her children lived and worked, like their father, as slaves in Maryland. So did her children's children and their children.[25]

The 1664 law itself lasted a far shorter time. The Maryland colonial legislature repealed it in 1681, very soon after Nell's marriage. For one thing, as a lawyer arguing on behalf of freedom for Nell's progeny—an effort that failed later explained, it was repealed "to prevent persons from purchasing white women and marrying them to their slaves for the purpose of making slaves of them."[26] Perhaps, too, the thought occurred to slave owners that their investment in a slave man might be in jeopardy if a white wife took it into her head to terminate her servitude by ending his life.

During the time that the 1664 Maryland law was in effect, an offending white woman's interracial marriage subjected her to being expelled from the land of freedom into the world of slavery—or from servitude for perhaps seven years to servitude until her husband died—and, in effect, from a white racial identity to a black one. Though she had been born free as well as white, her children, partly "black" and partly "white," would be born into lifetime slavery—not free, as neighboring Virginia's 1662 law provided, nor even subject to a mere 30 or 31 years of servitude, as Virginia's 1691 and 1705 laws might have imposed. Before the repeal, the 1664 law had been in place for 17 years, and under it any number of people became slaves. The 1664 Maryland act, though it laid down the law of race and marriage for only a few years, made all the difference between slavery and freedom for many hundreds of mixed-race people through the next two centuries.

Irish Nell and Her Mixed-Race Descendants—Slave or Free?

By the time of the American Revolution, the law of race and marriage in Maryland and Virginia had long been producing slaves and long-term servants. But perhaps the law of racial lineage could be turned against slavery. The 1664 Maryland law, followed by its repeal in 1681, led to a variety of freedom suits during the eighteenth century and after, as the descendants of Irish Nell—and descendants of some other white women in her situation—sought their freedom. Irish Nell's marriage took place while the 1664 act was still in effect, but the 1681 repealed that act, and her children were all born after it. The question was, must the law forever consider them to be slaves?

The matter could be argued either way, and it was. In 1763, a century after the 1664 act was passed, two of the people whom Richard Boarman held as slaves, William Butler and Mary Butler, began a freedom suit against him that, as historian Lorena S. Walsh writes, "threatened the livelihood of his family and frightened slaveowners throughout Maryland and northern Virginia."[27]

The Butlers failed in their attempt in the courts to secure their freedom, but a number of subsequent efforts proved successful. In 1783, Eleanor Toogood won a freedom suit on the basis of her descent from Mary Fisher, a white woman who, more than a hundred years earlier, had married a slave named Dick. And as a result of the legal reasoning that led to Eleanor Toogood's victory, Mary Butler—daughter of the Mary Butler who had sued unsuccessfully for her freedom in 1763—won her freedom in 1791.[28]

A white woman, Elizabeth Shorter, married a slave named Little Robin in 1681, the same year Irish Nell married Negro Charles. The couple's children— all slaves—included Moll Shorter, whose daughter, Linda Shorter, became the mother of Basil Shorter, who, a few years after the American Revolution, went to court to see if he could secure his freedom. Basil Shorter came from a long line of slaves, but a Maryland court accepted the argument that, having descended in the female line from a white woman, he should not be held as a slave. In 1794, he became a free man. Across the quarter-century between 1783 and 1808, various Marylanders with mixed European and African ancestry shed their slavery in this way.[29]

The Crime of Giving Birth—and the Crime of Being Born

The child of a slave woman was also a slave. For a time, as we have seen, the child of a white woman and a slave man could be a slave. But those did not exhaust the legal possibilities. A Maryland woman who had a child with a black man might see that child born into servitude for a period identical to Virginia's terms of 30 or 31 years. The same 1664 law that made Irish Nell a slave also declared—in a way that more closely matched Virginia's 1691 law—that, regarding white women who had married slave men before its enactment, their children were to "serve the Master of their Parents till they be Thirty years of age and noe longer."[30]

Laws subsequent to 1664 and 1681 made similar provisions for long-term servitude for any mixed-race children of unmarried free women, whether those women were white, black, or mixed-race. Hannah Allen, a white woman from Scotland, was the mother, by a "negro," of a daughter also named Hannah Allen, who in turn had a daughter, also by a black man, named Jane Allen. In 1772, Jane Allen had a son, Nathaniel Allen, by a black man. Under the terms of Maryland laws dating from 1715 to 1728, she was sold that summer as a servant for 7 years, and the son, 5 months old at the time, was sold to Richard Higgins as a servant until the age of 31.[31]

In 1794, Nathaniel Allen sued for his freedom from Richard Higgins, and the Anne Arundel County Court—on the basis of Nathaniel Allen's descent from a free white woman, the first Hannah Allen, his great-grandmother—awarded him his freedom. Higgins appealed the decision, and the Maryland General Court reversed the lower court and consigned Allen to continued servitude. The record showed Jane Allen's conviction in 1772 for "having a mulatto bastard," the General Court ruled, and Nathaniel Allen had no claim to freedom until 1803.[32]

Miscegenation and Its Consequences: The Colonial and Revolutionary Chesapeake

In both Virginia and Maryland, beginning in the seventeenth century, racial identity had tremendous power to open up or close down opportunities for social advancement—to permit upward mobility or to force downward mobility. In both Virginia and Maryland, laws imposed severe penalties for whites who married across racial lines, for white women who had mixed-race children, and for the children of white women by black men.

In Maryland, white female ancestry had not prevented people from being held in slavery. In fact, such ancestry—descent from a white woman married to a black man—could be precisely why a person was a slave. But, beginning during the era of the American Revolution, such ancestry offered a means out of slavery for some people. Maryland's treatment of freedom suits for several years beginning in the 1780s led to freedom for people descended from women who, it was argued, should not themselves have been held in slavery.

The next chapter returns our focus to Virginia and addresses Native Americans and the enhanced possibilities of freedom—for some mixed-race people—that the American Revolution produced.

Chapter 2

Indian Foremothers and Freedom Suits in Revolutionary Virginia

"American Indians are prima facie free; . . . where the fact of their nativity and descent, in a maternal line, is satisfactorily established, the burthen of proof thereafter lies upon the party claiming to hold them as slaves"

—Judge St. Georgia Tucker, Virginia Supreme Court of Appeals (1806)

Two women—both of them black, according to twentieth-century racial categories—had a conversation in 1937 in Petersburg, Virginia. One was Susie Byrd, a writer for the New Deal's Works Progress Administration, who was looking for former slaves to share their recollections. The other was Octavia Featherstone, who talked about her tri-racial background—part white, part black, part Indian—and about how, though legally nonwhite and surely born during slave times, she had, in fact, never been a slave. She closed the interview with this explanation: "I forgit to tell you how and why we was free. You see Gramma bein' a Indian, she came of de Indian Tribe which cause our freedom. You know Indians was never slaves, so dey chillun was always free, dat is cordin' to law."[1]

According to Featherstone, her Indian ancestry—and not her white forebears—made it possible for her to be born free in the 1850s. How did the law of slavery and freedom lead, despite her African ancestry, to her free birth? What exactly was the legal significance, if any, of her Indian ancestry? Featherstone's account, dating from the twentieth century, points back toward other stories from Virginia, before the Civil War and even before the American Revolution.

By no means was it true that no Indians in Virginia had ever been enslaved, but Octavia Featherstone was not making her story up. An Indian identity had, in fact, kept some people out of slavery. Moreover, Indian ancestry had supplied an avenue to freedom for any number of Virginians who, though born into slavery, were successful in court when they sued for their freedom. In Maryland, in a similar fashion (see chapter 1), a slave's descent in the maternal line from a white woman opened a possible path to freedom. The law of race, sex, and marriage generated a slim, yet expanded, range of possibilities for nonwhite southerners during the era of the American Revolution.

Indian Ancestry and the Prospect of Freedom

A 1790 court document sheds light on the question raised by Octavia Featherstone's account of her free birth. James Howarth, a white man from Stafford County, granted his slave Amy her freedom, on condition that she first work for him another three years with no pay except "necessary Clothes and Victuals." In the spirit of the 1782 law (see chapter 1) that permitted Virginia planters to free their slaves, Howarth went on to pledge that, after the three years had passed, "should the said Amy be incapable of maintaining herself through Age, Sickness, or Misfortune, I will allow her a Sufficiency to subsist" to protect her from becoming so poor that the county would have to support her as a pauper.[2]

Then, offering a clue to his motive in this gift of her freedom, Howarth noted: "Amy says she is originally entitled to her freedom, being descended of Indian parents as her colour somewhat shews." Howarth recognized that Amy might seek, perhaps with success, to "prove her right and title to her freedom."[3] Howarth and Amy both saw the possibility under Virginia law at that time. She no doubt accepted the deal so she would not need to sue and take the chance she might lose, while he made the offer because, if she sued and won, he would immediately lose her. She postponed her shot at freedom, but she guaranteed her eventual freedom as well as a subsistence that might otherwise prove unavailable to her.

Newspapers in late-eighteenth century Virginia often contained advertisements for fugitive slaves. Some of those ads called for readers' help in tracking down people who, having identified themselves as of Indian ancestry, might be claiming their right to be free on that basis. In October 1772, for example, Paul Michaux advertised from Cumberland County for "a Mulatto Man named Jim, who is a Slave, but pretends to have a Right to his Freedom." Michaux explained that Jim's "father was an Indian, of the name of Cheshire," and Jim would likely "call himself James Cheshire, or Chink." About 27 years old, Jim had "long black hair resembling an Indian's," and "when he went away I expected he was gone to the General Court to seek his Freedom." In April 1773, a 22-year-old man named David left his Dinwiddie County owner, William Cuszens, who then advertised that this "Mulatto Slave," who "says he is of the Indian breed," had gone "down to the General Court, as I imagined, to sue for his freedom, but has never returned."[4]

Court cases from eastern Virginia give us a clearer picture of race, sex, slavery, and freedom in the years around 1800. Slaves acted to gain their freedom on grounds of Indian ancestry, as Howarth no doubt anticipated that Amy might—and as Paul Michaux suspected of James Cheshire, and William Cuszens did of David—and took their owners to court. More often than not, according to the cases that went to the Virginia Supreme Court of Appeals, they won their freedom.

All these cases originated in eastern Virginia (that is, east of the Blue Ridge, in the Piedmont or Tidewater areas), where slavery was so dominant an institution, and affected so many people's lives, that in a number of counties slaves constituted a majority of all residents, and most white families owned slaves. Whenever a slave or group of slaves gained their freedom, they tilted the ratio among Virginians a little less toward slavery and a little more toward freedom. The growing number of Virginia residents in a special category, neither white nor slave, resulted in part from a window of freedom that Virginia judges opened through the way they interpreted the past in deciding what to do about suits for freedom in the present.

Robin v. *Hardaway*, a court case that arose in 1772 as relations between the colonies and England made their way toward the American Revolution, offers a glimpse of how the ideas of the Revolution could affect thinking about slavery and freedom for nonwhite Virginians. It also makes very clear that slaves with Indian ancestry might draw on that ancestry—and those ideas—to sue for their freedom. In the case of the slave Robin and his co-plaintiffs, according to the surviving records, Attorney Mason argued for their freedom.

"The Indians of every denomination were free," said Mason, "and independent of us; they were not subject to our empire; nor represented in our legislature; they derived no protection from our laws, nor could be subjected to their bonds." Mason related all those facts to white colonists' complaints against the British Empire in the years leading up to the American Revolution. "If natural right, independence, defect of representation, and disavowal of protection, are not sufficient to keep them from the coercion of our laws, on what other principles can we justify our opposition to some late acts of power exercised over us by the British legislature? Yet they [the British] only pretend to impose on us a paltry tax in money; we on our free neighbors, the yoke of perpetual slavery." In this case, the court determined that a 1705 law had repealed earlier legislation that permitted the enslavement of Indians, so that Indians brought into Virginia after 1705 could not be enslaved.[5]

Indian Ancestry and Freedom Suits in Post-Revolutionary Virginia

A case similar to Robin's reached the Virginia Supreme Court of Appeals in 1792, its record scant, its significance large. A number of slaves owned by William Jenkins, among them one named "Tom an Indian," sued for their freedom. They claimed descent from two Indian women, Mary and Bess, one the grandmother of the other, who, decades before, had been brought into Virginia and kept—wrongfully, it was argued—as slaves. Given the general rule under Virginia law that each child inherited the status, free or slave, of his or her mother, Bess's children all grew up as slaves. In similar fashion, her daughters' children were all slaves, and so on. If Bess had been free, however, her children, too, would have all been born free, and thus her daughters' children should be free.[6]

In Northumberland District Court, Jenkins's lawyer took the position that, under a 1753 statute, Virginia clearly permitted such enslavement, but the court corrected him. He was informed—to use the words reported in 1792—that "he misstated the law." The judge agreed that "there was a time at some period in the last century" when a law permitted the enslavement of Indians under certain conditions and, under that law, "many Indians were made slaves, and their descendants continue slaves to this day." But, he went on, "this law was some time after repealed; from which period, no American Indian could be sold as a slave," and all Indians who had been brought into Virginia as slaves since its repeal, "and who had sued for their freedom, had uniformly recovered it." The jury found for the plaintiffs. Their putative owner appealed the decision, but Virginia's highest court upheld the district court.[7] Jenkins lost his slaves, and Tom and the unnamed others gained their freedom.

Tom's case outlines a story that clearly included far more individuals than those involved in that particular case. In the 20 years between 1792 and 1811, the Virginia Supreme Court of Appeals heard 18 cases in which one or more Virginians challenged their enslavement. Six of those cases involved plaintiffs who called themselves Indians and who relied on their Indian ancestry as the basis for their claim to freedom. In every instance, the trial court or the appeals court or both sided with the plaintiffs and declared their right to freedom.[8] For example, "Dick and Patt, indians," won a freedom suit against Williamson Coleman in 1792, and the Supreme Court of Appeals upheld that decision the next year. A 1705 statute, the court said, constituted "a compleat repeal of all former laws on the subject," and "since that period, no American Indian, can be reduced into a state of slavery."[9] As late as 1831, cases like those of "Dick and Patt, indians," and "Tom an Indian" continued to come before Virginia's highest court.

Those cases point up the complexity of the law of slavery and freedom in post-revolutionary America. How, to begin with, did these kinds of cases ever get into the courts? Moreover, they identify an intriguing type of resistance to North American slavery. Resistance, after all, could take many forms,[10] and surely taking one's master to court—seeking a legal victory in a demand for freedom—was one such. In addition, they indicate a continuing strand in American social and cultural history that relates to the presence of a group in eighteenth-century Virginia known as "native American Indians."[11]

Race, Sex, and Claims to Freedom

A 1795 Virginia statute spelled out the procedure according to which people held in servitude could challenge their bondage and sue for their freedom. On presentation of a petition for recovery of freedom, the court assigned the person counsel, whose duty it was to investigate and "make an exact statement to the court of the circumstances of the case, with his opinion thereupon." If persuaded that the case should go forward, the court summoned the owner ("or possessor") to answer the complaint. Pending a trial, the owner had to give security, "to the full value" of the "complainant," to permit the plaintiff to appear in court. The Virginia Supreme Court of Appeals phrased the right in emphatic, though restrictive, terms: "Persons in the status of slavery have no civil rights, save that of suing for freedom when entitled to it."[12]

Shortly before enactment of the 1795 measure, the president (later called chief justice) of the Supreme Court of Appeals, Edmund Pendleton, observed: "Although suits for freedom may be instituted without the leave of the court, yet it is usual to petition for such leave." Then, he explained, the court would "require the opinion of the counsel upon the plaintiff's right; and if it appear, that the plaintiff has probable cause for suing, the court will [seek to protect] the plaintiff from the master's resentment, or ill treatment," for going to court.[13]

The same law that offered a remedy as well as procedural protection to the slave also offered protection to the owner. Historian Robert McColley has said of late-eighteenth-century Virginia's "true emancipators"—especially Quakers— that such people "diligently investigat[ed] the legal titles by which Negroes were held, and su[ed] for freedom whenever such titles were doubtful."[14] To counteract such activities, the 1795 law provided that, for each plaintiff who lost his or her case, anyone who had helped bring the suit was liable to pay the owner $100. And a subsequent amendment stipulated that no "member of any society instituted for the purpose of emancipating negroes from the possession of their masters" could serve as a juror in such a case.[15]

In formulating a response to suits for freedom by people who claimed Indian descent, Virginia judges created a history to guide their deliberations. As late as 1682, they knew, the Virginia legislature had provided for the enslavement of Indians. Yet a 1705 act had authorized "a free and open trade for all persons, at all times, and at all places, with all Indians whatsoever." In a 1787 case in which Hannah and other Indians sued for their freedom, the General Court decided that "no Indians brought into Virginia" since 1705, "nor their descendants," could be held as slaves there.[16] In a brief account of these developments, St. George Tucker—a Virginia lawyer, law professor, and judge, and a proponent of gradual emancipation—wrote a few years later that he had discovered an act, apparently passed in 1691, with the same language as the 1705 law, and thus "it would seem that no Indians brought into Virginia for more than a century [since 1691], nor any of their descendants, can be retained in slavery in this commonwealth."[17]

A frequent figure taking the cases of Indian plaintiffs in manumission suits, at least on appeal, was George Keith Taylor. Reputed to be one of the great orators of his generation, Taylor was a Federalist politician who served his native Prince George County in the state House of Delegates in the 1790s. He was also a son-in-law of Chief Justice John Marshall.[18] In the years that followed, this gifted orator took several leading cases to the Virginia Supreme Court of Appeals. One was the case of Jacky Wright and her family.

In 1805, Jacky Wright and her children—Maria, John, and Epsabar—brought suit to recover their freedom from Holder Hudgins. They won, and Hudgins appealed to the Virginia Supreme Court of Appeals. St. George Tucker was now a member of that court, where he propounded his thesis that the acts culminating in 1682 had been repealed in 1691, rather than 1705, that is, after only 9 years rather than 23. His colleague Spencer Roane found Tucker's position plausible, but concluded that accepting the earlier date was unnecessary in this case to find for the Wrights. A unanimous court, agreeing that Jacky Wright and her children were entitled to their freedom, affirmed the lower-court ruling.[19]

Presumption, Evidence, and Instruction

The case of *Hudgins* v. *Wrights* gave judges occasion to speak to several major questions about presumption and evidence in suits for freedom. The case came to the Virginia Supreme Court of Appeals from the High Court of Chancery, where George Wythe (an eminent lawyer, professor, and judge) presided, and where, on two separate grounds, he had ruled in favor of the Wrights. He pointed to section 1 of the Virginia Bill of Rights—what he called the state's "political catechism"—which began with the declaration that "all men are by nature equally free and independent." Thus, as his words were later reported, "freedom is the birthright of every human being," and, "whenever one person claims to hold another in slavery, the onus probandi [burden of proof] lies on the claimant."[20]

Quite aside from that line of argument, witnesses had testified that the family descended, in the female line, from "an old Indian called Butterwood Nan." Nan's daughter Hannah, they said, "had long black hair, was of the right Indian copper colour, and was generally called an Indian by the neighbours, who said she might recover her freedom, if she would sue for it." Chancellor Wythe inspected members of the family there in the courtroom and concluded that they—three generations of females—appeared more or less Indian, not at all African, and, in the case of Jacky Wright's youngest child, "perfectly white." Thus, without even having to rely on his radical statement of broader grounds for emancipation, he decided that they were entitled to their freedom.[21]

On appeal to the state supreme court, George Keith Taylor, counsel for the Wrights, argued that "from the beginning of the world till the year 1679, all Indians were, in fact as well as right, free persons." And if, he declared, "the appellees [the Wrights] are descended from Indians, it is incumbent on the appellant [Hudgins] to prove that they are slaves; the appellees are not bound to prove the contrary." In effect, the court agreed, though it "entirely disapprov[ed]" Chancellor Wythe's reasoning as it might apply to black Virginians. Judge Tucker made clear his premise that the Virginia Bill of Rights applied to "free citizens" and by no means "overturn[ed] the rights of property." And yet he—and the rest of the court—had no difficulty affirming the substance of Wythe's decree. The Wrights must benefit from a presumption of freedom; the burden of proof fell on Hudgins. The Wrights should go free.[22]

Judges Tucker and Roane each wrote an essay on "natural history" and elaborated on how "mere inspection" might establish a prima facie case—a presumption of slavery or freedom, to be rebutted by opposing evidence if such could be supplied. Judge Tucker concluded that "all American Indians are prima facie free; . . . where the fact of their nativity and descent, in a maternal line, is satisfactorily established, the burthen of proof thereafter lies upon the party claiming to hold them as slaves." According to Judge Roane's version: "In the case of a person visibly appearing to be a negro, the presumption is, in this country, that he is a slave, and it is incumbent on him to make out his right to freedom; but in the case of a person visibly appearing to be a white man, or an Indian, the presumption is that he is free, and it is necessary for his adversary to shew that he is a slave." And yet, Roane pointed out, Hudgins "brings no testimony to shew that any ancestor in the female line was a negro slave or even an Indian rightfully held in slavery."[23]

In another freedom suit, Rachel and 13 other slaves in Norfolk County challenged Nancy Butt's right to hold them in bondage. They were, they said, all descendants of Paupouse, "a native American female Indian" who had been brought to Virginia as a slave from Jamaica in about 1747. Rachel's case displayed the critical role that a trial judge's instructions to the jury could play. Butt's attorney sought an instruction that even "a native American Indian"—if held as a slave where he or she came from—could, in fact, have been brought during the late colonial era to Virginia as a slave. By contrast, plaintiffs' counsel urged the judge to instruct the jury that "no American Indian, brought into this state after the year 1691, could be a slave." The judge gave the plaintiffs' instruction, not the defendant's, and the jury found for Rachel and the others.[24]

Butt appealed. In the court of appeals, her counsel argued that such cases as those of Tom, Dick and Pat, and the Wrights had, to be sure, established the right to freedom for American Indians who could meet the appropriate test, but just as surely, he went on, a statute calling for "free trade with the neighbouring Indians" could not apply to Paupouse—who, to employ a traditional distinction, must have been brought in "by sea" and not "by land." George Keith Taylor, counsel for Rachel and her fellow slaves, countered by seeking to expand the court's construction of claims to freedom on the basis of Indian descent. "Since 1691," he declared, "no Indian could be held in bondage. I do not contend merely that Indians could not be reduced into slavery, but that they could not be held as slaves. This was the plain consequence of 'free and open trade with all Indians whatsoever, at all times and in all places.'" The reported decision in no way states how the judges viewed such an argument, but they did affirm the lower-court outcome. In 1814, therefore, 14 more slaves escaped bondage through their claims of descent from an Indian foremother.[25]

"Cordin' to Law"

The tenacity of the Virginians who went to court claiming Indian ancestry demonstrated Virginia slaves' quest for freedom in the years between the 1760s and the 1810s, including their efforts to adapt the law to the cause of freedom. George Keith Taylor's arguments regarding Indian ancestry sometimes sufficed, and sometimes did not, to win freedom for his clients. Either way, they gave evidence time and again that Indian ancestry was, as Octavia Featherstone knew, connected with a greater likelihood of freedom among nonwhite Virginians.

At least some of the "Indian" plaintiffs in Virginia's manumission cases were no doubt among America's "new people"—biracial, even triracial, descendants of people who originated in Europe, Africa, and America.[26] Most slaves, even of Indian descent, had no means of manipulating the legal mechanism that Virginia law provided for a time to some descendants of Indian women. The child of a son of an Indian woman could not hope to win a case on that basis, as only an unbroken maternal line would satisfy the requirements. Most slaves in Virginia, even among those with some Indian ancestry, could not hope to make their way through that escape hatch from slavery to freedom.

Some people held in slavery could, and did, make their cases in the courts and find their paths to freedom. Some no doubt retained that freedom, once they gained it. Moreover, free mothers gave birth to free children, so the multiplier effect of emancipating a slave woman continued to operate into the 1860s.[27] And, far more often than slaves, antebellum free nonwhites carried advantages in their cultural and economic baggage—in literacy and property holding, for example—into the post–Civil War world in which all Virginians were at last free.[28]

If we place the plaintiffs themselves at the center of the story, then the "true emancipators" were slaves themselves. Favorable outcomes in several of these cases—and the resulting rise in the number of free nonwhite Virginians—came as a consequence of actions that slaves themselves took. Emancipation, in this view, rather than resulting from initiatives taken by slaveholders large or small, had its roots in resistance by slaves against those masters.

Most nonwhite Virginians who lived free, though having been born slaves, gained their liberty only in the convulsive events of the 1860s, but having Indian foremothers provided a means for some slaves to obtain their freedom much earlier.[29] What has tended to fade from view is the complex past of the eighteenth century, when three races continued to mix, whatever the binary views of a later time, and when the law supplied an intermediate station (in addition to indentured servitude) between slavery—lifelong and inherited—and freedom.

An interracial relationship could make the difference between slavery and freedom for children, just as it could make the difference between freedom and unfreedom for a white woman who entered into a sexual relationship with a black man. Octavia Featherstone has led us to discover identities other than black or white, African or European, among Virginians and Marylanders. Not only were some nonwhite people in the Chesapeake region free during slave times, but they had used the law to maintain or even create their opportunities. They may have crafted those opportunities out of unpromising materials, but they crafted them nonetheless.

The Later Careers of the 1662 and 1691 Laws

Between them, Sarah Madden (chapter 1) and Jacky Wright embodied the triracial nature of Virginia society as late as the American Revolution and the early national era. Between them, they demonstrated the enormous power that race and sex, in various combinations, could have in shaping people's lives, in determining whether, when, and under what conditions they might live in freedom.

Sarah Madden exemplified the long-term unfreedom that some Virginians experienced, a status midway between starting out life free and being born a slave. The daughter of a European American woman and an African American man, she had to wait until the age of 31 to gain her own freedom in 1789, and another 18 years before the last of her unfree children grew old enough to become free in 1807.

Jacky Wright showed that, although born into lifelong slavery, one might still obtain freedom. Wright, who had Indian ancestry (whatever European and African ancestry she or any of her three children had), was a grown woman before she succeeded in wresting freedom for herself and her children in 1805 from Holder Hudgins.

In the years to come, the daughters of Sarah Madden and Jacky Wright would no doubt have children of their own, and those children, born to free mothers, would be born free. The Maddens would finally shake free of the burdens of the law of 1691 and its successors. The Wrights would finally see the law of 1662 operate to produce free Virginians rather than slaves.

By contrast, into the 1860s, most Virginians with African ancestry remained slaves. They could not enter into marriages—with people of any race—that the law recognized. And the law of 1662 declared their children, the children of slave women, to be born into lifelong slavery. The Virginia law of 1662 remained in force for two centuries—through at least six generations. The Virginia law of race and marriage as enacted in 1691, though it was amended from time to time, persisted even longer. Such laws as Virginia's emerged elsewhere, too, in British North America—in the northern colonies as well as in the South—and subsequently spread across much of the continent.

From Generation to Generation

The law of race and marriage in the Chesapeake region can be said to have gone through four phases between settlement in the seventeenth century and abolition in the nineteenth. In both Virginia and Maryland, after a prelude of a generation or two, the law of race first addressed matters of marriage in the second half of the seventeenth century. In Maryland, at least until the American Revolution, the law of race, marriage, and slavery consigned to perpetual slavery the mixed-race children, grandchildren, and great-grandchildren of a white woman who had married a slave man. In Virginia, the descendants of any woman—Indian, African, or mixed-race—who was held as a slave were born into slavery and remained slaves all their lives.

Then—in the third period, during the years of the American Revolution and the early national era—the law of race and freedom offered a way out of slavery for some people. The Revolution brought a period of promise that freed some of those descendants, if they could trace their lineage back through the female line to an Indian foremother in Virginia, or an Irish servant in Maryland. Irish Nell was a lowly servant Irishwoman in the seventeenth century, but by the time of the Revolution perhaps her racial identity as a white woman carried more significance.[30] Across the generations, she was able at last to do what she could not do in 1681—bequeath her progeny their freedom. At last, Irish Nell and Negro Charles could have great-great-grandchildren who were free. Similarly, at last, descendants of Bess as well as Butterwood Nan gained their freedom in Virginia.

By the 1810s, these three chapters in the law of race, marriage, and freedom had come to an end, and a new chapter was under way. In the final half-century before a general emancipation came in the 1860s, racial identity had little place in determining an individual's slavery or freedom. Under the law, racial lineage became irrelevant. Women held as slaves would continue to be slaves, and their children would be born into slavery and continue in slavery. Slaves might marry, but their marriages would not be legal relationships that anyone had to respect, would not bring rights or responsibilities that could be enforced in any court, nor would they bring penalties. And slavery would be lifelong and inherited, with no way out and no end in sight.

At each stage, people in Maryland and Virginia—slaves and their owners alike—might learn from their counterparts in the other jurisdiction, but lawmakers on each side of the boundary made up their own rules. Each colony could act for itself in fashioning laws governing race, sex, and marriage. So (as the next two chapters show) could the states from the American Revolution through the Civil War, although such matters could get caught up in larger controversies about race, power, and policy in the new nation's life.

CHAPTER 3

FROM THE CHESAPEAKE COLONIES TO THE STATE OF CALIFORNIA

"There is a difference of opinion respecting the proportion of African blood [that] will prevent a person possessing it from being regarded as white"

—Maine Supreme Court (1852)

"If the statute against mulattoes is by construction to include quadroons, . . . are we not bound to pursue the line of descendants, so long as there is a drop of negro blood remaining?"

—Alabama Supreme Court (1850)

Bryan v. *Walton,* a decision by the Georgia Supreme Court in 1853, prefigured the *Dred Scott* decision handed down by the U.S. Supreme Court four years later. Chief Justice Joseph Henry Lumpkin observed, "As yet, I believe, free negroes are not in any State in the Union, entitled to all the privileges and immunities of citizens." As for "marriage of whites with blacks," he continued, it was "generally prohibited" throughout the United States—a good indicator, he said, of the generally degraded status of black residents almost everywhere: "In no part of this country, whether North or South, East or West, does the free negro stand erect and on a platform of equality with the white man."[1]

The law's concern with race and marriage long outlasted the colonial era and reached far beyond the South. This chapter traces the spread of miscegenation laws outside the Chesapeake area, and it traces the career of such laws from the colonial era down to the eve of the Civil War. A collection of court cases will reveal the presence of interracial couples in pre–Civil War America; display the enforcement of miscegenation laws in the North as well as the South; demonstrate how such laws applied to many areas of life, including inheritance; and fore-shadow the developments of the century after the Civil War.

Laws or no laws, scholars have noted scattered instances of interracial mar-riages across the nineteenth century and in every corner of the country. Some families ran into trouble; others apparently did not.[2] For some families, racial identity may not have been a serious consideration in how they were accepted and viewed. Some families, by contrast, encountered physical violence or economic damage. Some encountered legal consequences of various kinds, as this chapter will reveal. Regardless of how individual families were perceived and classified, accommodated or attacked, interracial marriage surfaced again and again—in both the North and the South—as a political issue and a legal matter.

"Inspector of Colors"

In the North, as in the South, a number of colonies passed laws against interra-cial marriage. Most retained them after the American Revolution, even past the Civil War, and most new states in the North as well as the South enacted such laws as well. But some did not.

Colonial Pennsylvania acted against interracial marriage, so racial identity had great significance. According to a law dating from the 1720s, a preacher who presided at a marriage ceremony between a black and a white would be fined 100 pounds. Free blacks who married whites could be sentenced to slav-ery for life. Whites cohabiting with blacks "under pretense of being married" would be fined 30 pounds or sold for seven years, and blacks convicted of in-terracial fornication or adultery would be sold for seven years. Children of co-habiting interracial couples were subject to being sold for 31 years.[3]

Pennsylvania's allegiance to the antimiscegenation regime proved temporary, as it was the first of the 13 original states to act against the continuance of ei-ther slavery or miscegenation laws. Even while the American Revolution was being fought, the Pennsylvania legislature considered changes in the laws of race, marriage, and slavery. A proposal in 1779 would have retained provisions against interracial marriage but also would have reduced some of the penalties and would have launched the state on the road to emancipation. Under that proposal, interracial marriages could never be valid, and interracial cohabitation "under pretense that they are married" would subject the black party to seven years of servitude, while the white person would be fined 100 pounds or, if un-able to pay, sold for seven years.[4]

As enacted in 1780, however, the new Pennsylvania law repealed all racial re-strictions, including the miscegenation law, and provided for gradual emancipation and an eventual end to slavery. Some citizens objected that free black residents would have full voting privileges and the freedom to marry across racial lines. Pennsylvania had nevertheless demonstrated that a slave society could set itself upon a course to become a free society with none of the previous racial restrictions still in place, and other northeastern states emulated portions of the Pennsylvania program. Massachusetts, for example, abandoned slavery in the 1780s and repealed its miscegenation law in 1843, and Iowa (which had never legalized slavery) dropped its ban on interracial marriage in 1851.[5]

The fact that a state had repealed its miscegenation law did not mean that it never considered adopting a new one, just as states that never actually passed such laws might nonetheless consider doing so. Two generations after Pennsylvania's repeal of its restrictive law in 1780, a Democratic legislator introduced a bill in 1841 to impose a new ban on interracial marriage. Poking fun at the proposal, a Whig legislator suggested an amendment providing for an "Inspector of Colors," whose responsibility it was to calibrate people's skin color according to a graded color chart, and the darker the skin of the person with African ancestry, the greater the punishment to both offenders for the crime of marrying across a racial line. The Democrat urged that the House appoint the Whig to the new position. Pennsylvania did not, however, choose to restore its former allegiance to the antimiscegenation regime.[6]

The Republic of Liberty and the Antimiscegenation Regime:
Symbol and Substance, Demography and Culture, Race and Power

Before emancipation—which came to the North between about 1780 and 1830 and to the South in the 1860s—few African Americans were free. Black residents were disfranchised in many states regardless of whether they were free, so they had no effective say in either passing or repealing laws against interracial marriage. Whites made up the rules.

Three of the six New England states maintained miscegenation laws for many years. Massachusetts enacted a law against interracial marriage in 1705 and, after independence, reenacted that law in 1786. When Maine broke away as a separate state, one of its early pieces of business in 1821 was to enact a miscegenation law of its own. In the meantime, Rhode Island had passed such a law in 1798. None of the three states imposed a fine or jail sentence for interracial marriage, but all three declared such marriages void. Massachusetts and Rhode Island sought to enforce the law by providing for a penalty to be imposed on any minister who presided at an interracial wedding.[7]

Miscegenation laws sprouted up and down the east coast and then spread west. The ideas, even the language, that appeared in Virginia's 1691 law (see chapter 1) found echoes in other colonies' laws. Massachusetts, for example, in its 1705 law, spoke of the "Better Preventing of a Spurious and Mixt Issue." North Carolina's law of 1741 aimed at preventing "abominable Mixture and spurious issue."[8]

At the outbreak of the American Revolution, there were slaves in every state, but most lived in the South. Whether slave or free—and most were slaves—a majority of all nonwhite residents in the 13 original states lived in Virginia and Maryland. Between the American Revolution and the Civil War, slavery's center of gravity moved south and west. Across the South, slaves could not marry—or, rather, could not enter a marriage that the state would bind them to or that their owners could be counted on to recognize. If slaves could not marry at all, there was no need to say they could not marry across racial lines. For much of the time before emancipation and Reconstruction, interracial marriage was not a particularly compelling concern in the South. Most southern states had laws against interracial marriage, but some couples married regardless.[9]

The issue could appear at least as powerful in free territories—western areas outside the South.[10] As new states were organized in the West, most adopted miscegenation laws. Indiana fumbled at the matter for a time, enacting a law and then repealing it, trying out different penalties; but in 1842 it settled on penalties of a fine between $1,000 and $5,000 and a prison term between one and ten years. In 1850, the new state of California joined the antimiscegenation regime by enacting a law that established a fine of between $100 and $10,000, a prison term of from three months to ten years, or both.[11] California's ban on interracial marriages lasted nearly a century, though the criminal penalties did not last that long.

Even where black residents were few in number, miscegenation laws were often considered, and sometimes enacted, for their symbolic as well as their substantive value. They sent a message, as they were designed to, that black residents should know their place, and their place did not include an equal role in marriage, the most intimate of settings, as spouse of a white person.[12] Too much was at stake, it seemed, in terms of communal identity, accumulation of property, racial supremacy. The same white people who objected to black settlement in their midst also resisted black voting rights and supported an antimiscegenation regime.

It was vital to African Americans that they work with the materials at hand to reach freedom, maintain their families, and protect their property. Sometimes they succeeded, sometimes not. The materials varied from one place to another; often tipping the balance were people who demonstrated that not all whites were on the same side in matters of race or slavery. White voters and legislators who supported repeal of miscegenation laws, or who opposed the enactment of such laws, offered one kind of evidence. Lawyers like Virginia's George Keith Taylor (see chapter 2), who had his counterparts in Maryland, offered another.

Regardless of what kinds of allies emerged, interracial families in every corner of the nation found themselves caught up in situations that, on the basis of racial identity, threatened their liberty or their property. A sampling of cases will illustrate the geographic range, the kinds of problems, and the ways in which courts resolved questions that came before them.

Maine and Massachusetts

Of the couples that encountered the law because of their different racial identities, some did so in criminal court, where they were charged with violating a law against their marriage. Other interracial families encountered the law through civil proceedings having to do with property, especially inheritance. Two civil cases involving interracial marriage will serve to illustrate how much miscegenation laws could shape otherwise normal legal proceedings, and how far they ranged through time and space across the United States.

Between the American Revolution and the Civil War, in the North and in the South, people sometimes found themselves caught up in the rules of the antimiscegenation regime. Cases in New England dealt with two questions of property and the law. One question related to inheritance: whether children could inherit from their father if his marriage, allegedly interracial, was declared void. The other was pauper support: on what conditions had someone established a "settlement" in a town—that is, on what conditions a town was responsible for supporting a pauper.

Sometime before 1770, an African American named Ishmael Coffee and a white woman (we do not know her name) left Massachusetts, where a law banned marriages for such couples, and went to a neighboring colony, Rhode Island, which did not yet have such a law. They had a wedding ceremony there and returned "immediately" afterwards to Massachusetts. A half-century later, a dispute—one that hinged on the validity of the marriage—arose between two towns as to who was responsible for maintaining the couple as aged paupers. The town of Medway had given them some support, but had sought reimbursement from the town of Needham, which according to Medway was the place of their "legal settlement." Needham rejected the contention, arguing that it could be so only if the couple had a valid marriage, but since "he was a mulatto, and his supposed wife a white woman," their "supposed marriage" was as "void" as if the ceremony had taken place in Massachusetts. The trial court ruled the marriage valid, a ruling that was appealed. In upholding the trial court's judgment, the Supreme Judicial Court of Massachusetts ruled that a marriage, if valid "according to the laws of the country where it is entered into, shall be valid in any other country." It was "only void, if contracted within this state, in violation of its laws."[13]

Some years earlier, the same family had been in the courts over pauper support, this time not for the couple, but for their daughter and grandchild. Their mixed-race daughter, Roba Vickons, had married Christopher Vickons, a white man, in 1789 in Natick, where he had his legal settlement. But he later died, and by 1810 she and their child, described as "poor and indigent," were living in Medway, as were her parents. Seeking to shift the responsibility—or at least to determine whose responsibility it was to support Roba Vickons and her child—the town of Medway, which had been supporting them, sued the town of Natick.[14] The town fathers of Medway did not think they should presume to spend the local taxpayers' hard-earned dollars unless the legal responsibility to do so was clearly theirs, so they sought a ruling.

Medway agreed that, if Roba was a mulatto, and if the state law against marriages between whites and mulattos was constitutional, then she was Medway's responsibility, as she could never have acquired a legal settlement in Natick through her marriage. If, on the other hand, she was white, or if the law was unconstitutional, then Natick was responsible for her and must repay Medway its expenses for supporting the parent and child. The high court of Massachusetts ruled that it was not necessary to address the constitutional question, since she was not a mulatto. A "mulatto," the court determined, was, like her father, "half black and half white."[15] Since her father was a mulatto, and her mother white, she herself was not a mulatto, so she could legally marry Christopher Vickons.

In another New England case, Abigail Green and Tobias Jones were married in 1793 in the Maine District of Massachusetts. At that time, a Massachusetts law banned marriage between "a white person" and "any negro, Indian or mulatto." Many years later, after Tobias Jones had died leaving no will, the Maine courts were called upon to rule on the couple's racial identities and their marriage. When the trial judge declared the marriage void (which meant that Jones's children could not inherit from their father), the children appealed to the Maine Supreme Court, which handed down its decision in 1852.[16]

Chief Justice Shepley revealed that the court had to create law and impose definitions to render a judgment. He conceded, "There is a difference of opinion respecting the proportion of African blood, which will prevent a person possessing it from being regarded as white." Did it suffice that a person's "white blood predominated both in proportion and in appearance"? Even people "least disposed to consider a person to be white," he said, had admitted that a person no more than one-eighth black should be regarded as white.[17]

Tobias Jones's "proportion" was more than that. He was a "mulatto" with too much African ancestry to qualify as white—and must therefore be black—while Abigail Green was one-sixteenth Indian, which was too little, said the court, for her to be considered anything other than white. Thus the court ruled that their children were illegitimate. They had no claim on their father's property, for their parents had no right to marry under state law in the 1790s. Had no such rule regarding race existed, the question of the Jones children's legitimacy would never have come up, nor would their claim to an inheritance have been contested. Alternatively, had a more stringent test of racial identity been applied, both might have been defined as nonwhite and therefore capable of entering a valid marriage with each other.

One of the children of Abigail Green and Tobias Jones was Levi Jones, born in North Berwick, Maine, early in the nineteenth century. Levi Jones himself married a white woman. George A. Jones, their son, was at the center of a dispute between the Town of Raymond and the town of North Berwick a few years after the Civil War. What responsibility did North Berwick have for George Jones? The void marriage of his grandparents permitted the Maine Supreme Court to decide in 1871 that he could not have gained a "settlement," and thus a claim on the town, in North Berwick.[18]

The town of Raymond was on its own, because George Jones was on his own. What the court did not say was that George Jones might not have been a pauper had the courts not prevented his father from inheriting from Tobias Jones. The family's property failed to pass from one generation to the next. When a marriage was declared void because it was deemed interracial, the liabilities that accrued to the children descended through the generations.

A North Carolina Family

Alfred Hooper, a black North Carolinian, went on trial with his white wife in Rutherford County in 1842. They had been married for about ten years and were charged with adultery. The jury was stumped and advised the judge that, if the couple's marriage was valid, then they were not guilty but, if it was void, then they were guilty. Judge Bailey pointed toward an act of the legislature in 1838 that banned such marriages and concluded that, because the couple had married some years before 1838, the marriage was not unlawful. The prosecution appealed to the North Carolina Supreme Court, which determined that the trial judge had "overlooked" a previous statute dating from 1830.[19]

By some oversight, the North Carolina Supreme Court explained, the 1830 miscegenation statute was not reprinted in an 1836 compilation of North Carolina laws in force, so the act had been revived in 1838. The court calculated that, if the couple had been married for approximately ten years in May 1842, then the marriage probably took place after February 1831, when the 1830 law went into effect. Therefore the marriage was void and the couple should have been found guilty.

The Hooper couple, after evidently living together for a number of years without being challenged, appealed their convictions for violating a state law against their marriage. Unsuccessful in that effort, they paid the penalty—and went right on living together and acting as though, whatever the law, they were husband and wife. The 1850 census showed Alfred and Elizabeth Hooper still living together in Rutherford County, she listed as white and 36, he as mulatto and 54, a laborer who owned a farm worth $550. Living with them were their many children. The older ones were their two sons, Toliver, 18, and Henry, 17, together with their four oldest daughters: Charity, 14; Eliza, 12; Mahala, 10; and Martha, 8. The younger children—all born after the trial verdict and perhaps all but one of them since the state supreme court decision—were Amanda, 6; Mary, 4; Marilla, 2; and an infant, Arabella. Life went on, and, despite a miscegenation law, it could be good.[20]

Identity and Property in Maryland and Georgia

Nicholas Darnall was born a slave in Maryland because his mother was his father's slave. His father, Bennett Darnall, did what he could to give Nicholas his freedom and 596 acres of land, though the son was barely ten years old when the father died in 1814. Under Maryland law, the parents could not marry, but, under a 1796 manumission act, the father manumitted Nicholas, his brother Henry, and a number of other slaves. He also willed his two sons considerable land and other property. After Nicholas Darnall had come of age, he sold a plantation called Portland Manor for $13,112 to Claudius F. Le Grand.[21]

The story of Nicholas Darnall and his family made its way into the courts because questions arose as to whether Darnall had title to himself, let alone to the property that he had offered to sell. In view of his youth at the time of his father's death, went the question, could his father have lawfully left him his freedom or that property? A recent decision by the Maryland Court of Appeals had introduced doubt. The willing buyer and willing seller were in court, not because of wrangling or animosity, but to clear up the doubt about title to the land. As was reported at the time, "Le Grand is willing to pay if his title is a safe one," and "Darnall does not wish Le Grand to pay unless he can make a good title to him."[22] The lower court concluded that Darnall had good title, but the case went to the U.S. Supreme Court for another reading.

Justice Gabriel Duvall, who had long experience in Maryland as a lawyer and judge, spoke for the U.S. Supreme Court. He noted, for one thing, that, as witnesses had testified, young Henry had been old enough when his father died to work to support himself. More important, Justice Duvall noted that an older decision by the Maryland Court of Appeals had construed the manumission statute of 1796 as conferring freedom on any slave whose owner bequeathed him or her any property, real or personal. Therefore, any doubt about Nicholas Darnall's freedom vanished, as did any doubt about his title to the land in question. The lower court opinion was affirmed, and Darnall was free to sell the land to Le Grand.

Fifteen years after gaining his freedom and inheriting property when his father died, Nicholas Darnall was described as "well educated" and "living in affluence." Perhaps his mother loved her owner, or perhaps she felt more coercion than affection in her relationship with him. Perhaps she gambled on the most promising option available to her to see to her children's futures. However she felt, and whatever her motive, she helped establish the preconditions for her sons' successful adult lives in freedom, even if her mulatto son Nicholas, at least, had to navigate the legal system to safeguard his status and his property.[23]

Countless interracial relationships across the South—like that between Bennett Darnall and his slave, the mother of Nicholas—produced mixed-race children, and in some of those cases the white father did what he could to safeguard the children he had with their slave mother.[24] In a great many others, the child was just another slave. In most situations, no lawsuit developed, but sometimes one did—usually relating to the ownership of property.

Georgia displayed a variant example of the relationship between racial identity and the unrestricted right to own property. Shortly before Joseph Nunez died in December 1846, he conveyed six slaves—his wife Patience (though they could not legally marry) and their five children—to a white resident of Georgia, Alexander M. Urquhart, who then sold them to another white Georgian, Seaborn C. Bryan. All of that might have gone without judicial notice, except that the question arose as to whether Nunez was a "free person of color" who, under legislation dating from 1818 and 1819, had no legal authority to sell or give away any slaves he possessed, but could only pass them on to his lawful descendants, if any. A legal contest over his racial identity and those slaves rattled around the Georgia courts for years, almost to the end of the Civil War, almost to the end of anyone's claims to property in slaves.

All witnesses agreed that Joseph Nunez's mother had been white—or at least not black. One person said she was "a real Indian and no negress."[25] His legal right to have sold some of his slaves turned on whether his father (who had come to Georgia in the 1790s) had been a Portuguese immigrant, a Native

American, or a free African American. The definition of a "free person of color" in Georgia—a free person at least one-eighth black; that is, one of whose great-grandparents had been black—necessitated an exercise in genealogy to determine his rights.

One witness, Joseph Bush, said "James Nunez was an American; his father was a Portuguese; he passed as a white man." As for Joseph Nunez's mother, she was "a free white woman and a very pretty one too," who had formerly gone by the name Lucy Anderson but subsequently by Lucy Nunez. The couple "lived together as husband and wife." Other witnesses testified that Joseph Nunez's grandmother was white, and his mother as well, although his father, James Nunez, may have been "partly Indian and partly white"—his hair, according to one, was "not kinkey, but straight, black and smooth." Although some white neighbors had been concerned about Joseph Nunez because "he had for a wife a negro woman, his own slave," he had been "received" by those neighbors "on a footing with whites."[26]

Other witnesses insisted, by contrast, that Joseph Nunez's father had African ancestry, although the proportion might be disputed. James and Joseph Nunez alike, said Joseph Cosnahan, were "mulattoes—that is, white and negro mixed"; their hair "curled"; and, so far as he knew, had never exercised "the usual rights of white citizens." Charles Cosnahan similarly testified that neither of the Nunez men, he thought, had ever "voted or performed military duty," as they might have been expected to do had they been citizens, but, rather, they had been "regarded as free negroes."[27]

The case gave the Georgia Supreme Court an occasion to vent on a wide range of matters regarding race, marriage, and the law. The court determined that Joseph Nunez was a free person of color, subject to all the restrictions that applied to that group. Speaking for the court, Chief Justice Joseph Henry Lumpkin suggested that no black residents, even though free from slavery, had the legal capacity to contract a marriage. The court went so far as to equate black freedom and black slavery—except that "free" blacks had no owner. The legislature might "bestow" other rights on them, he said, but, until it did, they were not, for example, "capable of contracting, of marrying, of voting."[28]

Mixed Marriages in Alabama

Interracial marriages occurred with some limited frequency in pre–Civil War Alabama. Few marriages took place between whites and people of unmixed African ancestry, but a number of mixed-race women married white men, and a similar number of white women married mixed-race men. These marriages included two in Montgomery, where Isaac Merrett married Rachael Lantorn and Elias Evans married Catharine C. Reynolds.[29]

At no time before Reconstruction did Alabama outlaw such marriages, whether to impose criminal sanctions against them or to declare them null and void. Only in 1852 did the Alabama legislature act to place any impediment to interracial marriages. Until that year, Alabama law authorized certain officials to "solemnize the rites of matrimony between any free persons," with restrictions only on age and kinship. After 1852, the law approved marriages "between white persons, or between free persons of color," but not between a member of one of those two groups and a member of the other. The new law declared it a misdemeanor for a minister to perform a marriage ceremony "when one of the parties is a negro and the other a white person."[30]

But who was a "negro"? Also beginning in 1852, Alabama law specified that the term "negro" should be understood to include "mulatto," which it now defined as anyone at least one-eighth black. The urge to define "mulatto" can be traced directly to a ruling by the Alabama Supreme Court in 1850, in *Thurman* v. *State*, that Thurman could be clearly understood to be a "mulatto" only if he were half black and half white, the child of one white parent and one black. In the view of the court, the legislature had been insufficiently clear that it meant to cast a wider net and include the child of one white parent and one who was mixed-race:

> If the statute against mulattoes is by construction to include quadroons, then where are we to stop? If we take the first step by construction, are we not bound to pursue the line of descendants, so long as there is a drop of negro blood remaining? If not, the point where we should stop can only be ascertained by judicial discretion. This discretion belongs [instead] to the Legislature.[31]

Alabama lawmakers hastened to adopt a broader definition—anyone one-eighth black was black—that would include someone like Thurman.[32] Their twentieth-century successors (see chapter 9) would adopt, instead, a definition that the court had pointed toward and rejected, namely "pursu[ing] the line of descendants, so long as there is a drop of negro blood remaining."

The Antimiscegenation Regime in Pre–Civil War America

At least 38 states had miscegenation laws at some point, but not all did.[33] One by one, some states repealed them, beginning with Pennsylvania in 1780 and Massachusetts in 1843. Soon after Pennsylvania repealed its miscegenation law, however, Rhode Island inaugurated one. Soon after Massachusetts repealed its law, the new state of California adopted one and Alabama took a first step against interracial marriage. At the same time, therefore, that new states were enacting laws against interracial marriage, other states were repealing them.

Across the nineteenth century, the territory over which the antimiscegenation regime ruled kept changing—shrinking in one direction, growing in another, shifting location toward the south and west.[34]

Free African Americans lived in the South as well as the North. In both regions, issues in the enforcement of miscegenation laws—racial identity, interstate comity, the inheritance of property—appeared in some early court cases. Such court cases appeared with far greater frequency in the post–Civil War South than in the prewar era. Their early appearances prefigured the law of marriage in a later time, after the end of slavery.

The United States had no national law of marriage, and thus every marriage took place under the particular laws of an individual state. Whatever the Declaration of Independence said about the pursuit of happiness, an American couple's liberty and property could be jeopardized if they entered into an interracial marriage—regardless of whether they did so recognizing that they had different racial identities, and regardless of whether they knew interracial marriage to be against the law. As cases in this chapter have suggested, and as later chapters will develop in greater detail, there could be great doubt about an individual's racial identity under the law and great doubt, too, about what the law was and whether it was valid.

CHAPTER 4

RACE, MARRIAGE, AND
THE CRISIS OF THE UNION

Alexina Morrison "is proved to be of fair complexion, blue eyes, and flaxen hair. But the presumption of freedom, arising from her color, . . . must yield to proof of a servile origin"

—Louisiana Supreme Court (1861)

"I am now in my fiftieth year, and certainly never have had a black woman either for a slave or wife, and so it seems to me that it is quite possible for us to get along without making either slaves or wives of negroes"

—Abraham Lincoln (1858)

"Miscegenation" can refer to sex or marriage between people of different races, and it can refer as well to laws that long banned marriages between a person defined as white and someone of another racial identity. The term originated in the North during the Civil War (replacing "amalgamation"), when Democrats tried to worry voters during President Abraham Lincoln's 1864 reelection campaign that Lincoln and the Republican Party favored interracial marriage. The president had issued the Emancipation Proclamation and had directed that black troops be enrolled in the Federal army, and the Republican Party ran that year on a platform calling for a constitutional amendment to outlaw slavery throughout the nation.

Two Democratic newspapermen from the *New York World,* David Goodman Croly and George Wakeman, published a hoax pamphlet designed to portray Republicans as avowed advocates of interracial sexual relations, particularly between black men and white women. They titled their fabrication *Miscegenation: The Theory of the Blending of the Races, Applied to the American White Man and*

Negro. Its concoction and publication, in late 1863 and early 1864, demonstrated that the matter was expected to be a significant issue in a national election. So salient an issue, as Croly and Wakeman believed it to be, deserved so wickedly imaginative a creation. In addition, however, Croly wished to force the nation to confront the larger question of what kind of society might follow slavery. How *would* black Americans and white ones live together in a world in which slavery had been abolished?[1]

Republicans in the 1860s continued struggling to enhance the rights of African Americans, and their efforts continued to conjure images of black men marrying white women. The concern reached far beyond the South and could even be expected to play a significant role in national politics. National politics, in turn, had the potential of transforming the law of race and marriage in the states. This chapter examines the intertwined history of the crisis of the Union and the political and legal issue of interracial marriage in the 1850s and 1860s.

Language and Identity

Even the language of "black" men marrying "white" women can cause confusion. Twentieth-century scholars, like other people, tended to take at face value a lexicon that itself connotes a binary world that never existed. Despite the prevailing notion that "black" and "slave" were synonyms in slave states, such was never the case. It was more an assertion—a claim or a hope—than an accomplished fact, and it became less, not more true as the years passed. Some "black" southerners were free, not enslaved, among them Nicholas Darnall, the son of a white man and a slave woman, whose father, unlike many men in such situations, conferred freedom and considerable property on his mixed-race child. Some people, like Joseph Nunez (also chapter 3), though they may have had some African ancestry, held slaves and were therefore slave owners, not slaves themselves.

Slaves could be—and many were—more white than black. In pre–Civil War America, a person was defined as a slave not so much on the basis of racial identity but as being, simply, the child of a woman who was herself held as a slave, just as mixed-race Marylanders in the late seventeenth century could be born as slaves because their mother, a white woman, had married a man who was held as a slave (see chapter 1).

Perhaps no single statement captures this phenomenon better than a declaration by the Louisiana Supreme Court at the very time that one southern state after another was seceding from the Union over matters of power, race, and slavery. A young person, perhaps 15 years old, presented herself in New Orleans as a white female named Alexina Morrison, unjustly held as a slave by James White, who, she said, had kidnapped her from her home, where she had lived with her white parents. When a jury decided that she was in fact white, James White appealed the case to Louisiana's highest court, which in February 1861 determined that she "was born a slave, the offspring of a mulatto woman slave, and that she passed, by a regular chain of conveyances, from the possession of her original owner, the owner of her mother," to James White. She had moved from Texas to Arkansas to Louisiana, but she had not, after all, moved from slavery to freedom.[2]

Alexina Morrison could be three-fourths white, seven-eighths white, fifteen-sixteenths white, and still be a slave. The highest court in the new Confederate state of Louisiana acknowledged that she "is proved to be of fair complexion, blue eyes, and flaxen hair. But the presumption of freedom, arising from her color, . . . must yield to proof of a servile origin. The Legislature has not seen fit to declare, that any number of crosses between the negro and the white shall emancipate the offspring of a slave; and it does not fall within the province of the judiciary to establish any such rule of property."[3]

In the years surrounding the time of the quest by "Alexina Morrison" for free status and a white identity, courts throughout the land had occasion to rule on matters of black or white racial identity, free or slave status, and state or federal authority. In the politics of the pre–Civil War era, opponents of racial equality—in fact, opponents of any restrictions on the territorial expansion of slavery—threatened their audiences that any softening of the slave power would bring together white women and black men. The proponents of curtailing slavery's power were more inclined to project images of white men and black women—and then argue that, under their approach, such mixing would take place less often, not more.

Marriage, Citizenship, and the *Dred Scott* Decision

The U.S. Supreme Court ruled in *Dred Scott* v. *Sandford* (1857) that African Americans could not be U.S. citizens and that Congress could not restrict the expansion of slavery into western territories. Chief Justice Roger B. Taney—hostile to congressional restrictions on slavery's growth; hostile to the abolition of slavery; and hostile to black citizenship and racial equality—had much to say in his far-ranging opinion for the Court about the limitations that had been historically placed on U.S. residents of African ancestry. He marshaled evidence that in no American colony had African Americans been treated in a way consistent with citizenship. Many states, he could report, in the North as well as the South, had restricted interracial marriages as well as black voting. The chief justice did everything he could to draw an indelible line between "the citizen race . . . and the African race."[4]

Taney gave Massachusetts as an example, a jurisdiction that enacted a miscegenation law during the colonial era while slavery existed there. The 1705 law had banned marriage not between free people and slaves, he noted, but between any white person and "any negro or mulatto." In 1786, after independence was declared and the Revolution was over—and after slavery had been abandoned in Massachusetts—a similar law was enacted.[5] The chief justice did not bother to note that Massachusetts had repealed the law in 1843, but he had made his point that a key northern state, one that had moved quickly away from slavery during the American Revolution, had continued long after that to distinguish sharply between its white and nonwhite residents.

The law of race and marriage could, however, cut another way. In dissent, Justice Benjamin R. Curtis observed about Dred Scott's own marriage that such an action was hardly consistent with slave status. As slaves, Dred Scott and Harriet Robinson could never have contracted a marriage in Missouri. But Dred Scott's owner, Dr. John Emerson, took him to a free territory, Wisconsin Territory, and there, in 1836, Dr. Emerson consented to their marriage. As Curtis insisted, "In my judgment, there can be no more effectual abandonment of the legal rights of a master over his slave, than by the consent of the master that the slave should enter into a contract of marriage, in a free State, attended by all the civil rights and obligations which belong to that condition."[6]

The point was not that they had married interracially—that was not understood to be the case—but that they had been permitted to marry at all. According to Justice Curtis, their marriage should weigh heavily in support of their claim to freedom. His dissenting opinion did not speak for the Court, though it certainly represented an alternative view of the law of race, marriage, and slavery in pre–Civil War America.

Republican Rhetoric: Slavery the Source of "Amalgamation"

In 1857, Abraham Lincoln—a Midwestern spokesman for the new Republican Party, a political party that had emerged in opposition to the territorial expansion of slavery—had some things to say about the *Dred Scott* decision, which he understood as undercutting his party's authority to work toward its chief objective. Speaking in opposition to a fellow politician from Illinois, U.S. Senator Stephen A. Douglas, Lincoln acknowledged widespread opposition to "the idea of indiscriminate amalgamation of the white and black races." And he alleged that Douglas was trying to shore up his own political position by "appropriat[ing] the benefit of this disgust to himself."[7]

Chief Justice Roger B. Taney and Senator Stephen A. Douglas both argued that the founders of the Union had not meant to include African Americans as citizens or even potential candidates for citizenship. Lincoln sought to find a middle way that would make room for black freedom and citizenship and still accommodate the widespread concerns about "amalgamation." Republicans, he said, insisted that "the Declaration of Independence includes ALL men, black as well as white." Douglas, he noted, tried to tar Republicans with the image that, taking such a position, "they want to vote, and eat, and sleep, and marry with negroes!" Lincoln deflected the allegation: "Now I protest against that counterfeit logic which concludes that, because I do not want a black woman for a *slave* I must necessarily want her for a *wife*. I need not have her for either, I can just leave her alone."[8]

Lincoln hammered at the theme yet again: "Judge Douglas is especially horrified at the thought of the mixing [of] blood by the white and black races: agreed for once—a thousand times agreed. There are white men enough to marry all the white women, and black men enough to marry all the black women; and so let them be married."[9] Lincoln was not merely accepting the anti-amalgamationists' arguments, however, for he was using their rhetoric to undercut their arguments about race, slavery, and citizenship—by speaking of blacks as well as whites being permitted to marry, even if only within their own racial communities. That in itself, in the slave South, would be a huge advance.

Lincoln turned the anti-amalgamationist logic and fears back on his opponents. The 1850 U.S. census, he said, showed more than 400,000 mulattos—"nearly all of them sprung from black *slaves* and white masters." Dred Scott and his wife had two children, he observed, two daughters. Had the Republicans' wishes prevailed in *Dred Scott*—had the family been permitted a hearing on their freedom, and had the courts recognized them as free—then "the chances of these black girls, ever mixing their blood with that of white people, would have been diminished at least to the extent that it could not have been without their consent." Douglas, however, "is delighted to have them decided to be slaves," concluded Lincoln, "and thus left subject to the forced concubinage of their masters."[10] The persistence and expansion of slavery meant more interracial sex, not less, because people held as slaves could not legally marry and form their own families—and, in particular, women held as slaves could not put up much resistance against predatory masters.

Debating the Law of Race and Marriage in Illinois and Wisconsin

In the pre–Civil War years, the great political issue—in the South and the North—was not interracial marriage but slavery, yet both race and slavery had many meanings. Northerners widely insisted on keeping slavery from spreading to the west, and white southerners as earnestly feared that northerners were at-tacking the preservation of slavery itself. Northerners themselves divided over questions of black exclusion and racial equality. In the North, proponents of white supremacy and restrictive laws routinely portrayed black men with white women as the great bugaboo. Opponents of new laws, including supporters of black rights, downplayed the threat. Moreover, turning the image around, they depicted white men with black women.

In 1858, when Abraham Lincoln and Stephen A. Douglas were campaigning in their home state of Illinois for state legislators to be elected who would be fa-vorable to their competing parties (and their competing candidacies for the U.S. Senate—in those days, state legislatures chose U.S. Senators), the two con-tenders sparred on the subject. Much of the language was a reprise from the year before, in the wake of *Dred Scott.* Lincoln chided Douglas for alluding to "this tendency of mine to set the states at war, and to set the negroes and white peo-ple to marrying each other." At another point, Lincoln questioned Douglas's logic: "I do not understand that because I do not want a negro woman for a slave that I must necessarily want her for a wife." Why, Lincoln wanted to know, couldn't he "just leave her alone"? "I am now in my fiftieth year," he said, "and certainly never have had a black woman either for a slave or wife, and so it seems to me that it is quite possible for us to get along without making either slaves or wives of negroes."[11]

Lincoln observed, "I have never had the least apprehension that I or my friends would marry negroes if there was no law to keep them from it." He as-sured Douglas that he would "to the very last stand by the law in this State that forbids the marriage of white folks with negroes," but, if Douglas was so sure that blacks and whites would marry in Illinois "if there was no law to keep them from it," then the voters should keep Douglas in Illinois, elect him to the state legislature instead of the U.S. Senate, and then Douglas would be available, if a repeal measure came up at the next session, "to vote it off." In fact, Douglas went beyond supporting racial restrictions on marriage. As he said at one point, "I am in favor of preserving not only the purity of the blood, but the purity of the government from any mixture or amalgamation with inferior races."[12] There should be, he meant, neither interracial marriage nor black voters.

Racial attitudes and fears were often, as in the Lincoln-Douglas debates, at the center of political rhetoric. Nineteenth-century legislators were in the habit of entertaining themselves and their audiences with their use of the English lan-guage, all the more because that language often had an edge, such as a racial edge, to it. In 1859 in the Wisconsin legislature, for example, Frederick Horn, a Democratic representative from Ozaukee County, introduced a miscegenation bill. A Republican colleague named Beckwith, noting that the bill referred to "persons who are part African," asked Horn could he "tell us what part?" Another Republican, named Turner, noted that "the bill provides for asking persons about to be married whether they had any colored blood in them. Now if this question were asked of any good democrat, his dander would be up at such a question being asked." Horn countered that "the question is not necessary"; the bill included a provision, he said, that "if the party who is about to perform the ceremony was satisfied, he need not ask the question. Now if [Turner] was to come to me to be married, I should not ask him such a question; I should give him the benefit of the doubt."[13]

Other legislators expressed real concerns, though they, too, might be inclined to jab their colleagues about their racial identity. One opponent "was opposed to the bill because it was so indefinite. It did not state what proportions of the blood was to be colored—it said persons of color"—and he knew people "who had negro blood in them who were whiter than the gentleman from Ozaukee."[14]

Other Republicans also opposed the measure. In the House, one claimed, "When the bill was first introduced I thought it was done as a joke." Indeed, another Republican legislator expressed his opposition along the lines "that the passage of this bill would too fully endorse the decisions of the United States Courts on the subject of the rights of people of color." In the Senate, one Republican "opposed the bill on principle as relating to a matter of taste with individuals with which the State should not interfere."[15]

Delighted when a Republican leader in the House announced that he hoped the miscegenation bill would pass, a Democratic newspaper, celebrating his apostasy and jibing at his colleagues, observed that his "abandonment" of the doctrine of racial equality "knocks out the keystone, the foundation of the Republican organization." After all, it declared, the Republicans owed their unity to their opposition to the proslavery *Dred Scott* decision, including its declaration that no African American could be a citizen.[16]

Race, War, and Reconstruction

Within a decade of the *Dred Scott* decision, the political landscape was transformed. Abraham Lincoln's election to the presidency in 1860 led to secession by 11 of the southern states (that is, 11 of the states that maintained slavery)—all but Delaware, Maryland, Kentucky, and Missouri. For four years, what remained of the United States of America warred on the new Confederate States of America to keep—or bring back—the nation together. The Republican Party found that, having campaigned not for abolition but for an end to the extension of slavery into more of the West, it had to embrace abolition as a weapon of war. Winning the war for the Union ended up requiring the recruitment of slave men to fight that war, and thus the Emancipation Proclamation that President Lincoln issued in January 1863. Moreover, in part to prevent the issue of slavery from ever again disrupting national politics or occasioning fratricidal war, Congress approved the Thirteenth Amendment two years later and sent it on to the states for ratification.

During the 1860 presidential campaign, nobody could know any of that yet. In Mississippi, however, U.S. Senator Albert Gallatin Brown did what he could to appeal to white non-slaveholders' sense of vulnerability so they would sign on and support the radical proslavery ticket of John C. Breckinridge. Should emancipation come to Mississippi, Senator Brown warned his non-slaveholding readers, "The negro will intrude into his presence—insist on being treated as an equal—that he shall go to the white man's table, and the white man to his—that he shall share the white man's bed, and the white man his—that his son shall marry the white man's daughter, and the white man's daughter his son. In short that they shall live on terms of perfect social equality. The non-slaveholder will, of course, reject the terms. Then," Brown concluded, "will commence a war of races."[17]

The Civil War led to the death of slavery, beginning with the Emancipation Proclamation in January 1863 and ending with ratification of the Thirteenth Amendment in December 1865. Confederate defeat and the abolition of slavery did not, however, signal that the crisis of the Union was over. The Civil Rights Act of 1866, together with the Fourteenth Amendment, ratified in 1868, reflected the nation's continuing efforts to come to grips with the aftermath of the Union's victory and slavery's abolition. The early postwar years revealed a combination of idealism and practical politics animating Republican members of Congress as they addressed the social and political implications of emancipation. And the matter of race and marriage kept cropping up.

The southern states experienced enormous political discontinuity after the Civil War. Emancipation initiated great changes in social relations and the law, but Reconstruction, as it unfolded, brought further change. At first, an all-white electorate continued to choose public officials in every southern state, whether it had gone with the Confederacy or remained in the Union. President Andrew Johnson (who took office after Abraham Lincoln was assassinated just weeks into his second term) required in 1865 that each former Confederate state call a constitutional convention and ratify the Thirteenth Amendment outlawing slavery. Only whites voted in the elections to those constitutional conventions, and only whites participated in the elections to each state legislature that followed.[18]

Each of the former Confederate states enacted a Black Code, a new set of laws that included provisions to recognize slave marriages and regulate marital life among former slaves. Quite aside from the marriage portions, some provisions of the Black Codes struck most congressional Republicans as entirely too re-strictive—as having left too much of slavery in place. The region's white voters and legislators were committed to conceding as little as possible with regard to race in the postwar era, and to maintaining as much power and privilege as possible in every sphere. Mississippi, for example, though it permitted the acquisition of personal property (things like furniture and tools), denied freed people's access to farm land; former slaves would have to work on land owned by whites.[19]

In response, Congress passed the Civil Rights Act of 1866. Drawing upon its authority under Section Two of the Thirteenth Amendment to enforce emancipation, Congress offered a working definition of freedom for black southerners. Rebutting the U.S. Supreme Court's decision in *Dred Scott*, the Civil Rights Act declared African Americans to be citizens, and it outlined their core rights. Lyman Trumbull, chairman of the Senate Judiciary Committee, had the Black Codes in mind when he vowed "to destroy all these discriminations." The 1866 act focused on what were understood to be "civil rights" (not political rights)—among them the right to make contracts, own land, and testify in court, as well as black southerners' right to be free of criminal penalties that applied only to them. It also provided for the "full and equal benefit of all laws and proceedings for the security of person and property, as is enjoyed by white citizens."[20]

President Andrew Johnson vetoed the civil rights bill. He objected to the exercise of federal power in new areas, and he worried about the implications for miscegenation laws as well as political rights, the two areas about which Stephen A. Douglas had expressed concern in 1858. "I do not say that this bill repeals State laws on the subject of marriage between the two races," Johnson wrote, but he did inquire whether, "if Congress can abrogate all State laws of discrimination between the two races in the matter of real estate, of suits, and of contracts generally," might it not "also repeal the State laws as to the contract of marriage between the two races"? Moreover, if Congress could presume to legislate on "who shall hold lands, who shall testify, who shall have capacity to make a contract in a State," he charged, "then Congress can by law also declare who, without regard to color or race, shall have the right to sit as a juror or as a judge, to hold any office, and, finally, to vote."[21]

In the end, Congress passed the bill over Johnson's veto. It was the law of the land, but Republicans fretted that it might not survive future legislative or judicial assault. A subsequent Congress might pass a repeal measure, and a Democratic president would sign such a bill. Even if that did not happen, the Supreme Court might agree with Johnson that the act was unconstitutional.

Therefore, in part to put the Civil Rights Act of 1866 beyond the reach of a potentially hostile subsequent Congress and ensure that the courts would not declare it unconstitutional, Congress framed the Fourteenth Amendment, the key to making a postwar world that northern Republicans could view as safe for their interests and beliefs. Embodying the Civil Rights Act, Section One declared African Americans to be citizens and, to shield them from discriminatory state laws like the Black Codes, guaranteed them "the equal protection of the laws."[22]

Yet the Civil Rights Act was only one consideration impelling Republicans toward adopting the Fourteenth Amendment. The death of slavery raised new questions not only regarding legal and social relations between blacks and whites in the South, but also regarding political relations between the South and the nation. After the Civil War and emancipation, black southerners were no longer slaves. Former slaves would count full value, rather than three-fifths, in determining southern states' power in the House of Representatives and the electoral college. Republicans belatedly recognized this ominous fact. As one congressman put the question, "Shall the death of slavery add two-fifths to the entire power which slavery had when slavery was living?"[23]

Section Two of the Fourteenth Amendment tried to formulate a way of offsetting the danger that political southerners and their northern Democratic allies might—because of the shift from three-fifths to a full count—have more power in national affairs after the defeat of slavery than they had enjoyed before the war. Under Section Two, states could each choose whether to enfranchise their black citizens, but unless black men were permitted to vote, the black population would not count when members of the House of Representatives were apportioned among the states after each census. Blacks would vote their own representation, according to this formulation, or nobody would.

Congress proposed the Fourteenth Amendment as the foundation for Reconstruction. Among the 11 states of the former Confederacy, however, only Tennessee ratified it. Congress therefore moved in 1867 to establish new conditions for political restoration. Congress required that each of the ten states that had rejected the Fourteenth Amendment call a new convention, whose delegates would be chosen by a biracial electorate, rather than the all-white electorate of 1865. Those conventions had to write new constitutions that enfranchised black men, and those states had to ratify the Fourteenth Amendment.[24]

Only then, in the view of congressional Republicans, would it be safe to give all the southern states back their seats in the House and Senate; and only then might it be safe to leave black southerners in the hands of southern state governments. Black southerners would presumably vote Republican, and thus offset the votes of their white neighbors in congressional and presidential elections. They would have political rights and could thus represent their interests in state politics. And to protect their rights in the courts, they could rely on the Fourteenth Amendment. The needs of black southerners and northern Republicans combined to change the constitutional environment within which southern politics and policies unfolded in the years after the Civil War.

The recalcitrant states ratified the Fourteenth Amendment, and it went into effect. Deciding whether to ratify it in those states was hardly a matter of considering its potential impact on the law of race and marriage. Even larger questions were at stake. Once ratified, however, the amendment might well have a tremendous effect on the law of marriage. Or it might not, but that, too, remained to be seen.

Politics and Demography in the Postwar South

Women outnumbered men in the postwar South. So enormous were the Civil War casualties—more than a quarter million dead on each side—that the postwar sex ratio was way out of balance. A distinct shortage of white men resulted in the North as well as the South, but similar absolute losses in the North had less impact there than in the South, where the white population was far smaller to begin with.[25] War and emancipation led to a shortage of white men to marry or to vote.

When it came to marriage, men—white men and black men—suddenly had an inflated value. No longer was it true that, as Lincoln had said in 1857, "there are white men enough to marry all the white women," and some white women were more likely than they would have otherwise been to look for marriage partners across the racial divide. White women with black men—the white man's nightmare—struck the southern social and cultural landscape at just the time that postwar policies struck the southern constitutional and political landscape. By 1867 or 1868, black men were voting in elections, being elected as delegates to state constitutional conventions, and even, on occasion, marrying white women.

It was a curious historical truth. Sex ratios that were out of balance, whether it was white men or white women who were in surplus, could have similar results on the antimiscegenation front. In the seventeenth century, the surge of efforts to curtail the pairing of white women with black men had arisen when, with a shortage of white women, white men placed a premium on them and tried to curtail the competition for them from black men—who themselves faced a shortage of black women. In the postwar South, what was perceived as an urgent need to curtail interracial marriages arose in part from a shortage of white men that, combined with the end of slavery, created conditions in which white women, to find a man, might look to nonwhite men. In the late 1860s, black men were not only relatively numerous; they were citizens instead of slaves.

A shortage of white men during Reconstruction caused concerns similar to those the shortage of white women had led to two centuries earlier, when Maryland and Virginia first enacted laws against interracial marriage. In the immediate postwar years, a shortage of black men also heightened the uncertainty that people would behave in ways consistent with a ban on interracial relationships. "Colored" Virginians, like their white counterparts, displayed a deficit of men between the ages of 21 and 44. Therefore, while the enormous number of deaths of white Civil War soldiers was not the only force at work to skew the sex ratios, many white women—and perhaps black women, too—had reason to downplay race in their quest for marriage partners.[26]

Disputes over public policy, combined with changes in sex ratios, framed much of what went on in the postwar South. Many white men across the region took action to curtail social change and perpetuate their own constellation of privileges. As they had for 200 years, many held that white men should have exclusive access to white women—and that they should continue to have access to black women. Moreover, nobody—white or black, male or female—with one racial identity should be permitted to marry someone with the other racial identity.[27] The two questions—sexual access and prospective marriage partners—were addressed in postwar politics and law.

The legislative and judicial branches of the southern states might busy themselves enacting and applying laws to restrain people of both genders and all racial identities from marrying across racial boundaries. Then again, the participation of African American legislators and constitution makers might thwart whites' inclinations to use public power to regulate such matters. Moreover, the transformation of federal power and policy on race and slavery might change the rules as well. The Reconstruction era enhanced the perceived need to restrict racial equality among free people—including access to marital partners across racial boundaries—but it also reduced the likelihood that proponents of such measures could get their way, as long as large numbers of black southerners could vote.

Debating Civil and Political Rights in Arkansas

A debate erupted in the 1868 Arkansas constitutional convention after one delegate proposed a clause forbidding anyone in the state "to solemnize the rites of matrimony between a white person and a person of African descent." Opposing the clause, a Republican, James A. Hodges, who had moved to Arkansas from New York, took a libertarian approach. "If persons want to intermarry . . . they ought certainly to have that privilege."[28]

Then a black delegate, William H. Grey, spoke. His humor had a sharp edge. "I have no particular objection to the resolution," he said. "But I think that in order to make the law binding, there should be some penalty attached to its violation—kill them, quarter them, or something of that kind." In truth, Grey said, such a provision appeared "superfluous," in view of the great difference in "intelligence and wealth" of the two races in Arkansas. Moreover, such a law had long held in Arkansas, he observed, "but while the contract has been kept on our part, it has not been kept on the part of our friends; and I propose, if such an amendment is inserted in the Constitution, to insist, also, that if any white man shall be found cohabiting with a negro woman, the penalty shall be death."[29]

One of the notable features of the Arkansas debate was how much the term "miscegenation" had already made its way into use, just in the four or five years since the publication of the pamphlet by Croly and Wakeman. Other terms continued in use—a pairing like "social equality and amalgamation," as well as "miscegenation and mongrelism"—but it was a telling development that one newspaper, in particular, chose to condemn the Republicans as "miscegenationists." Both the political issue and the new term had great currency.[30]

The coupling of marriage with political rights revealed that, for some Conservative delegates, at least, there was no substantial distinction between "social equality" and "political equality." Those who would enfranchise black men, cried W. D. Moore, were inviting them "to marry our daughters." Joseph H. Corbell complained that "to confer the right of suffrage on the colored population" could not help "leading to amalgamation." "Political equality," warned J. N. Cypert, was "the stepping stone to miscegenation."[31]

The constitution that emerged from the convention recommended that the legislature act against miscegenation. That was a compromise measure. It left the question open, but at least it did not place in the constitution itself a ban against black-white marriage, so it accomplished delegate Gray's major purpose. Meanwhile, several Republican delegates had made it clear that they thought a miscegenation statute would violate the Civil Rights Act of 1866, which was already law, as well as Section One of the Fourteenth Amendment, ratification of which was pending. Conservatives, for their part, wanted to see the proposed constitution rejected because it gave black men the right to vote.[32]

Marriage in Black and White in Postwar Indiana

Even in the post–Civil War North, couples could jeopardize their freedom when they married across racial lines. In southern Indiana, on April 13, 1870, a man of African ancestry, Thomas Gibson, married a white woman, Jennie Williams. The Civil Rights Act of 1866 was on the books, as was the Fourteenth Amendment. Then again, so was a state law, dating from 1842, banning marriages between whites and blacks upon penalties of from one to ten years in the Indiana penitentiary and a fine of anywhere between $1,000 and $5,000.

Indiana law clearly disapproved of marriages such as that between Thomas Gibson and Jennie Williams, and, ten days after the ceremony, the grand jury in Vanderburgh County brought an indictment. Gibson's attorney asked, however, that the indictment be quashed. In view of the Civil Rights Act and the Fourteenth Amendment, the trial judge so ordered. His ruling did not end the matter, though. The state appealed the judge's action to the Indiana Supreme Court.[33]

The trial judge might consider the Indiana statute a dead letter. A unanimous Indiana Supreme Court ruled otherwise—reversing the trial judge, directing him to overrule the motion to quash the indictment, and ordering that Gibson be put on trial. "If the federal government can determine who may marry in a state, there is no limit to its power," the Indiana Supreme Court insisted. But the court rejected the premise. In its view, rather, "the state government controls all matters of a local and domestic character. The federal government regulates matters between the states and with foreign governments."[34]

The Indiana Supreme Court's decision had clear implications—whether ominous or promising depended on one's viewpoint—for legal developments in the South after the Civil War. No change in federal policy during the Reconstruction years, it seemed, had any bearing on Indiana's law against interracial marriage. Would similar determinations emerge elsewhere? Or would the approach taken at the Indiana trial court be more widely adopted?

Some people would surely lose their freedom if Thomas Gibson's experience at the Indiana Supreme Court proved widespread among interracial couples. Rather than a uniform national standard—whether one that banned interracial marriage or one that permitted it—the rule might well continue to vary from place to place and from time to time, depending on how legislators, judges, and juries chose to act. For Thomas Gibson, as he discovered, the state law of miscegenation had not changed in light of any changes in federal law. The Indiana law lived on into the 1870s as though nothing had changed there since the 1850s.

The Antimiscegenation Regime in a World without Slavery

Did the Civil Rights Act mean that people could legally marry each other regardless of their racial identities? What about the Fourteenth Amendment? Legislators, delegates to constitutional conventions, trial judges, appellate judges, men, women, blacks, whites, voters, non-voters—all could differ both on whether the rules had changed and whether change was a good thing. It might take some years before it was certain just what the rules were, whatever one thought of them.

When Croly and Wakefield published their pamphlet during the Civil War, "miscegenation"—the term and the issue—entered the national debate over the politics of race in a revolutionary decade whose major developments centered on race. In national politics, the issue remained near the center of controversy through 1866 and 1867, and it surfaced again on the road to the Civil Rights Act of 1875.[35] After that, the issue erupted from time to time in the politics of various states, and it proved of compelling interest to particular families whenever the law of race intervened in matters of marriage.

In the seventeenth century, each colony could act for itself in fashioning laws governing race and marriage. So could the states from the American Revolution through the Civil War. By the late 1860s and the 1870s, federal law might restrict such laws. Whether and how it did—what became of the miscegenation laws and how they operated, as well as how they finally came to an end—will be the subjects of subsequent chapters.

PART TWO

EQUAL PROTECTION OF THE LAWS

CHAPTER 5

POST–CIVIL WAR ALABAMA

"The civil rights bill now confers . . . the right to make and enforce contracts, amongst which is that of marriage with any citizen capable of entering into that relation"

—Alabama Supreme Court (1872)

"The former erroneous ruling of this court furnishes no excuse which we can recognize"

—Alabama Supreme Court (1878)

In 1858, Abraham Lincoln observed to white folks in Illinois that it seemed to him "quite possible for us to get along without making either slaves or wives of negroes."[1] After 1865, the Thirteenth Amendment said nobody could make anyone a slave. In later years, most people—whatever their racial identities—would demonstrate no particular interest in marrying across some racial line. But could white men, if so inclined, make "wives of negroes"? Would the law intervene if a black man and a white woman wished to marry? These were very real questions, and the answers could depend on what was happening in local politics as well as what had changed in federal policy.

During the quarter-century after the Civil War, the states of the former Confederacy went through three political phases. Between 1865 and 1867, to a large extent, each state had control over its own affairs. The Civil Rights Act of 1866, though, declared black southerners to be citizens and specified a wider range of rights that all citizens could claim. Then, in 1867, Congress took over Reconstruction. Republicans had proposed a Fourteenth Amendment, in part to put into the Constitution the central provisions of the Civil Rights Act, and, to secure ratification, Congress imposed new conditions on ten southern states. Black men obtained the right to vote and hold office there, and to a varying degree, black and white Republicans came to power in all ten states for a time.

For as many as ten years (though on average about half that), Republicans dominated the politics of all former Confederate states. By 1877, all the Republican governments had fallen, and the Democrats, or "Redeemers," had assumed power. In the years that followed, the power of the white Democratic Party became ever more complete, the South ever more "redeemed." Black political power vanished, and Reconstruction patterns and policies were ever more things of the past. Wherever political change took the South, the law of interracial marriage followed.

Was Interracial Marriage a Crime?

Was interracial marriage a crime in the Reconstruction South? Alabama exemplified the dominant features in the story line of interracial marriage and the law in the South—especially the Deep South—after the Civil War. Struggles between Republicans and Democrats, controversies between state and federal authority, constant concern with racial identity—in combination, these produced radical shifts in policy. Alabama embraced the antimiscegenation regime, repudiated that regime, and then returned to it. Rather than being unique, Alabama exemplified the postwar South. The discontinuity in the law of race and marriage in that one state—by pointing up the possibilities that changes in federal law brought—serves as a metaphor for Reconstruction.

Before 1865, although Alabama had enacted a penalty for anyone presiding at an interracial couple's wedding ceremony, it was no crime for a white person to marry a nonwhite. At the conclusion of the Civil War, the state wasted no time remedying its oversight. The Alabama constitution of 1865 directed the legislature to make interracial marriages between whites and people of African ancestry "null and void *ab initio,* and making the parties to any such marriage subject to criminal prosecutions."[2] So instructed, at its very next session, the Alabama legislature enacted a statute that outlawed interracial marriage.

The legislature established a penalty of two to seven years in prison for both members of any interracial couple. The law also established penalties for any probate judge who knowingly issued a marriage license for an interracial couple and for any justice of the peace or minister of the gospel who performed a marriage ceremony for such a couple.[3] Behavior that had been previously left up to individuals now became a question of criminal law. In this sense, race had more power to govern private relationships between free people in Alabama after emancipation than before.[4]

Throughout the years of Reconstruction and beyond, the Alabama courts ruled on various miscegenation cases. The fundamental right of individual citizens to marry, to live together, and to remain out of prison for doing so depended on how the courts ruled. What the law was, whether it was constitutional, and how it affected various individual relationships—questions like these generated considerable confusion in the late 1860s and the 1870s. In particular the Fourteenth Amendment, ratified in 1868, led to questions of whether miscegenation statutes had come under the ban.

The all-white electorate that controlled every southern state's politics in 1865 and 1866 lost its grip under the new political conditions that Congress created with the Reconstruction acts of 1867, and Republicans took power for a time in Alabama. Republicans controlled the constitutional convention that met in Montgomery in 1867 and, the next year, elected a governor and a majority of the legislature under the new state constitution. Whatever the changes that took place during the Republican interlude, Republican control proved short-lived in Alabama. By 1874, Democrats had retrieved control, and they retained control far into the twentieth century.[5]

These political changes during the postwar years governed the recruitment of judges to the Alabama Supreme Court. The court always spoke with one voice in miscegenation cases, and personnel changes fully account for the discontinuity that the court displayed in its decisions on such matters. Under the Alabama constitution of 1868, the voters elected three state supreme court judges to six-year terms. Beginning in 1869, three Alabama Republicans, all white, sat on the bench, and one result was a ruling that the Alabama miscegenation law was unconstitutional. After the 1874 elections, three Democrats replaced the Republicans on the Alabama Supreme Court, and the counterrevolution produced new results in civil rights cases.[6]

The Fourteenth Amendment offered protection against denials by state governments of "equal protection of the laws," "due process," and citizens' "privileges or immunities." In the *Slaughter-House Cases* (1873), however—shortly before the Democrats came back to power in Alabama—the U.S. Supreme Court construed very narrowly the "privileges or immunities" of citizens of the United States under the Fourteenth Amendment, an interpretation that raised doubts about the effectiveness with which the Fourteenth Amendment might protect individuals' rights against the power of a state.[7]

This dual context—the Fourteenth Amendment to the U.S. Constitution, followed by court rulings as to its meaning, together with violent shifts in power and policy within the states of the former Confederacy—frames the postwar history of litigation regarding the constitutionality of Alabama laws that threatened to make felons of both partners in interracial relationships.

Miscegenation and the Courts in Postwar Alabama

Alabama law imposed penalties that distinguished sharply between same-race couples and interracial couples. Under Section 3598 of the Alabama Code of

1867, two people, if of the same race and convicted of living "together in adultery, or fornication," were to be fined at least $100, and they could also be sentenced to as much as six months in the county jail or at hard labor. A second conviction "with the same person" subjected the offender to a minimum fine of $300 and a maximum one year in prison, while an additional conviction, again "with the same person," carried a mandatory sentence of two years, either in the penitentiary or at hard labor for the county.[8]

While Section 3598 covered same-race couples who lived together outside of marriage, Section 3602 covered interracial couples who lived together, regardless of whether they were married. Distinguishing neither married from unmarried, nor a first offense from a subsequent violation—and defining a nonwhite as a person with a black great-grandparent—Section 3602 mandated imprisonment, for a term of two to seven years each, of a white person and a "descendant of any negro, to the third generation," if they "intermarry or live in adultery or fornication with each other."[9]

Not long after Alabama's miscegenation law went into effect, Thornton Ellis and Susan Bishop, a black man and a white woman, went on trial in Lee County for violating Alabama's laws governing sexual relations. Unable to marry, they had managed to share their lives the best they could under Alabama law. A jury found Bishop and Ellis guilty of violating Section 3602, the interracial law—and imposed a $100 fine on each of them, as though they had been convicted under Section 3598, the same-race law.[10] No matter their racial identities, they had received the lightest possible penalty for the crime of which they stood convicted.

Nevertheless, they appealed their convictions. In June 1868, the Alabama Supreme Court upheld the convictions but reversed the trial court on the penalty it had imposed. The court suggested that the trial judge had believed Section 3602 to violate the Civil Rights Act of 1866, and it rejected that premise. The federal law, Chief Justice A. J. Walker wrote, "does not prohibit the making of race and color a constituent of an offense, provided it does not lead to a discrimination in punishment." As for Section 3602, it "creates an offense, of which participation by persons of different race is an element. To constitute the offense, there must be not only criminal intercourse, but it must be by persons of different race." The Alabama statute, which outlawed interracial liaisons for both the white partner and the black one and then imposed identical sentences for infractions, met the standard required under the 1866 Civil Rights Act, according to the Alabama Supreme Court.[11]

The state supreme court upheld the Alabama law and sustained the convictions, but it reversed the sentences and remanded the case, looking for a prison term rather than a fine. Thornton Ellis and Susan Bishop would have fared better if they had not appealed their convictions—or if their case had come to the

Alabama Supreme Court on appeal just one term later than it did. The June term in 1868 was the last one before a new court was elected. The new Republican court began its work in 1869. By that time, too, the Fourteenth Amendment had been ratified.

Burns v. State (1872)

The next miscegenation case to reach the Alabama Supreme Court developed in 1872 after a justice of the peace, James Burns, was indicted for presiding in Mobile over a wedding of an interracial couple. When Burns appealed his conviction, Justice Benjamin F. Saffold spoke for a court that viewed the miscegenation laws in a very different light than the court had four years earlier. In 1872, the court found that Section 3602 violated the state constitution, the Civil Rights Act of 1866, and the Fourteenth Amendment. "Marriage is a civil contract," Justice Saffold wrote. "The same right to make a contract as is enjoyed by white citizens, means the right to make any contract which a white citizen may make. The law intended to destroy the distinctions of race and color in respect to the rights secured by it."[12]

Justice Saffold, a Republican judge, relied on the U.S. Supreme Court's 1857 *Dred Scott* decision to bolster his interpretation of the law of freedom as it contrasted with the law of slavery. Chief Justice Roger B. Taney, he noted, had stressed state laws banning marriage between blacks and whites to support the conclusion that blacks were not citizens. As the Alabama judge stated, "an inhabitant of a country, proscribed by its laws, approaches equality with the more favored population in proportion as the proscription is removed." He applied that notion to the statute at hand: "Dred Scott was not allowed to sue a citizen because he was not himself a citizen. One of the rights conferred by citizenship, therefore, is that of suing any other citizen. The civil rights bill," declared Safford, "now confers this right upon the negro in express terms, as also the right to make and enforce contracts, amongst which is that of marriage with any citizen capable of entering into that relation." Whatever the authority of Congress to pass the Civil Rights Act in 1866, the Fourteenth Amendment enshrined "its cardinal principle" in the federal constitution. The second section of Article One of Alabama's constitution of 1868, Justice Saffold continued, had "the same effect." All citizens possessed "equal civil and political rights and public privileges," and James Burns was ordered freed.[13]

Rebuttal to Burns

A Huntsville lawyer, David Davie Shelby, soon challenged the ruling in *Burns*. Noting in 1874 that many states had miscegenation laws on the books, he observed that, in the few years since the Fourteenth Amendment had been ratified, "the validity of these statutes has been tested with varying results." In particular, he recounted the Indiana Supreme Court's opinion in *State* v. *Gibson* (see chapter 4), which he found compelling. Surely, he argued, it remained constitutionally permissible to draw "distinctions without inequality," and it wasn't like the penalties for black and white violators were dissimilar in either Indiana or Alabama.[14]

Shelby assumed that definite racial boundaries were in place, and he wanted those lines to persist. "It is an unnatural construction to place upon the Fourteenth Amendment to say that it abrogates the statutes," he insisted. "The Congress did not intend to destroy the purity of our races when it submitted this amendment to the people, nor did the people in adopting it vote for amalgamation." He cited the global distribution of the various races to make the claim that, not only had God "made the races dissimilar," but they were not meant to "overstep the line that he has drawn between them." To maintain that racial line, another line must be maintained, "a line of limitation" that separated the powers of the states and those of the federal government.[15]

Authority over marriage laws remained with the states, Shelby insisted, and the Alabama Supreme Court should not have ruled the way it did in *Burns*. Shelby was not alone in the position he took, and the Alabama judiciary soon followed the approach he had outlined.

A Partial Rollback

At about the same time as Shelby published his rebuttal to *Burns,* an unmarried interracial couple went on trial in Barbour County, Alabama. A white man named Ford and a black woman were tried, under Section 3602, on the felony charge of "living together in adultery or fornication" in an interracial relationship. They challenged the constitutionality of that statute, and they pleaded not guilty. Yet they were convicted and sentenced to the penitentiary. They appealed to the Alabama Supreme Court, where their lawyer, relying on the decision in *Burns,* argued: "The legislature had no power to make an act[,] which when committed by persons of the same race is only a misdemeanor, a felony when committed by persons of different races."[16]

John W. A. Sanford, who was still the Alabama attorney general in 1875 (he had argued the state's side in the *Ellis* and *Burns* cases), harked back to *Ellis* v. *State*. He insisted that Section 3602 contravened neither the state nor the federal constitutions. Relying on the U.S. Supreme Court's decision in *The Slaughter-House Cases,* he argued: "Every State has the right to regulate its domestic affairs, and to adopt a domestic policy most conducive to the interest and welfare of its people." As far as the decision in *Burns* v. *State* was concerned, he declared that it "should be overruled."[17]

The attorney general won a partial victory. The court stated that, "On the question involved in this case, we can add nothing to the thorough discussion it received" in the *Ellis* decision. Yet the court professed to see no "conflict" between *Ellis* and *Burns:*

> The latter case involved only the validity of the statute prohibiting marriage between whites and blacks. The validity of the statute prohibiting such persons from living in adultery was not involved. Marriage may be a natural and civil right, pertaining to all persons. Living in adultery is offensive to all laws human and divine, and human laws must impose punishments adequate to the enormity of the offence and its insult to public decency.[18]

The court spoke in its decision in *Ford* v. *State* as if the only question were whether "adultery or fornication" should be a criminal offense. It chose to ignore the racial component. It displayed no effort directly to address the difference between a misdemeanor offense, with a $100 fine, and a felony conviction that carried at least two years' imprisonment. By implication, the court ruled that "the enormity of the offence" was greater if the adulterous partners were of different races than if they were of the same race.

"The Former Erroneous Ruling of This Court Furnishes No Excuse"

In two cases in the December 1877 term, the court completed the counterrevolution that it had begun two years before. Like *Ellis,* but unlike *Ford,* each case involved the marriage of a black man and a white woman. Having chosen to distinguish between a statutory ban on interracial marriage (which had been struck down in *Burns)* and a similar ban on interracial adultery or fornication (which it had upheld in *Ford*), the court now threw out the distinction and upheld the statutes.

Aaron Green married Julia Atkinson in Butler County on July 13, 1876. On the basis that he was black and she was white, they were soon indicted for violating Section 4189 of the revised Alabama code of 1876, which, like its predecessor, Section 3602, banned interracial marriages and established greater penalties for fornication and adultery when the couples were interracial than when both partners were of the same race.[19]

Julia Green pleaded not guilty to the charge, but she did not dispute the facts. Judge John K. Henry instructed the jury that, "if they believed the evidence, they must find the defendant guilty." The jury convicted her, and Judge Henry sentenced her to two years in the penitentiary. Citing the *Burns* decision, Green appealed to the Alabama Supreme Court. Attorney General Sanford, as he had two years earlier in *Ford,* urged that *Burns* be overturned. He relied again on the Alabama decision in *Ellis.* He relied, too, on the Indiana decision, *State* v. *Gibson,* which had declared that the Fourteenth Amendment did not abrogate a statute making it a felony—with penalties of one to ten years in prison and a fine of $1,000 to $5,000—for any white person and anyone at least one-eighth black to marry each other.[20]

In March 1878, Justice Amos R. Manning spoke for the Alabama Supreme Court in a thoroughgoing rejection of the decision made by "our immediate predecessors" in *Burns.* He noted that, when the Civil Rights Act of 1866 was passed, many northern states had miscegenation laws on the books, and he declared that, during debate on the bill in Congress, no mention had been made of such laws. Returning to the court's line of argument in *Ellis,* he insisted that the Alabama law "no more tolerates" interracial marriage on the part of a "white person" than of a "negro or mulatto." Each, he insisted, "is punishable for the offense prohibited, in precisely the same manner and to the same extent. There is no discrimination made in favor of the white person, either in the capacity to enter into such a relation, or in the penalty."[21]

Going further, the court insisted that "the subject should be regarded with a broader view." Justice Manning raised the question whether marriage was "nothing more than a civil contract," and then he insisted that it was much more. He cited a Kentucky decision, for example, that stated that "marriage, the most elementary and useful" of all social relations, "is regulated and controlled by the sovereign power of the State, and can not, like mere contracts, be dissolved by the mutual consent only of contracting parties, but may be abrogated by the sovereign will, either with or without the consent of both parties, whenever the public good, or justice to both or either of the parties will be thereby subserved."[22] Marriages created "homes," wrote Justice Manning, and homes served as "the nurseries of States":

> Who can estimate the evil of introducing into their most intimate relations, elements so heterogeneous that they must naturally cause discord, shame, disruption of family circles and estrangement of kindred? While with their interior administration, the State should interfere but little, it is obviously of the highest public concern that it should, by general laws adapted to the state of things around them, guard them against disturbances from without.[23]

The judge conceded that "it depends very much, of course, upon the relative proportions and condition of the two races in any State, whether legislation of the kind in question is necessary there or not." He did not need to remind anyone in Alabama that, with regard to "relative proportions," people in that state who had no African ancestors (within recent generations) comprised only a small majority of all residents (the census figure was 52 percent in 1870).[24] As to "condition," virtually all black citizens of Alabama had recently been slaves. The implication, whether intended or not, was that, as slavery receded into the past, or as the black percentage of Alabama residents declined, or both, the need for such laws might diminish. In Alabama in the 1870s, however, and (the court assumed) virtually everywhere else in the nation at that time, the "conviction" prevailed that "the law should absolutely frustrate and prevent the growth of any desire" to enter into an interracial marriage. The law should do so

> by making marriage between the two races, legally impossible, and severely punishing those who perform, and those who, with intent to be married, go through the ceremonies thereof. Manifestly, it is for the peace and happiness of the black race, as well as of the white, that such laws should exist. And surely there can not be any tyranny or injustice in requiring both alike, to form this union with those of their own race only.[25]

Logic and law alike, Justice Manning contended, dictated that the court uphold the constitutionality of the Alabama laws. He cited various court decisions elsewhere, including the *Gibson* case in Indiana as well as two recent cases in North Carolina. And in view of his social commentary, he demanded, "How, then, can it be maintained that the States of this Union, in adopting" the Fourteenth Amendment, which makes "no allusion to such intermarriages, intended to deprive themselves of the important power of regulating matters of so great consequence and delicacy within their own borders for themselves, as it always was their undoubted right to do." On the contrary, the court declared, the Reconstruction amendments were "designed to secure to citizens, without distinction of race, rights of a civil or political kind only—not such as are merely social, much less those of a purely domestic nature." Thus, "No amendment to the Constitution, nor any enactment thereby authorized, is in any degree infringed by the enforcement of the section of the Code, under which the appellant in this cause was convicted and sentenced." As for "the decision made by our predecessors" in the *Burns* case, Justice Manning said, it "is hereby overruled."[26]

Later that term, the Alabama Supreme Court reiterated its new views on the constitutionality, the propriety, and even the urgent necessity of that state's miscegenation laws. Robert Hoover, a black man, had married Betsey Litsey, a white woman, on March 6, 1875, in Talladega County. The next year, the grand jury indicted them for living together in "adultery or fornication." Pointing to his marriage, Hoover had pleaded not guilty. Evidence showed that, during the year 1876, the couple had "lived together openly" in "a house containing only one room," and they "represented themselves to be married, and accepted each other as husband and wife."[27]

The state placed in evidence a marriage license signed by George P. Plowman, judge of probate, with a note affixed from a minister, John Livingston, that he had performed the wedding ceremony the same day. Hoover sought to introduce evidence that, before the marriage license had ever been issued, he had asked assurance from Judge Plowman that it was lawful for the two to be married and that "he had been informed that it was." Plowman had gone on to advise Hoover that the state "Supreme Court had decided the law forbidding such marriages to be unconstitutional." But the state objected to the introduction of such evidence, and the trial judge, John Henderson, upheld the objection.[28]

After both sides presented their cases, Judge Henderson, refusing the instructions that Hoover wanted, told the jury that "the marriage shown in this case was forbidden by law, is a nullity, and is no protection to the parties who are guilty as charged in the indictment, if the evidence shows, beyond a reasonable doubt, that Hoover is a negro man and Litsey a white woman, and that they have been cohabiting as husband and wife." The jury saw no reasonable doubt.[29]

When the case came to the Alabama Supreme Court, the state attorney general, the everlasting Mr. Sanford, cited the recent *Green* decision in arguing that the lower court should be sustained. By contrast, Hoover's attorney argued that, in view of the *Burns* decision, Hoover could not be criminally liable. He had been married "nearly three years after" that decision, which had, on constitutional grounds, negated the Alabama statute against interracial marriage, and his marriage had taken place before the *Ford* decision, let alone the court's ruling in *Green*.[30] (That argument, had it been accepted, should have relieved Hoover of his conviction, yet in view of the decision in *Green*, there was little hope of the couple's continuing to live together in Alabama without prosecution.)

In July 1878, Justice George Washington Stone spoke for the court in rejecting Hoover's contentions and, on every count, upholding the lower court. The attorney general had his way once again. The court read the decision in *Green* as having declared interracial marriages void. The Hoovers' "marriage being absolutely void, the offending parties must be treated as unmarried persons, and their sexual cohabitation as fornication within the statute." As the trial judge had instructed the jury, the Hoovers' wedding ceremony could offer "no protection" against the charge of living together without benefit of marriage.[31]

Nor, the higher court held, had the circuit court erred "in refusing to receive testimony that, before the alleged marriage, the probate judge counselled the defendant it was lawful for him to marry a white woman." Ignorance of the law is no excuse, the court insisted, "and the former erroneous ruling of this court furnishes no excuse which we can recognize."[32] As the Alabama Supreme Court noted, the statute at issue, though outlawed in the *Burns* decision in 1872, had been incorporated verbatim when Alabama revised its code in 1876.

In Alabama, by 1878, nobody identified as white could legally marry anyone identified as black. If such a marriage took place, the couple could be tried on the charge of living together without being married. If a couple living together outside of marriage was interracial, the charge, even for a first offense, was a felony, and conviction brought a sentence of at least two years in the penitentiary. In the years to come, countless people were indicted and convicted under the Alabama miscegenation laws. Among them were Jack Holden, a black man convicted in Dallas County in 1878 for "intermarrying races"; Mary Holden, the white woman who had married him, and who was imprisoned for "adultery and fornication"; and Joseph J. Bradley, a white man given a two-year sentence that year for "marrying [a] negress."[33]

By the 1880s, the offense was typically termed "miscegenation." Jefferson County produced many of the convictions, among them A. F. Doyle (a white man) and Jennie Street in 1884, and Terry Nelson (a black man) and Molly Guy in 1885. Nine convictions in Alabama during 1890 included two couples in Butler County, each of them involving a black man and a white woman, all charged with "felonious adultery" and each sentenced to three and a half years. The 1890 convictions also included two couples in Jefferson County, one involving a white man and a black woman, the other a black man and a white woman.[34]

The Trajectory of Miscegenation Legislation and Litigation

The politics of judicial recruitment could have a huge bearing on the ways in which southern appellate courts handled miscegenation cases. The period of greatest uncertainty came in the 1870s, when the new constitutional dispensation still offered the possibility—realized for a time in Alabama, when Republican judges controlled the state supreme court—that the Fourteenth Amendment controlled state action to the point of invalidating miscegenation laws. When Democrats resumed control of the Alabama court, a new approach to the Fourteenth Amendment quickly took shape. "Equal protection," in that view, permitted imprisonment for interracial marriage, at least so long as the law applied to both partners and imposed similar penalties.

Between 1868 and 1872, the Alabama Supreme Court reversed direction on the state's miscegenation laws; it did so again in the years that followed. By 1875, the Republican interlude of Reconstruction had ended in Alabama, and the state supreme court was again under the control of Democrats. In a series of cases between 1875 and 1877, the court overturned *Burns* and perfected a new interpretation of the law of race, freedom, and marriage. The new interpretation endured for nearly a century.

Alabama Attorney General John W. A. Sanford lost one, but only one, of all these cases. In every miscegenation case that reached the state's high court in the post–Civil War years, the trial court had convicted the defendant of violating some provision of the statutes. In the only case in which the state supreme court overturned the lower court conviction, a white justice of the peace named James Burns got off after presiding at the wedding of an interracial couple. The best that can be said about the other cases is that authorities did not seek to hit defendants with the greatest possible penalties. To the contrary, defendants seem to have been sentenced in most cases to two years' loss of liberty, rather than the maximum seven years.

The Rest of the South

Between 1868 and 1878, Alabama developed a line of argument defending an antimiscegenation environment against attacks based on the Civil Rights Act of 1866 or the Fourteenth Amendment. Alabama made a significant detour along the way, however, before settling down with that argument. Some other states' courts took a similar detour. Cases from Louisiana, Texas, and Mississippi—detailed in the next chapter—demonstrate that Reconstruction could make a huge difference in whether and how a state's miscegenation laws operated.

Moreover, the judiciary was not the only force for change in the former Confederacy. The same kind of political transformation that led to a renovated Alabama Supreme Court permitted some states to drop their miscegenation laws through other means. During Reconstruction, five states abandoned their allegiance to the antimiscegenation regime by repealing the old laws, or by simply leaving their miscegenation statutes out when revising their codes of laws. Between 1868 and 1870, three states—South Carolina, Louisiana, and Mississippi—repealed their laws against interracial marriage, and the ban against miscegenation in Arkansas simply vanished for a time when the state produced a new collection of its laws in 1874.

Florida, which as a territory had enacted a miscegenation law in 1832, was explicit in its rationale. In 1872, a new digest of Florida laws explained that "various provisions of the statutes in relation to marriages between white and colored persons are omitted out of deference to the opinion of those who think that they are opposed to our [state] Constitution and to the legislation of Congress."[35]

The statement from Florida, like the *Burns* decision in Alabama, revealed the possibilities that Reconstruction brought for a time to the postwar South. In all, in addition to Alabama, as many as six states of the former Confederacy abandoned their allegiance to the antimiscegenation regime for a time after Congress took control of the nation's Reconstruction policy in 1867. Put another way, of the seven original states of the Confederacy, all but Georgia went through changes of the sort that Alabama displayed.

CHAPTER 6

RECONSTRUCTION AND THE
LAW OF INTERRACIAL MARRIAGE

A. H. Foster and Leah Foster "continued to live together, habiting themselves as man and wife, until after the law prohibiting such a marriage had been abrogated by the 14th Amendment to the Constitution of the United States"

—Texas Supreme Court

"The Civil Rights bill . . . invested [Cornelia Hart] with the capacity to enter into the contract of marriage with E. C. Hart, a white man, and to legitimate her children by him born before said marriage, just as if she had been a white woman"

—Louisiana Supreme Court

The miscegenation cases from Reconstruction Alabama all had to do with criminal sanctions against people involved in black-white marriages—the bride, the groom, even the person who presided over the ceremony. Yet the law of race and marriage had many faces, and the civil matter of transmitting property from one generation to another—and from one racial identity to another—also played a significant role in shaping society and reflecting the new possibilities that came with the emancipation of slaves and the citizenship of black southerners.

Quite aside from criminal law, then, cases regarding interracial families and the inheritance of property—whether through a will or in the absence of a will—offered a measure of what (if anything) had changed, and when, and how, in the South in the early years after the Civil War. Cases from Mississippi, Louisiana, and Texas in the 1870s showed how much had changed—for a time—as a consequence of emancipation and Reconstruction.

Mississippi supplies an excellent example of the kind of change that could take place in one state along the path to the 1890s. In 1865, Mississippi enacted a prohibition against interracial marriage that carried a penalty of imprisonment "for life." Then the winds of politics changed direction, and the ban was lifted in 1870.[1]

"Former Impediments to Marriage between Whites and Blacks Ceased": Mississippi's Constitution of 1868

For a bright and shining decade, Mississippi had no law against interracial marriage. That did not mean that black-white couples never ran into extralegal difficulties, but the law provided a good barometer to the political change of the 1870s. The 1865 penalty, a life sentence for marrying across the color line, was eliminated, never to return. For a time, some black-white couples did marry and live in Mississippi without fear of the law.[2] In addition, the Mississippi Supreme Court ruled in an 1873 inheritance case that the state constitution of 1868 repealed the former rule.

L. P. Dickerson was one of many white men in Mississippi who had children with black women during slavery times. He evidently chose to live more or less openly with a woman named Ann and with their children from 1855 to 1871— during the time she was his slave and for several years afterwards. At his death in February 1871, he left "a large real and personal estate," and the question arose as to who should inherit his property. Susan Dickerson and Oliver Dickerson—Ann's daughter and son, and the deceased's only children—assumed that they should inherit. But his brother, P. C. Dickerson, had a daughter and son-in-law with very different ideas, and they won at trial in Coahoma County. They took possession of the Dickerson property and promptly began working the plantation.[3]

L. P. Dickerson's children did not give up, so the case went to Mississippi's highest court. Lawyers for the collateral claimants insisted that the children's parents had never married. A man could not marry his slave, and after emancipation their cohabitation was a crime. Even when the law was no longer an impediment, they had never taken any legal action to become husband and wife, and their long-term liaison constituted nothing better than "illicit intercourse"; it was "intentionally criminal." Since the "late universal emancipation of the colored race in the south," it was conceded, the state had acted to recognize marriages between former slaves and to legitimate their children; but Dickerson and his former slave, "living in adultery or concubinage," remained subject to criminal prosecution. Their relationship was criminal, not sanctified, and their children remained illegitimate and could not be the man's heirs at law.[4]

In the 1870s, the mixed-race children of a planter and his slave lived in a world in which they could go to court to press their claim to their father's property. The lawyer for the Dickerson children acknowledged that, for much of their parents' time together, they could not marry; their "marriage was void in its inception." But then things changed, and they had married. The only thing that prevented their marriage in the first place was that she was "a negro and a slave," and the "incapacity of the woman" to marry "was removed in the lifetime of Dickerson."[5]

The Fourteenth Amendment made Ann a citizen, it was said. An act of 1870 terminated the miscegenation law that prevented their marriage, and their relationship "ceased to be adulterous, and became a valid and legal marriage." In fact, the new state constitution, upon its ratification in December 1868, "validated this imperfect union, and pronounced them man and wife in the sight of man, as they already were in the sight of God and in the hearts of each other." The Mississippi constitution of 1868 declared, "All persons who have not been married, but are now living together, cohabiting as husband and wife, shall be taken and held, for all purposes in law, as married, and their children, whether born before or after the ratification of this constitution, shall be legitimate, and the legislature may, by law, punish adultery and concubinage." The new legal regime did not apply solely to black-black marriages, said the children's lawyer. Rather, the general statement "covers all who fall within its scope," all who were living together whose marriages had not previously been recognized under the law: "Indeed there are no black[s] and no whites in this State" under the law.[6]

The Mississippi Supreme Court had to pick its way between views so contrasting that upon their decision hinged not only whether the children were legitimate, and whether they inherited their father's estate, but also whether their parents' relationship was holy or criminal, and if the new legal regime had validated that relationship or repudiated it. "With the adoption of the present constitution," the court wrote, "former impediments to marriage between whites and blacks ceased." As for "matters of taste and propriety, like this, the people must determine for themselves"—but that was a private matter, and the judges had to work within the rule of law. Yet the court, although convinced that the couple could legally have married in Mississippi during Reconstruction, also had to determine whether they had done so. It accepted the idea that the constitution had meant to draw a line between, on the one hand, people legitimately living together as husband and wife, and on the other, people living "in meretricious cohabitation." But on which side of that line should this couple be located?[7]

The court had been asked by the collateral claimants to hold, in effect, that Mississippi had "one constitution for the whites, and another for the blacks," but to do that, the court objected, required making "a distinction precluded by recent events." The state constitution had "relieved the legislature and the courts to a great extent" of worrying about policy. The case hinged on a simple matter of fact, and "if these parties were 'cohabiting as husband and wife,' at the time of the present constitution," and if they continued to live together as before, "then their marriage was consummated and their children legitimated." Concluding that such was the case, the appeals court reversed the trial court's award of the property.[8]

Mississippi was by no means the only state from the former Confederacy to take such an approach to race, marriage, and inheritance during Reconstruction. The Mississippi Supreme Court ruled on the basis of the 1868 state constitution, which itself was the result of Republican power and was consistent with a statute subsequently passed by the Republican-dominated legislature. In Alabama, as the previous chapter showed, the legislature never passed a repeal law, and the supreme court ruled in a similar manner but on the basis of federal authority. Louisiana and Texas offer illuminating variations.

"Just as if She Had Been a White Woman": Race, Marriage, and Inheritance in Louisiana

E. C. Hart, a white man, died in 1869 and left a sizeable estate in Caddo Parish, Louisiana. Who should inherit that estate? Claiming to be his collateral heirs, and thus entitled to divide his estate among themselves, were Theodore Hart and other white relatives of the deceased. Cornelia Hart, however, a "colored person," claimed that she and her minor children, as Hart's wife and children, had a prior claim. There was little doubt that she had, for a number of years, been his concubine, and they had had children together. But was she in fact his wife, and were these his legitimate children? The Louisiana courts had to decide, and they had to forge new law if they were to decide in Cornelia Hart's favor. That may have seemed improbable, but she went ahead with her suit. The parish court ruled in her favor, but her rivals appealed the ruling to the Louisiana Supreme Court.[9]

As to the marriage in controversy, Cornelia Hart pointed to a ceremony in Shreveport in November 1867, a year and a half before E. C. Hart's death. In rebuttal, her rivals claimed that, as "a woman of color, she was prohibited by law from marrying E. C. Hart," and, even if she had recently formalized their long-term relationship, the gesture had done nothing to legitimate her children "subsequent to their conception and birth."[10]

The Louisiana statute against interracial marriage was incontrovertible—except for the possibility that the Civil Rights Act of 1866 and the Fourteenth Amendment, ratified in 1868, might have invalidated it. One side insisted that, "at the date of the alleged marriage," it "was prohibited by the laws of

Louisiana," so the "pretended marriage" was "null as having been entered into in violation of a prohibitory law." The other side took the position, by contrast, that "at the date of the marriage of E. C. Hart to Cornelia there was no law of Louisiana prohibiting the marriage." As for the children, Cornelia's attorneys argued that, if at one time "there existed an incapacity in them to occupy the status of legal heirs," the Civil Rights Act and the Fourteenth Amendment had "removed" such incapacity. The Civil Rights Act stated, in effect, that African Americans were henceforth citizens, and it declared that such citizens had "the same right . . . to full and equal benefit of all laws and proceedings for the security of persons and property as is enjoyed by white citizens."[11]

In turn, Cornelia's rivals characterized the Civil Rights Act as "unconstitutional" and the Fourteenth Amendment as having been adopted "after the marriage took place." Was the Civil Rights Act "unconstitutional," as those who claimed to be Hart's collateral heirs claimed?[12] Or was Louisiana's pre-emancipation law against interracial marriage overridden by federal authority and therefore no longer valid?

A majority of the Louisiana Supreme Court viewed the Civil Rights Act of 1866 as within the authority of Congress to enact and, as such, "paramount to any State law," and a state law in conflict with the federal law was "annulled." What if Cornelia and her children were not white and had once been slaves? "If Cornelia and her children were once slaves," the court ruled, "they became free persons under the State constitution of 1864" and "citizens" under the Civil Rights Act of 1866—citizens with "all the civil rights and privileges of white persons." The court concluded: "Cornelia Hart, therefore, in November 1867 was vested with the right to enter into a contract of marriage."[13]

What had been the intent of E. C. Hart with regard to his real estate and his mixed-race children? As the court observed: "The record abounds with evidence of the recognition and acknowledgment of these children by E. C. Hart. His solicitude to transmit his property to them is shown to have been strong." Testimony from a Catholic priest had been particularly persuasive, for he testified, as the court summarized it, that, "before marrying Cornelia, Hart desired him to take a conveyance of all his property in trust for his children. Hart's avowed object in marrying their mother was to legitimate them. They were baptized in the church as the children of E. C. Hart and Cornelia Hart."[14]

Chief Justice John T. Ludeling expressed the court's wish to bring "a termination of this protracted and fierce litigation." The rules had undergone fundamental change during the 1860s, and E. C. Hart's nonwhite family should benefit from his expressed wishes. The transformed law had emancipated him as well as his wife and children from their legal incapacity before the end of slavery and the advent of black citizenship:

The effect of the Civil Rights bill was to strike with nullity all State laws discriminating against them on account of race or color, and to confer upon them the rights and privileges which they would have under the State laws if they were white persons. It invested [Cornelia] with the capacity to enter into the contract of marriage with E. C. Hart, a white man, and to legitimate her children by him born before said marriage, just as if she had been a white woman.[15]

The chief justice reported that "E. C. Hart and Cornelia Hart, publicly and continuously, during many years, acknowledged their children. It is proved that Cornelia Hart was the concubine of E. C. Hart and resided with him in his house from 1854 until his death in 1869." As for the legitimacy of the children and their capacity to inherit from him, "the moment after the law forbidding marriages between white and colored persons was abrogated, it was lawful to legitimate them in every way that white children might be."[16]

Hart had done all he could while he lived, and he found powerful allies after his death. A court majority had spoken, and the miscegenation law was deemed no longer valid. Black citizenship transformed the law for whites as well as blacks—for collateral heirs who lost property as a consequence, and for E. C. Hart, his wife, and his children, who all won.

It was a close call, however. The vote was only 3–2, with Justices P. H. Morgan and W. G. Wyly dissenting. The transformation wrought by the Civil Rights Act took place not solely because Congress had acted, but because a slim majority of justices on the Louisiana Supreme Court, a court controlled by Republicans, chose to read the facts and the law in the manner that they did.[17] In Louisiana a miscegenation law fell, at least for a time—it was dropped from a revised code of Louisiana laws in 1870 and then declared unconstitutional in 1874 for the period between 1866 and 1870. Interracial marriages were not a crime. They were no longer void. A patriarch could get his way, and his wife and children—whatever their racial identities—could inherit his property.

Texas Revolution: "Abrogated by the 14th Amendment"

A. H. Foster died in Texas in 1867. Earlier, he had owned a number of slaves, among them a woman named Leah. He evidently loved Leah and wished to marry her, though no such marriage was possible in Louisiana, where he and she lived at that time. In 1847 he took her, together with several of her children, to Ohio, where he settled them in Cincinnati, emancipated them, and "provided them with the necessaries of life." When, on occasion, he returned to Ohio to visit them, he "spent his nights and frequently took his meals with the family." In 1851 he moved to Texas and brought his Ohio family with him, and in the years that followed Foster and Leah had at least two more children.[18]

All of this came to light after Foster died at the beginning of 1867 and "Leah Foster" claimed his property—for herself as widow and for her children as his rightful heirs. Her husband's estate, his executor reported, could not cover his debts, but she went to court, where she made her claim on the basis of a Texas homestead law that exempted some family property from being sold to cover debts. The trial judge observed that, at the time they all lived in Ohio, that state had no law that would prevent their marriage there, and that "their cohabitation while there might have raised a presumption of a marriage there." If so, he ruled, that presumption of marriage would not have been "destroyed by their subsequent removal to and residence in Texas," even though Texas had a law that would have prevented their marrying in their new state of residence.[19]

The trial judge's ruling was appealed, but the Texas Supreme Court agreed with his reasoning and unanimously upheld the verdict. "That Foster himself regarded this woman and her family in the light of a wife and children, cannot be doubted," wrote Judge Moses B. Walker for the court. Foster's will, which he made out in 1866, furnished "the strongest evidence" of a marital relationship. "He not only devises his property mainly to this woman and [her] children, but he provides by a clause (often found in the testaments of jealous husbands) that if Leah shall marry [again], she is to forfeit all her right and interest in his estate." The transformed legal environment in postwar Texas meant that the law as well as the facts supported Leah's claim, for the couple had "continued to live together, habiting themselves as man and wife, until after the law prohibiting such a marriage had been abrogated by the 14th Amendment to the Constitution of the United States. A marriage might then be presumed in the State of Texas upon the same state of facts, which would raise a similar presumption in . . . Ohio."[20]

Not only did the Texas state law not abrogate the Fosters' marriage; the Fourteenth Amendment had "abrogated" the miscegenation statute. According to Judge Walker and his brethren on the Texas Supreme Court in 1871–1872, the Fourteenth Amendment created a new legal world in which an interracial marriage could be contracted in Texas, and in which "the marital rights of the parties" could be enforced.[21] The Fourteenth Amendment had only been proposed by Congress in 1866, and not yet ratified by the states, but the Civil Rights Act of 1866 had become law by the time A. H. Foster died.

The Fosters' marriage had lasted from no later than 1847 until 1867. It had gone with them through Ohio, or at least had originated there, at a time when that state had no miscegenation law on the books; had endured into the postwar South; and had been recognized as valid by judges who were particularly taken with the deceased man's jealous stipulation that Leah not marry again. Absent any of those conditions, Leah Foster and her children would not have retrieved the family farm. As it was, because of her long liaison with a man who had once owned her as a slave, Leah's mixed-race children not only had grown up free, but they and their mother had an economic foundation on which to build their postwar lives.

"Occupied the Same Bed, and Ate at the Same Table"

One year after Leah Foster's case went to the Texas Supreme Court, another case, similar in some respects, went there, too. Again, Judge Walker spoke for a unanimous court in upholding the property rights of a black woman whose long-term relationship with a white man was the basis for her claiming his property after he died. John C. Clark died during the Civil War, however, not after it; he left an estate, including land and slaves, worth hundreds of thousands of dollars at the time of his death. Clark died before the Civil Rights Act of 1866 or the postwar constitutional amendments, so if the Fourteenth Amendment was going to help his family, it would have to do so in a very different way than it had in Leah Foster's case.

John C. Clark entered Texas as a single man sometime in the 1820s and settled in Wharton County, where he lived for the rest of his life. In 1833 or 1834, he bought a slave woman named Sobrina, and in the next few years she became the mother of three children, evidently his—Bishop, Lorinda, and Nancy. According to the three children, as well as many former slaves on the Clark place who testified in court proceedings in 1871, the couple lived together until his death in 1862.[22]

Sobrina died in 1869, the year that Texas produced a new state constitution under the rules established by Congress in the Reconstruction acts of 1867, which had been passed primarily to get the Fourteenth Amendment ratified. According to the 1869 Texas constitution, "All persons who, at any time heretofore, lived together as husband and wife, and both of whom, by the law of bondage, were precluded from the rites of matrimony, and continued to live together until the death of one of the parties, shall be considered as having been legally married; and the issue of such cohabitation shall be deemed legitimate."[23]

Slavery had ended, and black Texans as well as whites could marry. But how did those changes apply, if at all, to any marriage that Sobrina might have had with John C. Clark before his death in 1862? From the state's point of view, Clark left no heirs, and the property belonged to the state. Sobrina's three children with Clark did not see the matter that way. Moreover, three other claimants stepped forward, claiming to be Sobrina's children from an earlier relationship and therefore entitled to a portion of her half of the property she had shared with Clark.

Supporting the claims by Sobrina's three children by Clark were people, most of them former slaves on the Clark place, who testified that the couple had presented themselves as a couple, at least on the plantation. According to a summary of the testimony, several "testified that Clark and Sobrina habitually occupied the same bed, and ate at the same table." Moreover, "Sobrina carried the keys and exercised the authority of mistress of the house." Those witnesses even reported that Clark referred to Sobrina as his "wife," acknowledged her children by him as his own, and treated his family members in a manner that contrasted with his treatment of the slaves on the place.[24]

Testimony on the state's side—some from people who had known him for decades, others who had worked for him as overseers—painted a very different picture. Clark, they claimed, had never referred to Sobrina as his wife: "Some who had the best opportunities of knowing, never observed that Clark treated Sobrina and her children with any perceptible consideration." One man testified that he had been a census taker in 1850, and Clark had listed Sobrina, Bishop, Lorinda, and Nancy all among his slaves. Two witnesses reported that Clark had expressed regret that "he had never married," and one said, "Clark told me that he had nobody to give his property to." The state summarized the "general report in the neighborhood in those slavery times," that "Clark kept a negro woman, Sobrina, as men frequently did in those days." On two vital points, nonetheless, there was general agreement. Clark and Sobrina had a long-term sexual relationship, and he was the father of Sobrina's three grown children who lived there with her.[25]

The jury determined that Bishop Clark and his two sisters were "the legitimate children and lawful heirs of John C. Clark and Sobrina Clark; that John C. Clark and Sobrina were legally married in 1833 or 1834, and lived together as husband and wife" until his death. The "common property of John C. Clark and Sobrina Clark" should go to her children. Bishop Clark and his two sisters were not Sobrina's only heirs, however, for her three earlier children, Bishop Clark's half-siblings, were also her lawful heirs and should, together, get half of her estate.[26]

In the end, Judge Walker wrote for a unanimous court, just as he had the year before in the case of Leah Foster, and affirmed the decision of the lower court. The trial court had reviewed all the evidence and had concluded that Sobrina's children were "the true heirs of John C. Clark." The "mulatto woman, Sobrina," wrote Walker, was in Texas by 1830, after Mexico had abolished slavery and before Texas had obtained its independence and legally reintroduced the institution. Moreover, between 1828 and 1837, no law in Texas prevented the marriage of a black woman and a white man. According to the court, no subsequent law could, by itself, nullify any marriage they had contracted during that period, and from the 1830s into the 1860s, evidence suggested, Sobrina and Clark had lived together as husband and wife.[27]

The 1869 Texas constitution, said the court, was "intended to legalize the marriage of certain persons, and legitimate their offspring." The court identified the "persons" covered by that intent as "those who live together as husband and wife, and who, by law, were [previously] precluded the rights of matrimony." As for John C. Clark and Sobrina, the court pressed on, "the law and the evidence" showed them to be "precisely such persons," so their marriage had been "pronounced by the organic law of the state." The marriage was legitimate. So were the children: "The evidence shows that the appellees are the children of Clark and Sobrina, and the law says, being such, they shall be deemed legitimate; and the [con]sequence of their legitimacy is the right to inherit the property of their father."[28]

The Texas Supreme Court had done what could be done to throw out the state's antebellum miscegenation law and recognize interracial marriages for purposes of inheritance. Yet what the court created, it could undo, and the undoing was soon in coming.

Rollback

George E. Clements, a white man, executed a deed on some property in Galveston to secure a loan from E. E. Crawford, and as a consequence Crawford later took possession. Mary Clements, described as a mulatto woman, resisted. She and George Clements had lived together since 1868, she said, and thus before the constitution of 1869 went into effect. Therefore, she was Clements' wife. They and their children were living on the land in dispute, and she claimed it as their homestead, such that it could not be taken in payment of the loan. The judge instructed the jury that they must determine whether George Clements was a single man at the time he made out the deed. If he was, then they must find for Crawford. If, however, they concluded that George and Mary Clements were married at that time, then the homestead exemption must operate in their favor. Jurors looked at Clements, saw an unmarried man, and found for Crawford. The Clements couple appealed.

The appeal reached the Texas Supreme Court after the Democrats retrieved power in Texas. The transfer of power was unambiguous; so was the transformation in policy. A new panel of judges heard the case; though once again unanimous, they leaned the other way, and overruled their predecessors' decision in *Honey* v. *Clark*. The 1869 Texas constitution had in mind legitimating the children of two people "whose bondage had disabled them from legal marriage," wrote Justice Robert S. Gould for the court. The constitution used language about "both of whom" having been prevented from marrying, not "either of whom," so it could not apply to George Clements, for he had been free to marry under the law of the old regime. The constitution referred "only to those persons who were both precluded, not from intermarriage with each other merely, but from marriage with anyone else" as well. The court refused to interpret the state's constitution such that it would "confer on any parties, white or black, whose intercourse was illegal and immoral, the rights and benefits of lawful wedlock."[29]

The lower court decision was affirmed. The land was Crawford's. After the Democrats displaced the Republicans and took control of the Texas Supreme Court, the benefit of any doubt had moved to the other side, to narrow the likelihood that an interracial couple and their children would be recognized as legitimate.

"Never Intended to Abrogate"

In a story of interracial marriage that unfolded in 1875 in Gregg County, in northeast Texas, interracial marriage as matter of criminal law, rather than civil law, came to the fore. The law of race and marriage had taken a significant detour during the Republican years, but, over the longer run, the Gregg County case revealed the limits on change in the post–Civil War South.

Charles Frasher, a white man, married Lettuce Howell, an African American woman. Here were two people, both still very much alive and neither of them wrangling over any claim to property, trying to live together after a formal ceremony of marriage. In their case, the 1869 Texas constitution was not in dispute, and the Fourteenth Amendment, they discovered, no longer offered a shield. Rather, the prewar miscegenation law lived on and came into play.

Frasher went on trial for violating a Texas law—Article 386 of the Penal Code, enacted in 1858—that imposed a penalty of two to five years in the state penitentiary for a white person who knowingly married "a negro, or a person of mixed blood descended from negro ancestry" through the third generation, or, for that matter, had married such a person "in or out of the state" and continued "to cohabit" with that person in Texas.[30] The trial court admitted into evidence Frasher's marriage certificate and testimony from a witness to the marriage. Frasher was found guilty and sentenced to four years in the penitentiary. He was to be separated from his family and sent to prison for his crime—marrying the woman he loved—because he and she, the law insisted, had different racial identities.

Upon appeal to Texas's highest court, the law was upheld as entirely constitutional, though the conviction was reversed because of what the court saw as a faulty instruction to the jury by the trial judge. The Texas Court of Appeals surveyed post–Civil War cases from North Carolina, Indiana, and elsewhere and noted with approval their strong endorsement of the continued authority of states to restrict marriage on racial grounds. As for the current policy in Texas, the appeals court noted only two controlling events since 1858. The 1866 legislature, in repealing the antebellum laws "'relating to slaves and free persons of color,' expressly 'provided, nevertheless, that nothing herein shall be construed as to repeal any law prohibiting the intermarriage of the black and white races.'"[31] For subsequent changes in policy, the court pointed only toward the case of Mary Clements. That case had, of course, turned back the Republican-era interpretation that awarded property to Leah Foster and Sobrina Clark, property that under the post-Reconstruction regime would have been denied them.

Emile François fared worse. Convicted of violating the old 1858 statute, he was sentenced to the maximum five years in prison. Appealing the trial's outcome, he challenged the statute under both the Texas constitution and the U.S. Constitution. The Texas Court of Appeals was having none of it. The trial of François had been carried out in conformity with the guidelines in the *Frasher* case. What about the 1872 *Burns* decision in Alabama, the one that had declared miscegenation laws unconstitutional? It had been expressly overruled, said the Texas court, by the Alabama Supreme Court in the *Green* decision, which was cited with enthusiasm, as was *Frasher*.

As for the fact that the 1858 statute, under which François had been tried, provided a penalty only for the white party to a black-white marriage—"and this is the only question really involved in the case"—such discrimination was within the state's authority to regulate marriage in general and ban black-white marriage in particular. Texas had "never intended to abrogate this wise social provision; on the contrary, she has by recent enactment so extended the prohibition as to make it doubly effective, by making both the white and negro races alike amenable to punishment for such unlawful marriages." The new statute was "no evidence" that "our law-makers deemed" the old law "void, or that it was void."[32] The conviction stood, as did the five-year prison sentence.

Aftermath in Mississippi and Louisiana

Louisiana's experiment in overthrowing the antimiscegenation regime also came to an end, though the end came later than elsewhere in the South. Efforts in the Louisiana legislature in 1880 and 1888 failed to gain sufficient support for a new law against interracial marriage. In 1894, however, a majority of legislators voted to ban marriages between whites and persons of color.[33]

In Mississippi, too, the new dispensation vanished and a renewed restriction took effect. Beginning in 1880, anyone defined as white could not marry someone defined as not—someone with at least one-quarter African ancestry. In 1890, the requirement for a white racial identity was made more exclusive—anyone as much as one-eighth black was defined as black. Moreover, the ban was placed in the 1890 state constitution, together with the new definition of the color line.[34]

Never again, even in Mississippi, did the penalty for violating the state's miscegenation law extend to imprisonment for life. Yet no matter how much the fine or how long the confinement, no matter how severe the loss of property or of liberty, the threat of a trial and conviction loomed for any couple who—knowingly or even unknowingly—crossed racial boundaries when selecting a marriage partner. That was true in Mississippi after 1880; true in Louisiana after 1894; true, in fact, in every southern state before the end of the century. For a time, however, it was not true—in 7 of the 11 states of the former Confederacy.

In Seven Southern States, the Law of Love Was Blind

At some point in the early 1870s, the supreme courts of Texas, Alabama, and Louisiana overturned—refused to give force to—their states' miscegenation laws. By some other action between 1868 and 1874, the ban was removed in South Carolina, Mississippi, Arkansas, and Florida; and Louisiana also repealed its miscegenation law. Texas declared such measures unconstitutional in the case of Leah Foster. Louisiana did so in the case of Cornelia Hart (after the legislature had repealed the law). Alabama did so in the case of a minister named James Burns. Of the 11 states of the former Confederacy, 7 lifted their bans on black-white marriages for a time during Reconstruction.[35] Seven of the 10 states subject to Congressional Reconstruction did so—and all but Georgia among the original 7 states that seceded in 1860–1861 and established the Confederacy. Within a few years, however, the Republicans fell from power everywhere in the South and their opponents had free rein.

Maintaining miscegenation laws throughout the Reconstruction era were just four states of the former Confederacy—Virginia, North Carolina, Tennessee, and Georgia—together with all the states of the Border South: Delaware, Maryland, West Virginia, Kentucky, and Missouri. There, as the next chapter shows, Reconstruction brought no interlude, so the end of Reconstruction brought no reversal.

CHAPTER 7

ACCOMMODATING THE LAW OF FREEDOM
TO THE LAW OF RACE

Marriages between black citizens and white ones are "productive of evil, and evil only"

—Chief Justice Joseph E. Brown, Georgia Supreme Court (1869)

"Any white person who shall intermarry with a negro, or any negro who shall intermarry with a white person, shall be confined in the penitentiary not less than two nor more than five years"

—Law of Virginia (1878)

It seemed for a while after the Civil War that perhaps the rules had changed, and bans against interracial marriage could not be enforced. Any number of couples, from Virginia to Texas, married across racial lines, either because they did not recognize a difference in their racial identities or because they thought that racial boundaries were no longer relevant under the law. Subsequently, in many cases, they found themselves charged with violating a criminal statute for doing so. Despite a period of uncertainty, the rules soon hardened against forming and maintaining interracial families.

How free was free? After slavery, black southerners were free, but what they gained can better be understood as black freedom, not white freedom. And if blacks were not free to marry whites, the same rules curtailed the freedom of whites. Regarding the law of race and marriage, each state legislature made up its own mind, and each state judiciary decided—sometimes in one fashion, sometimes in another—whether and how the new rules from the federal government would apply to the local situation. What the Civil Rights Act and the Fourteenth Amendment might mean regarding marriage was by no means always certain, nor was it uniform across time and space. The same federal policies—congressional statutes, constitutional amendments—applied in principle everywhere, but from one state to another, and one time to another, states differed in how the broad policies were interpreted and put into operation.

Between about 1865 and the 1890s, southern states moved from one rigid antimiscegenation regime to another. At each end of that period, policy in southern states insisted upon a wide gap between black freedom and white freedom. Miscegenation laws demonstrated a concerted effort to construct a system of racial caste. White political power was translated into a separate world of white marriage and black marriage. In between those dates, however, seven states took a detour. This chapter focuses on the other southern states, the ones that did not waver—four states of the former Confederacy, plus the former slave states that had not joined the Confederacy. State supreme courts in Georgia and Tennessee, for example, held the line. There, throughout the post–Civil War years, the law of freedom was bent to conform to the law of race.

Georgia and Tennessee

In 1869, four years after slavery ended in Georgia, a black woman named Charlotte Scott returned from Macon to her home in Dougherty County, an overwhelmingly black county in the southwestern part of the state. Accompanying her was Leopold Daniels, a white man originally from France. A black preacher had performed a wedding ceremony for the pair in Macon, she reported, and her family recognized her as a married woman and accepted Daniels as her husband.

The state, however, did not—and charged Scott with "cohabitation" with Daniels. Terrified and bewildered, she insisted that they were married. If there were doubts about whether it was so, her attorney proposed that the judge perform a marriage ceremony for the couple there in the courtroom, "they being willing to marry." But the judge refused. Whether there had been a ceremony mattered not at all, he ruled, for an interracial marriage was null under Georgia law. The jury convicted her.[1]

Charlotte Scott appealed her conviction to the Georgia Supreme Court, but Chief Justice Joseph E. Brown, the former governor, wrote for a unanimous court that such marriages were illegal in Georgia. The Civil Rights Act and the Fourteenth Amendment had changed nothing in any state's laws against interracial marriages. Such marriages were "productive of evil, and evil only," and a state continued to have the authority to outlaw them. The "conquering people" of the Union had imposed an emancipation of all slaves, political rights for black men, and an "equality of civil rights," he wrote. But, he insisted, "they have neither required of us the practice of miscegenation, nor have they claimed for the colored race, social equality with the white race."[2]

Much had changed. Charlotte Scott, no longer a slave, could enter into a valid marriage—but it had to be with someone who shared her racial identity under the law. For Chief Justice Brown, the driving consideration in such cases was a perceived threat that black southerners presumed to claim "social equality" with whites. Black freedom from slavery was one thing, unwelcome but accepted, more or less, by white southerners. The exercise of civil rights in such matters as owning property and testifying in court was another. Political privileges—voting and even holding office—were yet another. In rapid succession, each of those three lines demarking the rights of whites and the denial of rights to blacks—the persistence of slavery, the denial of civil rights, and even the prevention of political rights—had been smudged if not erased. But "social equality with the white race"? The line had to be maintained somewhere, as Brown saw it, and he made it clear where he thought white southerners could and must draw that line.

Like Georgia, Tennessee gave short shrift to the significance of changes in federal law as they applied to state miscegenation statutes. The 1870 Tennessee constitution directed that the legislature enact a miscegenation law, and it did so. In January 1871, Doc. Lonas, a black man, having married Rebecca Teaster, a white woman, was arrested and charged with cohabiting with her in Knox County. Sentenced to the penitentiary for two and a half years, he appealed his conviction to the Tennessee Supreme Court. The statute violated his rights, he argued, under the Civil Rights Act of 1866 and the Fourteenth Amendment.[3]

The court differed. Black Tennesseans had all the rights in the world, the state's highest court conceded, so long as they did not presume to "marry or be given in marriage with the sons and daughters of our people." Congress had authority to regulate marriage in the District of Columbia and the territories, but nothing had changed that might "interfere with the rights of the States, as enjoyed since the foundation of the government, to interdict improper marriages." The Tennessee law condemning interracial marriage was "a valid and constitutional enactment."[4]

The cases of Charlotte Scott and Doc. Lonas revealed that state legislatures and state judiciaries were not necessarily going to act as though federal authority inhibited them in their inclinations regarding the regulation of marriage. In this view, nothing in a federal statute or the U.S. Constitution necessarily had anything to do with whether a state could enact and enforce a measure to ban interracial marriage.

Courts might choose to be bound by new authority. Not all southern states at all times took the approach that the Georgia and Tennessee supreme courts did on the constitutionality of laws against interracial marriage. As Alabama and Louisiana demonstrated, the Civil Rights Act of 1866 and the Fourteenth Amendment might make all the difference in the world in how a court ruled. But, as Georgia and Tennessee showed, it might just be that nothing had changed. North Carolina took a similar path to the new resolution.

Getting the Story Straight in North Carolina

During 1869, the same year as Charlotte Scott's encounter with the law in Georgia, a similar case unfolded in neighboring North Carolina as another interracial marriage was put on trial. Wesley Hairston, a black man, and Puss Williams, a white woman, went on trial in Forsythe County for "fornication and adultery." They claimed they were married, but the judge instructed the jury that no such marriage was valid in North Carolina. When the jury convicted both defendants, they appealed. The North Carolina Supreme Court declared: "The only question in this case is, whether the intermarriage of whites and blacks is lawful." The court dashed the couple's hopes, rejected the "pretended marriage," and unanimously upheld the convictions.[5]

A similar case, decided at the same time by the North Carolina Supreme Court, was *State* v. *Reinhardt and Love.* Shortly after Christmas 1868, Alice Love, a white woman, married Alexander Reinhardt, described as "a person of color within the third degree." They had done everything they were supposed to, followed all the rules, but in living together in Lincoln County as husband and wife they broke the law—or so it was charged. At their trial for fornication and adultery, Judge Logan determined that "the defendants had a right under the law, to enter into a contract of marriage," and he "ordered a verdict of not guilty to be recorded." The prosecution appealed the decision to the state's highest court, which held that, as in *State* v. *Hairston,* the couple could not legally marry and therefore could surely be tried for living together outside of marriage.[6]

The two North Carolina cases demonstrated that a trial could go either way; in one case the jury convicted, and in the other the judge directed an acquittal. Both trial outcomes were appealed to the state supreme court, however, and there the results were identical. An interracial couple had no right to marry, and therefore their acting as though they were married subjected them to criminal prosecution. The state supreme court, ironing out such differences as occurred at the local level when such cases came to trial, created a uniform law for the entire state. That uniform law for North Carolina, hardly distinguishable from the law in Tennessee and Georgia, declared that the Civil Rights Act and the Fourteenth Amendment had in no way softened the state's law against interracial marriage.

Stories from Georgia, Tennessee, and North Carolina revealed that some people fell in love and wished to marry across racial lines. Interracial couples sometimes went ahead and married in the belief that they were following the law, not violating it, but the supreme courts of all three states eventually disabused residents of such misapprehensions. In the meantime, appeals courts in other states might rule differently, just as, at their trial, Alice Love and Alexander Reinhardt had been acquitted. Each state made up its own rules, and for a time it remained unclear what those rules were. Virginia followed the general path that Georgia, Tennessee, and North Carolina took

Interracial Marriage and the Virginia Legislature

On the eve of the Civil War and the emancipation that followed, Virginia law sharply distinguished between free residents and slaves as well as between white residents and others. Two-thirds of Virginians (65.6 percent in 1860) were identified as white, and barely one in ten nonwhite residents were free. The law had free Virginians in mind when it banned any marriage between a "white" person and a "negro" or "colored person."[7]

Pre–Civil War Virginia law tried in three different ways to enforce the ban on interracial marriage. The 1860 Virginia Code declared it a crime for any clerk of court "knowingly" to "issue a marriage license contrary to law" (with penalties of a fine of up to $500 and prison for up to a year); a crime for anyone to "perform the ceremony of marriage between a white person and a negro" (there was a $200 fine); and a crime for any "white person" to "intermarry with a negro"—anyone of at least one-fourth African ancestry. Thus the law targeted the white partner alone; the penalties could be steep, or they could be nominal—a fine of up to $100 and confinement "in jail not more than one year."[8]

Virginia was a different place after the Civil War. Emancipation meant that no Virginian was a slave, and, with West Virginia having become a separate state, the population of what remained of Virginia was more than 40 percent nonwhite. Addressing the new dispensation, the 1865–1866 General Assembly applied the general Virginia laws on marriage to freed people. For a time, however, the legislature took only limited action to tighten the laws on interracial relationships. The Code of 1873 persisted in declaring miscegenous marriages "absolutely void," while the law continued to penalize only white partners in such marriages.[9]

Yet not only was marriage across racial lines banned, so was living together without benefit of marriage, and there, after the Civil War, the penalty could cut across racial lines. The 1860 code specified a minimum fine of $20 for any "free person" who committed "adultery or fornication," a provision that, after the war, applied to all Virginians. For longer-term relationships, the prewar code established a minimum fine of $50 for "any white persons, not married to each other," who "lewdly and lasciviously associate and cohabit together." After the war, the penalties for cohabitation were increased, and indictments could be brought against any couple—black, white, or interracial—who lived together outside marriage. The 1873 Code of Virginia stated: "If any persons, not married to each other, lewdly and lasciviously associate and cohabit together," they faced fines of from $50 to $500.[10] Authorities sometimes brought such charges and imposed such fines.

As early as 1866 and 1867, newspaper reports of interracial relationships in Virginia demonstrated that some men and women sought to forge marriages across racial lines and that the law sometimes intervened. In 1867, newspapers reported that black preachers officiated when "a negro man married a so-called white woman" in Wytheville and when a freedman from Winchester joined in "an amalgamation marriage" with a white woman there. In Bedford County in 1868, the county clerk refused to issue a marriage license to a black man, Henry Dunham, who intended to marry a white woman; when the clerk explained that Virginia law banned such a marriage, "Dunham became very indignant." In 1870 a Smyth County court convicted a black preacher of officiating at the marriage of a black man and a white woman, fined him $200, and jailed him for four months. In other reported instances, white men married black women. And a black man, Andrew Kinney, who married a white woman—they had gone to Washington, D.C., where no law prevented their marrying, but had returned to Virginia to live (see chapter 10)—was convicted of cohabitation and fined the maximum $500.[11]

At the 1877–1878 session, the Virginia legislature took stronger action against interracial marriages. An 1878 statute ended the lopsided nature of the Virginia prohibition on interracial marriage that had imposed criminal penalties only on the white partner, and it vastly increased those penalties:

> Any white person who shall intermarry with a negro, or any negro who shall intermarry with a white person, shall be confined in the penitentiary not less than two nor more than five years.

Thus the new law eliminated the cash fine, but it subjected whites and blacks alike to felony convictions. By the back door, Virginia had begun in this sense to apply equal protection across the color line. There was now a minimum penalty that exceeded the previous maximum, and the place of confinement was now the penitentiary, not the local jail. The law retained the $200 fine against presiding ministers as well as the penalties of as much as a $500 fine and a year in jail for an offending court clerk.[12] As for couples who chose—as Andrew Kinney and his bride had—to go to Washington, D.C., in hopes of evading the Virginia law against interracial marriage, the 1878 law applied to race the same provision that had previously been applied to brother-sister and other same-race categories of marriages banned under state law:

> If any white person and negro, shall go out of this state for the purpose of being married, and with the intention of returning, and be married out of it, and afterwards return to and reside in it, cohabiting as man and wife, they shall be as guilty, and be punished as if the marriage had been in this state. The fact of their cohabitation here as man and wife shall be evidence of their marriage.[13]

By 1878, the rules against enduring sexual relationships across racial lines in Virginia, whether within marriage or not, were fully developed. The laws that made marriage a felony, if between two people only one of whom was white, persisted in Virginia from the late 1870s to the time of the Lovings in the late 1950s.

"Every Chinaman, Indian and Hottentot"

In outline, developments regarding interracial marriage in Missouri resembled those in Virginia. Since the 1830s, Missouri had declared marriages between whites and blacks to be not only void but crimes subject to fine or imprisonment. In 1879, Missouri went further in defining the races and providing guidelines for sentencing offenders. The penalty for "knowingly" entering a marriage between a white person and a nonwhite—someone who was at least one-eighth black—could be two years in the penitentiary, a fine of at least $100, a minimum of three months in the county jail, or a combination of fine and imprisonment, "and the jury trying any such case may determine the proportion of negro blood in any party to such marriage from the appearance of such person."[14]

A Missouri case typified the uncertain legal environment regarding interracial marriage after the Civil War, but it also typified what had occurred across the South by the 1880s or 1890s. In 1880 a white woman was indicted in Cape Girardeau County for the crime of having married Dennis Jackson, a man "having more than one-eighth of negro blood." At trial, her attorney challenged the constitutionality of the law in view of the Fourteenth Amendment. When the judge agreed on the matter and let her go free, the state appealed his decision to the Missouri Supreme Court. That court declared that the Fourteenth Amendment had "no such scope as seems to have been accorded to it by the circuit court," remanded the case to the lower court, and directed that the woman be put on trial.[15]

States retained jurisdiction over marriage, the Missouri Supreme Court insisted. "Every Chinaman, Indian and Hottentot" who was a citizen had all the rights of a citizen of the United States under the Constitution. Yet, "If any provision of that instrument confers upon a citizen the right to marry any one who is willing to wed him, our attention has not been called to it."[16] Equal protection was assured by the statute as it was drawn, the court declared. Black could not marry white, nor white marry black, and violators, regardless of race, were subject to identical penalties. Confident that its ruling was in line with the mainstream of judicial interpretation elsewhere, the court could jibe that the U.S. Constitution provided no shield against such laws.[17] No one supposed, the court said, that, prior to the Fourteenth Amendment, there was "any provision of the federal constitution with which [miscegenation laws] were in conflict, and it is only by ascribing to that amendment a force and scope expressly denied it by the Supreme Court of the United States that any ground exists for questioning their validity now."[18]

If the strongest legal arguments failed to satisfy, the court called upon the best science to bolster its position: "It is stated as a well authenticated fact that if the issues of a black man and a white woman, and a white man and a black woman, intermarry, they cannot possibly have any progeny, and such a fact sufficiently justifies those laws which forbid the intermarriage of blacks and whites, laying out of view other sufficient grounds for such enactments."[19]

"Still in Force"

In 1874, an Arkansas man married a white woman there, and they raised a family in Pulaski County. Evidently unmolested by the law for many years, Thomas Dodson was arrested at last in 1891 as a black man cohabiting with a white woman as husband and wife, in violation of state law. Convicted and fined $25, Dodson appealed to the Arkansas Supreme Court. "The only questions in this case," said that court, were whether the statute was constitutional, whether it had been "in force at the time of the marriage," and whether it was "still in force." The law, enacted in 1838, had never been expressly repealed, and it had appeared in every digest of Arkansas laws since that time, including the current one, published in 1884—with the notable exception of the one in 1874, which had not been superseded until ten years later.[20]

Dodson's lawyer argued that the statute under consideration had been "repealed by implication" by the Fourteenth Amendment and by the Arkansas constitutions of 1864, 1868, and 1874. He cited the *Burns* case from Alabama, which had declared that changes in federal law during Reconstruction had rendered that state's miscegenation law unconstitutional. The antebellum statute arose from slavery, and the end of slavery, together with the extension of civil rights to former slaves, rendered marriage just another contract that citizens could freely enter into. Moreover, Dodson had "married in good faith, the statute in question not then [in 1874] being included in the digest of the statutes."[21]

The state saw the matter, every dimension of it, in an entirely different light. Miscegenation laws, the attorney general claimed, had "everywhere" been upheld against challenge under the Civil Rights Act of 1866 or the Fourteenth Amendment. As he reviewed some of the key decisions along those lines, he noted that the *Burns* decision in Alabama itself had been expressly overturned in 1878 in *Green* v. *State* (see chapter 5), a decision that also characterized a marriage as far more than a contract. As "a social and domestic relation," marriage was subject to regulation under the police power of the state. Arkansas's miscegenation statute had never been repealed, had never lost its validity, had always been in force.[22]

The Arkansas Supreme Court saw no reason to pause as it signed on with the prevailing trend in such litigation in the late nineteenth-century South. "Seeing no error," wrote the chief justice for a unanimous court, "the judgment of the lower court is affirmed."[23]

Driving toward a Southern Consensus on Interracial Marriage

The interracial couples whose stories are recounted in this chapter date from the three decades after the Civil War ended—after slavery was abolished in 1865, the Civil Rights Act of 1866 enacted, and the Fourteenth Amendment ratified in 1868. Legal changes during those years could lead couples to believe they were entirely law-abiding, yet some were sentenced to the penitentiary for the crime of marrying across racial lines. By the 1880s and 1890s, the antimiscegenation regime had consolidated its hold on the southern states. Meanwhile, some northern states were repealing their miscegenation laws, so that such laws were becoming more and more a regional phenomenon.

Four states of the former Confederacy kept their miscegenation laws in place throughout Reconstruction, but seven others did not. Yet each of the seven ended its postwar detour and returned to the main road of southern history. Florida, for example, dropped its ban for a time (see chapter 5), but then renewed its allegiance to the antimiscegenation regime in 1881. After that, if a white person married someone with as much as one-eighth African ancestry, both parties were subject to fines of from $50 to $1,000 and prison terms from six months to ten years.[24]

South Carolina, another state that dropped its law against interracial marriage for a time, suspended its previous ban in 1868 but adopted a new version in 1879. Under the new regime, for each partner to a marriage in which a white person married a nonwhite, the South Carolina law mandated a minimum fine of $500 or a minimum term of imprisonment of one year. Within the next three years, a white woman who married a black man was sentenced in Kershaw County to a year in jail; and a white man who married a black woman was convicted in Union County.[25]

Not all southern states had enacted laws that criminalized interracial marriage before the Civil War. Those that had not yet acted—Mississippi, Alabama, and South Carolina—wasted no time after the war in remedying the oversight. During the Republican years of Reconstruction, however, five states—Mississippi, Florida, South Carolina, Arkansas, and Louisiana—suspended those laws, whether by constitutional convention, legislative majority, or omission from a new digest of the laws. Moreover, the supreme courts of three states—Alabama, Louisiana, and Texas—ruled against the constitutionality of miscegenation laws in light of the Civil Rights Act of 1866, the Fourteenth Amendment, or both. In 7 of the 11 states of the former Confederacy, in short, miscegenation laws were suspended for a time after the Civil War.

Throughout Reconstruction and beyond, the states of the Border South all maintained their allegiance to the antimiscegenation regime, as did 4 of the 11 states of the former Confederacy. Whatever the course of a state through the Republican years, the return to power of white Democrats across the former Confederacy—Redemption, as southern Democrats liked to call it, which meant the virtual elimination from power of black or white Republicans—brought a resurgent impulse to construct a caste system along racial lines.

Within a few years after 1877, Mississippi and South Carolina enacted new laws against interracial marriage. Louisiana waited until 1894 to join the consensus. When Oklahoma became a state in 1907, one of the first acts of its legislature was to establish its own version of miscegenation legislation. By 1908, all 17 states of the Deep South, Upper South, and Border South had miscegenation laws in place. And all 17 retained those laws into the 1960s.

Public policy outlawed black-white marriage in the Jim Crow South. Year after year, people went to prison for violating the rules—or into the convict-lease system—and in various other ways encountered legal problems. Yet the continuing prosecutions for miscegenation—including prosecutions of black men who married or "cohabited" with white women—demonstrate that, in many cases across the South and throughout the era of Jim Crow, the formalities of legal procedure continued to be followed.[26] Lynchings occurred, to be sure, often on the premise—frequently the pretext—that a black man had in some way assaulted a white woman.[27] Yet such violence was by no means "inevitable," even when there was ample evidence to support a criminal charge of interracial cohabitation or marriage.[28]

These were grim options—to be convicted in a court of law or to be lynched by a mob. Either way, the world of the antimiscegenation regime could destroy freedom and happiness, could bring agony and anguish. Yet couples against whom criminal charges might have been brought did not necessarily face serious challenge, whether legal or extralegal. Thomas Dodson lived with his family in Arkansas from 1874 to 1891 before charges were brought. Surely some families escaped challenge entirely. What a family could not know was whether or when something terrible might happen.

Marriage and the Strange Career of Jim Crow

The southern states entered the postwar world with varying laws on matters of miscegenation, and they followed varying trajectories through the first postwar decades. By the 1890s, however, they had all arrived at more or less the same place. The latitudinarian interlude, such as it was in those states where it developed, proved fairly brief. But what happened in those intervening years suggested the range of possibilities after slavery ended, after black southerners acquired political rights, and after Congress changed at least some of the rules.

Racial segregation had a very different time line in marriage than it did in education or transportation. Historians have long argued about what C. Vann Woodward called "the strange career of Jim Crow." Focusing on public transportation—railroads in particular—Woodward discerned that legally mandated segregation emerged toward the end of the nineteenth century, after a generation of relative fluidity after the Civil War. Focusing instead on public education—elementary schools for black southerners started out segregated and stayed that way—Howard N. Rabinowitz spoke of a quick transition "from exclusion to segregation" with no intermediate state of integration.[29]

Marriage, by contrast, exhibited such an intermediate stage. Marriage resembled schooling in the quick emergence of a universal antimiscegenation regime in the immediate aftermath of the Civil War and the end of slavery, yet Reconstruction brought a relaxation of the antimiscegenation regime in most states of the former Confederacy. The law of race and marriage resembled the transportation model in that, after that time of relaxation, the end of the nineteenth century brought universal laws against interracial marriage in the South. The marriage model recalls Woodward's observation that segregation was not the inflexible rule, fully in place at all times and places in the post–Civil War South, though it came to appear as though it had been.

The chapters that follow explore various dimensions of life under the antimiscegenation regime during the century between the 1860s and the 1960s. Over time, the antimiscegenation regime became more and more a southern phenomenon. What might not have been predicted was that what emerged in the South in the twentieth century, following the consolidation of the three decades after the Civil War, was an even more rigid, more exclusive racial regime than the 1890s.

The territory ruled by the antimiscegenation regime focused during Reconstruction not on the Deep South, but on the Upper South, the Border South, and the North and West. Beginning by the 1880s, that pattern underwent dramatic change. One by one, states outside the South shed their laws. When the twentieth century dawned, every southern state had a miscegenation law. Not only did all the states in the South hold on, a number of them made their definitions of whiteness more exclusive than before, as chapter 9 will show.

CHAPTER 8

INTERRACIAL MARRIAGE AND THE FEDERAL COURTS, 1857–1917

"No State shall . . . deny to any person within its jurisdiction the equal protection of the laws"

—the Fourteenth Amendment (1868)

"Marriage . . . has always been subject to the control of the Legislature"

—the U.S. Supreme Court in *Maynard* v. *Hill* (1888)

In the Supreme Court's *Dred Scott* decision in 1857, Chief Justice Roger B. Taney gave no hint that miscegenation laws were in any way beyond the authority of a state to enact and enforce. To the contrary, in Taney's view, such laws demonstrated that, from the dawn of political independence, most American states, in acting to bar interracial marriages, had treated African Americans as lesser beings, hardly citizens.

Was the contrary perhaps true? After the war—under the Civil Rights Act of 1866 and the Fourteenth Amendment—African Americans were declared to be citizens. Did that mean—might federal courts therefore decide—that the miscegenation laws of the old regime could no longer be enforced? Certainly the Alabama Supreme Court viewed the matter that way in 1872 (see chapter 5).

Across the South in the years after the Civil War, state courts addressed the meaning, the constitutionality, and the application of miscegenation laws. So did federal courts. In some cases, the issue before the court stemmed from an indictment and conviction for miscegenation. In other cases, the federal courts—in particular, the U.S. Supreme Court—commented on the law of race and marriage while they considered other matters. Although there was, at first, some room for uncertainty about the law of race and marriage, federal judges had reached agreement before the end of nineteenth century. A case in Georgia pointed the way.

As early as 1871, an interracial couple took a case to federal district court in Georgia. Under Georgia law, they could not legally marry, but they had been living together—"cohabiting"—and thus they had been convicted of fornication. From their jail cells, they sought a ruling that, under the Civil Rights Act of 1866 and Section One of the Fourteenth Amendment, Georgia authorities could not constitutionally convict and penalize them for their actions.[1]

Judge John Erskine perused the case law of federal jurisdiction and the marriage contract, and he pondered the reach of the 1866 act of Congress and the 1868 amendment to the Constitution. The Civil Rights Act ought to be understood as relating primarily to property, he concluded, not to social relations. As for the Fourteenth Amendment, he ruled, marriage did not come under the privileges and immunities clause, nor did Georgia's laws violate the equal protection clause. Under Georgia law, an interracial marriage was "null and void as to both" the white partner and the black one. The penalty for fornication, if people lived together without benefit of marriage, was no different or greater for "the colored citizen" than for "the white citizen, the co-offender." Judge Erskine's federal court could not help these two people. They remained in a Georgia jail.[2]

Whites Who Married Black Texans

Not every federal judge would agree with Judge Erskine. In Texas a few years later, District Judge Thomas Howard DuVal had occasion to free Lou Brown, a white woman who had married a black man there. DuVal perceived that the Civil Rights Act of 1866 overrode the Texas miscegenation statute, which was "obsolete and inoperative," having been passed during slavery times when African Americans were not yet citizens. Moreover, the statute violated the Fourteenth Amendment, in that it imposed a penalty on the white person in an interracial marriage but not the black partner.[3]

A subsequent ruling by the Texas Court of Appeals, in the *Frasher* case (see chapter 6), caused Judge DuVal to change his mind about such laws. What a difference two years could make. DuVal declared in 1879, "The subject of marriage is one exclusively under the control of each state." That exclusive control had to be given wide latitude, he insisted:

> If a state thought proper to do so, I am not satisfied that she would be prohibited by any express provision of the federal constitution, or of the civil rights bill, from passing a law forbidding a marriage, among white persons, between an uncle and his niece, or between a Christian and a Jew, and imposing a penalty for its violation upon the man alone. If it

could do this, then it could certainly forbid the marriage between a white person and a negro, and affix a penalty for the act upon the former alone.[4]

Judge DuVal did not like the Texas statute. He had his qualms about its constitutionality, but by 1879 he did not feel that he could overturn it. That it was "unwise and unjust," he said, and "repugnant to the spirit of the constitution, and of the civil rights bill, both of which contemplate the equality of all persons before the law, and the equal protection of the law to all—I have no doubt." Yet, he continued, "I am not satisfied that it violates the letter of either. Unless it does so, I would not feel justified in declaring it to be unconstitutional."[5] It would be different if the law penalized the black party to the marriage but not the white one. In that case, the statute "would be clearly opposed to the civil rights bill, which expressly provides that the negro shall only be subject to the like pains and penalties as the white race. But is the converse of this proposition to be held as true in all cases? Upon mature consideration, I doubt whether this is so."[6]

At first, Judge DuVal perceived the statute's ban on interracial marriage as at odds with the new legal and constitutional order, but he put aside his doubts. He also thought it unconstitutional because it penalized only the white partner to the marriage —it exercised "discrimination against the white race"—but he rationalized that, too. "For such unnatural marriages," he wrote, "the whites are mainly to blame."[7] Perhaps, therefore, the legislature was not so far from the mark when it chose to impose a penalty only on the white party.

By 1879, Judge DuVal had come to believe that the Texas law of race and marriage dealt with "a subject over which the state has complete and exclusive control," and it violated only the spirit, not the letter, of the Constitution.[8] The federal judiciary would not, this time, intrude. Texas was free to go its own way. Texas chose, in fact, to equalize the penalties for interracial marriage. The ban itself was not up for reconsideration.

Equal Protection in Virginia

In March 1878, Virginia enacted a law that established prison terms for people who contracted mixed-race marriages. The penalties applied regardless of whether the ceremony took place in Virginia or the couple went outside the state in an effort to evade the Virginia statute. One Virginia case, related directly to that law, went to federal court.[9]

Edmund Kinney, a black man, had married Mary S. Hall, who was white, in Washington, D.C., in October 1878. They then returned to their home in Hanover County. Convicted of violating the 1878 statute against going out of state to get married, both parties were sentenced to the maximum penalty of five years at hard labor in the Virginia penitentiary. Kinney petitioned U.S. District Judge Robert W. Hughes for a writ of habeas corpus.

Judge Hughes rejected all constitutional grounds for intervention. What about the Fourteenth Amendment and its talk of privileges and immunities? Nowhere, declared Judge Hughes, did that amendment "forbid a state from abridging the privileges of its own citizens," a matter left to "the discretion of each state."[10] Comity would require recognition of most marriages contracted in another state, said Hughes, but there were exceptions—"marriages which are polygamous, incestuous, or contrary to public policy" and "made the subject of penal enactments." Edmund Kinney was "a citizen of Virginia amenable to her laws." Though married in the District of Columbia, he brought back with him to Virginia "no other right in regard to the marriage which he made abroad than he took away. He cannot bring the marriage privileges of a citizen of the District of Columbia any more than he could those of a citizen of Utah, into Virginia, in violation of her laws."[11] Virginia could choose to ban either miscegenation or polygamy among its residents, whatever other jurisdictions might choose to do.

Judge Hughes also rejected the relevance of the Fourteenth Amendment's equal protection clause, which, he said, gave "no power to congress to interfere with the right of a state to regulate the domestic relations of its own citizens." He continued: "But even if it did require an equality of privileges, I do not see any discrimination against either race in a provision of law forbidding any white or colored person from marrying another of the opposite color of skin. If it forbids a colored person from marrying a white, it equally forbids a white person from marrying a colored."[12]

"In the present case," Judge Hughes went on, "the white party to the marriage" was in prison, and so was "the colored person." They had received equal punishment for a crime of which both had been convicted. "I think it clear, therefore, that no provision of the fourteenth amendment has been violated by the state of Virginia in its prosecution of this petitioner." It did not matter to the judge that their crime could just as well be seen as a consequence of their color, not their behavior. Year after year, Virginia's penitentiary records showed the couple serving out their sentences.[13] Alabama generated a similar case in federal court.

To the U.S. Supreme Court: The Case of Tony Pace and Mary Cox

By 1878, nobody identified as white in Alabama could legally marry anyone identified as black. If such a marriage took place, the couple could be tried on the charge of living together without being married. As an interracial unmarried couple, the pair could be charged with a felony, and both parties, if convicted, would be sentenced to at least two years in the penitentiary. Between 1868 and 1878, the state had developed a line of argument defending such a legal environment against attacks based on the Civil Rights Act of 1866 or the Fourteenth Amendment. All of the Alabama cases were decided in state courts. If the U.S. Supreme Court ruled on the matter, would it rule differently?

Tony Pace and Mary Jane Cox spent time together near their homes in Clarke County, north of Mobile. They weren't married, nor could they marry each other under Alabama law. Maybe they wished to marry each other but knew that, under the law at that time and place, they never could. Maybe they consciously attempted to avoid falling into a trap under the law, so they chose not to share a home but, rather, visited from time to time and place to place. The law found them nonetheless.

In November 1881, the grand jury indicted them under two provisions of the Alabama Code, one that prohibited a man and a woman from living together outside marriage, and one that imposed a greater penalty if an interracial couple did so. When their case came to trial in April 1882, the court did not bother with the lesser charge but went after them as an interracial couple.[14]

After the evidence had been presented, the defendants hoped to sway the outcome with an instruction they urged the trial judge to give the jury. Jurors should consider "where the parties each lived, and with whom, and where the adulterous acts took place, if they did in fact take place," and they should consider, too, whether those acts "took place in a house controlled or occupied by either party or were mere occasional acts of illicit intercourse in out of the way places."[15] In short, the couple denied that they lived together, and thus they could hardly have been living together "in adultery or fornication with each other," even if they had a sexual relationship.

The judge refused the instruction. The jury convicted, and each defendant was sentenced to a term of two years in the state penitentiary. Like the Kinneys in Virginia, Pace and Cox in Alabama discovered a virulent form of "separate" as it related to "equal"—an equal punishment for failure to keep separate.

The couple appealed to the Alabama Supreme Court. Speaking for that court, Justice Henderson M. Somerville denied that the statute violated the privileges and immunities or equal protection clauses of the Fourteenth Amendment. In the case of sexual relations, penalties for same-race infractions did not have to be the same as for interracial crimes, for the crime was not the same. The nature of the crime was "determined by the opposite color of the cohabiting parties. The punishment of each offending party, white and black, is precisely the same." Interracial cohabitation jeopardized "the highest interests of government and society," for it could result in "the amalgamation of the two races, producing a mongrel population and a degraded civilization."[16]

The court produced a series of precedents supporting its approach to the case at hand. Among them were recent decisions—all of them upholding statutes that banned interracial sexual or marital relations—in Virginia, North Carolina, Texas, and Indiana, as well as the Alabama Supreme Court's rulings in a series of cases. Conspicuously missing was mention of the *Burns* decision, in which the Alabama Supreme Court—comprised of Republican appointees—had overturned the Alabama miscegenation statute as in conflict with federal law. *Burns,* the great aberration in Reconstruction Alabama, might as well have never happened. In the eyes of the couple's lawyer as well as the state supreme court, it had vanished without a trace.

The couple took their appeal to the U.S. Supreme Court. Representing them there, Mobile lawyer John R. Tompkins had no quarrel with the *Green* decision (see chapter 5), "on the intermarriage of the races," which in his brief he declared to be "good law." But he did object to two other precedents—*Ellis* and *Ford*—as "bad law," for they entailed "unequal punishments measured against different races according to color." He continued: "Marriage is a social blessing; adultery and fornication are social evils." He conceded that "marriage is a social institution subject to the regulation of the sovereign power of the State without violation of any provision of the Constitution." Yet he objected that, according to the law under which his clients had been convicted, "an ordinary misdemeanor is made a felony because one of the offending parties happened to be a negro." The Alabama law on interracial cohabitation had to fall, Tompkins insisted, because, under the Fourteenth Amendment, it mandated "an illegal discrimination between the offending party [who had had sexual relations across the black-white color line] and others of his own race who might commit a like offense with an Indian, a Chinese, a Corean or one of his own people."[17]

The state would have none of the distinction John R. Tompkins insisted upon. Repeating the language of the act at issue, which equally criminalized actions when an interracial couple "intermarry or live in adultery or fornication with each other," Alabama attorney general Henry Clay Tompkins declared the purpose to be twofold: "*First* to prevent the intermarriage of persons of the two races; and *second,* to prevent illicit intercourse between them, the end to be accomplished by each prohibition being the same—the prevention of the amalgamation of the two different races."[18]

Noting that the couple's attorney had conceded the ban on interracial marriage to be both constitutional and wise, the state insisted that he indulged in two fallacies in his approach to the cohabitation law. First, the couple's arguments to the contrary, there was, in the prosecution's case against them, "no discrimination against any race" and "no denial of any privilege belonging to any citizen." No such "privilege" as living in adultery or fornication "ever did or ever will exist," and the law imposed equal punishments on both parties in an inter-racial relationship. Second, the general law of sexual relations, the one related to same-race infractions, "refers and relates only to the crime of adultery when committed by parties between whom marriage is not forbidden." Where marriage was forbidden, whether in terms of race or incest, the state imposed greater penalties for "living together in adultery or fornication."[19]

The two sides argued over the application of the *Slaughter-House Cases,* where the reach of the Fourteenth Amendment had been contested. The couple's lawyer claimed that, according to *Slaughter-House,* the Fourteenth Amendment was designed to "reach precisely such cases as the one at bar," where racial distinctions resulted in discrimination in the law. The state, for its part, appreciated the *Slaughter-House* distinction between state and federal citizenship, insisted that many "privileges" remained the province of the state governments, and concluded that "the regulation of marriage is purely a power relating to internal police." Thus the state could argue that "the power to say who may and who may not marry is one of the ordinary police powers of every government, restrained only by legislative discretion," and "the policy of the law has always been to punish acts of criminal intimacy between those who are forbidden to marry with greater severity than where no such prohibition exists."[20]

The state laid out its arguments. First, each state had the power, "unlimited except by legislative discretion," to declare "who of its citizens may marry, when they may marry, and how they may marry." Second, the state's "power to forbid marriages between persons of different races carries with it the power to impose a greater punishment for acts of criminal intimacy between such persons than . . . for the same acts committed by persons between whom marriage is not forbidden." Third, since the power to regulate marriages resides in the states, "for the protection of his rights in connection therewith, if there are any such, the citizen must look to the States." And fourth, "a law which punishes persons of each race in the same manner and to the same extent for its violation is not a discrimination against either race, nor does it deny to any person the equal protection of the laws."[21]

The state claimed, as a matter of historical fact, that "the right of the State" to outlaw marriages "between persons of different races, or even different religions, has been exercised and sustained." The state went further, further than the truth could take it. "This question has never been before this court, but has been before several of the State courts and also several of the lower courts of the United States, and in every instance the validity of such laws has been upheld."[22] But neither side was mentioning *Burns,* and neither side was contesting the authority of the state to criminalize interracial marriage. The only question seemed to be whether the Fourteenth Amendment permitted the state to distinguish "criminal intimacy" between two unmarried people of different racial identities from that by members of the same race.

Writing for a unanimous Supreme Court, Justice Stephen J. Field rejected the argument that the Fourteenth Amendment's equal protection clause offered a shield. Rather, he adopted the Alabama court's line of reasoning. Viewing the two sections of the Alabama law, Justice Field found them "entirely consistent" and in no way racially discriminatory. Each, he insisted in all earnestness, dealt with a different offense. Section 4184 treated the races in an identical manner, in that it "equally includes the offense when the persons of the two sexes are both white and when they are both black." Section 4189 also treated the races in an identical manner, in that it "applies the same punishment to both offenders, the white and the black," in an interracial relationship.[23]

Section 4189, unlike 4184, the Court ruled, "prescribes a punishment for an offense which can only be committed where the two sexes are of different races. There is in neither section any discrimination against either race." The offense targeted by Section 4189 "cannot be committed without involving persons of both races," wrote Justice Field. "Whatever discrimination is made in the punishment prescribed in the two sections is directed against the offense designated and not against the person of any particular color or race."[24]

The decision in *Pace* v. *Alabama* did not rule directly on a statute barring interracial marriage. Yet its reasoning could have been applied—and could be understood to apply—to such a statute. According to the nation's highest court, therefore, the Fourteenth Amendment's equal protection clause had not terminated the power of a state to enact a law that, on racial grounds, barred an individual of one racial identity from marrying a person of another racial identity, at least if the penalties for violations were identical. By no means was it evident that a constitutional challenge to miscegenation laws could win unless the Supreme Court attributed to the equal protection clause a reach that the decision in *Pace* expressly denied.

Federal Jurisdiction and the Marriage Contract: *Maynard* v. *Hill* (1888)

Pace was not the only decision by the U.S. Supreme Court in the 1880s that proved vital to the constitutional history of miscegenation laws. In 1888, the U.S. Supreme Court addressed the nature of marriage, and the limited extent of federal authority with respect to it, in a case that seemed to have nothing to do with race.

The case began innocently enough with a marriage that took place in Vermont. What followed, however, was a tale related to the lure of the California

Gold Rush, a divorce secretly obtained in the Washington territorial legislature, and a parcel of land whose ownership was contested for a third of a century. After reviewing the American law of marriage, the nation's highest court rendered a decision that could have as much impact on matters of miscegenation as on the legitimacy of a divorce. Justice Stephen J. Field, the same justice who had written the decision in *Pace,* spoke again for the Court, though in *Maynard* the Court was divided, 6–2.[25]

The constitutional question was whether a territorial legislature—or, for that matter, any state legislature—had full authority to legislate a divorce. On that question, Justice Field saw no uncertainty. From the colonial era to the present, legislatures in America, like the British Parliament after which they were modeled, had exercised that power. "Marriage," he wrote, "as having . . . more to do with the morals and civilization of a people than any other institution, has always been subject to the control of the Legislature." State legislatures continued to govern the matter after the adoption of the U.S. Constitution in much the same manner as had their colonial predecessors. All that mattered in a divorce to render it effective, even unassailable, was that at least one of the parties be a resident of the jurisdiction whose legislature approved a dissolution of the marriage.[26]

The only constitutional question had to be whether, despite the settled acceptance of legislative prerogative, "the marriage was a contract within the prohibition of the Federal Constitution." Article IV, Section 1, declared: "Full faith and credit shall be given in each State to the public acts, records, and judicial proceedings of every other State." No state could invalidate a contract undertaken in another state. But the Court ruled that marriage was "not a contract within the meaning of the prohibition."[27]

Yes, Justice Field agreed, marriage was often characterized as a contract, a civil contract. But that definition had more to do with distinguishing it from the religious sacrament that often accompanied it than with deeming it nothing more than a "mere contract" between two consenting parties. In American law and culture, mutual consent was essential to entering into a marriage, but the marriage itself went beyond the contract:

> When the contract to marry is executed by the marriage, a relation is created between the parties which they cannot change. Other contracts may be modified . . . or entirely released upon the consent of the parties. Not so with marriage. The relation once formed, the law steps in and holds the parties to various obligations and liabilities.[28]

The same state power that recognized and reinforced the institution of marriage had authority, through the process of divorce, said Justice Field, to declare an end to any particular marriage.

The implications of *Maynard* for miscegenation were extraordinary. Marriage was not a federal matter. It was not a contract in any sense that was protected by Article IV, Section 1—the full faith and credit clause—so the application of a state's miscegenation laws could not be successfully challenged on the basis of that provision of the Constitution. In later years, when questions arose of interstate comity in cases of interracial marriage—of one state recognizing a marriage that had been contracted in another state—*Maynard* v. *Hill* could be called upon as evidence that the constitutional matter was settled.

Any state could choose to recognize a foreign marriage, including an out-of-state marriage. But no state could be required to recognize the validity of a marriage contracted elsewhere, if that marriage, though consistent with the public policy of the jurisdiction where it originated, violated the public policy of the state into which the parties wished to import it. In *Maynard* v. *Hill*, the nation's highest court validated the approach taken by Judge Hughes in federal district court a decade earlier in the Virginia case of Edmund Kinney and Mary Hall. Moreover, quite aside from the portability of an interracial marriage across a state line, the Supreme Court had left it to each state legislature to determine what the law of marriage should be in that state.

Return to Georgia

Soon after the *Maynard* decision was handed down, a federal case from Georgia demonstrated the law of the land regarding interracial marriage. The full faith and credit clause of Article IV failed to shield Charles Tutty and Rose Ward from prosecution. There was, they found, no general law of the land—only what each state chose to recognize or reject, regardless of whether a marriage arose within its borders or elsewhere.

Charles Tutty and Rose Ward wanted to spend the rest of their lives together; they wanted to do it legally; and they wanted to remain free of legal entanglements. That combination was asking entirely too much in the state of Georgia in the 1880s and 1890s. In Liberty County, one of Georgia's coastal counties just south of Savannah, they were both charged in April 1889 with fornication (sex outside of marriage). Georgia law specified that an interracial couple who lived together—necessarily without legal sanction, in view of the state's miscegenation law—would be charged with "fornication," although in other states the charge might have been cohabitation.[29]

The couple went to Washington, D.C., where they had a marriage ceremony. They returned to Georgia, where they took up residence in Chatham County. But he was white, and she was a former slave, and their trip to the nation's capital—and her styling herself Rose Tutty—carried no guarantee of satisfying

Georgia law, as Georgia's criminal justice system soon made clear. They took their case to federal court, where they challenged the state's refusal to recognize their marriage. They called on the U.S. Constitution and federal law, in particular the concepts of "equal civil rights" and "impairing the obligation of contracts," to shield them from prosecution. Surely, they argued, the state of Georgia could not ignore the evidence that they had a valid marriage under the laws of the United States in force in the nation's capital. The state, for its part, observed that they had been "married there in order to evade the laws of the state of Georgia."[30]

The federal appeals court observed that the case of Charles Tutty and Rose Ward could be decided on narrow grounds, but it determined not to do so: "It would, perhaps, be impossible to overstate the importance of this question under the grave and unsettled relations which exist between the distinct races now inhabiting a large portion of these United States, and it will be neither wise not patriotic for the court to evade the vital point of decision, as might perhaps be done in this case." Just a couple of years earlier, in *Maynard* v. *Hill,* the U.S. Supreme Court had left marriage to the states to regulate. Georgia, in its legislative discretion, had enacted its miscegenation law in an effort to "preserve . . . the purity and distinctiveness of the races inhabiting the state," and it had full authority to do so, the appeals court ruled. The couple, legally unmarried, would have to face the music in state court.[31]

Miscegenation and *Plessy* v. *Ferguson* (1896)

Homer Plessy became famous to students of American constitutional history and American race relations as a result of his arrest for violating a Louisiana law, passed in 1890, that required that black passengers take seats in a different railway passenger car than was set aside for whites. Plessy challenged the Louisiana law, and his case went all the way to the U.S. Supreme Court, where a thorough review was made of the arguments on both sides of the question as to whether a state could constitutionally mandate segregation of the races. Born in 1863, during the Civil War, Plessy was barely as old as emancipation was for most black southerners, and a failed challenge to racial segregation in transportation would signify a reversal of the tremendous growth of black freedom in the years after the Civil War.[32]

At the Supreme Court, Plessy's lawyers insisted on relating racial identity and interracial marriage to laws requiring separation of the races on the railroads. Louisiana had gone for a quarter-century without any law against interracial marriage, having just reimposed such a regulation in 1894, two years before the Supreme Court heard Plessy's case. Plessy himself was described as very fair, only one-eighth black. Conductors had the authority to determine whether a man of Plessy's appearance was white or black, and having made the determination, had the authority of law to assign him to a rail car on that basis.

Though interracial marriages could no longer be legally contracted in Louisiana, dozens, perhaps hundreds of such marriages had been formed in the preceding years. Moreover, regardless of whether the law permitted or banned interracial marriages, many people, like Plessy himself, were going to be of indeterminate racial identity under the law. The law offered no definition as to where to locate the boundary separating one racial identity from another, and even if it had, conductors might have good reason to be uncertain or, even if certain, ample opportunity to be wrong.

Moreover, even if all those matters were perfectly unambiguous, the railroad segregation law raised new questions. One of Plessy's lawyers, Albion W. Tourgée, offered an example that he thought should dispel any notion that the law ought to be permitted to stand: "A man may be white and his wife colored; a wife may be white and her children colored. Has the State the right to compel the husband to ride in one car and the wife in another? Or to assign the mother to one car and the children to another?"[33]

Another of Plessy's lawyers, James C. Walker, developed that approach. "A white man, married to a colored person, boarding the train has the right to enter and take his seat in the white coach with his black servant, if the servant be the nurse of his children; but the [mixed-race] children themselves . . . must occupy the colored coach, if the conductor please so to assign them." Meanwhile, Walker continued, "although the white man and his black servant, employed as nurse, may occupy the white passenger coach, not so is it permitted the colored wife." If traveling with her husband, she must travel separately from him, for "she is required to part with her husband at the coach door and take her seat in the coach intended for colored passengers." Walker concluded that "thus the bottom rail is on top; the nurse is admitted to a privilege which the wife herself does not enjoy, and which is refused to the children whom she is attending."[34]

In deciding the *Plessy* case, the Court itself took occasion to comment on the constitutionality of miscegenation laws. Justice Henry Billings Brown—making his way to a conclusion that state legislatures did not necessarily violate the Fourteenth Amendment by enacting laws requiring railroad facilities that were "equal but separate" for the two races—wrote: "Laws forbidding the intermarriage of the two races may be said in a technical sense to interfere with the freedom of contract, and yet have been universally recognized as within the police power of the State."[35]

Indicating no awareness of any exceptions to his generalization that miscegenation laws had been "universally" upheld, Justice Brown relied for his example of such rulings not on the Supreme Court's opinion in *Pace* v. *Alabama* but, instead, on one of the leading state court decisions on the subject, from Indiana. As Chief Justice Earl Warren would suggest many years later, *Pace* had not ruled directly on the constitutionality of laws banning interracial marriage. Yet in neither *Pace* nor *Plessy* had the Court noted any difficulties with such laws.

All Sides Agree on Miscegenation: *Buchanan* v. *Warley* (1917)

The constitutionality of miscegenation laws came up again in *Buchanan* v. *Warley*, a 1917 case in which the Supreme Court determined that municipal zoning ordinances segregating residential housing patterns by race violated the Fourteenth Amendment. Various cities—among them Louisville, Kentucky— enacted ordinances that directed citizens, if they wished to change residence, to move into areas in which their racial group predominated. Whites in mostly black areas did not have to move out, nor did blacks in mostly white areas, but neither group could move into a forbidden zone. The case arose when Charles Buchanan, a white homeowner in a white area of Louisville, was prevented from selling his house to William Warley, a black man who wanted to move there.[36]

When the case reached the Supreme Court, proponents of such ordinances argued that these regulations were just another expression of a state's police power, like other segregation laws, and that such "laws have existed for many years separating black from white in schools, in railroad cars[,] and in the matter of marrying." Opponents conceded that the issue was closed in education, transportation, and marriage, but they sought to distinguish housing as a separate issue, one that hinged on property rights.[37]

The Supreme Court—adopting the opponents' position, reasoning, and language—based its decision on "fundamental rights in property." The Court observed that residential separation "is said to be essential to the maintenance of the purity of the races," but it insisted: "The case presented here does not deal with an attempt to prohibit the amalgamation of the races."[38] Regardless, in *Buchanan* v. *Warley,* as in *Pace* v. *Alabama,* all sides operated from the premise that the laws against interracial marriage were safe from the Fourteenth Amendment. They differed, however, on other matters before the Court.

The Law of Interracial Marriage after 1917

Particularly after the U.S. Supreme Court gave what appeared to be its approval to miscegenation laws, the Fourteenth Amendment proved ineffective and the South's miscegenation statutes enduring. In view of *Pace* v. *Alabama* (1883) and

Maynard v. *Hill* (1888), miscegenation laws simply raised no constitutional issues that citizens could raise effectively in any quest to overturn them. Racial segregation in marriage and the family became just as central a part of American apartheid as did segregation on trains or in schools. From the 1880s into the 1960s, no state had to answer to federal authority for what it chose to do regarding the law of race and marriage.

The history of the post–Civil War antimiscegenation regime—in particular, the train of federal court decisions on race and marriage—revealed how little had changed since the time when *Dred Scott* ruled the law of race. Jim Crow did not necessarily govern matters of residence, where property rights (in the specific case of *Buchanan* v. *Warley,* the right of a white homeowner to sell some real estate) might override a segregation ordinance. Elsewhere in American life and law, race ruled everything, or at least it could.

African Americans could ride the same train—but not always in the same railway car. Both groups could marry—in fact, after the Civil War and the end of slavery, both were expected to—but, in more states than not, they could not legally marry across the boundary that separated a "white" racial identity from some other. All miscegenation laws restricted marriages between Caucasians and African Americans, regardless of whether other groups were also specified and regardless of whether there were criminal penalties for infractions.

The nation's high court accepted the main lines of argument that supporters of the Alabama miscegenation laws had developed from *Ellis* in 1868 to *Hoover* in 1878. By 1883, the aberration of *Burns*—in which the Alabama Supreme Court had overturned a miscegenation law as unconstitutional—had already become invisible to attorneys and judges. But it serves as a reminder, more than a century later, that the course of judicial history regarding laws against interracial marriage was not perhaps entirely inevitable—that the Lovings might have had an uneventful marriage, one into which the law of race never intruded.

Yet it is hard to see much likelihood that the U.S. Supreme Court would have ruled differently than it did in *Pace.* Justice John Marshall Harlan did not dissent from the ruling in *Pace,* though he was the sole dissenter from the Court's narrow construction of the Fourteenth Amendment in the *Civil Rights Cases*—decided in October 1883, just nine months after the *Pace* decision—and again in 1896 in *Plessy* v. *Ferguson.*[39]

The *Pace* decision was understood, from the 1880s to the 1960s, as reflecting a validation of state miscegenation laws. Yet only by implication had the ban against interracial marriage been addressed; the state had argued for stiffer penalties for cohabitation if a couple was prevented by state law from marrying. Regardless, the Supreme Court had upheld Alabama's miscegenation laws, and no southern state, for the next eight decades, displayed any inclination to repeal such laws. The Court's 1883 decision in *Pace* v. *Alabama* had an even more durable career in the American law of interracial sex and (by extension) marriage than the 1896 decision in *Plessy* v. *Ferguson* had in the law of segregated transportation and (by extension) education.

POLYGAMY, INCEST, FORNICATION, COHABITATION—AND INTERRACIAL MARRIAGE

" . . . lewdly and lasciviously associate and cohabit together"

—Law of Virginia

"Granted that [Jack] Johnson and Miss Cameron proposed to live together, was it better for them to be legally married or not?"

—W. E. B. Du Bois (1913)

A controversy in the 1836 presidential election prefigured developments in the half-century and more that followed the Civil War. The episode occasioned a wide airing of attitudes, beliefs, and concerns about interracial sex and interracial marriage; clearly differentiated between them; and demonstrated that interracial sex—particularly if between a white man and a black woman—was of far less public concern than was an actual marriage.

The Democrats nominated Richard Johnson, a resident of Tennessee, for the vice-presidency, but reports emerged that Johnson had maintained a lengthy sexual relationship with a slave woman named Julia Chinn, by whom he had two daughters, Adaline and Imogene—both of whom had married white men. Rumor had it for a time that Johnson had married a black woman and, if elected, would be bringing his wife and children with him to the nation's capital. Northern spokesmen for the political opposition expressed dismay at the prospect, and even southern Democrats were convinced that it would have been better had Johnson, like most white southern men in his place, kept his relationships private. His defenders took particular pain to insist that Johnson had never married anyone, especially a black slave. He had, therefore, never presumed to challenge the southern social order by treating a slave woman as if she were free and white. Richard Johnson was elected to the vice-presidency of the United States in 1836.[1]

The story of Richard Johnson and Julia Chinn raised questions that would emerge in a very different context in the half-century and more after the end of the Civil War and the death of slavery. In the late nineteenth century, and on into the twentieth century, would white Americans view interracial sex outside of marriage as better or worse than interracial marriage? How would people react if the man was black and the woman white? Beyond these questions, how did interracial marriage figure in a moral and legal calculus that included such infractions as polygamy and incest?

This interlude attempts to sort out such matters as occasional sex, cohabitation, illegal marriage, and legal marriage. Across the years between the 1870s and the 1950s, sexual relationships outside of marriage could be prosecuted anywhere, but race often added a component to these episodes that made them very different from what they would have been without the interracial dimension.[2] The saga of another Johnson, Jack Johnson, shows the way.

The Saga of Jack Johnson

John Arthur "Jack" Johnson was a boxer in the ring and a black man in America. In the ring, by pounding black men, and later white men, senseless, he ascended to the throne of the heavyweight championship. As a black man in America, he defied more powerful taboos by dating and even marrying white women. His first white wife, Etta Duryea, committed suicide in September 1912. His marriage in December that year to his second white wife, Lucille Cameron, occasioned a furor across the land.[3] There were calls for new state laws against interracial marriage, and Congressman Seaborn Anderson Roddenbery of Georgia even urged adoption of an amendment to the U.S. Constitution that would outlaw such marriages (see chapter 9).

Jack Johnson's marriage to Lucille Cameron led W. E. B. Du Bois to wade into the fray with his own observations about interracial marriage. If, Du Bois wrote, "two full-grown responsible human beings propose to live together as man and wife, it is only social decency not only to allow, but to compel them to marry." Why would Georgia's Congressman Roddenbery, for one, respond to Jack Johnson by promoting a constitutional amendment that would outlaw marriage between two people just because one happened to be black and the other white? Du Bois offered a suggestion: "Let those people who have yelled themselves purple in the face over Jack Johnson just sit down and ask themselves this question: Granted that Johnson and Miss Cameron proposed to live together, was it better for them to be legally married or not?"[4]

Johnson's bride offered her own observations on the madness all around her. Regarding the priorities of the congressman from Georgia, she wondered, why hadn't it seemed to him at least as important to stop southern white men, and northern white men too, from "raising colored children out of wedlock"?[5] Lucille Johnson had reason to be puzzled—generations later, many people would tend to share her bewilderment at such turmoil as her marriage occasioned. Moreover, the fact that she married Johnson in the first place, and then wondered at folks' fury, demonstrated that some white Americans were immune to the antimiscegenation craze.

Yet, at that time, vast numbers of people were troubled by the Jack Johnson story, even deeply so. White folks were generally the most perturbed—white men might see their entitlement to a monopoly on white women flouted when Johnson gained sexual access to one and then another—but they were not alone. Black men and black women might admire Jack Johnson's flamboyant life and take pride in his success in the ring, but, at the same time, they could worry that a ruckus of the sort that surrounded this one black man endangered all African Americans, especially black men.[6] Moreover, black women might ask why they weren't good enough for a black man—why, when a black man met with great success, at least in Johnson's case, he evidently placed a greater value on white women than on black women.

What was happening revealed a peculiar manifestation of family values in Progressive Era America. Johnson's very public pursuit of white women made him vulnerable in the first place—in the court of public opinion and in the nation's courts of law—but marriage made it worse. One has to guess that, had Jack Johnson been white and Lucille Cameron black, there would have been less furor among white Americans. Or had the pair quietly got together only once, or on occasion, there would have been far less concern. Sex inside marriage was, in Johnson's case, worse than sex outside marriage.

The miscegenation laws, in their application, generally targeted sustained relationships rather than episodic encounters. In those states subject to the antimiscegenation regime, interracial marriage was the primary target, whatever and wherever the actual ceremony. Formal marriages having been outlawed, the law proved just as eager to punish instances in which marriage was acted out in the absence of a marriage certificate, as Tony Pace found out in Alabama (see chapter 8). More casual sexual relationships outside marriage, especially interracial encounters, could be prosecuted, too; but in the absence of evidence that the relationships approached the marriage model, even if convictions were secured, appeals courts sometimes decided that the laws had not been meant to be applied in such a way. Two cases each from Virginia and Alabama illustrate the possibilities.

Occasional Acts or Cohabitation—Virginia and Alabama

In Virginia, William H. Scott was convicted in Culpeper County in 1882 of "unlawful, lewd and lascivious associating and cohabiting" with Retta Jackson and fined $75. Scott appealed his conviction to the Virginia Supreme Court, but that court rejected every argument he mounted. Writing for the court, Judge Thomas J. Fauntleroy noted that "Scott, a *white* man, admitted that Jackson, a *colored* woman, was *his wife;* that they lived together; that he, Scott, admitted that Jackson's daughter was *his child.*" Other witnesses testified that Scott "carried her mail to her from the post-office," that "he familiarly associated with the woman, Jackson," and that he lived with her "as man and wife."[7] The appeals court upheld the trial court's conviction.

The couple had lived as husband and wife, and everyone seems to have been convinced that one was white and the other not. They might have been charged instead with interracial marriage, but the cohabitation charge was easier to prove, and it sufficed to demonstrate that public authorities were prepared to enforce the racial boundary. Even in the absence of racial considerations, the conviction could well have been sought and upheld, though—a critical distinction—two people of the same race had the option of marrying to avoid prosecution. The law against formal marriage meant that people in an interracial relationship were vulnerable regardless of whether they entered a formal marriage or, unable to manage that, simply acted as they would have had they been able to marry.

Another decision, two years later, also written by Judge Fauntleroy, reversed the conviction of D'Orsay Jones for "lewd and lascivious cohabitation"—outside of marriage—with Kate Oliver. Though he was black and she was white, the appellate court's opinion does not even suggest a racial component. And although they may have had sexual relations, the court took pains to insist that the offense charged in the indictment had not been fornication or adultery but that they did "lewdly and lasciviously associate and cohabit together." For the more serious charge to stick, there had to be *"cohabitation,"* wrote Judge Fauntleroy, and it had to be *"lewd and lascivious"*; "there must be a living together." And yet testimony had gone no further than the "mere implication that he might possibly have had some intimacy with her," and "the facts certified prove that he did *not* cohabit with her."[8]

The law of interracial sex outside marriage nabbed a good many couples, and some, once convicted, stayed convicted. Two cases that arose in the 1920s in Alabama, where interracial liaisons were prosecuted as aggressively as in any state in the nation, illustrate the considerations that determined whether miscegenation laws should be used against all interracial liaisons.

Hint Lewis was white and Bess Adams black. Neither was married. They lived just a quarter-mile apart, it was said, and spent a lot of time together. Witnesses reported his caring for at least one of her children and claiming that the child was his. Should Hint Lewis have been convicted and sentenced to two-to-three years in the penitentiary on the charge that "he lived in a state of felonious adultery and fornication with Bess Adams"? In affirming the conviction in 1921, the Alabama Court of Appeals observed that, "as has been stated many times before," no testimony was required by witnesses who had seen the defendants "actually engage in sexual intercourse." All that was required was that the jury be "satisfied beyond a reasonable doubt that there was an act of sexual intercourse and an agreement between the parties, either express or implied, that they would continue the relation when the occasion offered or they so desired."[9]

For a conviction to stick, an appeals court might demand that there be both "an act of sexual intercourse" and such "an agreement between the parties." Thus the Alabama appeals court reversed the conviction of Alexandra Markos, "a Greek woman," where the prosecutor had insisted in court, and the judge had agreed, "The only issue is whether or not [Markos's co-defendant] had intercourse with this woman and whether or not she is a white woman and he is a negro." Overturning the trial court verdict, the Alabama Court of Appeals in 1930 insisted instead that there be evidence of "cohabitation," meaning "some living together in a state of adultery or fornication." Just "one act," the court continued, or even "the occasional act, without the intention to live together in a state of adultery or fornication, would not make out the offense. It is a question of intention. One act would be sufficient if they intended to live together, but there must be some evidence to show that." In this case, the evidence showed the opposite.[10]

The trial court had convicted, but the appeals court held the evidence to a higher standard. As in the earlier case of D'Orsay Jones and Kate Oliver in Virginia, Alexandra Markos got off on appeal when the evidence showed something less than "cohabitation." Sexual relations between a black person and a white did not necessarily lead to a conviction that an appeals court would uphold—even when it was the man who was black and the woman white, even in the Deep South state of Alabama in the 1920s. A relationship that looked a lot like a marriage, however, might well lead to charges, a conviction, and a refusal to overturn the conviction. William H. Scott and Hint Lewis each learned that lesson—and both were white men.

Distinguishing Crimes of Race, Incest, and Polygamy

States might choose to enact miscegenation laws, or they might not. That was a matter of policy, not constitutional law. A major problem of challenging the constitutionality of miscegenation statutes lay in the entanglement of race with other considerations. State appellate judges, in particular, had a way of declaring that either states had authority over matters of marriage and family, or they did not.

In the 1870s, the Tennessee Supreme Court confronted a case in which an interracial couple claimed a legitimate marriage they had contracted in neighboring Mississippi, and it rejected the claim. Otherwise, the court warned, every time an out-of-state couple chose to move to Tennessee, the state would be entirely dependent on the whims of some other jurisdiction as to who could lawfully live in Tennessee as a married couple. The court's logic made some sense, though the contingencies it named seemed unlikely: "Extending the rule to the width asked for by the defendant," the court declared,

> and we might have in Tennessee the father living with his daughter, the son with the mother, the brother with the sister, in lawful wedlock, because they had formed such relations in a State or country where they were not prohibited. The Turk or Mohammedan, with his numerous wives, may establish his harem at the doors of the capitol, and we are without remedy. Yet none of these are more revolting, more to be avoided, or more unnatural, than the case before us.[11]

In another case in the 1870s, the Tennessee Supreme Court observed that Congress had similar power over the territories, a power that at that very time was "being exercised in Utah, in the suppression of polygamy." In short, Tennessee's authority "to interdict improper marriages" reflected a broader concern than post–Civil War race relations.[12]

In 1883, the Missouri Supreme Court protested that, "if any provision" of the U.S. Constitution "confers upon a citizen the right to marry any one who is willing to wed him, our attention has not been called to it. If such be one of the rights attached to American citizenship," the court went on, then "all our marriage acts forbidding intermarriages between persons within certain degrees of consanguinity are void, and the nephew may marry his aunt, the niece her uncle, and the son his mother or grandmother."[13] How, in short, to single out race? If the racial boundary in marriage was brought down on constitutional grounds, the court claimed to see no basis for legislation restricting marriage on other grounds.

Legislatures tried to prohibit and punish liaisons that were between two people who either were too different in racial identity or too close in blood relationship. Various courts wrapped interracial marriage together with incestuous marriages and polygamous marriages as a collection of "improper marriages" that the state either had, or did not have, authority to regulate.[14] Whereas the Republican Party, in its 1856 platform, had spoken of "twin relics of barbarism" in the western territories—polygamy and slavery—postwar judges seem to have adopted the concept of "twin relics" and applied it to polygamy and miscegenation.

In short, race was hardly the only barrier legislatures sought to establish in either sexual or marital relations. Was race to be privileged as a category less subject to state control than incest or bigamy?[15] The answer for many years was "no," whether because people did not want the answer to be "yes," or because they could not see quite how to make the distinction. Again and again, states acted as though, and used language as if, to lose the power to prevent miscegenous marriages meant also to lose the power to regulate marriages of any other sort. Language to that effect appeared in countless court decisions during the post–Civil War years. In this regard, courts' upholding of the constitutionality of miscegenation statutes was less a matter of intentionally thwarting black aspirations to social equality than it was of maintaining state authority over marriage and the family in ways that went far beyond race. And yet the matter kept coming back to race.

Interracial Sex and Interracial Marriage

The language, as from Georgia, about the need to maintain "the purity and distinctiveness of the races"[16] was belied by distinctions between casual sex and either cohabitation or formal marriage. The semblance of full equality—as represented by sustained close relationships between a man of one racial identity and a woman of another—was far more likely to draw the wrath of the law. If, that is, one person was identified as black and the other as white, even one spouse was one too many.

Miscegenation laws continued to serve their multiple purposes—even though not all interracial couples were indicted, not all indictments led to convictions, and not all convictions were upheld on appeal. The laws curtailed growth in the number of interracial couples, as the law defined them. They provided boundaries—not always certain, not always enforced—that delimited the range of legitimate behavior that people, whatever their racial identities, could consider engaging in. And they rendered doubtful a couple's ability to move from one state to another.

On racial grounds, miscegenation laws banned marriages that were, in other respects, entirely legal. The law of race and marriage permitted people to be charged with "fornication," "adultery," or "cohabitation" who believed and claimed that they had in fact married, or who were prevented from carrying through on their wish to marry by the very laws under which they were charged. It rendered "criminal" and "lascivious" behavior that, aside from the matter of racial identity, was entirely legal, normal, respectable. For living together outside marriage, two people could be charged with fornication. For living together inside marriage, they could be charged with fornication. The fact of a marriage could be immaterial.

Into the 1950s, authorities in Alabama, Mississippi, Louisiana, and Virginia prosecuted cases of interracial cohabitation or interracial marriage.[17] Into the 1960s, miscegenation laws lived on, as people in many states were denied a marriage license because of their racial identities. King Color still presumed to rule people's relationships on the basis of their racial identities. Such laws covered most American states at least for some period, and they covered some states for generations, even centuries—from the colonial era to the year 1967. As laws shaped lives, the antimiscegenation regime governed affairs both public and private.

Under the antimiscegenation regime, interracial sex outside of marriage was bad enough, but interracial marriage was worse. As for the question Du Bois posed—"Granted that Johnson and Miss Cameron proposed to live together, was it better for them to be legally married or not?"—the antimiscegenation regime replied, "not." The regime placed a particular premium on the utter exclusion of black men from sexual access, on any terms, to white women. The only safe sex for a black man was with a black woman. If, though, a black man were to have sex with a white woman, what ranked next in terms of preference was sex on an episodic basis. Dead last in terms of preference was anything approaching the marriage model. Regarding white men and their sexual access to black women, the regime could go along with either utter exclusion or unlimited access. But dead last, once again, was anything approaching the marriage model.

PART THREE

PROBLEM OF THE COLOR LINE

CHAPTER 9

DRAWING AND REDRAWING THE COLOR LINE

"The problem of the twentieth century is the problem of the color-line"

—W. E. B. Du Bois (1903)

"Intermarriage between negroes or persons of color and Caucasians or any other character of persons within the United States . . . is forever prohibited, and the term negroes or persons of color . . . shall be held to mean any and all persons . . . having any trace of African blood"

—Proposed amendment to the U.S. Constitution (1912)

In late 1912, Seaborn Anderson Roddenbery should have been pleased at his recent reelection to the U.S. House of Representatives from his district in southwest Georgia, and he must have been gratified that Democratic candidate Woodrow Wilson, a native of Virginia who had grown up in Georgia, had just defeated Theodore Roosevelt and William Howard Taft for the presidency. Yet, to his mind, events were by no means all moving with the right current.

So enraged was Congressman Roddenbery at the images of Jack Johnson not only beating white men senseless in the boxing ring, but also marrying white women, that he introduced an amendment to the U.S. Constitution to fix, if not both problems, then at least one of them. In a speech before Congress, Roddenbery exclaimed, "We can do no greater injustice to the negro than to let our statutes permit him to entertain the hope that at some future time he or his offspring may be married with a woman of the white race."[1]

Such aspirations would, the congressman was certain, be acted upon, and such actions would bring an apocalyptic outcome. "The consequences," he said, "will bring annihilation to that race which we have protected in this land for all these years"; whites would take the gloves off and end all such protection.[2] Meanwhile, the congressman hoped many of his colleagues would sign on and show their rage and determination. What better opportunity to go national with a ban on marriages like Johnson's with Lucille Cameron?

It was the image of a black man with "a woman of the white race," not a white man with a black woman, that catalyzed Roddenbery's antics and proposals. Roddenbery had been elected from Georgia, but he aimed his message at a wider audience, beyond the South. The easygoing approach to race relations in the North, he thought, had brought the chickens home to roost. "The negro question" demanded answers that cut across regional lines; only a change in federal law would suffice. White women across the land needed protection from the likes of Johnson. Who knew which one of them he would want to marry next? The congressman warned his colleagues from the North that "Johnson's marriage in Chicago" presented them with "as grave a negro question as ever confronted your brethren in the South."[3]

Roddenbery therefore proposed an amendment that would ban such marriages in every state. In full, the resolution calling for the amendment read:

> That intermarriage between negroes or persons of color and Caucasians or any other character of persons within the United States or any territory under that jurisdiction is forever prohibited, and the term negroes or persons of color, as here employed, shall be held to mean any and all persons of African descent or having any trace of African blood.[4]

Presumably, enforcement legislation would establish appropriate penalties, and such marriages would be void even if there were no criminal penalties. At the time Roddenbery proposed his amendment, 19 of the 48 states had no miscegenation law on the books, but the governors of several of those states had recently spoken out in favor of such laws. If the amendment could gain the approval of two-thirds of both houses of Congress, and then go on to be ratified by three-fourths of the states, the question of criminal penalties by way of enforcement could be addressed by a simple majority in Congress.

Roddenbery wanted to set the racial boundary between "any and all persons . . . having any trace of African blood" and everyone else. Not only Caucasians, but all other non-blacks, were to be protected from the taint of African blood. Western states, if they wished, could retain their bans on marriages between Caucasians and people of Asian ancestry. That question did not interest Congressman Roddenbery. But no state should, like Illinois—or Massachusetts or New York or Pennsylvania—permit a marriage of the sort that Jack Johnson had just contracted. Not only in Atlanta, Memphis, and New Orleans, but also in Boston, New York, Philadelphia, Chicago, and Washington, D.C., such marriages must be declared against public policy.

Like the 1857 *Dred Scott* decision regarding slavery, Roddenbery's proposal pointed toward a nationalization of Jim Crow marriage laws. This was no time,

Roddenbery was saying, to think about the niceties of state rights. Enshrined in the Tenth Amendment, the concept of state prerogative was always available to be deployed, particularly when the South's racial regime took a defensive posture against federal intrusion. Yet the congressman from Georgia was prepared to override state rights when states failed, in his view, to use their power appropriately—when they failed to ban black-white marriages. The "redemption" of the South from black power and racial equality should be taken to the entire nation.

The amendment that Roddenbery proposed, had it been adopted, would have established a national law of marriage as it related to race. Such a development would have inverted the approach taken by previous supporters of miscegenation laws, who held that the Fourteenth Amendment left matters of marriage in the hands of state legislatures and state judges and, therefore, left state miscegenation statutes intact in the face of challenges under the Fourteenth Amendment. It would have undone, in that respect, the Supreme Court decision in *Maynard* v. *Hill* (1888), according to which marriage remained solely within state jurisdiction—a decision that suddenly looked progressive in its implications regarding the antimiscegenation regime, not facilitating a challenge to it but at least permitting a containment of it.

And Roddenbery's proposed amendment would have created a legal environment starkly at odds with the alternative that emerged during Reconstruction. State supreme courts in Alabama, Texas, and Louisiana had declared their states' miscegenation laws invalid in light of the Civil Rights Act of 1866, the Fourteenth Amendment, or both, and any number of trial judges, from Indiana to Tennessee, had ruled that way, too, though their decisions had often been overturned on appeal.

Roddenbery's proposed constitutional amendment captured a number of significant developments in the United States in the generations preceding and following the turn of the century. By the time of Johnson's marriage in Chicago, Illinois had repealed its pre–Civil War law against interracial marriage, and Roddenbery's proposal would have restored it. In the last few years prior to Roddenbery's proposed definition of the color line, such states as Virginia, Alabama, and Louisiana had moved the boundary so as to make more exclusive the legal definition of whiteness. Roddenbery proposed to move it further still.

W. E. B. Du Bois surely seemed to have it right when he wrote at the dawn of the century that "the problem of the twentieth century is the problem of the color-line."[5] According to Roddenbery, the color line had to be defined, and it had to be enforced. According to Du Bois, it was to be recognized, negotiated, transcended.

Like a firecracker on the Fourth of July, Roddenbery's proposal shot high and exploded. It made a lot of noise at the time, though it left little trace. While it was in the sky, it illuminated much of what was going on around it. Jack Johnson—and Congressman Roddenbery—had hit a nerve. Yet the Constitution, when it was changed in the next few years, included statements about income taxes and women voters and the election of U.S. senators, but the only prohibition to be commanded had to do with alcoholic beverages, not interracial marriage.

In the aftermath of Johnson's marriage and Roddenbery's response to it, sympathetic statements by various state governors pointed in the direction that the congressman had indicated, as did similar proposals in various state legislatures. Remarkably little new legislation emerged, however. The congressman floated in on high tide, but the surf receded. His rant on the floor of Congress in December 1912 came as the antimiscegenation tide in American law and culture crested.

Currents ebbed and flowed across the next few decades, but—in the longer view—the antimiscegenation crusade had already reached its greatest strength in 1912 and 1913. It maintained that power through the 1920s and 1930s. But the twentieth century proved to be one in which, though the color line remained exceedingly important, laws against interracial marriage receded everywhere except the South, and then were abruptly declared no longer enforceable even there.

The Marital Color Line in America

In the aftermath of the Jack Johnson brouhaha and Congressman Roddenbery's response to it, the National Association for the Advancement of Colored People (NAACP)—with which W. E. B. Du Bois was closely associated—fought the expansion of the antimiscegenation regime into new states, and it did so with substantial success. Between 1913 and the late 1920s, miscegenation measures continued to be introduced in various state legislatures outside the South, but only Wyoming signed on with the antimiscegenation regime, in 1913. From time to time, as late as the 1920s, a southern member of Congress introduced federal legislation to outlaw interracial marriages in the District of Columbia. Such measures were approved in the U.S. House of Representatives in 1913 and 1915, but they stalled in the Senate, and subsequent efforts were turned back as well.[6]

In the realm of miscegenation laws, the North and South increasingly diverged. In the generation after the Civil War, various northern states repealed their laws—Illinois in 1874, Rhode Island in 1881, Maine and Michigan in 1883, and Ohio in 1887.[7] During the 1880s, then, just when the South was closing ranks in legal opposition to interracial marriage, northern states were withdrawing their support for the antimiscegenation regime. From the 1880s on, by contrast, the South refined its miscegenation laws and its commitment to racial regulation. By the time the new state of Oklahoma enacted a miscegenation law, all 17 southern states, the states that retained such laws until 1967, had them in place.

Moreover, some of those 17 states redefined "white" in ways more specific or more exclusive than before. According to a 1927 act of the Georgia legislature, for example, whites could not legally marry "persons of color"—a group previously defined as one-eighth black, but who were redefined as "having any ascertainable trace" of nonwhite ancestry. A "white person" was a "Caucasian," and, to secure that racial designation, people had to have "no ascertainable trace" of "Negro, African, West Indian, Asiatic Indian, Mongolian, Japanese, or Chinese blood in their veins."[8]

With that new law, Congressman Roddenbery's home state had implemented his view of what constituted whiteness—no African ancestry whatever. Having moved the boundary in that fashion, however, Georgia applied a white-non-white division, rather than Roddenbery's proposed line separating black from non-black. Although varying in particulars, other states acted at about the same time and in similar ways to redefine "white."

Marriage and the Color Line in Virginia

In nineteenth-century Virginia, the legal definition of a white person required less than one-fourth African ancestry, but a 1910 Virginia law redefined the races by adjusting the boundary that separated white from nonwhite. The new statute left the definition of an Indian unchanged—"every person not a colored person" who had "one-fourth or more of Indian blood." But henceforth, the law insisted, "Every person having one-sixteenth or more of negro blood shall be deemed a colored person."[9] Thus Virginia's quest for racial purity took it from a one-fourth fraction to one-sixteenth.

Under the nineteenth-century rule of one-fourth, three full-blooded white grandparents sufficed to make a person white only if the fourth grandparent were part Indian or part white. Under a one-eighth rule, seven of eight great-grandparents would have been required in addition to whatever margin the eighth could offer. Now fifteen white great-grandparents out of sixteen would fail to satisfy the definition of a white person, unless the sixteenth could help out at least a little. The intent, of course, was to make the definition of a white person more exclusive, a change that would make it much more difficult for a person of both African and European ancestry to qualify for marriage to someone who satisfied the more rigid requirement as a white person.[10]

The practical significance of Virginia's new law could be more complicated. A mixed-race person less than one-fourth black who, under the law before 1910, could marry only a white person—that is, who was barred from marrying a "colored person" under penalty of indictment for a felony—could now marry only another person of color and, if marrying a white person, would be subject to prosecution for that choice. Two mixed-race people who, under the previous dispensation, might have legally married each other as white people (if, for example, each were seven-eighths European and one-eighth African), might still marry each other, but it would be as nonwhite people. Finally, two mixed-race Virginians who could not have married across the previous barrier—for example, if one had one-half and the other only one-sixteenth African ancestry— might now legally marry each other. Genealogical tests to determine who could marry whom had taken on even greater complexity than in the past.

The Virginia Supreme Court may have suffered confusion under the 1910 law. A white woman, Lucy May, had married a white man, I. B. Grasty, and borne two white children, Madeline and Ruby, but Grasty died. Later, she and John Moon had gone to Washington, D.C., and been married there. Authorities subsequently challenged her right to retain custody of the two children. John Moon qualified as "white" under the "one-quarter rule" but, being one-sixteenth African, could not meet the new racial standard for "white." Now that the mother was involved in an interracial marriage, her white children would be associating with "persons of mixed blood" and "would be deterred from association with gentle people of white blood." The trial court ordered their removal to the Children's Home Society, which was required by law to take into custody all children found to be living in "vicious or unsalutary surroundings."[11]

Speaking for a unanimous state supreme court in 1911, Judge John Alexander Buchanan reported all this but, declining to recognize that the case at hand might be affected by the new standard, overruled the trial court and awarded custody of the children to their mother. As Judge Buchanan concluded his opinion, "It is not pretended in this case that the step-father was a colored person within the meaning of our statute, or that he and the mother of the children were guilty of any crime in intermarrying, or were not persons of good character."[12]

Two Virginia lawyers responded with distaste to the state supreme court's decision. All right, they said, maybe Moon was a white man under the law when she married him, but by the time the court spoke, he was white no more. The court, they wrote, had "restored these children to the control of their mother, whose husband, although legally white when she married him[,] is now a negro under the law, and these children are thus condemned for the future to associate with persons who are in the eyes of the law negroes." The 1910 statute had "changed the status of these Moons . . . from white to colored," and the court should have done the same. "The power of the legislature to make this legislation retroactive so as to affect the validity of a marriage such as that of [Lucy Grasty to John Moon] may well be doubted," the critics conceded. They insisted, nonetheless, that the judges should have let the new law govern their disposition of the case.[13]

The authors understood the difficulty that, as they saw it, the judges must have faced, given the legislature's attempt "to establish a dividing line between white and colored persons which does not coincide with that established by the universal consensus of the public opinion of the state, so that . . . there is a considerable class of citizens who are in the eye of the law white, but by the judgment of society are colored." The legislature had, in 1910, "taken a step" in the right direction, they wrote, but it was not enough. "This difficulty will continue to exist until the legislature adopts the rule enforced by public sentiment"—until, that is, the legislature "recognizes and declares to be members of the colored race all having an appreciable amount of negro blood."[14] The critics' formula begged the question, of course, as to how to define and ascertain what they called "an appreciable amount of negro blood."

After the 1910 statute, the Virginia General Assembly further redefined race in the Old Dominion. It did so by moving the "dividing line" in very much the way that had been called for in the wake of the *Moon* case, but it took a number of years to do so. After throwing out the old one-quarter rule by adopting a one-sixteenth threshold in 1910, the legislature redefined "white" in 1924 to exclude anyone of any traceable African ancestry.

With interracial marriage in mind, the 1924 "Act to Preserve Racial Integrity" required all Virginians to register their racial identities with a local registrar as well as with the state registrar of vital statistics. The process was cumbersome and designed to be fail-safe. Any trace of nonwhite ancestry whatever meant that a person was defined as nonwhite and thus incapable of marrying someone who still qualified as white. The sole exception related to the so-called "Pocahontas defense," given that a number of "white" Virginians had long admitted, even celebrated, their descent from the seventeenth-century union between Pocahontas and John Rolfe. Any otherwise white Virginian, if possessing no more than one-sixteenth Indian ancestry—and no African ancestry—would still qualify as a "white person." The key people involved in passage and implementation of the new law were John Powell, whose Anglo-Saxon Clubs of America screamed about racial purity, and Walter Plecker, the hard-driving director of Virginia's Bureau of Vital Statistics.[15]

The 1924 statute did not specify any races other than "white," "negro," and "Indian." Legislators' central concern, after all, related to European and African ancestry. But the exclusive language brought Asians, too, into the binary world of Virginia's racial laws, and it placed Asians on the nonwhite side of the racial boundary. Thus a "white" person and someone of Asian birth or ancestry could no longer contract a valid marriage under Virginia law.[16]

Virginia law had long classified as "white" anyone of European descent who was less than one-fourth African—the fraction that had shaped earlier litigation. The redefinitions of 1910 and 1924 moved the boundary that determined racial identity under the law. Every time a state moved the boundary that separated one racial identity from another, it demonstrated how flexible the legal definition was, and how arbitrary was the entire enterprise of legislating identity.

The 1924 law redefined race—supplied a new definition of "white"—as it related to marriage, but otherwise left interracial marriage as it had been since 1878, a crime carrying a penitentiary sentence of two to five years.[17] In the summer of 1924, the clerk of court in Rockbridge County denied Atha Sorrells and Robert Painter a marriage license. Painter was white, it seemed, but was Sorrells? Told she could not marry Painter because she had some African ancestry, she sued.

Walter Plecker was determined to win the case and see the Racial Purity Act continue to do its work, and he expected to win on the strength of testimony from local people who had known generations of the Sorrells family. He had recently won a similar case in the same county involving Dorothy Johns and James Connor. This time, though, a number of local people opposed Plecker and proved just as determined to win as he was. His main witness failed to show up at the trial to testify, "afraid that his barn will be burned or other injury done to him or his property." The presiding judge, Henry Holt, therefore ruled in favor of Sorrells and directed the clerk to issue the license.[18] The threat of violence, like the use of the courts, could cut more than one way when it came to racial identity and marriage licenses.

In May 1928, an Amherst County jury convicted Mary Hall, a "white woman," and Mott Hamilton Wood, a mixed-race man who was reportedly one-sixteenth black and had lived all his life as a white man. The couple were each sentenced to the penitentiary for two years.[19] He had been born white, but then the law made him black, and he paid a big penalty for marrying someone who had remained white.

Some juries, though, failed to convict, uncomfortable with the reach of the statute and the two-year minimum sentence. Therefore, the 1932 legislature made one last change in Virginia's miscegenation law, reducing the minimum sentence for a violation to one year.[20] Whatever the penalty, individual Virginians would continue to find themselves vulnerable to prosecution, and judges and juries would continue to have to determine how the law should be applied.

The 1924 law's more stringent definition of whiteness moved the legal boundary that separated one racial identity from another, but it did not end uncertainty as to what the law might mean for one Virginian or another. The law of racial identity and marriage in Alabama went through a transition much like Virginia's.

Marriage and the Shifting Color Line in Alabama

Under Alabama law, beginning with the Code of 1852, a "mulatto" was a mixed-race "negro" who had "descended . . . from negro ancestors, to the third generation inclusive, though one ancestor in each generation may have been a white person."[21] That definition persisted into the twentieth century, but then it was tightened. First came a law by which Alabama, like Virginia, shifted by two generations the minimal requirement for being defined as white. In 1907, at about the same time that Virginia's quest for racial purity took it from a one-fourth fraction to one-sixteenth, Alabama abandoned its one-eighth fraction of the previous half-century in favor of one thirty-second.[22]

In 1927, the Alabama legislature—made up of white legislators representing white constituents—moved aggressively to change the racial boundary again and also apply the new definition to marriage. A new law made the definition of a white person in Alabama more exclusive than ever before. Scrapping the one-thirty-second rule, it stipulated that a "negro" was a person "descended on the part of the father or mother from negro ancestors, without reference to or limit of time or number of generations removed."[23] Another statute applied the new language to miscegenation: "If any white person and any negro, or the descendant of any negro intermarry, or live in adultery or fornication with each other, each of them shall, on conviction, be imprisoned in the penitentiary for not less than two nor more than seven years."[24] The penalty, at least, remained unchanged from Alabama's inaugural miscegenation law, enacted right after the Civil War.

In 1927, the Alabama legislature completed its work in defining the black and white races and in banning marriage between them. Back in 1850, the Alabama Supreme Court had balked at defining someone one-fourth "negro" as a "mulatto," and had instead preferred to interpret the term as applying to someone half-white and half-black. "If the statute against mulattoes is by construction to include quadroons," worried the antebellum court, "then where are we to stop? If we take the first step by construction, are we not bound to pursue the line of descendants, so long as there is a drop of negro blood remaining?"[25]

The court had left it in 1850 to the legislature to define racial terms in some other way, should it see a necessity. Over the next 77 years, the Alabama legislature exercised that authority and, by 1927, had in effect determined to "pursue the line of descendants, so long as there is a drop of negro blood remaining." During that 77 years, Alabama had established a marital color line, and then, by stages, had moved it to the logical endpoint that the court had resisted in 1850.[26]

Georgia, Virginia, and Alabama were hardly alone in drawing the line between "white" and "black" at a point where any African ancestry whatever sufficed to categorize a person as black.[27] Oklahoma law had adopted the "one-drop" definition of black racial identity even earlier.

The Oklahoma Variant: African Ancestry?—Check "Yes" or "No"

In 1938, an African American woman named Patsy Perryman told an interviewer that, about 1858, she had been born a slave in the Cherokee Nation, in what became eastern Oklahoma. She and her parents, brothers, and sisters belonged to a Cherokee family named Taylor, she said, until emancipation came in the 1860s. After statehood in 1907, Oklahoma's population ran more than 85 percent Caucasian, but the 1860s and 1870s that she recalled from her youth were very different. "There was nobody around the place but Indians and Negroes," she remembered. "I was a full-grown girl before I ever saw a white man." In a post-emancipation world of Native Americans and African Americans, her "brother Lewis married a full-blood Indian woman in the old Cherokee country," she reported, and she herself married three times—"Charley Clark, a full-blood Creek Indian," a "black African" whom she did not name, and finally Randolph Perryman, a Creek freedman.[28]

Patsy Perryman faced no legal impediment in the nineteenth century to marrying either a Native American or an African American. The 1907 Oklahoma state constitution, however, classified residents in a way that would have banned her from wedding Charley Clark, the "full-blood Creek Indian." A section on "Definition of Races" declared:

> Wherever in this Constitution and laws of this state, the word or words "colored" or "colored race," "negro" or "negro race," are used, the same shall be construed to mean or apply to all persons of African descent. The term "white race" shall include all other persons.

These terms set up the law of race and marriage in Oklahoma. According to a statute enacted in the new state's first legislative session,

> The marriage of any person of African descent, as defined by the Constitution of this state, to any person not of African descent, or the marriage of any person not of African descent to any person of African descent, shall be unlawful and is hereby prohibited within this state.[29]

Oklahoma placed Native Americans on the white side of the racial boundary, distinguishing blacks from non-blacks rather than whites from nonwhites.

The law of racial identity in Oklahoma resembled the one Congressman Roddenbery had in mind, in that it separated people with African ancestry from all others. It varied, however, from the norm in many states, where "white" was separated from all—or at least most—other racial identities. Patsy Perryman lived long enough for the racial categories of the world that she remembered from her childhood—with "nobody around . . . but Indians and Negroes," and where she never saw "a white man"—to take on a very different meaning. "Indians" had not been "white" when she was a child. Nor had "Indians" been "white" when she herself married "Charley Clark, a full-blood Creek Indian." But from 1907 on, "full-blood" Indians like Charley Clark were defined as "not of African descent" and therefore of the "white race."

Oklahoma was typical of American states in treating people with African ancestry as particularly inappropriate candidates for marrying whites. Oklahoma was by no means typical, however, in assigning a white racial identity to anyone who had no traceable African ancestry. Elsewhere, policymakers expressed concern about the whiteness quotient even of many people from Europe—and certainly they rejected the notion that people from East Asia should be classified as white. Again and again, the questions arose. Who was white, and who was not? Who should be permitted to marry a white person? In particular, who should be permitted to marry a white woman?

Race, Immigration, and Marriage:
Asians and Caucasians along the Color Line

Experts on immigration in the early twentieth century, convinced that American society would reflect its immigrants, urged the nation to shape the outcome by shaping the inflows. According to Harry Laughlin—the "expert eugenics agent" for Congress's House Committee on Immigration and Naturalization—national policy should permit immigration by people whose racial characteristics "are compatible with our prevailing races for mate selection."[30]

If "the American people" were "to remain American," Laughlin said, the nation could "successfully assimilate in the future many thousands of northwestern European immigrants," although "only such of these as are carefully inspected and selected." By contrast, the nation could assimilate only a small number of immigrants from other parts of Europe—and from "the colored races practically none." Beyond controlling immigration, Laughlin went on, the nation could depend for its continued social development on mate selection, which could itself be "controlled or directed to a small degree by the several individual states in their marriage laws." John Sharp Williams, U.S. Senator from Mississippi, stated in this context, "You have got to have a population which is at least potentially assimilable in lawful wedlock." Williams no doubt spoke with his state's laws in mind, laws that restricted marriages between Caucasians and people of either African or "Mongolian" ancestry.[31]

Concerns about race and marriage, then, went beyond African Americans. Some western territories had acted as early as the 1860s to curtail marriages between whites and Asians or Asian Americans, as well as between whites and African Americans. In 1861, Nevada imposed penalties for couples that, whether they were cohabiting or formally married, included a Caucasian and someone African American, Native American, or Chinese. Idaho enacted a similar measure in 1864. So did Arizona in 1865, though the Asian category it used was "Mongolian." California, Oregon, Utah, and one southern state, Mississippi, acted later in the nineteenth century. States inaugurating similar restrictions in the twentieth century included Missouri and Montana in 1909; Nebraska, South Dakota, and Wyoming in 1913; and Georgia in 1927.[32]

Across the country, and from the mid-nineteenth century through the midtwentieth century, men of Asian ancestry were far more numerous than were women of Asian ancestry. Thus it was, in particular, that Filipino men often dated and sometimes married white women. Men from the Philippine Islands began coming to the continental United States—some as students, most as workers—soon after the Spanish-American War. Filipinos could not become citizens, but, living in what had just become part of the American empire, they were not subject to general U.S. immigration laws. The number of Filipinos living on the mainland leapt from 5,603 in 1920 to 45,208 ten years later—30,470 in California. The Great Depression caused immigration to slow. Moreover, the 1934 Tydings-McDuffie Act, while promising the Philippine Islands their eventual political independence from the United States, immediately slashed annual immigration to the United States from no limit to 50.[33] But the people already in the country largely remained there.

The Filipino population in the United States was overwhelmingly male—in most communities, by a factor of between ten and twenty to one—and the women they dated were, whatever their ethnicity, mostly "white." White daughters of immigrant families in the city—young women with limited occupational choices or income, especially during the Depression years of the 1930s—sometimes escaped their authoritarian families to work at dance halls, where they could socialize and earn a little extra money dancing. Filipino men found that, at those dance halls, as historian Barbara Posadas has phrased it, "money might buy the feminine companionship" that "their skin color prevented elsewhere."[34]

Tensions often surfaced over relationships between Filipino men and white women, and over a period of years in California there was considerable jockeying over whether to permit such mixed-race couples to obtain marriage licenses. In 1932, Salvador Roldan wanted to marry Marjorie Rogers, but the Los Angeles county clerk's office—seeing a "Mongolian" wishing to marry a white woman in violation of state law—refused to issue them a license. Roldan took the matter to local court, where it was determined that, as a person of Philippine ancestry, he was not a member of the "Mongolian" race and therefore not subject to the state's ban against marrying a Caucasian.[35]

State authorities appealed the case to the California Supreme Court, which, in a 3–3 tie, left the lower court ruling in place. The appellate judges who sided with Roldan's contention, when they recounted the legislative history of the California law, concluded that lawmakers had not meant to include "Malays" in the term "Mongolian." Lawmakers proceeded to correct the oversight, and the California law henceforth banned marriages between Caucasians and "members of the Malay race," which included Filipinos. Marriages between a white and a Malay were henceforth "illegal and void."[36] Roldan and Rogers won their case, but as a consequence the state extended the reach of its law against interracial marriage.

The story from California demonstrates that the color line in the law of marriage persisted well into the twentieth century, even outside the South. It also shows that—particularly in the West, where residents of Asian ancestry often outnumbered those of African descent—racial differences under miscegenation laws could go beyond "black" and "white." And it shows that, into the 1930s, state legislatures—again, even outside the South—were prepared to add to the list of proscribed groups to keep white women from marrying nonwhite men.

California was not alone in any of those respects. Arizona extended the coverage of its miscegenation laws in 1931 to include "the Malay race." So did Maryland, in 1935, and finally Utah, in 1939. Maryland established three groups of people, and every member of each group could legally marry only someone from within that group. Whites could not marry blacks or Malays, and blacks could marry neither whites nor Malays. Violation remained an "infamous crime" that carried imprisonment for between 18 months and 10 years.[37]

The Color Line: Definitions and Redefinitions

From the 1860s to the 1960s, Americans struggled over state laws against interracial marriage. Some people sought to enact new laws, broaden their application to new groups, or redefine "white" in a more exclusive manner. Others sought to eliminate all such laws as bad policy. Some people, finding themselves targeted by those laws, resisted them, arguing that they did not fall under the ban as it was stated, or that the ban itself was unconstitutional.

Under the antimiscegenation regime, an individual's racial identity under the law was always subject to change. It could change through a person's migration across a political boundary, or it could change because a legal boundary had been redefined or relocated. An interracial couple who could legally marry in Pennsylvania could not do so across the state line in Maryland. Moving the legal boundary—for example, in Alabama, Louisiana, and Virginia in the years around 1910—led to a redefinition of some people from white to black, like John Moon in Virginia. Moving the color line in California, Maryland, or Arizona to redefine people classified as "Mongolians" or "Malays" made them suddenly inaccessible to potential marriage partners who had retained identities as white people. Although racial identity could be changed, under the official rules it could be changed only by the authority that had imposed it in the first place, not by a person who opted for another category.

Into the twentieth century, many, even most states outside the South had miscegenation laws. In the West, as late as Wyoming in 1913, more states adopted such laws. Moreover, into the 1930s, a number of states, especially in the West, added some people of Asian ancestry to the ranks of residents who could not legally marry people defined as Caucasians.

Yet by 1912, the geographical color line in matters of marriage had begun to take up a position not only along the Mason–Dixon line (between Pennsylvania to the north and Delaware and Maryland to the south) but also along the Ohio River (between Ohio and Illinois to the north and Kentucky and West Virginia to the south). With a repeal by Maine in 1883, no New England state still had a miscegenation law, and after Ohio's action in 1887 only Indiana retained such a law in the Old Northwest. Even in states with no laws regarding interracial marriage, however, the nation's immigration policy influenced citizens' marriage choices by shaping the size and nature of immigrant groups.

Meanwhile, the antimiscegenation regime in the United States thrived, even after it stopped expanding into new territory. Miscegenation laws were implicated—whether under state laws or through national policies—in every facet of American life, from immigration to education to inheritance.[38] Marriage served as a metaphor for the color line throughout American law and culture.

CHAPTER 10

BOUNDARIES—RACE AND PLACE
IN THE LAW OF MARRIAGE

"To be a negro is not a crime; to marry a white woman is not a crime; but to be a
negro, and being a negro, to marry a white woman is a felony"

—Virginia Supreme Court (1885)

"A law like . . . ours would be very idle if it could be avoided by merely stepping over
an imaginary line"

—North Carolina Supreme Court (1877)

Wherever a line was drawn against interracial marriage, other lines had to be determined. Boundaries—cultural and geographical—governed the ways in which race shaped the law of marriage. What was the racial identity of each partner in a putative marriage? Sometimes that question was the crux of a case, and conviction or acquittal depended on the court's answer. What was the law of race and marriage where their ceremony took place, and was their marriage portable, could it be brought across state lines? Some cases hinged on those issues. Once raised, these were momentous questions for any couple.

Is She Black or Is She Guilty?

In October 1881, John Crawford and Maggie Dancey went on trial for violating South Carolina's new law against interracial marriage. After courting in North Carolina, they had decided to marry. They had heard that North Carolina had a stringent law against their doing so, but, believing that South Carolina had no such law, they thought they had a remedy. He moved back south across the state line to his home in York County, and she soon followed from her family's home in Mooresville, just north of Charlotte. They approached a black preacher, Edward Lindsay, about their wishes, and he assured them that they could marry in South Carolina. The ceremony took place. Their arrests soon followed.

The newlyweds' marriage did not involve the question of comity, of whether a contract undertaken in one state was viewed as valid in another—though it very well might have had they moved back to North Carolina. But it definitely involved the thorny issue of racial identity. John Crawford testified that the fair-skinned woman he had married came from a family that, back in her home-town, was regarded as mixed-race. He had seen his wife's grandmother, a "bright mulatto," he said. The family attended a black church; they associated only with African Americans; and despite their color, they seemed to fall on the black side of the great racial divide. In short, his wife, described as of "fair complexion," with "flaxen or light auburn hair and light blue eyes"—though far lighter than he, a "dark mulatto"—was also a person of color, and therefore they had not, after all, broken the law of whose existence they had not known.[1]

One defendant's statements about the other left the court perplexed. The fact that Maggie Dancey went on trial some distance from her family's residence meant that no local witnesses could help the court with testimony regarding the Dancey family's racial reputation.

The judge called upon a white medical doctor, W. J. Whyte, to offer his ex-pert testimony, but the doctor, after a brief examination in the waning light of day, reported the woman's racial identity difficult to pin down. The judge held the trial over to the next morning. The doctor tried again but complained that the microscope with which he examined the woman's hair and skin seemed in-adequate to the task. If forced to choose, he held to his opinion that Maggie Dancey was a white woman, but he could not be certain.

The judge put the matter in the hands of the jury. He told them that, if they were unsure, they should resolve their doubt in "favor" of the woman—what-ever he or they might think that meant in this case. If they decided that she should go free, then she must be black, not white. If they found that she was white, then she stood in violation of the law under which she and Crawford had been charged. After an hour's deliberation, the jury reported its verdict. Maggie Dancey was white. John Crawford was not. Both were guilty.

The kind of question that Maggie Dancey's trial raised could never vanish as long as the law of marriage insisted on dividing people into two discrete racial categories, categories that can perhaps better be understood as existing along a continuum. A few years after the convictions of Crawford and Dancey, delegates to the South Carolina constitutional convention of 1895 encountered similar problems when they considered whether to incorporate the miscegenation statute into the fundamental law. One proposal would have classified as white only those residents without "any" African ancestry. Another would have set the boundary so that anyone with less than one-quarter African ancestry qualified as white. The convention settled upon a boundary at one-eighth, so that having one African American great-grandparent could result in classification as black.[2]

Anyone living in a jurisdiction that had a miscegenation law might have to consider: which people were available under the law as potential marriage partners? who was forbidden from marrying whom? Enforcement of a miscegenation law depended on having a boundary that separated one racial identity from another. Being subject to prosecution and conviction depended on where the boundary was set between those who could not cross it to marry—and, perhaps, where a jury chose to locate a person with regard to that boundary. Anyone at all was at risk, for even if one person's racial identity was agreed upon by everyone, the racial identity—under the law—of that person's choice of marriage partner might be challenged.

Wherever the line was situated, Maggie Dancey was vulnerable to indictment, and therefore John Crawford was, too. The arbitrariness of the line's location exemplified the cultural definition of race—as opposed to a biological definition—in the various state miscegenation laws.[3] Cases from Virginia and elsewhere further illustrate the difficulty of sorting out racial identities under the law—and the extraordinary power that the law had to punish what a trial determined to be an errant choice of marriage partner.

When brought to court, therefore, some people challenged the claim that they did not share one racial identity, and argued that, since they were both black or both white, their marriage was lawful. Others argued that they had entered a valid marriage and, having moved into another state, should not be subject to the enforcement of its laws against interracial marriage. This chapter explores racial identity and interstate comity, two of the main problems in enforcing—or escaping conviction under—laws against interracial marriage during the hundred years after the Civil War.

"To Be a Negro Is Not a Crime":
Assigning Racial Identity Can Be Hard To Do

In the 1870s and 1880s, cases arose in Virginia regarding race, sex, and marriage, in some of which the delineation of the racial boundary proved of central importance. The case of *McPherson* v. *Commonwealth* arose across the James River from Richmond in the city of Manchester, where Rowena McPherson and George Stewart faced charges of "living in illicit intercourse" with each other. They were convicted and fined despite their insistence that they were legally married. The trial court determined that, while he was white, she was not, and thus their marriage had no validity and could supply no shield in their defense.[4]

According to a unanimous state supreme court, to the contrary, the facts suggested that McPherson was not, in fact, "a negro." Her father was white (the court seems to have taken that as meaning he was 100 percent of non-African ancestry); her maternal grandfather was also white; and thus already she was three-fourths white. To be sure, that fraction would leave her nonwhite in the eyes of the law at that time in Virginia. To be legally "white," she had to be less than one-quarter black.[5]

The case hinged on the racial ancestry of Rowena McPherson's maternal grandmother, for if she had been entirely African in ancestry, then McPherson was nonwhite, but, if not, then McPherson qualified as white. Testimony from the family declared that the maternal grandmother's mother—McPherson's great-grandmother—was "a brown skin woman," "half-Indian." Thus, the court concluded, "less than one-fourth" of Rowena McPherson's "blood" was "negro blood." And "if it be but one drop less, she is not a negro." Because she had, therefore, not married across the racial boundary provided under Virginia law at that time, the marriage was valid after all. The pair were not guilty.[6]

A case from Montgomery County, in western Virginia, also raised the complicated matter of racial identity and jeopardized two Virginians' freedom. In February 1883, Isaac Jones obtained a license to marry Martha Ann Gray. The license listed both parties as "black"—the form, which assumed that both parties would be of the same race, supplied only a single blank line to be filled in.[7] The Rev. Charles S. Schaeffer performed the marriage ceremony at "the colored Baptist church near Christiansburg," where Schaeffer, a former Freedmen's Bureau agent, had ministered since shortly after the Civil War. All had perhaps gone well enough at first in the new couple's married life, but then they were indicted in September 1883 for "feloniously" marrying—he was "a negro," she "a white person"—across the racial divide.[8]

Convicted in county court, Isaac Jones was sentenced to the penitentiary for two years and nine months, his would-be wife for the minimum two years. They appealed their convictions to the Montgomery County circuit court—which affirmed the decision of the trial court—and then to the state supreme court. They asserted that Virginia's 1878 miscegenation statute violated the U.S. Constitution, and they denied, in any case, that the statute applied to them. Jones claimed to be mixed-race and not "negro," and Gray claimed to be mixed-race and not "white." Certainly she "was accustomed to associate and attend church with the negroes," it was said, and the church pastor had acknowledged that some "colored persons attending his church" were "whiter" than she.[9]

Speaking on July 24, 1884, for a divided court, Judge Thomas T. Fauntleroy noted that Jones stood "convicted of a crime, not only against the law of Virginia, but against the just sensibilities of her civilization."[10] Yet the state had failed, he said, to carry the burden of proof beyond a reasonable doubt. Thus the appeals court reversed the couple's convictions and remanded their case to Montgomery County for a new trial.

On August 3, ten days after the appeals court's reversal, the county court came to the same judgment it had the year before. The circuit court again confirmed that decision, and "the prisoners" again appealed. The following June, the state supreme court again reversed and remanded. It rejected Isaac Jones's contention that the statute did not apply to mixed-race Virginians, but insisted nonetheless that the law applied solely to two people only one of whom was at least one-fourth black.[11] What was his racial status under the law? What, for that matter, was hers? The court could not tell.

This time—again with the hard-liner, Judge Drury A. Hinton, dissenting— Judge Benjamin Watkins Lacy wrote:

> The charge against Isaac Jones is, that he is a negro, and that being a negro he was married to a white woman. To be a negro is not a crime; to marry a white woman is not a crime; but to be a negro, and being a negro, to marry a white woman is a felony; therefore, it is essential to the crime that the accused shall be a negro—unless he is a negro he is guilty of no offence.[12]

Isaac Jones had both European and African ancestry, and the crucial question was how much of each; but the prosecution had developed, wrote Judge Lacy,

> no evidence of his parentage except that his mother was a yellow woman. If his mother was a yellow woman with more than half of her blood derived from the white race, and his father a white man, he is not a negro. If he is a man of mixed blood he is not a negro, unless he has one-fourth at least of negro blood in his veins, and this must be proved by the commonwealth as an essential part of the crime.

Because, Lacy wrote, "every accused person is to be presumed to be innocent until his guilt is proved, this person must be presumed not to be a negro until he is proved to be such."[13] Two years and three months after their wedding, the couple's freedom to live together as husband and wife—and out of prison for doing so—remained in the hands of the Virginia courts.

A Marriage, Valid in the State Where Contracted: Must It Be Recognized Elsewhere?

State boundaries affected the law of interracial marriage in multiple ways. At any one time, some states permitted interracial marriages, and some did not. If an interracial couple moved from a state where they had a valid marriage into a state that banned such marriages, did their marriage survive the move? Alternatively, might a marriage be valid if a couple deliberately went out of state to evade the law, married, and then returned to their home state?

J. P. Bell, a white man, married an African American woman in Mississippi at a time when that state had no law against such marriages. The couple moved to Tennessee, where he was indicted under an 1870 Tennessee law banning interracial unions. At his trial, his motion that the indictment be quashed was granted in view of the evidence, stated in the indictment, that the couple had been married in Mississippi, not Tennessee. The state appealed.[14]

The sole question was, the state highest court observed: "Does a marriage in Mississippi protect persons who live together" in Tennessee "in violation of" its marriage laws? If the parties had the legal capacity to marry under Tennessee law, then the precise location or ceremony would little manner. But, the court ruled, they had no such legal capacity in Tennessee.[15] The trial judge had ruled in the couple's favor, but the Tennessee Supreme Court ordered a new trial. Moving to Nashville had been a mistake. Perhaps they should have stayed in Mississippi, where their marriage was recognized as valid. In other states, variations on the theme of J. P. Bell's experience in Tennessee were played out.

The case of Andrew Kinney, a black man, and Mahala Miller, a white woman, supplied Virginia's major precedent regarding miscegenation cases in the late-nineteenth and twentieth centuries. By 1874, Kinney and Miller had lived together long enough to have had three sons born since 1867. Perhaps seeking to avoid charges of unmarried cohabitation, yet unable to find a preacher who would marry them in Virginia, they left their home in Augusta County in November 1874 and traveled to Washington, D.C., to get married.[16]

The gesture failed to protect them from prosecution. Virginia authorities charged Kinney with "lewdly associating and cohabiting" with Miller. Kinney claimed to be married to Miller, and his attorney urged the trial judge to instruct the jury that the marriage was "valid and a bar to this prosecution." Instead, the judge instructed the jury that the marriage was "but a vain and futile attempt to evade the laws of Virginia," laws that banned any marriage between a white resident and an African American. Convicted and fined $500—the maximum penalty under the law—Kinney appealed the decision, first to the circuit court and then to the Virginia Supreme Court.[17] As with J. P. Bell in Tennessee, the question regarding Andrew Kinney was: Did the defendant have a valid marriage that gave him an effective defense against the charge he faced? Or was his living as though he were married precisely the basis for that charge?

The appeals court viewed Andrew Kinney's action as "a violation of [Virginia's] penal laws in this most important and vital branch of criminal jurisprudence, affecting the moral well being and social order of this state." As to whether the law of Washington, D.C., or that of Virginia—"the lex loci contractus or the lex domicilii"—governed the case, Judge Joseph Christian, speaking for a unanimous court, declared: "There can be no doubt as to the power of every country to make laws regulating the marriage of its own subjects; to declare who may marry, how they may marry, and what shall be the legal consequences of their marrying."[18] In this case, the "country" was Virginia, and Kinney the "subject."

Judge Christian reviewed the precedents, English and American, and only one seemed to support Kinney. In that case, which also involved one black partner and one white, he and she had left colonial Massachusetts, which banned such marriages, and gone to a neighboring colony, Rhode Island, which did not; had a wedding ceremony; and then returned to Massachusetts. A Massachusetts court had ruled many years later (see chapter 4), as Kinney now asked the Virginia court to, that a marriage, if valid according to "the laws of the country where it is celebrated, is valid in every other country."[19]

Speaking for the court, Judge Christian rejected this proposition. If the ritual itself were at issue, the marriage should be recognized as valid. Kinney, however, faced a problem not of "the form of the contract," or of "rites and ceremonies," but of "essentials," and "the essentials of the contract depend upon . . . the law of the country . . . in which the matrimonial residence is contemplated."[20] As the judge noted,

> The purity of public morals, the moral and physical development of both races, and the highest advancement of our cherished southern civilization, under which two distinct races are to work out and accomplish the destiny to which the Almighty has assigned them on this continent—all require that they should be kept distinct and separate, and that connections and alliances so unnatural that God and nature seem to forbid them, should be prohibited by positive law, and be subject to no evasion.[21]

What "God and nature" had sundered, let no man seek to bring together. The state of Virginia would allow no such marriage as Andrew Kinney and Mahala Miller had contracted to persist—at least in Virginia: "If the parties desire to maintain the relations of man and wife, they must change their domicile and go to some state or country where the laws recognize the validity of such marriages." Despite the heavy fine and the possibility of further prosecution, the Kinneys stayed together. The 1880 census showed the couple—now in their forties and the parents of five sons, Will, James, John, Tom, and Harrison—still living together in Augusta County.[22]

Having gone to the Virginia Supreme Court and generated widespread publicity, the case jolted the Virginia General Assembly into taking further action.

The new legislation enacted in March 1878—criminalizing the behavior of both parties to a black-white marriage, and converting the penalty from one taking property, such as Andrew Kinney's $500, to one taking liberty, with two to five years in prison[23]—might be termed the "Andrew Kinney bill," and prosecutions soon commenced under it (see chapters 7–8). Expressly going beyond criminalizing interracial marriages contracted in Virginia, the 1878 statute imposed the same new penalties on Virginians who went outside the state to evade the law and then returned to Virginia to live together as husband and wife.[24]

These two cases from Tennessee and Virginia may have seemed to make the outcome clear in matters of comity and its connection to marriage, but other possibilities remained open, at least under some circumstances.

Two Views from North Carolina

Two cases, both decided in 1877 by the North Carolina Supreme Court, illustrate the doubtful validity of interracial marriages in view of different states' conflicting laws. North Carolina had a constitutional provision and a statute that banned marriages between black and white citizens, and the state's authority to enact such a law was not challenged in these two cases. At trial, nonetheless, one interracial couple was found guilty and the other acquitted. In both cases, the losing side appealed to the state supreme court, and that court—in each case, with an opinion written by the same judge—upheld the lower court, though in one case with a divided voice. The question came up because South Carolina, at that time, permitted interracial marriages, while North Carolina did not.

Two citizens of North Carolina—Isaac Kennedy, a black man, and Mag Kennedy, a white woman—went to South Carolina to get married. Immediately after their wedding, they returned to North Carolina, where they were indicted for fornication and adultery and tried and convicted in Mecklenburg County, just across the state line from South Carolina. Speaking for a unanimous supreme court, Justice William R. Rodman noted that their domicile, both before and after their marriage, was North Carolina. Had they left with the intent to evade the North Carolina law? Justice Rodman found the question immaterial, for they had never established another domicile. Speaking of his state's law against such marriages, he said, "A law like this of ours would be very idle if it could be avoided by merely stepping over an imaginary line." As the judge noted, "when it is conceded as it is, that a State may" pass such a law as North Carolina's, "the main question is conceded."[25] How could this particular pair be anything but guilty?

Yet an exception might be permitted, as Justice Rodman himself decided that same term. In May 1873, Sarah Spake, a citizen of North Carolina, went to

Spartanburg, South Carolina, to marry Pink Ross, a citizen of that state. They married that month, lived "as man and wife" in South Carolina for three months, and then moved to Mecklenburg County, North Carolina. There they were charged with fornication and adultery, but Judge David Schenck found the couple not guilty, even though he had decided otherwise in the case of Isaac Kennedy and Mag Kennedy. The Rosses had a valid marriage, he said.[26]

The state appealed the decision, but Justice Rodman spoke for a majority of the supreme court in upholding Judge Schenck. The appeals court understood the central question to be "whether a marriage in South Carolina between a black man and a white woman *bona fide* domiciled there and valid by the law of that State, must be regarded as valid in this State when the parties afterwards migrate here? We think that the decided weight of English and American authority requires us to hold that the relation thus lawful in its inception continues to be lawful here."[27]

"Our laws have no extra territorial operation," Rodman wrote. When the woman married a man from another state, she immediately acquired his domicile, and when they moved into North Carolina, they came as citizens of that other state. "We are under obligations of comity to our sister States," he said, and the marriage remained valid when the couple moved into the state. "Upon this question above all others," he concluded, "it is desirable . . . that there should not be one law in Maine and another in Texas, but that the same law shall prevail at least throughout the United States." As for Pink Ross and Sarah Spake, their "cohabitation," although "unnatural and immoral," met the standard of "lawful."[28]

Justice Edwin G. Reade wrote a vigorous dissent, one that suggested that the court's approach in that case would hardly prevail everywhere and might not last long in North Carolina. The state attorney general had argued that this interracial marriage ought to be treated in the same way that an incestuous or polygamous marriage would—it should be criminalized under North Carolina law. According to Justice Reade, comity had its limits; it was "secondary to the public good," which was "paramount."[29]

North Carolina, with its clear declaration of law on the subject, had no need to recognize a neighboring state's laws in this respect. Justice Reade asked, "If such a marriage solemnized here between our own people is declared void, why should comity require the evil to be imported from another State? Why is not the relation severed the instant they set foot upon our soil?" Any "individuals who have formed relations which are obnoxious to our laws can find their comfort in staying away from us."[30]

Justice Reade went further in his statement of the limits of comity. The Fourteenth Amendment's privileges and immunities clause, he wrote, "does not mean that a citizen of South Carolina removing here may bring with him his South Carolina privileges and immunities; but that when he comes here he may have the same privileges and immunities which our citizens have. Nothing more and nothing less." Reade felt betrayed, he said, by the majority's views in this case. "We give to comity all the force of a constitutional provision when we allow it to annul a statute. Indeed we put it above the [North Carolina] Constitution itself; as I believe one of the late amendments prohibits the intermarriage of white and colored."[31]

The differences of opinion on the North Carolina Supreme Court in the case of Sarah Ross and Pink Ross—and the contrast between that case and the one concerning Isaac Kennedy and Mag Kennedy—revealed that the question of recognizing an out-of-state marriage could go either way. Certainly there was no guarantee that an interracial marriage, if banned under one state's laws, would be recognized—under any circumstance whatever—under another state's laws.

Among other states with miscegenation laws, Maryland and Virginia typified courts' rulings on out-of-state marriages. Discussing the circumstances in which interracial marriages might be recognized under the general principle of comity, the Maryland Court of Appeals observed in 1895:

> The statutes of Maryland peremptorily forbid the marriage of a white person and a negro and declare all such marriages forever void. It is, therefore, the declared policy of this State to prohibit such marriages. Though these marriages may be valid elsewhere, they will be absolutely void here so long as the statutory inhibition remains unchanged.[32]

Virginia's highest court made a similar assessment nearly half a century later. A 1939 ruling, one that had nothing directly to do with race, reviewed the kinds of marriages (bigamous ones, for example, as well as miscegenous ones) that, void in one state, could be denied any recognition in its courts even if validly celebrated elsewhere: "One state . . . cannot force its own marriage laws, or other laws, on any other state, and no state is bound by comity to give effect in its courts to the marriage laws of another state, repugnant to its own laws and policy."[33]

Racial Identity and Miscegenation Cases in Twentieth-Century Virginia

Through the 1930s and 1940s, the Virginia courts continued to be the scene of prosecutions, made possible by a miscegenation law and perhaps rendered more likely by the twentieth-century redrawing of the color line so that any African ancestry at all rendered a person nonwhite (see chapter 9). The law against miscegenous marriage lived on, ready to pounce on couples said to be interracial. Two examples will suffice.

Grace Mohler, age 19, married Samuel Christian Branaham, age 26, in 1937 in Fincastle, Virginia. Both were later indicted for violating the state's ban on interracial marriage. She escaped conviction when she testified that she had not known that he was of African descent. He testified that he was not, in fact, of mixed race, yet other testimony contradicted him. Some witnesses stated that his family "came from Amherst County, where they lived to themselves, even today, and were colloquially known as 'issues.'" The sheriff from Amherst County, A. B. Watts, informed the court that "the Branahams of his county once were forced out of membership in a white church because they were of Negro extract." And birth certificates for some of Branaham's alleged kinsmen designated them as nonwhite.[34] Clearly he had considerable European ancestry—perhaps enough to have met the nineteenth-century test for white (that is, less than one-fourth African ancestry)—but that could offer no support to his claim in 1938 to be exempt from the ban.

Judge Benjamin Haden declared him to be black, not white, and imposed a one-year prison sentence, the shortest possible under the law. Then he suspended that sentence. But he "stipulated the suspension was to be for 30 years, revocable at any time during that period should he again live with the woman he married or marry another white woman." Thus, as one newspaper account put it, having been "adjudged a Negro," Samuel Branaham was ordered "never again to live with the pretty young white woman he married here a year ago under penalty of serving a year's suspended sentence."[35]

Sometimes charges were brought that did not stick. Was Willie E. Purcell white or black? A 33-year-old truck driver living in Richmond, he married Stella May Rhoton—everyone agreed that she was white—in Richmond City Hall on December 31, 1948. The bride's mother, Ada Rhoton, charged that he was black, and that he had thus broken the statute against miscegenation. Mrs. Rhoton had been excluded from the wedding—her daughter, in obtaining the marriage license, had said she was 21, she was born in Tennessee, and her parents were dead. In fact, she was 18, born in Scott County, Virginia, and her mother was very much alive in South Richmond.[36] Charges were pending against the daughter for perjury. But what of Mrs. Rhoton's charge against her putative son-in-law?

At a trial in police court, the evidence proved mixed. A number of police records appeared to be evenly divided as to Purcell's race, with "about half" listing him as black and half as white. More conclusive in the eyes of the court were his Army discharge papers, which indicated that he was white; his birth certificate, which listed both of his parents as white; and his father's testimony that both he and Purcell's mother were white. Concluding that Willie Purcell was white, Judge Harold C. Maurice dismissed the case against him.[37]

Identity, Comity, and the Calma Couple

Within a few years, Virginia courts faced the case of an interracial couple that included a Caucasian and someone of Asian/Pacific ancestry. Virginia's miscegenation laws came into play in a civil case in the context of an out-of-state marriage that, it was judged, failed to satisfy in-state requirements. Rosina Calma and Cezar Calma—she Caucasian, he Filipino—had married in New Jersey in 1954 and had relocated to Virginia.[38] Virginia authorities did not arrest them, yet the law of interracial marriage nonetheless affected their private lives.

When Rosina Calma sought to end their marriage, Virginia courts refused to recognize its validity, and thus it could not be terminated through divorce in the new state of their residence. She took her case to the Virginia Supreme Court, where she argued that "the action of the lower court in failing to recognize the marriage performed in New Jersey as valid in Virginia was in violation of the full faith and credit clause of Article IV, Section 1, of the Constitution of the United States." She argued, too, that the refusal to recognize her marriage violated "the rights guaranteed to her by the equal protection and due process clauses of the fourteenth amendment."[39]

In December 1962, the Virginia Supreme Court—declaring that "we do not reach and decide the constitutional issues" Rosina Calma had raised—upheld the lower court's disposition of the case, on procedural grounds.[40] It seems improbable that Rosina Calma could have convinced any court in Virginia to recognize her marriage.

Basing an argument such as Rosina Calma's on the full faith and credit clause—seeking validation of a marriage that violated a state's policy—held little promise of success. The U.S. Supreme Court had long ago, in *Maynard* v. *Hill* (1888), ruled that marriage was not a contract in the sense that the Constitution's full faith and credit clause had any application to it. Rather, it was left to each state to devise the law of marriage as it applied to people within that state, even if they had moved there from elsewhere. As for the Fourteenth Amendment, the equal protection clause had emerged by the early 1960s as a powerful tool in cases of state action and racial discrimination (see chapter 13)—but not, or at least not yet, in matters of marriage.

Should the antimiscegenation regime finally fall, the boundaries of race and place would no longer have any legal bearing on a marriage between a man of one racial identity and a woman of another. As long as miscegenation laws remained in force, however, the boundaries of race and place—and the linkages between them, as in the Calma case—would remain vitally important to the law of marriage.

The Many Faces of Miscegenation Laws

The Calmas had reason to wish they had never married, or never left New Jersey and moved to Virginia, or both. They were not a black-white couple, yet they fell subject to Virginia's miscegenation laws. They were not trying to start a marriage, or to stay together; yet finding that they had no legal marriage in Virginia, they could not end their marriage through the customary legal procedure. The combination of their different racial identities and Virginia's non-recognition of interstate comity must have driven them to distraction as they tried to divorce.

The next chapter emphasizes another dimension of the manner in which miscegenation laws affected multiracial families. Just as the law of racial identity could have enormous impact on two people who thought they were a married couple, the combination of the law of inheritance and the law of race and marriage could powerfully influence the transfer of property from a dead person to a live one and from people of one racial identity to those of another.

(left) Figure 1. Virginians have long celebrated the interracial marriage in 1614 between John Rolfe and Pocahontas, and many "white" Virginians have claimed descent from the union through Thomas Rolfe, their son. This image is an engraving made in 1616 by Simon van de Passe. National Portrait Gallery, Smithsonian Institution / Art Resource, NY.

(right) Figure 2. According to Chief Justice Roger B. Taney in the Supreme Court's Dred Scott decision (1857), miscegenation laws in northern states from the era of the American Revolution showed that white Americans had never considered African Americans, whether free or enslaved, to be citizens. Courtesy of the Library of Congress.

ABRAHAM LINCOLN.

(left) Figure 3. After the Dred Scott decision in 1857, and again in a political debate with Democratic U.S. Senator Stephen A. Douglas the following year, Abraham Lincoln, a Republican, asked why whites couldn't get by "without making either slaves or wives" of African Americans. This image is a woodcut by Franklin H. Brown (based on an 1857 photograph by Alexander Hasler) that was mass-produced and distributed in 1860. Courtesy of The Lincoln Museum, Fort Wayne, IN (#2024).

WHAT MISCEGENATION IS !

—AND—

WHAT WE ARE TO EXPECT

Now that Mr. Lincoln is Re-elected.

By L. SEAMAN, LL. D.

WALLER & WILLETTS, Publishers,

NEW YORK.

Figure 4. What Miscegenation Is! *(1865). The word was widely adopted soon after its introduction in the 1864 presidential election year, and this pamphlet—its caricature of an African American man with a Caucasian woman reflecting, and designed to foster, fears of black men mixing with white women—came out soon after Abraham Lincoln was reelected. Courtesy of the Library of Congress.*

(left) Figure 5. Justice John Marshall Harlan was the U.S. Supreme Court's sole dissenter in The Civil Rights Cases (1883) and again in Plessy v. Ferguson (1896), but in Pace v. Alabama (1883), also about the Fourteenth Amendment and "equal protection of the laws," he failed to dissent, so the Court unanimously upheld a miscegenation statute. Courtesy of the Library of Congress.

(below) Figure 6. The South was solid in its allegiance to the antimiscegenation regime in 1866—one year after the Confederacy's defeat in 1865 and one year before Congress passed the Reconstruction acts of 1867. But many states outside the South also had such laws at that time. Some of the former Confederate states had just inaugurated such laws during the previous year; and seven whether by legislative or judicial action—soon dropped their miscegenation laws for at least a few years. Produced by John Boyer, geography department, Virginia Tech.

Figure 7. Of the 37 states in 1874, at least 9 (of 21) in the North and another 9 (of 16) in the South had miscegenation laws. Many western territories (not shown here) also had such laws, but most states of the Lower South had lifted them. Produced by John Boyer, geography department, Virginia Tech.

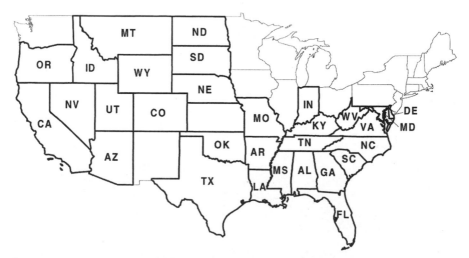

Figure 8. Between 1913 (when the last state enacted such a law) and 1948 (when the California Supreme Court overturned that state's law), the antimiscegenation regime's power was at its peak, and its territory held at 30 of the 48 states. Produced by John Boyer, geography department, Virginia Tech.

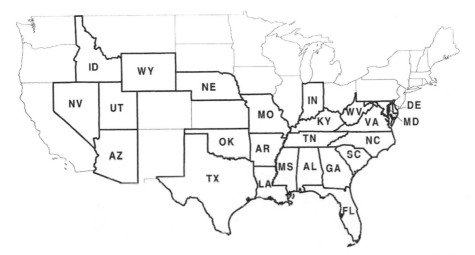

Figure 9. *When the Lovings were arrested in 1958 in Virginia for their interracial marriage, 24 of the 48 states still had miscegenation laws on the books. Virginia's law dated all the way back to 1691, Wyoming's only to 1913. Produced by John Boyer, geography department, Virginia Tech.*

Figure 10. *By 1966, the territory controlled by the antimiscegenation regime had shrunk to one-third of the nation—17 of the 50 states, clustered in the South. Into the 1960s, laws that banned interracial marriage continued to be enforced in those states. Produced by John Boyer, geography department, Virginia Tech.*

Figure 11. Oklahoma's miscegenation statute defined people "not of African ancestry" as "white." Marriages between Caucasians and Native Americans were legal, as both, by that definition, were "white," but members of neither group could marry black Oklahomans. Thomas N. Athey Collection, #5056, Oklahoma Historical Society, Oklahoma City.

Figure 12. As the circuit court judge of Caroline County (1941–1965), Leon F. Bazile (1890–1967) loomed over the lives of the Loving family. He presided over the Lovings' trial in January 1959 and their rehearing in January 1965. He retired later that year (the year this picture was taken) and died in March 1967, three months before the Supreme Court overturned his decision. Grey Villet/TimePix.

Figure 13. The Loving children—the youngest, Peggy; Donald; and Sidney, the oldest—during the time (between 1965 and 1967) when Mr. and Mrs. Loving awaited the outcome of their appeal of their conviction and exile for marrying across a line that, under Virginia law, banned people with a white racial identity from marrying anyone not white. Grey Villet/TimePix.

MR. & MRS. GUY SMITH / An Interracial Wedding

Figure 14. The wedding in California, in September 1967, of Margaret Elizabeth Rusk—whose father was Dean Rusk, a native of Georgia and secretary of state for President Lyndon B. Johnson—and Guy Gibson Smith was perceived as so significant that it made the cover of Time. *TimePix.*

CHAPTER 11

RACIAL IDENTITY AND FAMILY PROPERTY

"Being in doubt as to whether they were entitled thereto"

—Executor of a Virginia estate, in view of an interracial marriage (1882)

Given their different racial identities, "William Yates acquired no legal rights by his Arkansas marriage with Emily Lewis, and upon her death, had no inheritable interest in her lands"

—Court ruling in Oklahoma (1924)

John D. Walker married Chur-ga, according to the law of the Pima people, on her reservation in Arizona Territory in 1871. Their daughter, Juana Walker, was subsequently born there, a child her father always recognized as his own. Chur-ga died when Juana was young, and John D. Walker died in 1891. That is when Walker's brothers and sisters presented themselves as the rightful claimants to his property. According to them, Juana Walker was no heir at all.

The Pinal County probate court declared in Juana Walker's favor in 1893, but her rivals appealed. In district court, on the grounds that in 1871 a state law prohibited marriages between whites and Indians, they objected to evidence of a marriage between John D. Walker and Chur-ga. The judge sustained the objection, but he allowed evidence that Walker had recognized and supported the young woman who claimed to be his legitimate daughter and rightful heir. The case made its way to the Arizona Supreme Court.

That court had no difficulty ending the long dispute. No valid marriage could have taken place in Arizona in 1871 "between a Pima Indian squaw and a white man, either by ceremony as provided in [the Arizona] statute . . . , by the customs of said Indian tribe, cohabitation, or any other method. Such marriages were null and void." Whether such a marriage had taken place on an Indian reservation, according to custom there, had no bearing on the case: "The law reached white men in every part of Arizona, and forbade such marriages."[1] The decision was not unanimous, but the court majority denied Juana Walker's claim to be an heir. Her father had left an estate of some sort. His siblings would divide it.

The Law of Race, Marriage, and Inheritance

Decisions in several state supreme court cases in Texas, Mississippi, and Louisiana during Reconstruction so transformed the law of race and marriage that mixed-race children could inherit property from their white father. The undoing of Reconstruction—the end to the Republican interlude—did much to block inheritance from a white person by people with a nonwhite racial identity, although it did not necessarily operate that way everywhere.

In general, people can inherit on the basis of a legitimate family relationship with the person who died and left property, although sometimes disputes arise. Laws about racial identity introduced an additional consideration into matters of inheritance. Was there a valid marriage? If not, a person could not inherit on the basis of that marriage. A family's ability to accumulate property from one generation to another might be contested on the basis of individuals' racial identity. As a group, nonwhite people might come up short in matters of property ownership as a result of challenges to the legitimacy of interracial marriages or mixed-race children.

When the law intruded with regard to racial identity and the inheritance of property, a case was a matter of civil law, not criminal law. In the cases recounted in this chapter, no one had been prosecuted for entering into an interracial marriage; nor does the evidence suggest that the interracial couples had suffered extralegal violence. These controversies reached the courts because one set of relatives challenged the legitimacy of another set of relatives. The law of race and marriage provided a weapon for one side to attempt to cut another out of a slice of the pie.

The law of interracial marriage could—and often did—prevent the conveyance of wealth from white to nonwhite. Whiteness brought wealth—absorbed it, retained it, kept it out of the hands of people who, aside from their racial identity, had an entirely legitimate claim on property they nonetheless could not get. In effect, the law of interracial marriage imposed a tax by one group on another, an estate tax that tended to apply to nonwhite people, who paid the tax to whites. The law of racial identities contributed to a flow of wealth—property; economic well-being; resources and access to them—from one community to another.

Providing the rules of a zero-sum game, miscegenation laws kept some people wealthier—and other people poorer—than they would otherwise have been. On one side of the exchange, some people suddenly had more property than they would have otherwise. On the other side, the surviving spouse was left bereft of both partner and property; the next generation might have to start all over in its quest to build up property. Such consequences of the application of miscegenation laws might result from the absence of a will—or they might even emerge in the face of a will.

A Devise of Property to the "Unfortunate Issue" of an Outlawed Marriage

Mary James died in Stafford County, Virginia, around 1831, and left an inheritance that went to a man who died a half century later. At that point, the laws governing comity, racial identity, and the inheritance of property all came into play. Years after the Civil War came to an end and brought an end to slavery, and years after the Civil Rights Act of 1866 and the Fourteenth Amendment spoke of property rights and equal protection, the mixed-race children of a white man went to court to claim the property that their father had intended to leave them according to his will.

Mary James had property and wished to leave it to her family. She put the bulk of that property in trust for the use of her brother, William S. James, and then for the use of her married sister, Nancy Hooe. After Nancy Hooe's death, the trust was to go to the use of Nancy Hooe's sons, Dade and George, and if one of them died without children, then the entire estate was to go to the survivor and then, in fee, to his children. William and Nancy died, as did George Hooe, unmarried and childless. That left Dade Hooe. Married and with 11 children, he died in 1881. The estate that had originated with Mary James consisted of $1,000 invested in Virginia state securities. For many years, the interest had gone to Dade Hooe. Now the principal itself, according to the trust, should be divided among his children. Or should it?

There was a hitch. Around 1840, Dade Hooe had begun a lifelong relationship with Hannah Greenhow, and she, the mother of his children, was not a white woman. In November 1875, the couple, by then elderly, went to Washington, D.C., to marry, as much as anything so as to legitimize their children; they then returned to their home in Stafford County. They had stayed together during a period of approximately two decades before the beginning of the Civil War and then for another two decades, and in their final years together they were a married couple, at least according to the ceremony in the nation's capital.

It seems Hooe and Greenhow had never been prosecuted for living together without being married or, for that matter, for claiming to be married in violation of a law that banned such marriages. They had done what they could to stay together, raise their children, and legitimate them for purposes of inheritance. But the fact remained that their marriage could never have been legally contracted in Virginia, and Virginia law never could have been assumed to recognize a marriage that they contracted in a place they had visited solely to evade the ban on interracial weddings in Virginia.

Mary James had put her estate in the hands of two executors: R. C. L. Moncure, who later served on the Virginia Supreme Court but who had died by the time Dade Hooe did, and W. Peyton Conway. Conway had no problem with handing over the property to its new owners, and then his responsibilities to the estate would at long last be over. Yet he hesitated. "Being in doubt as to whether they were entitled thereto," as was later said about him, he "refused to deliver said securities to them without first having the question judicially settled." So the case went to the circuit court at Fredericksburg, where Conway "simply submitted himself to the direction of the court." It wasn't as if any alternative heirs presented themselves and claimed the money. The sole question was whether these 11 people had a claim—that is, a claim that the court would recognize—on the money the use of which Dade Hooe had inherited from Mary James. The trial court ruled against Hooe's children, and they appealed to the Virginia Supreme Court.[2]

Dade Hooe had left a will. In it he said: "I give my property, of every kind whatsoever, real and personal, . . . to the children of Hannah Greenhow, a woman of color, who is now and for many years has been living with me, the said children being eleven (11) in number, and being my natural children, or to such of the said children as may be living at my death, and the issue then living of such as may then be dead."[3]

Was Dade Hooe empowered to leave to these 11 claimants that $1,000, money the use of which he had inherited from his aunt and that, according to her will, was to go now to his "children"? Were they his legitimate children for purposes of inheriting that particular property? Perhaps the other property, real and personal, went to the children without any problem, but as for that $1,000, a 50-year-old restriction put the matter in doubt.

The Virginia Supreme Court determined that Hooe's children could not inherit that money. Their parents' marriage was not only "absolutely void" but "criminal," wrote Judge Drury A. Hinton, and the circuit court's decree was "plainly right and must be affirmed."[4] Dade Hooe's patriarchal authority as a white man and a property owner did not extend to an ability to pass along to the next generation that particular piece of property, because they did not qualify as legitimate children for purposes of inheriting it.

The court had spoken, but it spoke with a divided voice, 3–2. Judge Robert A. Richardson wrote a dissenting opinion that was not only vehement in tone but far longer than the majority opinion. True enough, he agreed, the couple could have been indicted for violating the law against their marriage, though that evidently had not happened. Yet, even if a marriage was "deemed null in law," went one provision of the Virginia Code, "the issue . . . shall nevertheless be legitimate."[5]

For Judge Richardson, the fact of the marriage, even if not recognized as valid in itself, should confer legitimacy on the children. "Certain rights," he wrote, "may flow from a void marriage." He pointed toward the provision regarding bigamous marriages—subject to an even longer prison sentence than were interracial marriages. Bigamous marriages were void, but the issue was considered legitimate. Why then, he wondered, make an exception of interracial marriage and deny the same benefits? The law provided for a punishment for the crime of bigamous or interracial marriage, but it did not, he argued, punish the "unfortunate issue of the marriage which in law is void." To the contrary.[6]

Dade Hooe had "lived a life greatly offensive to the law and society," Judge Richardson conceded. Yet, the judge continued, in his "old age" Hooe "did what in the eye of the law and good morals was perhaps the best thing he could do under the circumstances." Hooe "doubtless did what he thought was best in attempting to advance the interest of those who had the greatest claim upon his affection and bounty." The dissenting judge concluded his remarks with the declaration, "In view of all the circumstances, I am of the opinion, that by virtue of the marriage of Dade Hooe to Hannah Greenhow, in the city of Washington, and the continuous recognition of their children, the appellants, both before and after said marriage by Dade Hooe, their father, they are his legitimate children, and as such entitled to the fund in question; and that therefore the decree of the court below should be reversed and annulled."[7] But the decree was upheld.

Kansas or Florida: The Costs and Benefits of a Felonious Marriage

Matters of racial identity, interstate comity, and family inheritance likewise came into play after Elizabeth Anderson, a woman "who had one-eighth or more of negro blood in her veins," died in Kansas early in the twentieth century. Long a resident of Pensacola, Florida, she owned a town lot there, and she continued to own it after she moved to Leavenworth, Kansas, where she married a white man, W. J. Grooms. She could never have married Grooms in Florida (which, in the state constitution as well as in a statute, banned interracial marriages), but Kansas had no such restriction, and they lived together as husband and wife until she died. She left no will, but she left a mother, a husband, and that lot in Pensacola. Grooms sold the lot to R. E. L. McCaskill, but Anderson's mother, Josephine Whittington, challenged the sale and sought to recover the lot. She took the position that, in view of her daughter's interracial marriage, which had no validity in Florida, Grooms could hardly inherit the lot.[8]

The Escambia County circuit court upheld the marriage, the widower's claim to the lot, and therefore McCaskill's right to the property that he had bought from Grooms. Whittington appealed the decision to the Florida Supreme Court, but that court, too, recognized the marriage as valid and the property as belonging to Grooms, who therefore had every right to convey it to McCaskill. As far as the Florida courts could see, Anderson had not left Florida with an intent to evade that state's law by marrying Grooms. When she married, she had been a resident of another state, a state with no racial restriction on the kind of marriage that she entered, and neither she nor her husband ever subsequently resided in Florida.

The Florida Supreme Court recognized that authorities were not all in agreement on the law that applied in a case such as this one, but it quoted two Florida statutes that seemed to govern the situation. "Foreigners" (that is, residents of other states), said one statute, "shall have the same rights as to the ownership, inheritance and disposition of property in this State as citizens of the State." Another law provided that "if there be no children or their descendants, and the decedent be a married woman and her husband survive her, all the property, real and personal, shall go to the husband."[9]

In the years to come, surely Josephine Whittington had occasion to ponder whether the law would have been interpreted in the same way had the racial identities of the partners to the marriage been reversed. A marriage that, had it taken place under Florida law, would have been declared void and a felony, was recognized for the purpose, or so it seemed, of conveying to a white man a piece of property that would otherwise go to a black woman.

Other courts might well have interpreted the "rights" accruing to citizens of Florida as in no way including the right to contract an interracial marriage and then inherit any property on its basis. Almost certainly, Anderson and Grooms could not have imported their marriage to Florida. Comity did not extend that far. But the Florida Supreme Court recognized the marriage, valid in Kansas, as controlling the disposition of property in Florida. Josephine Whittington lost more than her daughter when Elizabeth Anderson died. She also lost her claim to the Pensacola land that her daughter had owned.

Died in Missouri: The Will That Could Not Convey

From the late 1840s through the end of the century, Eli Keen lived in Missouri. When his father died at mid-century, Keen bought a slave named Phoebe and her daughter, Martha, from the estate. Beginning soon thereafter, and continuing for the next third of a century, Phoebe and Eli Keen lived together as husband and wife. During the 1850s and 1860s they had eight children together, four sons and four daughters, and he recognized them all as his own.

In 1882 or 1883, however, for whatever reason, he broke off the relationship with his black almost-wife and went for a short time to West Virginia. There, in Wood County, on August 22, 1883, he married a white woman, Sophronia K. Barrett, with whom he lived out the remainder of his long life back in Missouri. Upon his return, however, he provided for Phoebe and their four daughters. In a deed dated November 22, 1883, he conveyed the farm home they had shared for so long to "Phoebe Keen" and provided that, after he and she had both died, the farm should belong to Lettie Ann Skinner, Phoebe Wise, Mary Phillips, and Alice Cora Brown. Phoebe Keen died in 1896.

Eli Keen never told Sophronia about Phoebe or the eight children until late 1900. In September that year, he made out a will that provided Sophronia with more than the minimum she would have received had he died without a will. The rest of his estate he devised to his "beloved children"—his children with Phoebe—with a tract of farm land each going to his sons Ellis, Reason, Mathew, and Mark, all of whom had been living on the land they were now to own outright.[10]

Eli Keen died in February 1901, and Sophronia Keen contested the will. She claimed the tract of land on which her husband's oldest son, Ellis Keen, lived. Sophronia Keen insisted that she and Eli Keen had had no children themselves and that her late husband had no other children with anyone else who were capable of inheriting from him. Ellis Keen, for his part, went to court to defend his claim to the land according to his father's last will and testament.

The circuit court judge in St. Charles County, E. M. Hughes, determined that Phoebe and Eli Keen had never been married, that Ellis Keen was therefore not a legitimate son, and that Sophronia Keen should get the land. Still unwilling to relinquish the land his father had meant for him to have, Ellis Keen took the case to the Missouri Supreme Court. That court affirmed the trial court. The two courts agreed that Phoebe and Eli Keen could never have been married under Missouri law, either before emancipation—when Phoebe was a slave and therefore had no capacity to contract—or afterwards. Throughout the years the two had lived together, Missouri law had always declared interracial marriages to be void, and an 1879 statute made them a felony.

For trial court and appeals court alike, the only material question was whether the couple had ever been married. That question could have no answer other than a negative. It would seem, of course, that the judges could just as easily (in fact, more readily) have determined that the question was irrelevant, that there did not need to be any family relationship whatever for Eli Keen to will property to Ellis Keen.

Ellis Keen had every reason to defend his claim, and in fact he took the case to the U.S. Supreme Court. Speaking for the nation's highest court, however, Justice Henry Billings Brown, who had authored the majority decision in *Plessy v. Ferguson,* claimed that "it is difficult to see any facts upon which to found our jurisdiction of the case." No proper federal question had been raised, he said, and "the question of what facts constitute a common-law marriage is purely a local one." Ellis Keen would have to move. Sophronia Keen had triumphed over the last will and testament of her late husband. She had won a legal victory over her husband's long relationship with Phoebe Keen.[11]

Weapons among the Weak: Mixed-Race, White, and Black in Louisiana

The law of interracial marriage was an all-purpose tool. In matters of criminal law, it could fine people or put them in the penitentiary—deprive them of property or liberty—as well as force families apart or into exile. In matters of civil law, it could force, or prevent, the movement of property across racial boundaries. The cases from Virginia and Missouri exemplify the loss of wealth that people of nonwhite racial identities under the law could experience. But, as in so many matters in miscegenation law, it was not always or only a simple matter of black and white.

Various civil cases in Louisiana revealed not only that a considerable number of "black"-"white" couples lived in that state in the late nineteenth and early twentieth centuries, but that people of one nonwhite racial identity could seek to wield the weapon of miscegenation laws to extract or retain property from people who had other nonwhite racial identities. When it came to inheriting property, people who were white under the law—or, for that matter, people who were black—could attack the children of interracial couples. Three examples of decisions by the state supreme court will illustrate the law of race, marriage, and inheritance in Louisiana in the years around 1900. The first two of them were handed down in 1913 and the last one in 1923.

John Yoist, a "white" man, "lived together in concubinage" with Eudora Bergeron, a woman of "color," from 1870 until his death in 1910. Yoist specified in his will that most of the property was to go to his two children, Henry J. Yoist and Eudora Yoist, both of whom he had legitimated in 1905. His collateral heirs disputed the will, and the trial court found in their favor. But the children appealed to the Louisiana Supreme Court, which reversed the trial court, rescinded the award of the property to the white relatives, and instead found in favor of the man's mixed-race children. It held that the two children, both of whom had been conceived at a time when the couple could legally have married, were capable of inheriting from him, given his acknowledgment and legitimation of them—even though that had not happened until after Louisiana's miscegenation act of 1894 had gone into effect.[12]

Joseph C. Segura, a "white" man, lived with Mary Miles, "a colored woman," from sometime before the Civil War until her death in February 1912.[13] They had their first two children while Mary Miles was still Segura's slave—and therefore also before Louisiana's miscegenation law was rescinded during Reconstruction—and they had one more in 1873, at a time during which they could have legally married. Under Louisiana law, they could not have married before Reconstruction or after 1894, and they never did marry during the quarter-century that provided a legal window. In August 1912, Segura legitimated their four children, and in December that year, at the age of 93, he died.

Segura left no will. Particularly in view of his estate, valued at nearly $77,000, his numerous white relatives challenged his children's legal capacity to inherit from him. At trial, the court ruled in the children's favor. The 1894 law had terminated the parents' capacity to marry each other, the court ruled, but it had not terminated their capacity to legitimate their children, who therefore could inherit from them.

The white relatives pursued their interest in the case to the Louisiana Supreme Court. That court observed about the trial court record that Segura had clearly lived his own life. He had lived alone much of the time—often sleeping out somewhere on his cattle ranch—and he had lived with black folks the rest of the time. As for his white relatives, he appeared to have had little regard for them and little communication with them. The appeals judges, like the trial court, displayed every inclination to respect the wishes of this "peculiar and eccentric" old man, even though they expressed distaste for his lifestyle. He had insisted on legitimating his "own dear children," as he had expressed it, and the court saw no legal impediment to their inheriting his estate.[14] An act passed in 1870 had provided for the legitimation of children born to a couple who—because of slavery as well as the existence of a miscegenation law—had previously been unable to marry. As for the 1894 act, it did nothing retroactively to affect the legal capacity of any children of an interracial couple.

Segura's numerous collateral heirs could not break through the insistence of the Louisiana judiciary that the legal changes of the post–Civil War years had transformed the ability of children of mixed race, like Segura's, to inherit property from their parents. The estate went to the man's children. In both *Yoist* and *Segura*, white collateral heirs of a deceased white man had battled an interracial couple's mixed-race children to control the dead man's property. At trial, the man's children had prevailed in one case, the man's white relatives in the other.

In both cases, though, the state supreme court had interpreted the contours of Louisiana's post–Civil War legal history as one that called for victories by the children. Into the twentieth century, Reconstruction continued to make a difference in various multiracial families in Louisiana.

But what if the collateral heirs, the people who contested the mixed-race children's right to inherit, were black? Dave Murdock, "a single man, of the Caucasian race," had a son, Kire Murdock, with Fannie Williams, "a colored woman."[15] Kire Murdock was born in 1889, at a time when Louisiana law would have permitted his parents to marry, but they never did. His mother died in 1896, when he was seven—two years after Louisiana revived its miscegenation law—and he grew up with his mother's mother, Eliza Williams. He was already an adult when his grandmother died in 1918.

Neither Fannie Williams nor her mother left a will, but Eliza Williams left another daughter, Helen Potter. After the death of Eliza Williams, both her estate and that of her daughter Fannie were awarded to Helen Potter "as the sole and only heir of the two decedents."[16] Kire Murdock was prepared to recognize Helen Potter as a legitimate heir who should get half of her mother's estate, but he insisted that he ought to get the other half, and he ought also to get his own mother's entire estate, whatever there was of it. Helen Potter resisted his overtures. He took the matter to court, and at trial his position prevailed.

Potter appealed the lower court outcome to the Louisiana Supreme Court. There, Kire Murdock relinquished his claim on a half-interest in his grandmother's estate but defended his claim to his own mother's estate. Potter continued to deny that her sister's natural child had any claim on anything. How, she wanted to know, could he be a legitimate heir of his mother if, as she interpreted the Louisiana law of marriage and inheritance, his parents could not have married in 1896 (the year she died) and therefore he could not be legitimated "under the laws existing at the time of the opening of her succession"?[17]

The court rejected Potter's claim to her sister's entire estate. Dave Murdock and Fannie Williams could have legally married in 1888, when their son was conceived. Fannie Williams always "recognized him as her child, cared for him, and held him out to the world" as her son "from his birth in 1889 until her death in 1896."[18] At the time of his conception, his parents could have married; his mother acknowledged him as her son; and therefore he had the capacity "at the time of the opening of her succession" in 1896 to inherit from her.

In the case of Kire Murdock and Helen Potter, a black woman was first awarded the entire estate left by her black sister and black mother, but she had mixed success in her bid to overcome a mixed-race man's challenge to her claims. Kire Murdock, because his parents had never formally married, was unable to hold on to a half of his grandmother's estate, so one portion of his victory in the trial court proved fleeting. Because, however, he had been conceived during the window of time when a black woman could have legally married a white man in Louisiana, he did inherit half his mother's estate.

Interracial Transfers of Family Property

These various cases—from Virginia, Missouri, and elsewhere—demonstrate ways in which the matter of miscegenation could and did intrude upon civil matters, quite aside from criminal law. Might the laws invalidating interracial marriage sometimes curtail African Americans' ability to benefit from the transfer of property from one generation to the next? Certainly. Could a person leave his property to his children? Not necessarily. In the absence of a will, who should get the deceased person's property? Racial considerations might determine the answer.

Throughout the nineteenth century and much of the twentieth, dozens of cases like the ones in this chapter were appealed to state supreme courts, and countless others never went past trial court. Sometimes the miscegenation law ended up being the basis for denying claimants such property as would otherwise have gone to them. Sometimes it did not. But whenever a case was lost when it would have been won had it not been for a law against interracial marriage, the loss revealed the antimiscegenation regime's estate tax at work as it altered the distribution of wealth, legal rights, and economic well-being.

A case from Oklahoma showed how, when connected with racial identity, alimony as well as inheritance—and also interstate comity—could be put in play under the antimiscegenation regime. Ernestine Baker had, by the end of 1936, been married to Billy Baker for so many weeks she could not stand it anymore. They married in Independence, Kansas, on September 12, 1936, but, home again in Oklahoma, on December 19 she filed for divorce on the grounds of his habitual drunkenness and extreme cruelty. She said he had property worth about $50,000. She wanted cash, she wanted the car, and she wanted more, too, and Judge Harland A. Carter of the Okmulgee County Superior Court ordered that he make temporary payments.[19]

In Oklahoma, the racial boundary under the law separated people with African ancestry from everyone else, including Indians (see chapter 9). Billy Baker wanted to part with his wife, not with any property. So he filed a motion to dissolve the court order, on the grounds that he was "a full-blood Seminole Indian," and thus not even a minor fraction black; she was "of African descent"; and thus their "purported marriage" was "null and void."[20] He insisted that he be heard on the matter before he be compelled to obey the order, but the judge refused to listen. So he took his case, now directed against the judge, to the Oklahoma Supreme Court, where he found a more accommodating authority.

The supreme court remanded the case to superior court and directed that Judge Carter give Billy Baker his hearing on the matter of race: "If it is a fact that [Ernestine Baker] is of African descent and [Billy Baker] is a full-blood Indian, then their marriage is a nullity." That was true, moreover, "even though the marriage was contracted in another state," since the parties were residents of Oklahoma. Marriage might or might not be till death do us part; but divorce is an option only for people who are in fact married. Someone "who clearly never was a wife" cannot insist on alimony or any property settlement, even from a man she thought had been her husband.[21]

In another Oklahoma case, Emily Lewis, a Choctaw Indian, had accompanied William Yates, an African American, to Arkansas. Both states had miscegenation laws, but the couple could not marry in their home state, yet could in a neighboring state. The newlyweds returned to Oklahoma in 1914, where they lived at her place in Haskell County until her death the following year. She left no children and no will, but she left her land, her husband, and her parents. A legal tussle over who should get the land ended in a judicial determination that "William Yates acquired no legal rights by his Arkansas marriage with Emily Lewis, and upon her death, had no inheritable interest in her lands."[22]

The state of Oklahoma generated other cases, too, in which the law of race and marriage intersected with the law of property, as the next chapter shows. The cases from Oklahoma—where Indians were legally "white"—were all like *Murdock* v. *Potter,* in that they were posed as interracial conflicts, even though none of the contestants were Caucasian. The developments in Oklahoma reveal as well that, as late as the 1940s, federal courts were upholding miscegenation laws.

CHAPTER 12

MISCEGENATION LAWS, THE NAACP,
AND THE FEDERAL COURTS, 1941–1963

"It seems clear that the statute involved is unconstitutional . . . [yet] review at the present time would probably increase the tensions growing out of the school segregation cases"

—Harvey M. Grossman, Supreme Court law clerk (1954)

"My own personal view is that interracial marriages are constitutionally protected, but they affect such small numbers of people that their consideration might very well be postponed at this critical time in the lives of our citizens"

—James M. Nabrit Jr., Howard University president (1963)

Through the 1920s and 1930s and into the 1940s, 30 states maintained laws against interracial marriage, and individuals' liberty or property hinged on whether those laws were enforced. Despite great changes in American politics and in the scientific understanding of race, as well as the emergence of new constitutional protections to individual privacy and against racial discrimination (see chapter 13), racial identity remained central to the law of marriage.

Into the 1940s, neither state courts nor federal courts seemed in any way interested in reconsidering the constitutionality of miscegenation laws, so the Fourteenth Amendment looked much as it had in the days of *Pace* v. *Alabama* (1883). And no national organization battled to obtain a breakthrough decision in the courts. From the 1910s to the 1940s, with the laws against interracial marriage as fully in place as they ever would be, the antimiscegenation regime neither gained nor lost territory. Yet challenges kept coming. Cases from Oklahoma, Alabama, and Virginia in the 1940s and 1950s raised the issue again and again, in state and federal courts alike.

The Color of a Will: *Stevens v. United States* (1944)

Under Oklahoma state law, everyone was either "of African descent" or "not of African descent," and nobody in one group could marry anyone in the other.[1] Across the 1920s and 1930s, a series of appellate court cases arose involving Native Americans, African Americans, and the inheritance of family property. None of these cases involved a Caucasian, though each involved a "white" person—that is, a person "not of African descent"—and a nonwhite. The results in the Oklahoma cases were inconsistent as to whether property was permitted to flow, or prevented from flowing, between people defined as "white" and those who were not. And, as in every state with miscegenation laws, great uncertainty could develop regarding an individual's racial identity. Regardless, racial identity under the Oklahoma law was crucial to the outcome in these cases.[2]

In the absence of a will, Oklahoma law provided that a half-share of a deceased person's property would go to the surviving spouse; the other half would go to collateral heirs—siblings, nephews, and nieces. To inherit under a marriage, however, the marriage had to be valid, and on that point a contest over racial identities sometimes developed. In *Blake* v. *Sessions* (1923), for example, James Grayson and Myrtle Segro were each three-fourths Indian, but the other fourth proved decisive. The law prevented Segro, a "white" woman, from inheriting land from Grayson, a man "of African descent."[3]

Stevens v. *United States* (1944), an Oklahoma case that was decided in federal court, addressed the question of whether the property of a reportedly Native American woman could go to her African American husband. Stella Sands, who was enrolled as a Creek Indian, owned some land (her allotment of Creek lands) as well as some other property when she made out a will as a single person in December 1935. A year later, she and William Stevens went together to Independence, Kansas, where they married. They returned to Ocmulgee County, Oklahoma, and lived together there until she died on November 7, 1941, at the age of 41. She had no children, and her parents had died.[4]

Who would inherit her property? In the earlier case of James Grayson and Myrtle Segro, race had entered the matter of a dead person's property in the absence of a will. In the case of Stella Sands and William Stevens, by contrast, race entered the matter of a dead person's property in the presence of a will—a will that named Sands's sister, Lorena Thompson Minyard, the sole beneficiary. As widower of the deceased, Stevens knew that his marriage should have revoked that will, and he should by rights be named her administrator and get half of her estate. Instead, the sister took the will to probate in Ocmulgee County and expected to inherit the entire estate.

William Stevens contested the will because it predated their marriage and did not name him as an heir. Under a 1926 federal law, because Indian allotment lands were involved, Stevens's attorney, A. L. Emery, advised the Superintendent of the Five Civilized Tribes of the proceeding, and the case was moved to federal court. The U.S. District Court for the Eastern District of Oklahoma heard the case.

The United States took the position that, while Stella Sands was a "full-blood Indian," William Stevens, though also listed on the Creek rolls, was indicated as a "Creek freedman" and therefore was a "person of African descent." The couple could have had no valid marriage under Oklahoma law. Stella Sands "left surviving no husband, nor issue, nor father nor mother, but left surviving as her sole and only next of kin" her sister Lorena, to whom, in the will being contested, she had left her entire estate.[5]

Stevens's lawyer counterattacked with an arsenal of arguments. True, Stevens was a "person of African descent," but so was Stella Sands. Moreover, Oklahoma had no authority to restrict marriages—and therefore access to inherited property—as the state's 1908 legislation was now being called on to do. First, the U.S. Constitution's supremacy clause (Article VI) privileged the nation's treaties—as well as Congress's Enabling Act that led to Oklahoma's statehood in 1907—over the Oklahoma constitution and statutes. Second, the Fourteenth Amendment denied any state the authority to prevent Stevens from inheriting solely because he was "of African descent."[6]

On every count, District Court Judge Eugene Rice adopted the position of the United States and ruled against William Stevens. In December 1943, he concluded that "a void marriage does not revoke a will," and the will should be admitted to probate.[7] The sister, he ruled, should get the property.

Miscegenation Laws and the NAACP

Stevens and Emery were not finished. Perhaps the National Association for the Advancement of Colored People would help. Emery sought help from the NAACP Legal and Educational Fund to take the case to the Circuit Court of Appeals. In a long letter in January 1944 to NAACP special counsel Thurgood Marshall, Emery outlined the facts and his major contentions. As for racial identity, he explained that all of the "towns, so called, . . . included full blood Indians, colored or Freedmen, and mixed bloods." The parents of Stella Sands, because they "belonged to a so-called Indian town," were "placed on the Indian roll as full-bloods," whereas, because William Stevens "belonged to a Freedman town, he was placed on the Freedmen roll." And yet, Emery underscored in his letter, "both are and were mixed bloods."[8]

Emery knew, though, that Marshall would be more interested in the broad legal arguments than in the local facts. "The property involved is little," he said—"the entire estate . . . does not exceed $6,000"—"but the principle involved is great." He brought up the supremacy clause and the Fourteenth Amendment to bolster his claim that the marriage had been valid. And he insisted that Stevens had been denied his rightful half "simply, solely and only because he was of African descent." As Emery put it, if Stevens "had been a white man, a yellow man, a brown man—if he had belonged to any race on Earth except a colored man, his right to inherit would not have been questioned," and there would have been no occasion for legal action. Emery needed expertise, and he needed funds: "I am convinced with your help, we shall win and the colored race in Oklahoma will be accorded their rights as American citizens— rights for which they fight in Italy against the Germans and in the Pacific against the Japs."[9]

Thurgood Marshall supported sending Emery a sum toward expenses he had incurred. And he assured the man that "this is most certainly the type of case we are vitally interested in and it will be a pleasure to serve with you."[10] A. L. Emery, responding in late January 1943, said he was "glad" to know the money was coming to pay certain court costs:

> I shall be happy to have you and your organization participate in every step for I feel sure, in the end, we shall win. I can readily understand why the trial court held against us—he is a one man court and only a trial court and he did not want to hold unconstitutional a provision of the state constitution and a state statute. He is just passing the buck to an appellate court.[11]

That, however, proved the high-water mark of the collaboration between Emery and the NAACP. Marshall conferred with such colleagues as William H. Hastie and Milton R. Konvitz, and the case looked less and less promising. The team worked up considerable acquaintance with the Oklahoma precedents on race, marriage, and inheritance, and the NAACP came to see "a great likelihood and danger of creating an unfavorable Appellate Court precedent." Emery's case was of "great interest," he was told in April, "but we are afraid of raising the issue in an Appellate Court in a case such as this case at the present time."[12]

Some of the NAACP's concerns are clearly visible in various memoranda and letters. What was there to gain that offset a likely setback? Were the circuit court to credit the testimony that Stella Sands shared William Stevens's racial identity as "of African ancestry," Stevens would win on the facts but no victory of principle would have been achieved. Should it credit the supremacy clause, the law of interracial marriage might be altered in Oklahoma, but nowhere else. Only if the arguments from the Civil Rights Act of 1866 and the Fourteenth Amendment were accepted by the court was there even a chance of a useful decision of national significance. And even then, should Emery's approach prevail, the ruling might apply only to Oklahoma and Indian lands and have no necessary wider application.

Emery replied that the letter was a "knock out" blow to him, but he refused to stay down. In continuing communications, he urged the NAACP to reconsider. Konvitz assured Emery that "we feel as you do that miscegenation laws should be held unconstitutional," yet "it would be extremely hazardous at this time" to press the matter. Emery himself conceded at several points that it was only the peculiar nature of Oklahoma's laws that drove him on— and, as Konvitz wrote Marshall three months later, "First of all, we cannot for a moment concede that the statutes of other states are constitutional." Emery needed help, but the NAACP was not going very far down that road at that time.[13]

Emery pressed on. Marshall wrote him in May that the organization would give him a final $100 toward expenses, given the interest Emery had shown in the case and the fact that "it is the type of case which should be fought." But the near-term prospects remained gloomy; there was "very little chance of success because of the precedents involved."[14]

The Court of Appeals—More of the Same

Nearly another year passed and Emery continued, alone. Then, the Tenth Circuit Court of Appeals handed down its decision. The appeals court reviewed the history of the case, the decision of the district court, and the statutory history of Indian Territory and the state of Oklahoma. Was the supremacy clause an obstacle to Oklahoma's enacting and enforcing laws like those William Stevens found himself up against? No, it was "clear that the marriage relations of Creek Indians in Oklahoma are subject to the laws of the state."[15]

Did Oklahoma law violate the Fourteenth Amendment or the Civil Rights Act? *Pace* v. *Alabama* neutralized the Civil Rights Act, as the appeals court saw it: "There is no discrimination against the colored race, within the purview of the Civil Rights Bill." *Maynard* v. *Hill* left matters of marriage in the jurisdiction of the states, and a train of precedents, dating back to the 1870s and 1880s—the usual suspects from Indiana, Alabama, Virginia, and elsewhere— shielded the Oklahoma statute against attack from the direction of the Fourteenth Amendment. The court explained that "within the range of permissible adoption of policies deemed to be promotive of the welfare of society as well as the individual members thereof, a state is empowered to forbid marriages between persons of African descent and persons of other races or descents."[16] As the NAACP lawyers had anticipated, the precedents, like it or not, governed the outcome.

A series of state cases from Oklahoma left no doubt whether William Stevens could have ever entered into a valid marriage with Stella Sands—if she was "white" and he was not—and the fact that their wedding took place in another state in no way added to its validity. The law was clear, but the court still had to address the central fact, the couple's racial identities. Should the Creek rolls be deemed conclusive when it came to racial designations? According to William Stevens, both he and Sands were of mixed ancestry, "part Indian and part Freedman," so neither could be classified as white, and they could legally marry. The appeals court was not buying any of this argument, though it did not say there was no truth in it. The court was going to accept the racial identities, as given by the tribal rolls, of Stella Sands and of William Stevens:

> It would not serve any useful purpose to review the evidence at length. It is sufficient to say that a painstaking examination of the record convinces us that the findings are supported by substantial evidence and are not clearly erroneous, due regard being had for the opportunity of the trial court to observe the witnesses, appraise their credibility, and to determine the weight to be given their testimony. Therefore the findings are not to be overturned on appeal.[17]

So the court of appeals affirmed the decision of the district court. As for the facts, the appeals court accepted the district court's determination that Stella Sands—a "full-blood Creek Indian"—was "white." As for the law, William Stevens could constitutionally be deprived of an inheritance, as his lawyer had put the matter, "simply and only because he is of African descent."[18] Under Oklahoma law, William Stevens had never been married to Stella Sands. Her will, made out before she married him, remained in effect, and he had no claim on her property. All this because he was deemed "of African ancestry," and she was not.

Windmills

In March 1945, A. L. Emery wrote Thurgood Marshall about the circuit court's adverse decision, upholding the district court. Emery was bewildered that he had lost. After all, he insisted, the Civil Rights Act of 1866 "plainly says that a negro shall be accorded the same rights as a white person. In Oklahoma, a white person can marry and inherit from an Indian but a negro cannot." And he was deeply troubled by the experience, which had been "almost too much for me last summer. I regret now that I ever took the case. I am sure it will be my last along these lines. I am going to let such battles to others in the future."[19]

He received a final letter, written in soothing tones, from Edward R. Dudley, NAACP assistant special counsel. "We certainly share with you," Emery was told, "the keen disappointment of having the Court render an adverse decision." But experience had led the NAACP lawyers to see that they "must proceed with caution in that the case must not only be the right type of case, but it must also be brought at the right time."[20]

The Oklahoma case was messy—it did not raise the right issue, it did not raise it in the right way, and it did not raise it at "the right time." The relationship between A. L. Emery and his potential backers in the NAACP gives a pretty clear idea of how the leading civil rights organization of the time viewed the feasibility of mounting an attack on the constitutionality of state laws restricting interracial marriage. Not only were other matters more urgent, but there seemed far greater likelihood of success in pursuing them, and a failed effort would be substantially worse than just leaving things alone.

To judge from Emery's unhappy experience in *Stevens* v. *United States,* no national organization was prepared to give serious support to a challenge to the constitutionality of state laws that restricted marriage on the basis of racial identity. Nor was any federal court yet ready to reconsider the constitutionality of those laws. Moreover, as a party to the suit in *Stevens,* the federal government went to court to argue in support of their constitutionality—to insist that they be enforced.

The decision in *Stevens* in the Tenth Circuit Court of Appeals wrapped up the constitutional status of miscegenation laws at the close of World War II. The laws were constitutional. The precedents remained intact. So did the antimiscegenation regime. A decade later, miscegenation cases from Alabama and Virginia reached the U.S. Supreme Court. Would a federal court at last overturn such a law?

Not at This Time: The Case of Linnie Jackson

Linnie Jackson probably should have stayed away from A. C. Burcham. She was black. He was white, not to mention married to someone else. Alabama law was no more friendly toward interracial relationships in the 1950s—especially when they persisted—than it had been in the 1880s, and, as a consequence, Linnie Jackson was convicted of miscegenation and sentenced to the Alabama penitentiary.

E. B. Haltom Jr., Linnie Jackson's lawyer, did what he could to challenge the constitutionality of the law under which she had been tried. He called upon a long train of twentieth-century civil rights decisions from the U.S. Supreme Court to help Jackson. Nonetheless, the Alabama Court of Appeals (a twentieth-century appellate court below the Alabama Supreme Court) surveyed the history of decisions in miscegenation cases in the Alabama courts; declared that, after all, the nation's highest court had affirmed the Alabama Supreme Court's decision in *Pace* back in the 1880s; and noted that "the decisions of the [Alabama] Supreme Court shall govern the holdings and decisions of this court." It upheld her conviction.[21]

Jackson did not give up. She took her case to the Alabama Supreme Court, which rebuffed her as well, and then to the U.S. Supreme Court. There she found that the justices were by no means eager to push an equal-rights agenda on the matter of miscegenation. Focused as they were on the school segregation cases that had been decided in 1954, they recognized that, were they to take on miscegenation, they might only get in their own way. The first decision in *Brown* v. *Board of Education* came in May 1954; the second, implementing decision came in May 1955. Linnie Jackson's case went to the Court between those two dates.[22]

Harvey M. Grossman, law clerk to Justice William O. Douglas, expressed his conflicted response when advising his boss on the *Jackson* case. "It seems clear that the statute involved is unconstitutional," he wrote on November 3, 1954. And yet, he continued, "review at the present time would probably increase the tensions growing out of the school segregation cases and perhaps impede solution to that problem, and therefore the Court may wish to defer action until a future time. Nevertheless, I believe that[,] since the deprivation of rights involved here has such serious consequences to the petitioner and others similarly situated[,] review is probably warranted even though action might be postponed until the school segregation problem is solved."[23]

Later that month, the Supreme Court dodged the bullet and decided not to hear the case. Three justices voted to hear it: Hugo Black, William O. Douglas, and Chief Justice Earl Warren. But five others voted not to: Harold Burton, Thomas Clark, Felix Frankfurter, Sherman Minton, and Stanley Reed.[24]

Seven decades had elapsed between *Pace* v. *Alabama* (1883) and *Jackson* v. *Alabama* (1954), and still nothing, it seemed, had changed. The precedent of *Pace,* such as it was, remained intact. The Court was prepared to let Linnie Jackson spend years in the penitentiary for violating Alabama's miscegenation law. The next year, the Court faced another miscegenation case, one that came from Virginia.

A Battered but Sturdy Fortress: The Case of Ham Say Naim

On June 26, 1952, Ham Say Naim, a Chinese sailor, married a white woman from Virginia, Ruby Elaine Lamberth, in Elizabeth City, North Carolina, where they had visited briefly from Norfolk, Virginia. Like Virginia, North Carolina banned marriages between whites and blacks, but, unlike Virginia, it permitted marriages between Caucasians and Asians. For some months, the Naims made their home back in Norfolk, although he was often away at sea. Then she decided that she wanted out. On September 30, 1953, Ruby Elaine Naim filed a petition seeking annulment on grounds of adultery, and if that effort failed, she asked that an annulment be granted on the basis of Virginia's ban on interracial marriages.[25]

Judge Floyd E. Kellam of the Portsmouth Circuit Court knew an easy case when he saw one. Here was a marriage between a white person and a nonwhite. The couple had gone to North Carolina in order to evade the Virginia law, as much a crime as having had the ceremony in Virginia. Of course the marriage was void, and he granted the annulment Mrs. Naim sought.[26]

Now it was Mr. Naim's turn to go to court. On the basis of his marriage to an American citizen, he had applied for an immigrant visa, and unless he remained married he could not hope to be successful. His immigration attorney, David Carliner, mounted a test case in the Virginia Supreme Court.[27]

On the face of it, the case was about the 1924 Racial Purity Act, but Virginia's legislation curtailing interracial marriage dated back to 1691. Its constitutionality had never been successfully challenged, and a unanimous ruling in 1955 revealed that nothing had changed. Justice Archibald Chapman Buchanan, writing for the Virginia Supreme Court, relied on the Tenth Amendment to fend off the Fourteenth. "Regulation of the marriage relation," he insisted, is "distinctly one of the rights guaranteed to the States and safeguarded by that bastion of States' rights, somewhat battered perhaps but still a sturdy fortress in our fundamental law, the tenth section of the Bill of Rights."[28]

What about *Brown* v. *Board of Education* and its interpretation of the equal protection clause, that segregation could no longer pass constitutional muster? No problem, Justice Buchanan assured Virginia authorities: "No such claim for the intermarriage of the races could be supported; by no sort of valid reasoning could it be found to be a foundation of good citizenship or a right which must be made available to all on equal terms." He could find nothing in the U.S. Constitution, he wrote, that would "prohibit the State from enacting legislation to preserve the racial integrity of its citizens, or which denies the power of the State to regulate the marriage relation so that it shall not have a mongrel breed of citizens." Rather than promote good citizenship, he suggested, "the obliteration of racial pride" and "the corruption of blood" would "weaken or destroy the quality of its citizenship."[29]

The Tenth Amendment, "that bastion of States' rights," may well have been, as Justice Buchanan wrote, "somewhat battered" after *Brown* v. *Board of Education,* but—even if trumped by the Fourteenth Amendment on education—

it remained "a sturdy fortress" against a challenge to Virginia's marriage laws. The Virginia court was not about to make any concession in its reading of the Tenth Amendment or the Fourteenth—despite the decision in *Brown,* in fact especially in view of it. If the nation's highest court should rule another way, the Virginia judiciary would nonetheless have done its job, as the justices all saw it. So the state court upheld the constitutionality of the state legislature's handiwork.

Refusing to give up, Naim appealed to the U.S. Supreme Court. Unhappily for Naim, his case came to the Supreme Court only one year after *Jackson,* and the court was no more eager to confront the issue then than it had been the year before. Law clerks for various justices saw the inauspicious timing. Justice John Marshall Harlan's clerk worried, "I have serious doubts whether this question should be decided now, while the problem of enforcement of the [school] segregation cases is still so active." Justice Harold M. Burton's law clerk struck much the same tone: "In view of the difficulties engendered by the segregation cases it would be wise judicial policy to duck this question for a time."[30]

The observations by the Court's justices and their clerks make it clear that a number of them, at least, were inclined to view miscegenation laws as unconstitutional.[31] Justice Felix Frankfurter, however, weighed in on the side of inaction. Bringing a tortured prose to the deliberations, he spoke to his brethren of pressing "moral considerations," which he proceeded to identify as, "of course, those raised by the bearing of adjudicating this question to the Court's responsibility in not thwarting or seriously handicapping the enforcement of its decision in the segregation cases." He felt certain, he said, that every member of the Court would agree with him that "to throw a decision of this Court other than validating this legislation into the vortex of the present disquietude would . . . seriously, I believe very seriously, embarrass the carrying out of the Court's decree of last May."[32] Frankfurter was referring to the implementation decision in *Brown,* handed down in 1955.

Justice Frankfurter knew that several states outside the South, as well as every state in the South, still had a miscegenation statute more or less like Virginia's. Bound up in the miscegenation question were attitudes regarding race and policies regarding marriage. Even aside from the school desegregation cases, Frankfurter was unconvinced that the time had come for the Court to take on the issue that Naim's case sought to force. The time might come to face the matter directly and declare such statutes unconstitutional—but not yet. He concluded that "as of today one can say without wrenching his conscience that the issue has not reached that compelling demand for consideration which precludes refusal to consider it."[33]

The Supreme Court neither accepted nor refused the case. Rather, it sent the case back to Virginia. Claiming to have determined the record insufficiently clear or complete to address the question Naim raised, it directed the Virginia Supreme Court of Appeals to remand the case to Portsmouth for further proceedings. But Virginia's highest court refused to cooperate with the request—or, rather, it helped the Court out of its dilemma. It remonstrated that "the record before the Circuit Court of the City of Portsmouth was adequate for a decision of the issues presented to it. The record before this court was adequate for deciding the issues on review. . . . The decree of the trial court and the decree of this court affirming it have become final so far as these courts are concerned."[34]

The *Richmond Times-Dispatch* published an editorial about the standoff. Acknowledging that the Virginia court had "used some rather tart language in refusing to comply," it insisted nonetheless that "the Virginia court has not defied the nation's highest tribunal." Rather, the paper noted, the state court had simply declared that "it had *no* legal means of conniving with the Federal court's order." Noting "many" Virginians' "displeasure" with the Supreme Court's recent rulings on public school segregation, the editorial observed that those "many Virginians . . . also applaud the Virginia court in rebuffing the Federal court's attempt to operate in an area of State affairs over which it has no jurisdiction."[35]

Naim took his case back to the Supreme Court, but it died there. The nation's highest court simply noted that the response of the Virginia Supreme Court "leaves the case devoid of a properly presented Federal question." The Virginia court had helped get the U.S. Supreme Court off the hook.[36] No judicial reconsideration took place by the Supreme Court in the 1950s regarding miscegenation laws in Alabama, Virginia, or anywhere else.

The NAACP: First Things First

Attorney E. B. Haltom had assiduously pressed Linnie Jackson's case without guidance or support from any national organization. He evidently figured his chances were better if he sailed alone, at least in the Alabama courts, and did not travel freighted with baggage such as the NAACP might have represented—or, for that matter, the American Civil Liberties Union (ACLU). Much of the litigation challenging the constitutionality of miscegenation laws in post–World War America, however, proceeded under the tutelage of such civil rights groups, including the American Jewish Congress and especially the ACLU. Unlike attorney Haltom in Linnie Jackson's case, David Carliner did not sail alone. Carliner sought help, and his role led to extensive involvement by the American Civil Liberties Union.[37]

The NAACP, by contrast, although it had acted to prevent passage of new legislation early in the century, was slow—as in the *Stevens* case, and even in the 1950s—to take an aggressive stance toward miscegenation laws already in place. It was a question of priorities. Viewed one way, the NAACP was leery of getting in its own way, in much the way that the Supreme Court ducked the *Jackson* and *Naim* cases so as not to add to the difficulties of seeing the school desegregation decisions implemented. Viewed another way, desegregation on the marriage front seemed far less pressing a matter than did progress in educational opportunity or voting rights.

Leading spokesmen for black America said as much at the time. Walter White, long a leader of the NAACP, was one. White presented himself as an African American, though he was said to be one sixty-fourth black, and he himself had married a white woman. When asked in 1954, shortly after the first of the two decisions in *Brown* v. *Board of Education,* whether he thought integrated schools would lead to more frequent intermarriage, he replied:

> That could be true. When human beings get to know each other and to respect each other, friendships develop and some of those friendships develop into love and into marriage. But there has been no noticeable increase in such friendships in the States where there has been no segregation. I think it will not materially increase the number of such instances.

Whether he thought that the laws against such marriages should stand was another matter. Asked whether the NAACP planned legal challenges to such laws, White replied without directly answering the question: "We've always opposed such laws on the basic ground that they do great harm to both races," he said. "If two people wish to live together, it is most un-Christian to say they must live together in sin instead of holy wedlock." Yet, mounting a constitutional challenge to the miscegenation laws was a low priority for his organization.[38]

Four years later, in 1958, NAACP executive secretary Roy Wilkins was also asked about white southerners' expression of fears that school desegregation would lead to interracial marriage. Asked on the Columbia Broadcasting System's "Face the Nation" about his own attitude toward the prospect of "complete intermingling of the races over a period of years," he told his national television audience, "We have no feeling one way or the other on intermarriage. That is what they are talking about. If they are talking about intermingling, then it strikes me they are a couple of hundred years late." Intentionally tweaking the beaks of all people who professed such concerns at such a late date, he pointed at the large numbers of mulattos living in southern states like Mississippi and South Carolina under slavery: "So that, if anybody is concerned about this matter unduly in 1958, I would have thought they would have become concerned about it before now."[39] The great era of "miscegenation" had occurred long before, when white men "intermingled" with their slave women back before the Civil War; it was even before the word "miscegenation" had been invented.

Five years later, some weeks after the 1963 march on Washington, another black spokesman, Howard University president James M. Nabrit Jr., was asked to comment on the continuing unease on the racial front. "To an individual, marriage is a major interest," Nabrit explained, although "there just doesn't seem to be much desire for intermarriage on the part of either group." As for the constitutional status of miscegenation laws, he went on, "My own personal view is that interracial marriages are constitutionally protected, but they affect such small numbers of people that their consideration might very well be postponed at this critical time in the lives of our citizens." Far more pressing, he thought, was racial discrimination in a broad range of other areas—education, employment, housing, voting, transportation, criminal justice, public accommodations—all of them "too critical for a diversion of scarce legal talent into . . . the relatively minor area of interracial marriage."[40] Public life—not private—should be the focus of the campaign for racial change.

The NAACP did not view miscegenation laws as a high priority in its litigation campaign against racial discrimination. Moreover, cases from Oklahoma, Alabama, and Virginia in the 1940s and 1950s had revealed how, into the 1960s, nothing, it seemed, had changed regarding the constitutional standing of those laws since the 1930s or even the 1880s.

President Truman and a Four-Foot-Long Word

In the summer of 1963, Harry S. Truman was visiting New York City, where his daughter lived. As he went for an early morning walk, a reporter caught up with him, and among the questions asked of the former president was whether he thought interracial marriage would become "widespread."[41]

"I hope not," Truman replied. "I don't believe in it. What's that word about four feet long? Miscegenation?" Truman, well known for his bluntness, redirected the question. "Would you want your daughter to marry a Negro?" The reporter replied that he'd want her to marry "the man she loved." Truman, not satisfied with this response, snapped, "Well, she won't love someone who isn't her color," and then he explained, "You'll edit the man she goes out with. I did, and mine married the right man."[42]

The reporter, writing the story up, described Truman as having long been "an advocate of integration in other respects." In 1948, Truman had ordered the desegregation of the U.S. military, and he and his administration had taken various actions to support the civil rights of African Americans, including voting rights for black southerners. But clearly there were limits, even 15 years later.

Truman thought whites should marry whites, and blacks should marry blacks. Interracial marriage, he said, was inconsistent with the "teachings of the Bible."[43] Truman's statements in 1963 summed up how little had changed regarding interracial marriage since 1948—in many people's attitudes, in decisions in the federal courts, or in the antimiscegenation regime's hold on the South. Even since 1941—the year that Stella Sands died in Oklahoma, the year the United States entered World War II—much had remained unchanged.

Between 1941 and 1963, however, another story line had been unfolding. In 1941, black labor leader A. Philip Randolph called for a march on Washington to obtain equal employment opportunities, particularly in defense plants at a time when the nation was coming out of the Great Depression and gearing up for possible entry into World War II. As a consequence, Randolph secured from President Franklin D. Roosevelt an executive order opening up defense plant jobs to black workers. Seven years later, in 1948, a similar initiative by Randolph led President Harry Truman to issue the executive order that began the desegregation of the U.S. armed forces. In 1963, Randolph was the titular leader of a "March on Washington for Jobs and Freedom," at which the Rev. Dr. Martin Luther King Jr. gave his "I Have a Dream" speech.[44] The war on miscegenation laws should be understood as an important component of the Civil Rights Movement, even if many spokesmen for the movement saw greater urgency in dethroning King Color in other areas of life.

During the 15 years between 1948 and 1963, yet a third story line took shape—one that, consistent with the Civil Rights Movement, belied the image that nothing had been happening regarding miscegenation laws over those years. Highlighting that other story line were actions by the American Civil Liberties Union and decisions made by some state courts in the West, especially the California Supreme Court.

PART FOUR

IF THE RIGHT TO MARRY IS A FUNDAMENTAL RIGHT

CHAPTER 13

A BREAKTHROUGH CASE IN CALIFORNIA

"If the right to marry is a fundamental right, then . . . an infringement of that right by means of a racial restriction is an unlawful infringement of one's liberty"

—Justice Jesse Carter, California Supreme Court (1948)

At the end of World War II, no state had repealed a ban on interracial marriage since Ohio in 1887. Moreover, Supreme Court decisions from the 1880s—*Pace* v. *Alabama* (1883) and *Maynard* v. *Hill* (1888)—continued to hold sway (see chapter 8). *Pace* was understood to have held that miscegenation statutes—banning whites from marrying blacks, and imposing equal penalties on both parties for violations—in no way contravened the equal protection clause of the Fourteenth Amendment. *Maynard* expressly left authority for regulating marriage in the hands of the states. Well into the 1940s, for state and federal judges alike, matters of marriage simply did not seem to raise federal questions under the U.S. Constitution.

Multiple efforts in the 1940s failed to get an inheritance case involving miscegenation laws before the U.S. Supreme Court. Antoinette Giraudo had married a Caucasian man, Allan Monks, in Arizona in the 1930s, and the subsequent case—tried in California in 1939, regarding her eligibility to inherit from him—hinged on her racial identity. It was determined that she had "one-eighth negro blood," and therefore could never have contracted a legal marriage in Arizona with Allan Monks. Appellate courts in both California and Massachusetts ducked her appeals, one in 1941 and the other in 1945. The Supreme Court, too, rebuffed her, in 1942 and again in 1946.[1]

As late as *Stevens* v. *United States* (1944), federal courts—a district court and a circuit court of appeals—upheld the constitutionality of Oklahoma's miscegenation law. The NAACP had been urged to intervene in support of th constitutional challenge in that case but had declined to do so, fretful that a negative outcome would only make it harder to mount a successful attack later on. In that sense, little had changed from the Jack Johnson era, when the NAACP had exerted itself to contain the empire of miscegenation but had not chosen to seek any kind of rollback.

In fact, containment had finally been achieved, and that in itself was a new development. After the 1930s, no new miscegenation measures were enacted—after 1913 no states inaugurated such laws, and after 1939 no new group in any state was defined as nonwhite for purposes of restricting marriage. No state since the 1880s had renounced its loyalty to the antimiscegenation regime, but at least the size and scope of the racial regime were no longer expanding.

As World War II came to an end in 1945, a new phase of repeal was about to begin. Yet the new phase of removing laws against interracial marriage was like the old phase of enactment. What happened in the states depended entirely on developments in those states—and not at all on initiatives in Congress or in the federal courts. Laws against interracial marriage vanished from the statute books in various states in the years to come. Until the 1960s, however, they usually did so as a result of action in the legislatures, not in the courts—and certainly not in the federal courts.

State action in the 1940s, 1950s, and 1960s weakened the antimiscegenation regime by reducing the number of states with laws restricting interracial marriage. To complete the job—to end miscegenation laws in states that showed no inclination whatever to remove them on their own—would take federal action of the sort that the U.S. Supreme Court decision in 1967 finally brought. But before the antimiscegenation regime could be brought down in its entirety, two changes had to occur. One was in the law of race, the other in the law of marriage. By World War II, both changes were under way, although only in the early stages of development.

Federal Courts, Racial Segregation, and an Emerging Right to Privacy

By the first few years after World War II, the Supreme Court had acted against certain forms of racial discrimination. In *Buchanan* v. *Warley* (1917), it had ruled against municipal ordinances that restricted land ownership by racial identity, although it had arguably done so more because the restrictions undercut white homeowners' ability to find purchasers than because the laws thwarted potential black purchasers' equal access to good housing. In *Smith* v. *Allwright* (1944), the Court declared white Democratic primaries unconstitutional, and more black southerners were soon voting in primary and general elections alike. 'n *Shelley* v. *Kraemer* (1948), the Supreme Court threw out the judicial enforcement of restrictive housing covenants (the preferred means to achieve residential segregation after city ordinances were banned). *Shelley* v. *Kraemer* identified judicial enforcement as deploying "state action" in support of private prejudice and therefore at odds with the Fourteenth Amendment's pledge that "no State shall . . . deny . . . the equal protection of the laws."[2]

Those cases demonstrated that the Supreme Court could not be counted on to uphold measures that defined people's opportunities on the basis of their racial identities. Transportation and education offered the best examples of how the Fourteenth Amendment might be relied on to support enhanced black access instead of unequal opportunities or outright exclusion. Supreme Court decisions in the 1940s were curtailing the constitutional basis on which train companies and interstate bus lines could assign separate seats or separate cars to black riders. A 1938 case from Missouri directed states to provide black residents with substantially equal in-state graduate programs in higher education or, as an alternative, to admit otherwise qualified black applicants to previously "white" graduate programs. By mid-century, other decisions further ratcheted up the Constitution's requirements in higher education.[3]

Higher education offered the best example of how the old "separate-but-equal" formula from *Plessy* v. *Ferguson* (1896) lived on into the 1940s. But it also showed that the nation's highest court was increasingly prepared to support African Americans' efforts to secure an enhanced definition of "the equal protection of the laws." Through the late 1940s, the Court had not taken the position that segregation in educational facilities was itself unconstitutional, but that time came in the 1950s. The world of segregation was coming under mounting challenge, and it remained to be seen how long marital segregation could be maintained by state law. No constitutional challenge to miscegenation laws had been successful since the 1870s. Success in one state appellate court would apply to that state only. Success in a case that went to the U.S. Supreme Court would apply across the land.

While courts grappled from time to time with the constitutionality of miscegenation statutes and other measures that restricted people's freedom on the basis of race, a separate train of cases was in motion. American constitutional law developed what would come to be known as a right to privacy, a right that emerged in the 1920s and came of age in the 1960s and 1970s.

By the 1940s, the Supreme Court had ruled on various cases in the area of individual privacy. How much control should people have over their lives, and how much power should state governments have to restrict people's freedom? What, if any, fundamental rights did Americans have that were not spelled out in the U.S. Constitution? The Court declared that people had the right to teach their children a foreign language (*Meyer* v. *Nebraska*, 1923) and the right to send their children to private schools (*Pierce* v. *Society of Sisters,* 1925). In a list of "privileges long recognized at common law as essential to the orderly pursuit of happiness by free men," *Meyer* expressly included "the right . . . to marry." Moreover, married people had the right to have children; the Court voided a law that mandated that people convicted of certain types of crime be sterilized (*Skinner* v. *Oklahoma,* 1942).[4] These three privacy cases provided a backdrop to the late 1940s, when a judicial reconsideration of the constitutionality of miscegenation laws began.

Racial Categories, Religious Freedom, and the Right to Marry

In October 1947, a California couple attempted to obtain a marriage license, were denied, and took legal action. Under California law, Sylvester S. Davis was black and Andrea D. Perez was white, and they did not contest those racial identities. The state prohibited marriages between whites and blacks, and it banned the issuance of licenses for interracial couples to marry, so J. F. Moroney, the Los Angeles County clerk, refused to issue the license. Davis and Perez were not on trial themselves. Rather, putting Moroney and the California laws on trial, they went to court to force the county clerk to issue them the license.[5]

The couple argued that their Fourteenth Amendment rights were violated if, solely as a consequence of any differences in their racial identities, they were denied the right to marry. Unlike most other couples challenging restrictive laws, they also argued from the First Amendment. Davis and Perez were Catholics, and they argued that they were being denied their religious freedom if they could not "participate fully in the sacraments" of their religion.[6]

The case was in the California courts from August 1947 through October 1948. Two changes in the clerkship of Los Angeles County—from J. F. Moroney, who resigned, to Earl O. Lippold, and then W. G. Sharp—meant that the case was known successively as *Perez* v. *Moroney, Perez* v. *Lippold,* and finally *Perez* v. *Sharp.* All manner of developments in recent years—even while the court decision was pending—shaped the arguments and influenced the outcome.

Arguing the Perez Case

Los Angeles County lined up all the traditional authorities to sustain its position. *Maynard* v. *Hill* left the regulation of marriage up to the states, and in *Stevens* v. *United States,* just three years earlier, a federal court had turned back the argument that racial restrictions violated the Fourteenth Amendment. A Supreme Court decision that had upheld a congressional ban against Mormon polygamy, *Reynolds* v. *United States* (1879), allowed California to distinguish between belief and behavior in matters of religious freedom, so the state's restrictions on interracial marriage did not abridge anyone's First Amendment rights. Moreover, a Supreme Court decision on eugenics and sterilization, *Buck* v. *Bell* (1927), permitted a state to do what it could, California argued, to curtail marriages that "might lead to the conception of defective or socially maladjusted offspring."[7] These and other arguments permitted the state to argue that there was, in fact, no basis for the court to declare the California miscegenation law unconstitutional. A first pass at this argument in August 1947 seemed increasingly inadequate, so the state followed it up with a fuller version in October.

Oral argument took place on October 6, 1947. The couple's attorney, Daniel G. Marshall—who shared the plaintiffs' Catholic faith, and was active in the American Civil Liberties Union—highlighted what seemed the weakest points in the state's argument.[8] Was the kind of behavior they wished to be permitted at odds with universal moral codes? Eighteen of the Union's 48 states had no such policy. He pointed out the inconsistencies in the California law as to who could marry whom—Native Americans could marry anyone; whites could marry only other whites or Native Americans; and as for all the other racial categories, they could marry among themselves without legal restriction. Race, after all, was the only issue in the case. And it was "arbitrary," Marshall insisted, "to premise legislation upon myth and superstition."[9]

Charles C. Stanley Jr., deputy counsel of Los Angeles County, encountered heavy weather in his own oral argument, to judge from the questions that interrupted him. On the matter of equal protection, he reached back to *Pace* v. *Alabama,* in which a miscegenation statute had been upheld on the basis that, under it, blacks and whites were equally restricted and, if convicted of being in violation, equally penalized. Justice Roger J. Traynor wanted to know what was meant by the words "negro" and "mulatto" in the statute, and Stanley had to confess that it would have been better had the legislature more carefully defined its terms, because then people of mixed racial background would be more sure whom they could and could not marry. Traynor asked, too, "How do you answer the argument that the statute in reality amounts to a 'carfare' statute, that if the parties went to Mexico and were married, the marriage would be recognized as valid upon their return to California?"[10]

Marshall and Stanley clashed most sharply over what Marshall had called the "myth and superstition" of race. Marshall suggested that the arguments for upholding miscegenation laws stemmed in large part from a Georgia case in 1890, *Tutty* v. *State* (see chapter 8). He quoted its language about "amalgamation," an "inferior race," and "deplorable results," and he juxtaposed it to similar language from a much more recent rant, Hitler's *Mein Kampf.* Should California now follow "the dogma of the Tutty case" and its echo in *Mein Kampf,* he asked, or, rather, "the sublime expressions of our national aspiration" that stemmed from the Declaration of Independence? Stanley nonetheless wanted to talk about the "biological and medical considerations" that might, he hoped, provide cover for the statute: "There is a definite showing—I do not like to say it or to tie myself in with 'Mein Kampf'—but it has been shown that the white race is superior physically and mentally to the black race, and the intermarriage of these races results in a lessening of physical vitality and mentality in their offspring."[11]

Justice Traynor had displayed substantial skepticism about Stanley's evidence and arguments. No matter how Traynor decided the case, other judges would have to side with the petitioners, or *Perez* would end up just another case in which a miscegenation statute's constitutionality was upheld. Attorney Marshall tried to prod more members of the court in the direction that Justice Traynor seemed inclined to go. True, he conceded, the Supreme Court had upheld eugenic sterilization in *Buck* v. *Bell,* but more recently it had ruled, in another sterilization case, *Skinner* v. *Oklahoma,* in a way that cast doubt that the Court would now "unblinkingly follow" *Buck.*[12] In any case, there was *Meyer* v. *Nebraska,* with its explicit guarantee of the right to marry and raise children.

As to who should be permitted to marry whom—without legal restriction—Marshall wanted to know, why were certain interracial pairings singled out for proscription? Surely there were other kinds of pairings that could lead to "social tensions," he said: "The wedding of May and December, . . . of the cultured to the ignorant, of the sick to the strong, of the poor to the rich, of the handsome to the ugly, of the Jew to the Gentile, of the Protestant to the Catholic, in none of these does the state venture to express a judgment."[13]

Stanley had cited with much favor an Alabama Supreme Court decision from the 1870s, *Green* v. *State,* with its strong language about the right and the need for a state to regulate black-white marriage. Marshall therefore pointed out—"lest it be thought" that the Alabama judiciary had never ruled any other way—the case of *Burns* v. *State,* the 1872 decision in which the same court had, for a time, ruled the state's miscegenation law unconstitutional. Moreover, every case that Stanley had called on as precedent for the constitutionality of miscegenation laws, Marshall insisted, proceeded "upon the same hallucination of race which is found in the *Stevens* case, the *Tutty* case, and *Mein Kampf.*" Regarding any group's quest for racial purity, Marshall concluded: "Myth and superstition are not rationality. 'Master races,' reflection of the community mores or not, are constitutionally forbidden when they are sought to be created and preserved under its aegis by state action."[14]

The Perez Decision

Nearly a year passed. When the California Supreme Court handed down its decision at the beginning of October 1948, three judges went through the con-

ventional argument, resting on *Pace* v. *Alabama, Maynard* v. *Hill,* and other court decisions that would leave intact a restrictive law like California's. "Such laws," they insisted, "have been in effect in this country since before our national independence and in this state since our first legislative session. They have never been declared unconstitutional by any court in the land although frequently they have been under attack." After a survey of previous decisions, their opinion concluded: "The foregoing authorities form an unbroken line of judicial support, both state and federal, for the validity of our own legislation, and there is none to the contrary."[15]

The judiciary should not tamper with the legislature's handiwork, these three judges held. It was a plausible exercise of state power, and any question as to whether it was a good policy ought to be left to the wisdom of the legislature. Speaking for the people of California, the legislature had acted as early as 1850, when it declared marriages between whites and blacks void, and as recently as 1933, when it had responded directly to the *Roldan* decision by bringing white-Malay marriages under the ban (see chapter 9). Perhaps the time would come for the statute to be repealed, but the legislature, not the court, should make that determination.

While three justices supported the California law, however, four went another way. Writing for the majority, Justice Roger Traynor recalled the U.S. Supreme Court's statement in *Meyer* v. *Nebraska* about the right to marry. Calling, moreover, on *Pierce* v. *Society of Sisters* and *Skinner* v. *Oklahoma,* Justice Traynor wrote: "The right to marry is as fundamental as the right to send one's child to a particular school or the right to have offspring." Traynor turned on its head the traditional phrasing about marriage being more than a contract and therefore subject to state regulation. Instead, he insisted, marriage was "something more than a civil contract subject to regulation by the state"; it was "a fundamental right of free men."[16]

Traynor surveyed recent decisions by the U.S. Supreme Court on segregation in housing, education, and transportation, building on them in some places and distinguishing them at other points. The Supreme Court had, on various occasions, taken the position that segregated facilities were constitutionally permissible if blacks, excluded from one facility, had access to a substantially equal alternative. Such an approach, however, the court insisted, could hardly apply to marriage:

> A holding that such segregation does not impair the right of an individual to ride on trains or to enjoy a legal education is clearly inapplicable to the right of an individual to marry. Since the essence of the right to marry is freedom to join in marriage with the person of one's choice, a segregation statute for marriage necessarily impairs the right to marry.

Appearing to make a dangerous concession, Traynor was intending instead to bolster his case when he suggested: "If miscegenous marriages can be prohibited because of tensions suffered by the progeny, mixed religious unions could be prohibited on the same ground." When all was said and done, according to the court majority, California's miscegenation provisions "violate the equal protection of the laws clause of the United States Constitution by impairing the right of individuals to marry on the basis of race alone."[17]

Justice Jesse Carter wrote a concurring opinion, in which he addressed the other side's central arguments. As to the "'sociological' reasons" for maintaining a miscegenation law—that interracial families might face ostracism on any and all sides—he declared about a prospective bride and groom:

> If they choose to face this possible prejudice and think that their own pursuit of happiness is better subserved by entering into this marriage with all its risks than by spending the rest of their lives without each other's company and comfort, the state should not and cannot [constitutionally] stop them.

As to the "medico-eugenic" argument, Carter drew in part on international developments to make his case. He quoted Hitler's declaration in *Mein Kampf* that the "most sacred human right, . . . the most sacred obligation," was "to see to it that the blood is preserved pure." Carter contrasted Nazism, just recently defeated, with the values Americans had defended in the American Revolution and Union soldiers had fought for in the Civil War:

> To bring into issue the correctness of the writings of a madman, a rabble-rouser, a mass-murderer, would be to clothe his utterances with an undeserved aura of respectability and authoritativeness. Let us not forget that this was the man who plunged the world into a war in which, for the third time, Americans fought, bled, and died for the truth of the proposition that all men are created equal.

Relating the case to the emerging Cold War, Carter observed, "The rest of the world never has understood and never will understand why and how a nation, built on the premise that all men are created equal, can three times send the flower of its manhood to war for the truth of this premise and still fail to carry it out within its own borders."[18]

The majority decision was therefore, Carter said, "in harmony with the declarations contained in the Declaration of Independence which are guaranteed by the Bill of Rights and the Fourteenth Amendment . . . and reaffirmed by the Charter of the United Nations." Addressing what he called "the only question before us," he concluded, "It seems clear to me that it is not possible for the Legislature, in the face of our fundamental law, to enact a valid statute which proscribes conduct on a purely racial basis." Therefore, Carter wrote, "If the right

to marry is a fundamental right, then it must be conceded that an infringement of that right by means of a racial restriction is an unlawful infringement of one's liberty."[19] To Carter, the path seemed clear, the conclusion evident. There was no "if" about it. The right to marry was indeed a fundamental right. Therefore the racial restriction was an unlawful infringement.

The state petitioned for a rehearing, so attorney Daniel G. Marshall had occasion to answer. In the same kind of rollicking language he had deployed all along, he castigated all attempts "to exhume the cadaver of these pseudo statutes . . . whose burial site the instant decision marks." Mindful of the way in which the legislature had responded to the earlier decision in *Roldan*, he suggested that the other side was attempting "to obtain certain shoal markings for the draftsmen of other racist marriage legislation."[20]

Marshall called on *Shelley v. Kraemer*—a 1948 Supreme Court decision that had not been available for use back when the briefs were written and oral argument made in late 1947—as authority to forestall either a reconsideration by the court or another pass in the legislature. Comparing *Perez* to *Shelley*, he found that "another fundamental right, the right to marry and procreate," was at stake. The racial restriction in *Perez*, like the one in *Shelley*, was, "*per se*, a violation of the Fourteenth Amendment," said Marshall. "Just as no court may enforce a restrictive covenant[,] the respondent here is forbidden, since he is an agent of the state, to refuse a license for reasons of race or color no matter what the statutes upon which he relies say." He ended by asking: "But what purpose is to be served by a further refutation of the cult of the worship of the purity of the blood?"[21]

The Significance of Perez

By the narrowest of margins, 4–3, Andrea Perez and Sylvester Davis had won their case in the California Supreme Court. Had they lost in California, the couple had been prepared to carry their case to the U.S. Supreme Court—though it is hard, looking back, to see how they could have won there at that time. Even when they won in the California Supreme Court, they knew that their victory was not yet secure. The state might appeal to the nation's high court. California decided not to, however, so Davis and Perez were free to marry in California—and free to live in California as husband and wife.[22] They could not assume, though, that they had the freedom to move as an interracial family to any state that still had a miscegenation law on its books.

Was *Perez* a breakthrough decision? Certainly it transformed the law of race and marriage in California, but it had no immediate effect anywhere else. As to whether it broke judicial precedent, Justice Traynor distinguished the Supreme

Court decision in *Pace* from the case at hand by noting that *Pace* had dealt not with marriage but with sex outside marriage. Justice Carter could announce that "there are no decisions of either this court or the Supreme Court of the United States which uphold the validity of a statute forbidding or invalidating miscegenous marriages."[23] As for all those state court decisions from places like Georgia and Alabama, California had no need to be bound by them—no need to be governed by the cumulative consensus that such decisions seemed to represent.

The dissenters, on the other hand, stated: "Research has not disclosed a single case where a miscegenetic marriage law has been declared invalid."[24] With that declaration, they neglected relevant state appellate decisions during Reconstruction in more than one state in the South. In fact, the petitioners' attorney had specifically called attention to the 1872 *Burns* decision in Alabama, so the dissenters' claim that no court had ever declared a miscegenation statute unconstitutional was not merely wrong on the facts but, one gathers, willfully misleading.[25] The minority was correct, though, in pointing to an unbroken line—from as early as *Pace* v. *Alabama* to as recently as *Stevens* v. *Oklahoma*—in which federal courts had upheld such statutes against constitutional challenge.

Several considerations permitted a divided court in California to come to the conclusion it did. Justice Traynor's passionate leadership was critically important; had a defender of the statute sat in his place, the court would have ruled, by at least 4–3, in favor of the law. Inconsistencies in the California law and its enforcement meant that a weak commitment to the antimiscegenation regime could be undercut entirely. Unlike many states with laws restricting interracial marriage, California in the 1940s did not prosecute interracial couples who had gone outside the state to marry. In fact, for many years, there had been no criminal penalty in California for marrying interracially or living together as an interracial couple.[26] Restrictions had been real—Perez and Davis could testify to that—but the relative lightness with which the antimiscegenation regime ruled in California made it easier for a court majority to rule that it should not rule at all.

With one split decision by the state supreme court, California's miscegenation law became suddenly unenforceable.[27] Elsewhere in the West, state legislatures soon began repealing their miscegenation laws. Oregon did so in 1951, Montana in 1953, and North Dakota in 1955 (see appendix 1). But such laws lived on in all 17 southern states, as well as 9 states outside the South. Legislative repeal was not a viable option in the South, nor would a state appellate court there act as the California high court had. Challenges to southern laws would therefore have to be taken to federal court.

The Antimiscegenation Regime Continues to Shrink

Justice Jesse Carter of the California Supreme Court used the phrase in *Perez,* "If the right to marry is a fundamental right." Half of his colleagues accepted his premise, so a slim 4–3 majority converted the conditional clause into a declarative statement. In 1948—only 15 years after having expanded its miscegenation law's scope by restricting marriage between Caucasians and "members of the Malay race"—California joined states like Vermont and Wisconsin, which had never had laws restricting interracial marriage, and states like Pennsylvania and Massachusetts, which had repealed their miscegenation laws as long ago as 1780 and 1843. For the first time in the twentieth century, an American court ruled a miscegenation statute unconstitutional. Yet a majority of American states—29 in all—retained such laws into the second half the twentieth century.

One by one, western states relinquished their place in the antimiscegenation regime. In Nevada, labor leader Harry Bridges and Japanese American Noriko Sawada flew into Reno in December 1958 expecting to get married and ran smack into a miscegenation law preventing them from obtaining a marriage license. When they took the matter to court, Taylor H. Wines, a local judge, agreed with the logic of *Perez* v. *Sharp* and ordered the clerk to issue the license. As an afterthought, Judge Wines's ruling held blameless the person who would perform the ceremony, for, as the judge commented, "the license would do no good if no one could marry" the couple. The incident launched a repeal effort in the legislature, successful early the next year.[28]

Although *Perez* v. *Sharp* had an immediate impact nowhere outside California in 1948, Nevada felt the influence ten years later. The California decision, available to attorneys in other states to deploy in local cases, convinced Judge Wines in Nevada that his state's law should go, too. Every time another state withdrew its allegiance to the antimiscegenation regime, the count switched in favor of continuing the trend.

Until the 1948 California decision, 30 states still had miscegenation laws. When Harry Bridges and Noriko Sawada went to Nevada ten years later, the number had dropped to 24—exactly half of the 48 states at that time. Then Nevada dropped its ban, and so did Idaho. Also in 1959, Alaska and Hawaii became states, and they had no miscegenation laws. Beginning in 1959, for the first sustained period in the nation's history, the antimiscegenation regime had the support of only a minority of states. The lower the number became, the easier it was for judges and legislators elsewhere to note a decline in public support for such laws. Those lower numbers helped get the number down still more.

Soon after the events in Nevada, a similar sequence unfolded in Arizona. In December 1959, another Japanese American and Caucasian couple applied for a marriage license and were turned back. Herbert F. Krucker, another local judge, declared the Arizona miscegenation law unconstitutional, and Mary Ann Jordan and Henry Oyama were able to get a marriage license. In 1962, the legislature passed a repeal bill.[29]

Outside the South, the antimiscegenation regime was in retreat.[30] A split decision in California, reflecting any number of recent world events and constitutional developments, showed how much had changed since 1912, when Congressman Roddenbery proposed an amendment to the U.S. Constitution that would have banned black-white marriages everywhere across America. One after another, western states were taking down their legal obstacles to marriages between either Asian Americans or African Americans and people identified as white.

CHAPTER 14

CONTESTING THE ANTIMISCEGENATION REGIME—THE 1960S

"Eventually, . . . interracial marriages will become as acceptable as interfaith marriages are today"

—Farley W. Wheelwright, a northern minister (1962)

"I think it is simply not possible for a state law to be valid under our Constitution which makes the criminality of an act depend upon the race of the actor"

—Potter Stewart, Supreme Court justice (1964)

Into the 1960s, the law of racial identity could affect a wide range of family matters—from obtaining a marriage license to inheriting property to child custody.[1] Viewed from a wider perspective, the law of racial identity shaped opportunity across a broad spectrum of public activities as well. The Civil Rights Movement focused its energies on racial restrictions in the public realm—such as voting, education, transportation, and lunch counters—but interracial marriage was often what opponents of change voiced as their central concern.

In 1962, at the height of the Civil Rights Movement in the South, the Rev. Farley W. Wheelwright gave a sermon at a Unitarian–Universalist church in New York about race in American life. Just back from three days in Albany, Georgia, which he had visited at the invitation of the Southern Christian Leadership Conference, Wheelwright predicted that segregation in public accommodations would fall, and when it did, segregation in marriage would fall as well. "Eventually," he said, "when schools, restaurants, hospitals and cemeteries are integrated, it is inevitable that interracial marriages will become as acceptable as interfaith marriages are today."[2]

In view of the uncertain acceptance of interfaith marriages in the early 1960s, Wheelwright was not predicting that race would disappear as a determinant of marriage partners. In fact, he observed that black residents of Albany weren't really interested in miscegenation. Speaking of the typical black man in southwest Georgia, Wheelwright observed, "What he really wants today is the vote."[3]

Yet, in suggesting that interracial marriage would become more "acceptable," Wheelwright was voicing something that the most fervent supporters of segregation and disfranchisement—the most committed opponents of the Civil Rights Movement—had been warning about in Georgia. Wheelwright and the segregationists differed fundamentally on whether public policy should continue to curtail intermarriage. Regardless of those differences, formal desegregation in the law of marriage would mean that two people could marry across a racial boundary, not that they necessarily would.

In the 1960s, increasing numbers of Americans challenged the law's authority to govern interracial marriage, though others resisted any change. In state after state, legislatures repealed miscegenation laws, until only the 17 states of the South held on. Couples in Georgia, Maryland, and elsewhere encountered the law and did what they could to bypass it. In Florida, Oklahoma, and Virginia, court battles developed over whether to dismantle the antimiscegenation regime once and for all. Lawyers from the American Civil Liberties Union continued to assist in court challenges, and the National Association for the Advancement of Colored People signed on, too. Moreover, the Supreme Court of the United States began to reconsider the antimiscegenation regime's constitutionality under the Fourteenth Amendment.

The Rise of Religious Opposition to Miscegenation Laws

The discourse in the 1960s regarding interracial marriage in the United States is illuminated if it is related—as the Rev. Wheelwright did—to interfaith marriage. Individuals' choices to marry outside the faith encountered religious authorities' strong objections that such behavior threatened communal identity, confused the children, and endangered eternal souls. Some of the same religious leaders who spoke out against miscegenation laws argued that people of their particular faith should not choose marriage partners of another faith. Questions regarding the manner in which children would be raised, combined with a feared loss of communal identity, arose time and again.[4] Those concerns were related to religious authority in American life, but not directly to state power.

In the long history of the United States, race generally trumped religion as the basis of individual identity and communal conflict, but other nations did not necessarily share the American approach. (See appendix 3 for an example from the Middle East.) Even in the United States, the fact that, in every era, some individuals had crossed the boundaries of racial identity—boundaries that other people thought impassable, and had acted to keep that way—showed that race did not govern all human activity. Such partnerships sometimes heightened communal conflict (the Jack Johnson effect, discussed in chapter 9), but they could instead ease tensions across intergroup lines (the Pocahontas effect, seen in chapter 1).

In the 1960s, various religious figures, together with groups of church people, voiced a growing opposition to laws and attitudes that would ban interracial marriages. For example, the National Catholic Conference for Interracial Justice insisted at its annual meeting in 1963 that interracial marriage was entirely compatible with the doctrine and canon law of the Roman Catholic Church. "Diversity of faith" was an impediment to marriage, in this view, but race and color were not. "Races do not marry," declared an official statement; "only persons marry." As long as individuals did not violate the "impediments" regarding incest ("consanguinity"), bigamy ("already existing marriage bonds"), or "diversity of faith," they should have "the right to decide to marry and the right to decide whom to marry," with neither their family nor the state stepping in to thwart their choices in these matters.[5] From this perspective, the marriage in Arizona in 1959 between Henry Oyama and Mary Ann Jordan (see chapter 13) was not a mixed marriage after all, for both were Catholics, as were Sylvester Davis and Andrea Perez in California a decade earlier.

The National Catholic Conference for Interracial Justice recognized society's frequent expressions of what it termed "cruelty"— hostile attitudes and behavior— toward interracial families. But whereas the supporters of miscegenation laws used such attitudes and behavior to justify bans against interracial marriage, this group turned the argument around to chastise the prevalent social practices and call for their "reform." It explained: "The Catholic conscience condemns . . . the underlying racist philosophy" that so often led to such behavior. Instead, "the Catholic dogma, revealed by God, of the unity of the [human] family cries out against this pagan ideology."[6] Not content with statements of faith and prescriptions for toleration, the group called for action against conditions—like miscegenation laws— that had come to be seen as incompatible with the group's understanding of its religious beliefs and social mandates.

Some Protestant groups took a similar approach to miscegenation laws. The 1965 General Assembly of the United Presbyterian Church, a denomination that was described as "overwhelmingly white in its membership," adopted a statement denying that there were "theological grounds for condemning or prohibiting marriage between consenting adults merely because of their racial origin." Moreover, the Church condemned what it called the "blasphemy . . . of racism," that is, "the deliberate or unconscious assumption that a human being's worth is conditioned by his racial derivation." The Assembly's newly elected moderator, William Phelps Thompson, said that such prohibitions "deny basic human rights." The group did not wish to be misunderstood as actively en-couraging interracial marriage, for it recognized that such marriages could "bring all kinds of tensions within the family," but the matter should be an op-tion left to individuals to weigh, not foreclosed by law.[7]

The United Presbyterian Church called on its members to work for the "re-peal or nullification" of miscegenation laws. Not only should they urge their leg-islators to vote for repeal if their state still had such a law; the call seemed to suggest that members should support litigation to overturn the law in states that failed to act on their own to end the legal bans. In their communities and their churches, in electoral and judicial politics, Christians should enlist in a battle to end a system of unjust laws.[8] Church leaders and church followers adopted the statements they did because they knew miscegenation laws to be alive and well in many states—and because, in the 1960s, growing numbers of Americans viewed such laws as evil rather than good, codes that should be opposed rather than tolerated or promoted.

The shifting orientation among various religious groups revealed—at the same time that it fostered—changes in public opinion that permitted repeal of laws restricting interracial marriage in one northern state after another. Between 1913 and 1948, the number of states with miscegenation laws held steady at 30. By the end of the 1950s, 8 of those states had withdrawn their allegiance to the antimiscegenation regime, but 22 held on into the 1960s. Then, in 1962, Ari-zona repealed its miscegenation law, and Utah and Nebraska followed the next year. That left 19 states, among them Wyoming and Indiana. In 1964, for the first time since the 1930s, Indiana voters elected both a Democratic governor and a Democratic legislature, and Governor Roger D. Branigin led the charge of "let's catch up" and create "a New Indiana." Among the many fossils of ear-lier times that fell in early 1965 during the crusade was the state's nineteenth-century law against interracial marriage. Wyoming acted the same year. Finally, every state outside the South had dropped its ban on interracial marriage. Only the 17 southern states remained.[9]

The South defined itself in two ways in racial policy. One was the 17 states' allegiance to the antimiscegenation regime past 1965. The other was that, alone among American states, those 17 maintained fully segregated systems of public schools, from the elementary grades through higher education (especially be-tween 1890 and 1935).[10] The twin concerns—education and marriage—were often connected, as is revealed in a story that unfolded in Georgia at about the time that the Rev. Wheelwright visited Albany.

Desegregated Schools and Interracial Marriage

Furious rhetoric greeted the Supreme Court's desegregation rulings in *Brown* v. *Board of Education* in 1954 and 1955 and the efforts at implementation in elementary and secondary schools in the decade and more that followed. It was said that integrated settings that put little boys and girls (and older boys and girls) together, day in and day out, on terms of equality, would lead—as Georgia governor Herman Talmadge put it in 1956—to "the mongrelization of the races."[11] There was, of course, some truth to what was said, whatever one thought of it, in the sense that integration could lead to intermarriage. People who grew up together were more likely than not to marry within the group, however it might be defined—in terms of class, religion, or race. In a racially mixed environment, people were a bit more likely to marry across racial lines.

Similar resistance was mounted to the desegregation of higher education.[12] Then, in 1963, a story burst on the scene that seemed to give substance to the worries. It surely occasioned posturing on matters of race, law, and marriage. At the same time, it revealed, once again, that people drawn powerfully to each other did not necessarily pay much respect to social or legal proscription.

Under federal court order and amidst threats of violence by whites, the University of Georgia admitted two black transfer undergraduates—Hamilton Holmes and Charlayne Hunter—in January 1961. They were admitted to classes, but not necessarily to anything else. Hunter was permitted to live in a dorm room; in fact, university regulations required all female undergraduates to live on campus. But she had to go back to court to gain access to eating places on campus.[13] The newsmen eventually went away, and both students went on to graduate in June 1963.

In September 1963, Charlayne Hunter was back in the national news. During her senior year, she revealed, she had married a classmate in the Journalism School—Walter Stovall, a white man from Douglass, Georgia—and they were now living in New York City and expecting their first child in three months' time. She was working as an editorial assistant at the *New Yorker* magazine, and he had just arrived in the city after spending the summer working as a reporter for the *Atlanta Journal.*[14]

They had met during the summer of 1962, when she was eating in a coffee shop at the Continuing Education Center, and he asked if he could join her. They began dating that fall, and in March—they declined to give specifics—they had a wedding ceremony somewhere and, as Stovall said, spent their "honeymoon on the turnpike" heading back to campus for classes. After she graduated, they tried to have another wedding—"on advice of counsel," explained Stovall, because of "the effect of racial laws" in the original "place of marriage." On June 8, one week after her graduation, they had a wedding in Detroit.[15]

Walter Stovall, the young journalist, soon issued a statement to the press to clarify matters—and in the hope that the air might be cleared of speculation, that the couple might thereafter be "left alone," and, as he put it, "so that we can live normal lives." "We have not wanted to embarrass, humiliate or disturb our families or anyone else," he said; he knew full well that his own family in Georgia was deeply disturbed at the revelation. "We are two young people who found ourselves in love and did what we feel is required of people when they are in love and want to spend their lives together. We got married."[16]

Their marriage—wherever, whenever—was no ordinary marriage, if it was any marriage at all, as officials in Georgia made very clear. Georgia law would not recognize their marriage, and they would be subject to arrest, prosecution, and fine and imprisonment if they tried to return to their home state and live as a married couple there. State Attorney General Eugene Cook, who declared all these things, was investigating whether the couple had violated a state law by living together as a married couple while students. The assistant attorney general, however, was reported to have decided that, in view of the reported marriage date a few days after their graduation, no university rules had been broken. Regardless of whether Hunter and Stovall had broken a state law or a university regulation, Governor Carl Sanders called the marriage a "shame" and a "disgrace."[17]

O. C. Aderhold, the university president, also weighed in. He was "greatly surprised and shocked," he exclaimed, by the news of their marriage. "Interracial marriage is prohibited by Georgia law," he insisted, "and secret marriages are contrary to the University of Georgia regulations." Had their marriage come to the attention of school authorities before Hunter graduated, "dismissal rules would have applied" to both of them. As it was, Stovall would not be "permitted to return" to the university to take the remaining classes required for graduation. Then again, from the Stovalls' perspective, other considerations overrode the university's rules. The couple could not live in Georgia. Their daughter would begin life in New York.[18]

The law of the color line did what it could to shape Charlayne Hunter's life. She gained unwanted fame when she broke through a barrier that, for a century and a half, had kept African Americans out of the University of Georgia. She soon went back to court, where a federal judge specified that the order under which she became a student brought with it full access to student eating facilities on campus. While eating at one such place, she met the man she would marry. But they had to leave the state to marry, and they had to stay out of the state to live as husband and wife. By no means did a court order to desegregate a state university extend to the state's miscegenation law.

Asian/Pacific Ancestry and White Marriage Partners in the 1960s:
Navigating the Miscegenation Laws of Maryland and Missouri

Other Americans, too, encountered miscegenation laws in the 1960s. In Maryland in 1964, for example, Elizabeth Medaglia and Benjamin A. deGuzman were planning to marry. Refused a license, they contested the miscegenation law. Embracing the language of the Fourteenth Amendment, she claimed that she had been denied due process of law. The statute was unconstitutional, she said.

Circuit Court Judge W. Albert Menchine pondered the situation. The statute declared that "members of the Malay race" could not marry whites, but it failed to define "Malay." That deGuzman was a medical doctor was perhaps not relevant, but that he had a white grandmother might well be. Instead of addressing the statute's constitutionality, Judge Menchine simply decided that it did not apply to Dr. deGuzman. "Assuming that in general a Filipino is a member of the Malay race," he declared, "it is very clear that this Filipino is not." One day before Valentine's Day in 1964, he directed the clerk of courts of Baltimore County, just outside the city of Baltimore, to issue the license.[19] Dr. and Mrs. deGuzman may well have lived happily ever after, but their court victory left the statute in place.

In 1965, Diane Greenwald and Benjamin Aguinaldo wanted to marry in St. Louis, but the law of race stepped between them. Aguinaldo was part Filipino, and authorities told them that a Missouri law banning marriage between whites and Mongolians barred their wedding. Rather than go to court and fight the statute or its application to them, the couple crossed the river into Illinois— which had long before repealed its miscegenation law (and had never barred marriages between Caucasians and Asians)—and had their ceremony at the Holy Family Church in Cahokia.[20]

In 1966, Jo Ann Kovacs and Meki Toalepai ran into the same problem with Maryland's miscegenation law that Elizabeth Medaglia and Benjamin A. deGuzman had two years earlier. She was a nurse at Baltimore General Hospital, and he was a professional entertainer who hailed from American Samoa. Denied a license in Baltimore because she was white and he was not, rather than contest the law they went to the nation's capital. The Rev. Frederick James Hanna, of Baltimore's Emanuel Episcopal Church, made the drive to the nation's capital so that he could perform the ceremony at Washington Cathedral. Neither the minister nor the ritual had to change, but the venue had to.[21]

All three of these couples managed to marry. Each could find a way—in the Border South—to bypass the racial restriction. Two of the three, however, had to go outside their state. The other couple obtained a license to marry only after a judge redefined them so that both were white. In none of the three cases was one partner African American. These six people—about three of whom nobody expressed any doubt that they were "white," and three others with Asian and Pacific ancestry—found that, in the mid-1960s, they had to navigate miscegenation laws dating from generations earlier.

Maryland struggled over whether to keep its ancient law. In 1966, Verda Welcome, a Democrat from Baltimore and the sole African American in the Maryland Senate, sponsored a bill to repeal the law. Observers were surprised when the bill was approved in the Senate's Judicial Proceedings Committee, for never before had such a measure advanced that far. In fact, the full Senate passed it, and it went to the House of Delegates. But there it was rejected 66–50 after one representative urged passage "if we want to make this country a brown race."[22]

The next year, however, the state legislature had been reapportioned, and rural areas like the Eastern Shore had less representation. In March 1967, both houses passed a repeal measure, and Governor Spiro Agnew signed it. The law would go into effect on June 1.[23] After 303 years with laws penalizing interracial marriage, Maryland joined the empire of liberty. One of the 17 southern states—and the first colony in British North America to enact such a measure—had at last abandoned its allegiance to the antimiscegenation regime. Viewed another way, little more than 18 years elapsed from California's split-decision judicial rejection of that state's miscegenation law to the Maryland legislature's repeal of its law.

In the 1960s, the U.S. Supreme Court, like the Maryland legislature, displayed a new willingness to take on the issue of miscegenation. Recovering from the paralysis it had suffered in the mid-1950s, the Court drove toward total demolition of the structure of Jim Crow in American public life—and thus, to a degree, in private life as well. In the *Pace* decision in the 1880s, the Court had unblinkingly upheld Alabama's miscegenation law. In the 1950s, it had refused to deal with the question. The Court began to confront it in 1964.

Dewey McLaughlin and Connie Hoffman

The first of the 1960s Supreme Court cases was *McLaughlin* v. *Florida.* The Legal Defense Fund of the National Association for the Advancement of Colored People (NAACP) took the lead in pursuing it, and the American Civil Liberties Union (ACLU) was delighted to see it do so. Dewey McLaughlin and Connie Hoffman, after living for a few weeks in an efficiency apartment in Miami, had been indicted under a Florida statute, Section 798.05, that said: "Any negro man and white woman, or any white man and negro woman, who are not married to each other, who shall habitually live in and occupy in the nighttime the same room" were each to be sentenced to imprisonment for up to a year or a fine as high as $500. Convicted, the couple were each sentenced to 30 days and a $150 fine. They appealed their convictions, but the Florida Supreme Court relied on the authority of *Pace* v. *Alabama* and upheld the trial court.[24]

In refusing to reconsider the constitutionality of Florida's miscegenation measures, the state supreme court used language that summed up the stance of southern states on that question. For the Florida court, the 1883 Supreme Court decision in *Pace* v. *Alabama* was still good law. The convicted couple's lawyers had intimated that, failing to get the right answer in Florida, they would carry the case to the nation's highest court. The Florida court responded that perhaps it was "a mere way station on the route to" the U.S. Supreme Court—and perhaps a different decision would be obtained there—but it could not help that. "This Court," it said, "is obligated by the sound rule of stare decisis and the precedent of the well written decision" in *Pace,* which it quoted at length. If a new rule were to be applied and a new outcome achieved, "it must be enacted by legislative process," said the unanimous court, "or some other court must write it."[25]

McLaughlin and Hoffman took their case to the U.S. Supreme Court. There they objected, first, that they had been prevented in Florida from mounting the defense that they had a common-law marriage, for the trial judge had insisted that, as an interracial couple, they had no freedom to marry under Florida law. Second, they argued that they were denied equal protection of the law, as they had been convicted under a statute that applied only to interracial couples. Finally, they contended that no conclusive evidence had been introduced to identify McLaughlin as being at least one-eighth of African ancestry, as would be necessary under Florida law for them to be an interracial couple.[26]

A unanimous U.S. Supreme Court struck down their convictions. With regard to the issue of equal protection, the Court objected that the conduct criminalized under Section 798.05 related only to interracial couples. Writing for the Court, Justice Byron White noted three elements of the couple's offense, "the (1) habitual occupation of a room at night, (2) by a Negro and a white person (3) who are not married." The provision under which they had been indicted and convicted, he observed, fell among several other sections designed to "deal with adultery, lewd cohabitation and fornication," most of them "of general application." But this particular provision specified an interracial couple and, unlike any of the others, "does not require proof of intercourse along with the other elements of the crime."[27]

The Court had to deal with the ancient legacy of *Pace.* As the Court now saw things, though, "*Pace* represents a limited view of the Equal Protection Clause which has not withstood analysis." The Court in 1883 had apparently been untroubled that an Alabama law "did not reach other types of couples performing the identical conduct" or by "the difference in penalty established by otherwise identical offenses," one committed by a single-race couple and the other by a black-white couple.[28]

The Court in 1964 was deeply troubled by such questions. Justice White wrote: "The courts must reach and determine the question whether the classifications drawn in a statute are reasonable in light of its purpose—in this case, whether there is an arbitrary or invidious discrimination between those classes covered by Florida's cohabitation law and those excluded. That question is what *Pace* ignored and what must be faced today." As he explained, relying on *Brown* v. *Board of Education* and other recent cases, "the central purpose of the Fourteenth Amendment was to eliminate racial discrimination emanating from official sources in the States." Yet, he said, "We deal here with a racial classification embodied in a criminal statute."[29]

Other provisions of Chapter 798, Justice White wrote, "neutral as to race," adequately expressed Florida's "general and strong state policy against promiscuous conduct, whether engaged in by those who are married, those who may marry[,] or those who may not. These provisions, if enforced, would reach illicit relations of any kind and in this way protect the integrity of the marriage laws of the State, including what is claimed to be a valid ban on interracial marriage." No compelling state purpose, he wrote, could support the offending law.[30]

Would the Court overturn the convictions on narrow grounds related solely to the law against interracial cohabitation, or would it rule more broadly to throw out all miscegenation laws? Plaintiffs and the state alike had attempted to tie together Florida's laws against interracial nonmarital cohabitation and interracial marriage—the plaintiffs on the basis that marriage was not an option available to them, the state on the grounds that the "interracial cohabitation law . . . is ancillary to and serves the same purpose as the miscegenation law itself."[31]

The Court insisted on untying the two bans: "We reject this [Florida's] argument, without reaching the question of the validity of the State's prohibition against interracial marriage or the soundness of the arguments rooted in the history of the [Fourteenth] Amendment." The justices invalidated the statute under which the pair had been convicted, but they did so, they took pains to make explicit, "without expressing any views about the state's prohibition of interracial marriage." In the case at hand, "the state police power . . . trenches upon the constitutionally protected freedom from invidious official discrimination based on race."[32]

The Court ruled that a state could not use a miscegenation statute to prosecute an interracial pair for "habitually liv[ing] in and occupy[ing] in the nighttime the same room." Justice Potter Stewart appeared to go further—he seemed ready to overturn all miscegenation laws—in a concurring opinion in which Justice William O. Douglas joined: "I cannot conceive of a valid legislative purpose . . . which makes the color of a person's skin the test of whether his conduct is a criminal offense." He reiterated his objection, based on the equal protection clause: "I think it is simply not possible for a state law to be valid under our Constitution which makes the criminality of an act depend upon the race of the actor. Discrimination of that kind is invidious *per se.*"[33]

Justice John Marshall Harlan also found the interracial cohabitation measure unconstitutional, but he thought *McLaughlin* "a very bad case" for overturning laws against interracial marriage.[34] As late as 1964, it was not possible to obtain a decision—certainly not a unanimous decision, certainly not in that particular case—in support of extending *Brown* that far.

Maybe the state's marriage law was permissible under the Fourteenth Amendment, and maybe it was not. That question did not need to be answered, the Court contended, to reach a conclusion in *McLaughlin.* Florida escaped a loss in its strategic gamble, and proponents of change lost their opportunity to obtain a wider-ranging decision. The Court proved less timorous than in the 1950s cases of Linnie Jackson and Ham Say Naim, but it was unprepared to go all the way.

McLaughlin was a crucial decision, in that the Supreme Court expressly overturned the *Pace* precedent on interracial cohabitation, and yet the Court sidestepped the central question. One might say that it had done little better in *McLaughlin* than it had in *Pace.* Dewey McLaughlin and Connie Hoffman could still not marry under Florida law without subjecting themselves to time in the penitentiary. If they continued to live together in Florida as an unmarried couple, authorities could bring charges against them for a sexual relationship outside marriage as "any man and woman" rather than as "any negro man and white woman."

In the meantime, another miscegenation case was in the courts, the case of the Lovings in Virginia. It, too, eventually made its way to the Supreme Court. This one involved a "white man and negro woman," to use Florida's language, two people who—like so many couples over the years—had thought they had contracted a marriage and found they had committed a felony.

In addition, a promising case was taking shape in Oklahoma, also involving a "white man and negro woman." Building on the decision in *McLaughlin* v. *Florida,* the Virginia and Oklahoma cases each attacked a state law against interracial marriage as unconstitutional.[35] The ACLU, pursuing its longtime commitment to eradicating all miscegenation laws, was centrally involved in both cases.[36]

Frances Aline Jones and Jesse Marquez

Many cases stemming from Oklahoma's miscegenation law developed after someone had died and were concerned with inheritance (see chapter 12). The case of Jesse Marquez and Frances Aline Jones, by contrast, began because two people, both of them still very much alive, loved each other and wanted to marry. Canadian County's largest town, some 25 miles west of Oklahoma City, is El Reno. There, though unmarried, Jesse Marquez and Frances Aline Jones lived as husband and wife in the 1960s. They had two children. By the time a third was on the way, they had attempted but failed to obtain a marriage license.

Jesse Marquez was a Catholic, Frances Aline Jones a Baptist. More to the point, he was of Mexican descent, she of African ancestry, and Oklahoma law declared: "The marriage of anyone of African descent . . . to any person not of African descent . . . shall be unlawful."[37] Jones and Marquez encountered several obstacles in their quest for a marriage license, but they claimed that they had been refused on racial grounds. They went to court to overturn the legal obstacles and obtain a license, and the ACLU gave them friend-of-the-court support in their challenge. Thus they moved into the main current of a small river of litigation brought by interracial couples who wished to marry in the United States. Perhaps their case would force a change in the course of that river. For their own sakes, they hoped so. The American Civil Liberties Union hoped it would alter the course of American constitutional law.

Oklahoma law required several things of people who wished to marry, and the couple did not satisfy all the requirements. Their ages caused difficulty. Jones was 22 years old, and Marquez 19. Had he been her age, and she his, that would have posed no problem. Oklahoma law required that the prospective groom be at least 21 years of age or that he have the written consent of a parent, and his parents refused to give their consent. Moreover, both the man and the woman had to pass physical examinations for syphilis, although, if both parties were at least 25 years old, they might request a waiver of that requirement.

On January 28, 1965, Jones and Marquez went to the county judge, Virgil M. Shaw, and pointed out that Section 3 of the law supplied a way around the problem of parental permission. It permitted the judge to authorize a marriage between underage people, even without parental permission, "when the unmarried female is pregnant, or has given birth to an illegitimate child."[38] When Judge Shaw refused to permit the marriage, Jones and Marquez challenged his decision. Arguing that he had declined to cooperate solely because of their differing racial identities, they appealed their case to the Oklahoma Supreme Court. Working with the ACLU, attorneys Bernard Cohen and Philip Hirschkop assisted the couple's local counsel, Jack P. Trezise.

Cohen and Hirschkop were taking time away from *Loving* v. *Virginia* to challenge the constitutionality of Oklahoma's miscegenation statute. In much the way that the court majority in *Perez* v. *Sharp* had done in 1948, the ACLU attorneys pulled together the separate tracks of Supreme Court rulings on race and privacy. What had happened since 1948 included the 1954 and 1955 decisions in *Brown* v. *Board of Education,* which had thrown out *Plessy* v. *Ferguson's* defense of separate-but-equal and had inaugurated desegregation in public schools. The 1964 decision in *McLaughlin* v. *Florida* meanwhile had overturned *Pace* v. *Alabama* and ruled against the Florida miscegenation statute as it applied to an unmarried interracial couple living together.

Relying on *McLaughlin,* the ACLU argued that the Fourteenth Amendment's equal protection and due process clauses made enforcement of the Oklahoma statute impermissible. *McLaughlin,* according to the ACLU, had "reaffirmed the idea that race alone could not be made the basis of punitive statutes." In addition, the ACLU relied on two of the early privacy cases, *Meyer* v. *Nebraska* and *Skinner* v. *Oklahoma* (see chapter 13), in both of which, as the ACLU put it, the Supreme Court "had expressed the view that marriage is a fundamental right of the individual and is protected by the Fourteenth Amendment."[39]

The Oklahoma Supreme Court justices were impressed with the work of Trezise, Cohen, Hirschkop, and the ACLU. Vice Chief Justice Floyd L. Jackson saluted the organization: "On this question [regarding the statute's constitutionality] we have been favored with excellent briefs by the applicants and by amicus curiae, the American Civil Liberties Union." But all that was beside the point, for the court did not budge on the statute's constitutionality. Speaking for a unanimous court on April 20, 1965, Jackson went on to announce, moreover, that "these briefs entirely ignore the cited statutory requirements concerning parental consent for the marriage of minors, the premarital examination for syphilis, and the discretionary power of the County Judge to order a waiver of these requirements."[40]

Jones and Marquez and the ACLU were not ready to give up. The couple requested a rehearing, and within weeks, on May 11, the court denied that rehearing. Trying again, they directed their attention toward obtaining an order from the state's highest court directing the court clerk of Canadian County, Dorothy Lorenzen, to issue them a marriage license. First they took care of everything that was in their power; presumably, they took and passed the medical examination.

And then Jones and Marquez went back to the state supreme court. By this time Marquez was 20 years old and the third child had been born. He and Jones claimed that Lorenzen "has refused and still refuses" to issue the license "for the sole reason that 'mixed marriages' are forbidden" by state law. Lorenzen filed a response conceding that "petitioners are entitled in all respects to be issued a marriage license," except for the law governing interracial marriages. The court agreed to hear the case and this time address the constitutional question. Again speaking for a unanimous court, Vice Chief Justice Jackson explained: "Since the facts are undisputed[,] no useful purpose could be accomplished by requiring petitioners to first file their action in the trial court and subsequently present the question to this Court on appeal," and "petitioners have already been delayed in receiving an answer to the question."[41]

The outcome, on November 23, 1965, was nonetheless substantially the same. Petitioners had urge First Amendment considerations of freedom of religion. Rejecting this position, the court declared that "freedom of conscience and freedom to believe are absolute but freedom to act is not." As far as the Fourteenth Amendment was concerned, the Oklahoma court had no intention of going beyond what the U.S. Supreme Court required—and that court had never ruled that states could not ban interracial marriages. Tallying "approximately nineteen states" that retained miscegenation statutes, the court insisted that "the great weight of authority from both federal and state courts is that they are constitutional," and it would not change its position until forced to do so:

> In view of this court's traditional practice of upholding its former decisions which involve questions of constitutional law, and in view of the fact that the great weight of authority holds such statutes constitutional, and the Supreme Court of the United States not having decided the question, we feel duty bound to again hold the statutes in question constitutional.[42]

The couple's lawyers attempted twice to persuade the Oklahoma court to rehear the case. Rehearings were denied on December 14, 1965, and again on March 8, 1966. The ACLU prepared to appeal the decision to the U.S. Supreme Court, the only court that might still make it possible for Jesse Marquez and Frances Aline Jones to obtain a marriage license. The Oklahoma court having rebuffed Jones and Marquez, Marquez then foiled Jones and the ACLU. According to the ACLU's doleful report, "plans to appeal the case . . . were frustrated when Marquez married someone else," a white woman.[43]

Bernard Cohen and Philip Hirschkop returned to Virginia to look after other business.

CHAPTER 15

VIRGINIA VERSUS THE LOVINGS—
AND THE LOVINGS VERSUS VIRGINIA

"Almighty God created the races white, black, yellow, malay and red, and he placed them on separate continents. . . . The fact that he separated the races shows that he did not intend for the races to mix"

—Judge Leon M. Bazile (1965)

"Mr. Cohen, tell the Court I love my wife, and it is just unfair that I can't live with her in Virginia"

—Richard Loving (1967)

In August 1963, a reporter asked President John F. Kennedy whether, in his "crusade" against racial discrimination, he would "seek to abrogate" the miscegenation laws that were still on the books in some 20 states, and, if so, "how would you go about it?" The president did not bite. Kennedy's evident discomfort with the subject had primarily to do with his having to get legislation through a Congress dominated by southern members of his own party. If there were an interracial marriage, he posited, and "if any legal action was taken" against the couple, then presumably they would take their case, if necessary, all the way to the Supreme Court.[1]

Kennedy implied that the Court would eventually rule against such laws and thus put an end to them. Regardless, the Justice Department had no particular role to play in the matter. And in no way did he suggest that the civil rights bill then under consideration might address the question. The responsibility for changing the legal environment regarding race and marriage rested, it seemed, with some interracial couple who had been charged under a state miscegenation law—a couple like the Lovings in Virginia.

Arrest

In Caroline County, Virginia, on July 11, 1958, Commonwealth's Attorney—the Virginia equivalent of a district attorney—Bernard Mahon obtained warrants for the arrest of Richard Loving and "Mildred Jeter," each for a felony associated with their marriage on June 2 in Washington, D.C. Then, late at night, Sheriff Garnett Brooks and two officers went to make the arrests.[2]

The three law officers entered the Lovings' bedroom and awakened them that July night. "We were living with my parents," Mildred Loving would later recall, in "a guest bedroom downstairs":

> I woke up and these guys were standing around the bed. I sat up. It was dark. They had flashlights. They told us to get up, get dressed. I couldn't believe they were taking us to jail.[3]

There was an interlude before they actually left the house. First, "I went upstairs, sat on the bed, talked with my mother," she remembers. "Make them go away," she pleaded to her mom. But the intruders had ascertained that the two were indeed living together as husband and wife. The couple did not share a racial identity, and yet they shared a bed. The men "explained we had broken the law," Mrs. Loving says, and "they took us to jail." Richard was let out after one night, but Mildred, all alone, was kept for several more days. Each posted $1,000 bail.[4]

Trial

The Lovings encountered what was called the Racial Integrity Act of 1924, the latest version of Virginia's law against black-white marriage that dated from 1691. There was no doubt in anyone's minds as to the racial identities, white and black, of the people who claimed to be Mr. and Mrs. Loving. They could just as easily have been charged under the 1878 law (see chapter 7)—which defined a black Virginian as someone at least one-fourth black—rather than under the more demanding racial definitions of 1910 or 1924, which first moved the fraction to one-sixteenth, and then adopted the "one drop" rule. Certainly the statute that made it a crime to evade the law, by going out of Virginia to marry and then immediately returning to the state and claiming to be married, dated from 1878.

The only way in which the Lovings' case was clearly affected by the twentieth-century changes in the law was in the penalty they faced. Beginning in 1878, the penalty was a term of two to five years in the penitentiary. In view of instances of difficulty in securing convictions under the 1924 law, the minimum penalty was reduced in 1932 to a single year.

The Caroline County grand jury brought indictments at its October 1958 term. At their trial on January 6, 1959, the Lovings pled "not guilty" at first and waived a jury trial. But then they changed their pleas to "guilty," and Circuit Court Judge Leon M. Bazile sentenced them to one year each in jail. In accordance with the plea bargain, Judge Bazile suspended those sentences "for a period of twenty-five years"—all the way to 1984—provided that "both accused leave Caroline County and the state of Virginia at once and do not return together or at the same time to said county and state for a period of twenty-five years."[5]

The suspended sentence did not mean that, after 25 years, the Lovings could return home to Caroline County as a married couple. If they lived together anywhere in Virginia, even after the 25 years had elapsed, they would face prosecution just as they had in 1958.

Exile

Richard Loving and Mildred Jeter, as the court knew them in Virginia, moved to Washington, D.C., where they resumed their identities as Mr. and Mrs. Loving. Either Mr. Loving or Mrs. Loving could visit Caroline County, but both could not legally do so at the same time. Regardless, they returned home from time to time, and Mrs. Loving was in Virginia for the births of all three of their children—Sidney, Donald, and Peggy. But the family had to live and work outside the state, and the couple longed to live in Caroline County. As Mrs. Loving later explained, "I wanted to come home. My family was here, and my husband's family was here." Moreover, she said, "I hate to live in the city."[6]

After four years of exile, the Lovings began to contest their fate. In 1963, Mildred Loving wrote Robert F. Kennedy, Attorney General of the United States, for assistance. As she recalled many years later, "I told Mr. Kennedy of our situation" and asked "if there was any way he could help us."[7] It was time, she felt, that her family move back home, and she had no doubt heard of a civil rights bill bobbing around in Congress—although the Civil Rights Act of 1964, when it became law the next year, left marriage as the one remaining pillar in the legal structure of Jim Crow.

The Justice Department redirected her letter to the National Capitol Area Civil Liberties Union with the suggestion that, although the federal government could not help the Lovings, perhaps the American Civil Liberties Union (ACLU) could. That organization had been pushing litigation since the *Perez* case in California in the late 1940s to rid the nation of miscegenation laws like Virginia's.[8]

ACLU member Bernard S. Cohen, a young lawyer practicing in Alexandria, Virginia, welcomed the opportunity to take the couple's case. In fact, he found it irresistible. Here were two people who clearly loved each other and wanted to live together and raise their children in familiar surroundings, and he wanted to help make things work out for them. Moreover, they were bringing the perfect test case for attacking the nation's miscegenation laws. The name of the case itself enthralled him: Loving versus Virginia.[9]

Return to Court

Cohen had to figure how to get the Lovings' case back into the courts. They had pleaded guilty, had been sentenced, and now wanted to re-open their case. Fortuitously, Cohen came across a Virginia Supreme Court decision from some years before that addressed reviving a case in which there had been a suspended sentence. The court had ruled that the Virginia law "providing for the use of probation and suspension of sentence in criminal and juvenile courts" permitted such cases to be reviewable as "still in the breast of the court."[10] Cohen tried that approach, and Judge Bazile evidently accepted it. Meanwhile, the Lovings returned home to the Caroline County area, though they faced uncertainty there, actually stayed in an adjacent county, and kept their sanctuary in Washington, D.C., at the ready.[11]

In November 1963, Cohen filed a motion in Caroline County Circuit Court to set aside the original convictions and sentences. Cohen knew that he would have to be creative to overturn a century's worth of adverse precedents. Of course he deployed the Fourteenth Amendment's equal protection clause to contest the constitutionality of Virginia's miscegenation statutes. He argued, too, that the suspended sentence "denies the right of marriage which is a fundamental right of free men"; that it constituted banishment and thus violated due process; that it constituted "cruel and unusual punishment" in violation of the Virginia Constitution; and that 25 years exceeded the "reasonable period of suspension" permitted by Virginia law.[12]

Judge Bazile was in no hurry to second-guess himself, so for some time nothing happened. In mid-1964, another young ACLU attorney, Philip J. Hirschkop, joined Bernard Cohen in the case and, no action having been taken on the petition in state court, Cohen and Hirschkop began a class-action suit in October 1964 in the U.S. District Court for the Eastern District of Virginia.[13] Cohen and Hirschkop requested that a three-judge court convene to determine the constitutionality of Virginia's miscegenation statutes and to prohibit the enforcement of the Lovings' convictions and sentences under those laws. Pending a decision by a three-judge panel, they requested a temporary injunction against the enforcement of those laws, which they said were designed "solely for the purpose of keeping the Negro people in the badges and bonds of slavery." District Judge John D. Butzner Jr., however, saw no "irreparable harm" to the Lovings while awaiting the panel's decision and rejected a motion for a temporary injunction. Recognizing that the federal panel was due to meet soon, Judge Bazile finally set a date to hear arguments on Cohen's motion.[14]

In January 1965, six years after the original proceedings, Judge Bazile presided at a hearing on the Lovings' petition to have his decision set aside. In a written opinion, he rebutted each of the contentions that might have forced reconsideration of their guilt. Pointing back to an 1878 Virginia Supreme Court decision, *Kinney* v. *Commonwealth* (see chapter 7), he insisted that the Lovings' marriage was "absolutely void in Virginia" and that they could not "cohabit" there "without incurring repeated prosecutions" for doing so. Relying on the Virginia high court's 1955 decision in *Naim* v. *Naim* (see chapter 12), Bazile stated that marriage was "a subject which belongs to the exclusive control of the States," and he noted that the U.S. Supreme Court had done nothing to overturn the Virginia decision or to undermine any other state's laws against interracial marriage.[15] By way of conclusion, Judge Bazile wrote:

> Almighty God created the races white, black, yellow, malay and red, and he placed them on separate continents. And but for the interference with his arrangement there would be no cause for such marriages. The fact that he separated the races shows that he did not intend for the races to mix.[16]

Writing history of a sort, this Caucasian judge held forth in Virginia—on a continent where "Almighty God" had placed the "red" race until Europeans moved there and forced Africans to settle there, too, and mingle among them.

The Virginia Supreme Court

The Lovings' case moved on from Judge Bazile's court, for his was not the last word. First, lawyers for the state convinced the federal court that the case should next be heard in the Virginia Supreme Court. So the Lovings took their case to the state's highest court, and the lawyers for both sides rehearsed arguments that, everyone well knew, were likely to be heard again before long at the U.S. Supreme Court.

In mounting one of their arguments, Cohen and Hirschkop quoted from *Perez* v. *Sharp*, the 1948 California Supreme Court decision against the constitutionality of miscegenation laws: "If the right to marry is a fundamental right, then it must be conceded that an infringement of that right by means of a racial restriction is an unlawful infringement of one's liberty." They went on to assert:

> The caprice of the politicians cannot be substituted for the minds of the individual in what is man's most personal and intimate decision. The error of such legislation must immediately

be apparent to those in favor of miscegenation statutes, if they stopped to consider their abhorrence to a statute which commanded that "all marriages must be between persons of different racial backgrounds."

Such a statute, they claimed, would be no more "repugnant to the constitution"—and no less so—than the law under consideration. Something "so personal as the choice of a mate must be left to the individuals involved," they argued; "race limitations are too unreasonable and arbitrary a basis for the State to interfere."[17]

The Virginia Supreme Court's opinion rejected the Lovings' arguments and largely adopted the brief of the state of Virginia. Its reasoning and conclusion from a decade earlier in the case of Ham Say Naim remained, as the court saw things, entirely viable. On March 7, 1966, a unanimous court declared: "We find no sound judicial reason . . . to depart from our holding in the Naim case."[18] As far as the court was concerned, the state law against interracial marriage was as sound in the 1960s as it had been in the 1880s.

The Lovings had exhausted their appeals in the Virginia courts, and their convictions remained intact. They were still not allowed to "cohabit as man and wife" in Virginia, so they appealed their case to the U.S. Supreme Court.[19]

The Lovings Take Their Case to the U.S. Supreme Court

The Lovings were reluctant parties to the case that bears their name. This is not to say that someone had to convince them to bring the case, for they were committed to their marriage. Rather, they would have much preferred for the question never to have been raised—so very rudely raised—back in July 1958, when they were awakened in their bedroom and hauled off to jail. All they had ever wanted was to be left alone. Richard Loving, a private and taciturn man, explained their position in 1966, after the Virginia Supreme Court had rejected their position: "We have thought about other people," he told a reporter in Virginia, "but we are not doing it just because someone had to do it and we wanted to be the ones. . . . We are doing it for *us*—because we want to live here."[20] So they pressed on.

Bernard Cohen and Philip Hirschkop, in their jurisdictional statement to the U.S. Supreme Court, pointed out why the case should be heard there. "The elaborate legal structure of segregation has been virtually obliterated with the exception of the miscegenation laws," they said. "There are no laws more symbolic of the Negro's relegation to second-class citizenship. Whether or not this Court has been wise to avoid this issue in the past, the time has come to strike down these laws; they are legalized racial prejudice, unsupported by reason or morals, and should not exist in a good society."[21]

While the Court was considering whether to hear the case, Justice John Marshall Harlan's clerk wrote that "the miscegenation issue . . . was left open in *McLaughlin,* and appears ripe for review here. If the Court's traditional test that discrimination based on race must be examined carefully for any justifiable state interest, I doubt whether this statute can stand."[22]

On December 12, 1966, the Court agreed to hear the case.

Briefs

The time had come for Hirschkop, Cohen, and the ACLU to prepare a written argument to convince the Court to invalidate the Virginia law under which the Lovings had been indicted and convicted. Yet the power of miscegenation laws to affect interracial couples in the United States went far beyond the Virginia laws and far beyond the Lovings. The ACLU wished to secure a ruling from the Court broad enough to address the wider issues and invalidate every state's miscegenation laws.

Hirschkop and Cohen played important roles in crafting the ACLU brief in *Loving,* but they were not alone. For example, William D. Zabel wrote Arthur L. Berney at the Boston College Law School about his thoughts on how to proceed. The ACLU attorneys were in agreement that the Lovings' case should provide a vehicle for attacking all miscegenation laws. *McLaughlin* had produced only a narrow ruling, and Zabel warned, "We should not assume that the Court will try to avoid a narrow holding" in *Loving.* Zabel argued, however, against stressing the kind of sociological evidence that had been deployed in *Brown* v. *Board of Education.* In *Loving,* he said, "there is no separate but equal problem." As he explained: "Two consenting, competent adults ought to have the right to marry regardless of race and there can be no separate but equal opportunity for them."[23]

The written arguments brought the two sides of the controversy into clear focus. One side emphasized how far the Fourteenth Amendment could reach, the other the limited intent of its framers. Where the ACLU emphasized the reasoning in *Brown* v. *Board of Education* and in *McLaughlin* v. *Florida,* Virginia emphasized the doctrine in *Maynard* v. *Hill* that states had authority over the regulation of marriage. One side recounted the history of privacy cases from the 1920s into the 1960s. The other spoke instead of an unbroken string of federal cases in which statutes banning interracial marriage had been upheld, most recently in the 1940s in *Stevens* v. *United States.*

The NAACP Legal Defense Fund—which was very much involved in the case when it reached the Supreme Court—bore in on the Virginia court's statement in *Naim* v. *Naim* that the 1924 law's purpose was to "preserve the racial integrity" of Virginia's citizens. Rebutting that position, the NAACP argued that "there is no rational or scientific basis upon which a statutory prohibition against marriage based on race or color alone can be justified as furthering a valid legislative purpose." Revealing an interest in the question that went beyond black-white marriages and the law, the Japanese American Citizens League also submitted a brief as a friend of the court. Cohen and Hirschkop, in their brief, reviewed the history of Virginia's miscegenation laws from the seventeenth century to the twentieth and characterized those statutes as "relics of slavery" and, at the same time, "expressions of modern day racism."[24]

Oral Argument

In oral argument on April 10, 1967, the state did what it could to convince the Court that miscegenation laws should be left up to the states. Once again, a state mounted the old steed, the Tenth Amendment, to joust with its adversary, mounted on the Fourteenth. The Tenth Amendment, Virginia argued, and not the Fourteenth, ought to govern marriage. But while *Maynard* v. *Hill,* which declared marriage to be subject to state legislation, could be trotted back out for another fray, its twin from the 1880s, *Pace* v. *Alabama,* had died three years before in *McLaughlin* v. *Florida,* so was no longer available to assist. And talk about the need for racial purity sounded even less convincing in 1967 than it had in oral argument before the California Supreme Court in 1948.[25]

The ACLU lawyers argued, of course, that Virginia's miscegenation laws could not pass constitutional muster. Philip Hirschkop focused on the equal protection clause, Bernard Cohen on the due process clause. Hirschkop argued from the legislative history of the Virginia laws that their intent to secure the racial purity of the "white" race, and their intent to demean and control black Virginians, violated the Fourteenth Amendment. Cohen concentrated on the personal impact of the laws on the Lovings. He spoke of their "right" to marry, as he and they saw it, and their wish to live together in peace in Virginia. And he referred to their terror and humiliation at being dragged out of bed and off to jail for living as husband and wife.[26]

Cohen summarized some of the civil penalties (quite aside from the criminal penalties) that automatically attached to the couple under Virginia's laws. "The Lovings have the right to go to sleep at night," he declared, "knowing that should they not awake in the morning their children would have the right to inherit from them, under intestacy [in the absence of a will leaving them their parents' property]. They have the right to be secure in knowing that if they go to sleep and do not wake in the morning, that one of them, a survivor of them, has the right to social security benefits." The "injustices" that necessarily followed from the Virginia law, Cohen argued, "amount to a denial of due process," for those rights were being arbitrarily denied the Lovings.[27]

Cohen highlighted his argument by conveying to the Court the words of Richard Loving: "Mr. Cohen, tell the Court I love my wife, and it is just unfair that I can't live with her in Virginia."[28]

Loving v. Virginia

Two months later, on June 12, 1967, Chief Justice Earl Warren delivered the opinion of a unanimous Supreme Court. The Court rejected each of the state's arguments. The historical record, the judicial precedents, and legal logic of the state's brief had been incorporated in the decision of the Virginia Supreme Court. By contrast, those of the Lovings' attorneys, as well as the NAACP and the Japanese Americans Citizens League, made their way into the decision of the U.S. Supreme Court.

The Virginia court's decision in Naim v. Naim to the contrary, the chief justice wrote, the Tenth Amendment had to yield to the Fourteenth when it came to the claim of "exclusive state control" over the "regulation of marriage." As for the narrow construction of the Fourteenth Amendment, dependent as it was on the state's reading of the intent of the framers, the Court harked back to its statement in 1954 in Brown v. Board of Education that the historical record was "inconclusive." That Virginia's "miscegenation statutes punish equally both the white and the Negro participants in an interracial marriage" could no longer satisfy the standard of constitutionality.[29]

Warren gave the back of the hand to the state's contention that "these statutes should be upheld if there is any possible basis for concluding that they serve a rational purpose." The burden of proof rested on the state, for "the fact of equal application does not immunize the statute from the heavy burden of justification" required by the Fourteenth Amendment, particularly when racial classifications appeared in criminal statutes.[30] The doctrine voiced in Maynard v. Hill still held general sway, but the Fourteenth Amendment of the 1960s, unlike that of the 1880s, negated it when race entered the equation.

The chief justice declared that "we find the racial classifications in these statutes repugnant to the Fourteenth Amendment, even assuming an even-handed state purpose to protect the 'integrity' of all races." As Warren put it, "The clear and central purpose of the Fourteenth Amendment was to eliminate all official state sources of invidious racial discrimination in the States." Quoting from the McLaughlin case, he wrote: "Indeed, two members of this Court have already stated that they 'cannot conceive of a valid legislative purpose . . .

which makes the color of a person's skin the test of whether his conduct is a criminal offense.'"[31]

Warren was sure of the Court's recent history in civil rights cases: "We have consistently denied the constitutionality of measures which restrict the rights of citizens on account of race. There can be no doubt that restricting the freedom to marry solely because of racial classifications violates the central meaning of the Equal Protection Clause." As for the due process clause, the chief justice noted that "the freedom to marry has long been recognized as one of the vital personal rights essential to the orderly pursuit of happiness by free men."[32]

Connecting race with privacy, Chief Justice Warren explained: "To deny this fundamental freedom on so unsupportable a basis as the racial classifications embodied in these statutes, classifications so directly subversive of the principle of equality at the heart of the Fourteenth Amendment, is surely to deprive all the State's citizens of liberty without due process of law." Giving the Lovings and their lawyers everything they had asked for, the chief justice wrote that the Fourteenth Amendment "requires that the freedom of choice to marry not be restricted by invidious racial discriminations. Under our Constitution, the freedom to marry, or not marry, a person of another race resides with the individual and cannot be infringed by the State." Therefore, he concluded, "These convictions must be reversed."[33]

Free Now

A phone call brought the news. From their farm home in Bowling Green, east of Fredericksburg, Virginia, Mr. and Mrs. Loving drove north to Alexandria for a news conference at their lawyers' office. There he said, "We're just really overjoyed," and she, "I feel free now." A photographer snapped a picture, law books in the background, of two happy people sitting close together, his arm around her neck. "My wife and I plan to go ahead and build a new house now," said Richard Loving, the construction worker, about the new home in Caroline County that Richard Loving, the husband and father, wanted his family to live in.[34]

The new house, in which the Lovings' three children grew up, symbolized the family's freedom to have a permanent dwelling where they could live in peace in their home state. As Mildred Loving later put it, "The Supreme Court decision changed our life a lot. We moved our family into our community in Caroline County without fear of going to prison."[35]

Other families, too, shook free of the law of interracial marriage and could make permanent plans. According to the *Loving* decision, race would no longer be the basis for county clerks to deny applications for marriage licenses. No longer could men or women, once married—whether of European, African, or any other racial ancestry—be separated by the courts because of the racial identity of their partners in marriage. The penitentiary no longer awaited newlyweds for the crime of interracial marriage. Nowhere in the United States would such marriages be put on trial.

The major white newspapers in Virginia greeted the Supreme Court's ruling with equanimity, black newspapers with congratulations. "Anti-miscegenation laws go back three centuries," the *Virginian-Pilot,* Norfolk's white newspaper, explained in an editorial on the decision. "In the beginning their purpose was to force mulattoes into the slave system, not to prevent what white-supremacists now call 'race-mongrelization.'" One might note, of course, that the seventeenth-century laws were in fact designed to achieve both objectives, or at least to prevent "race-mongrelization" on the "white" side of the boundary.[36]

The *Virginian-Pilot* went on to prophesy that "social discouragements to mixed marriages . . . will not quickly disappear," but it also suggested that "Virginia in recent years had allowed . . . its law to lose vitality." By that it meant to say that only black-white couples like the Lovings were challenged in court, though "the restriction they defied applied also to whites and members of brown and yellow races, including Chinese and Filipinos." The paper pointed out that "Virginia was inclined to arrest only whites and Negroes, although it withheld such marital civil rights as adoption, inheritance, and divorce from other racially mixed couples as well." The editorial concluded with a celebration of sorts that the topic of interracial marriage had now "been removed, as it had to be, from the field of jurisprudence."[37]

The *Journal and Guide,* the voice of Norfolk's black community, led off its front page with the headline "Top Court Junks Marriage Bars" and ran an editorial on "Freedom of Choice at the Altar." That paper, too, predicted "no noticeable increase in the number of mixed marriages in Virginia," but it rephrased the explanation. "Prospective grooms" would continue to enjoy "the privileges of withholding their requests for the bride's hand," it said, and brides would retain "the privilege and authority to prevent mixed marriages simply by saying 'no.'"[38]

The *Journal and Guide* nonetheless insisted on the importance of the court's ruling: "What makes this Supreme Court decision so desirable is that it lifts an onerous and brutalizing stigma from Negro Virginians by knocking down that psychological barrier which, in effect, told them and the world that no Negro is good enough to be the husband or wife of a white Virginian."[39]

And it saluted the Lovings: "They have done an incalculably great service for their community, their state, and their nation. Had they been less persevering, the legal battle to end Virginia's oppression on the marital front might have been forfeited long ago."[40]

Virginia after *Loving*

A few days after the Supreme Court decision, Phil Hirschkop wrote ACLU legal director Melvin Wulf to express the two Virginia attorneys' appreciation for Wulf's "congratulations extended over the phone the other day. Lest you think our heads are getting swelled, we realize we had a good case and a good Supreme Court brief to work with."[41]

The Supreme Court decision affected many couples in many states, not only in Virginia. Bernie Cohen and Phil Hirschkop perceived, however, that the victory in the Loving case required follow-up to secure the gains. Hirschkop wanted agreement with Wulf as to whether Wulf saw any need to go "back to the three judge court for a declaratory judgment, declaring all the sections of the [Virginia] Code relating to these laws to be unconstitutional and further for injunctive relief against the state trying to enforce any of these laws." He added: "The Supreme Court said everything that apparently had to be said and I am not sure if there is any use in this further procedural step."[42]

Wulf was slow to get back to Hirschkop, who wrote again in mid-July to remind Wulf of the unanswered question of whether to go back to the three-judge court, and also to say, "Bernie and I have . . . discovered that the Clerks in the state courts are still handing out forms concerning information on getting married in Virginia [that say] that interracial marriages are prohibited. We are asking a state legislator to get an attorney general's opinion on this."[43]

Wulf got back to Hirschkop this time. "I feel as you do that it would be useless—certainly at this point—to go back to the three-judge court for enforcement." Wulf continued: "Presumably even Virginia will comply with the Supreme Court's ruling in this case, though there may be some bureaucratic lag. I think that if one or two letters to the Attorney General do not get the desired results, we could then talk about more litigation. I hope it won't be necessary."[44]

And indeed, it proved unnecessary. William R. Durland, the member of the House of Delegates to whom Hirschkop had referred, followed through on contacting the attorney general, Robert Y. Button, and Button offered his assurances. No, he answered, clerks of court could no longer refuse, on racial grounds, to issue a license to a couple who wished to enter into an interracial marriage; no, a person performing a wedding ceremony between a white person and a nonwhite could no longer be punished under Virginia law; and yes, the children of an interracial couple would now be legitimate if the marriage was otherwise valid.[45]

As for "Virginia Marriage Requirements," the official publication about which Hirschkop had expressed concern, Button stated: "While the pamphlet to which you refer may still be issued, the references contained therein to Virginia's anti-miscegenation requirements should be deleted, or the attention of the recipient drawn to the fact that the Virginia anti-miscegenation statutes have been invalidated by the decision in the *Loving* case. In future editions . . . , any reference to the requirements of the Virginia anti-miscegenation statutes should be deleted."[46]

A little later that August, Virginians were informed about "the first known partners to an interracial marriage in Virginia" since the *Loving* decision was handed down two months earlier. In a ceremony at Kingdom Hall Church, described as "a Negro Jehovah's Witnesses church" in Norfolk, a white woman, Leona Eve Boyd, married a black man, Romans Howard Johnson.[47] Thanks to the Lovings' persistence and the decision of the U.S. Supreme Court, the Johnsons had no need to leave the state to get married. Nor did they have to face the prospect of midnight arrest, felony conviction, or long-term exile. A federal court decision had forced a change in public policy in Virginia such that the Johnsons' decision, like that of the Lovings, was now a private matter.

On July 14, 1968, 13 months after the *Loving* decision, Marian E. Wright married Peter Edelman in Virginia, across the Potomac River from the District of Columbia. Edelman, a white lawyer, had served as law clerk to Supreme Court Justices Felix Frankfurter and Arthur J. Goldberg, as a special assistant at the Justice Department, and as legislative researcher and speechwriter in Robert F. Kennedy's 1964 campaign for a U.S. Senate seat from New York. Wright had been an aide to the Rev. Dr. Martin Luther King Jr., and she was the first black woman to be admitted to the practice of law in Mississippi. As Marian Wright Edelman, she later became widely known for her work with the Children's Defense Fund.[48]

Although the ceremony was bittersweet for all who attended—King and Kennedy had been assassinated only weeks before—a more graphic demonstration of how much had changed in the law of marriage could hardly be imagined.

The Law of Slavery and the Law of Freedom

Richard and Mildred Loving had a compelling case, able lawyers, and the good fortune to take their case to the U.S. Supreme Court at an auspicious time in the history of the United States. Cohen and Hirschkop made a remarkable team. Bernie Cohen—the Lovings' first lawyer after Mildred contacted the ACLU in 1963—bonded with them, found a way to breathe new life into the case, and saw it through to the end. His partner in the effort, Phil Hirschkop, who joined the effort the next year, brought experience in the federal courts, and the federal connection prodded Judge Bazile to rule on the case. Together the two young lawyers made their way through the Virginia Supreme Court and on to the U.S. Supreme Court, where both participated in the oral argument.

In addition to good timing and good lawyers, the Lovings also had the commitment to see their case through. Ten days after their ninth wedding anniversary, the Court handed them the victory they had longed for. It put an end to their banishment from Virginia and their odyssey through the judicial system. Not only could the Lovings live in Virginia without fear of prosecution for their interracial marriage, but laws similar to Virginia's fell in 15 other states as well.

In much of the nation, King Color's power to govern who might marry whom lived on in full force into the second half of the twentieth century. Everywhere in the South, in particular, miscegenation laws persisted into the 1960s. Only then, in the area of marriage and family relations, did it become true—as Justice Potter Stewart insisted in *McLaughlin* v. *Florida* and then again in *Loving* v. *Virginia*—that "the criminality of an act" could not "depend upon the race of the actor."[49] Only then could it no longer require an exercise in genealogy to scrutinize whether two people fell into the proper racial classifications that they might legally marry.

Reporting on the 1967 *Loving* decision, the *New York Times* noted its larger significance: "In writing the opinion that struck down the last group of segregation laws to remain standing—those requiring separation of the races in marriage—Chief Justice Warren completed the process that he set in motion with his opinion in 1954 that declared segregation in public schools to be unconstitutional." Bernard S. Cohen offered a similar benediction on the proceedings. At his clients' press conference, he said: "We hope we have put to rest the last vestiges of racial discrimination that were supported by the law in Virginia and all over the country."[50]

By the time the *Loving* case arrived at the Supreme Court, state action had already eliminated miscegenation laws everywhere outside the South. Maryland repealed its statute in early 1967. But until the Supreme Court's decision, miscegenation statutes persisted in all 11 states of the former Confederacy plus Delaware, Kentucky, Missouri, Oklahoma, and West Virginia.

The 1964 Civil Rights Act failed to address the matter of miscegenation laws. By 1967, state action had gone about as far as it could in removing them. In the 1960s, only the U.S. Supreme Court could take on the issue. In contrast to its approach a decade earlier, when it had ducked the *Jackson* and *Naim* cases (see chapter 12), it proved ready to address the one major area in which Jim Crow legislation lived on. A decade and more after the decisions in *Brown* v. *Board of Education,* it did what it had avoided in the 1950s. It decided to deal with the Virginia statutes, to rule against their constitutionality, and to do so in a broad rather than narrow manner. The chief justice, no doubt remembering with more clarity than comfort the Court's wish to hide from the matter early on in his tenure, observed: "This case presents a constitutional question never [previously] addressed by this Court."[51]

By the middle of 1967—one hundred years after Congress had, in effect, directed ten former Confederate states, among them Virginia, to ratify the Fourteenth Amendment—the twentieth-century case against Jim Crow had been initiated, argued, and won. The law of race and slavery, dating in Virginia from the seventeenth century, had given way to the law of freedom, and the Lovings could return home and live together in Virginia. Their banishment under Virginia law came to an end when the U.S. Supreme Court decreed that, even with regard to marriage, Jim Crow—America's apartheid—be banished from American law. After *Loving* v. *Virginia,* couples with any combination of racial identities could legally marry and live together in any state in the nation.

CHAPTER 16

AMERICA AFTER *LOVING* V. *VIRGINIA*

" . . . a sound public policy which gives to every person of age and discretion, white or black, male or female, the right of marriage to another of the same race and of the opposite sex"

—South Carolina Supreme Court (1941)

"In accordance with this clear mandate of the Supreme Court of the United States . . ."

—Oklahoma Supreme Court (1967)

Loving v. *Virginia* brought to an end several chapters in the history of the American experiment. By toppling the antimiscegenation regime, ending its long reign across much of North America, *Loving* brought the law of race more or less back to where it had been in the mid-seventeenth century—before any colonial assembly became consumed with concern about "abominable mixture and spurious issue"; before the disparate racial identities of two parents could consign a child to 30 or 31 years of servitude; before the freedom suits of the American Revolution; before the time when birth from a slave mother, whatever her racial background, could consign a child to a lifetime of slavery; before the turmoil and uncertainty that came with emancipation and Reconstruction; and before the long century from the Fourteenth Amendment to the high points of the Civil Rights Movement.

After the Supreme Court's decision in *Loving* v. *Virginia,* marriage between people of different racial identities became a private matter. At least, people who entered such marriages could no longer be prosecuted, or denied any rights as married people, for doing so. Interracial marriages could nonetheless still be page-one news. In September 1967, for example, the *Richmond Times-Dispatch* printed a front-page story that Margaret Elizabeth Rusk, daughter of

U.S. Secretary of State Dean Rusk, had married a black man, Guy Gibson Smith, in California. And in June 1968, the *Richmond News Leader* told Virginians that, in Massachusetts, Donald Hasler, "who is white," had married Remi Brooke, the mixed-race daughter of Edward W. Brooke, U.S. Senator from Massachusetts.[1]

California and Massachusetts had at one time maintained miscegenation laws, but both abandoned them well before the Supreme Court decision in the *Loving* case—California through judicial action 19 years earlier (in 1948), and Massachusetts through legislative action a century before that (in 1843). The *Loving* decision had not changed the laws of those two states. But as late as the day before the Supreme Court handed down the *Loving* decision, miscegenation laws were still on the books, and still shaped people's lives, in all 11 states of the former Confederacy plus 5 states of the Border South. Moreover, black-white couples from California or Massachusetts could not freely move to Virginia until the Lovings themselves could.

Loving had many meanings. Some were obvious from the beginning; others took a while to develop. State by state, the old laws crumbled and the old practices faded. The decision in *Loving* meant that miscegenation laws could no longer be the basis for prosecutions for marrying someone of a different racial identity; nor could they be the basis for denying an inheritance, or alimony, or death benefits.

Within a few years, local authorities ended their practice of denying marriage licenses to black-white couples. After some years, the U.S. Supreme Court applied the reasoning in *Loving* to child custody. Meanwhile, beginning in the 1970s, growing numbers of citizens sought to have courts extend *Loving* to validate same-sex marriage. *Loving* ended the three-century history of the antimiscegenation regime, and it rippled into the future with various implications for the law of marriage.

Death Benefits and the Federal Government after *Loving*

The *Loving* decision proved a godsend to people in many states. Until *Loving,* even the federal government had continued to act in accordance with state miscegenation laws. Mrs. Ida Nell Waters, a black woman, discovered this in the 1960s when her husband, a white man, died while on active duty with the U.S. Army. The couple had been married in Texas. When the widow sought death benefits, the U.S. Comptroller General denied her application on the basis that, given the Texas miscegenation statute, the couple had no valid marriage.[2]

But in light of *Loving,* the comptroller's office reversed its previous ruling and approved the payment of death benefits to Mrs. Waters. The ACLU, expressing its "outrage" in 1967 at such blatant discrimination by an agency of the federal government, sought an executive order from President Lyndon B. Johnson against such behavior as the Comptroller General had displayed.[3] Perhaps there were other such wrongs to be righted.

In an explanation of its earlier stance, the Comptroller General noted that, "in the absence of a controlling judicial decision holding the state anti-miscegenation statute to be invalid, we 'should make no determination as to the validity of Private Waters' marriage.'" (Of course, the government did in fact make just such a determination—that the marriage had no validity.) The agency explained that "the validity of the payments involved" depended on his marital status, and in view of the Texas statute "the matter of such status was held to be too doubtful to warrant the authorization of such payments."[4]

Mrs. Waters obtained a widow's death benefits from the federal government. The Lovings could live together in Virginia, and the newlywed Smith and Hasler couples could move there if they wished. Yet remnants of the old laws remained.

Postscript in Delaware

The decision in *Loving* made many marriages possible that would otherwise have been out of the question, and it changed the outcomes in some proceedings already in the courts. For example, it had an immediate impact on the law of marriage in Delaware. There, William Wesley Davis, a "Negro" under Delaware law, and Sandra Jean Drummond, a "white person," wanted to marry each other. On March 21, 1967, they had gone to the office of Mabel V. Roman Gately, the New Castle County clerk of the peace, to obtain a marriage license but were turned down "solely because of race."[5]

That same month, Davis and Drummond took their case to federal court. Race was the only impediment, Gately later testified, but it was "the invariable practice of her office" to reject applications from black-white couples. In this, she and her staff may, or may not, have been acting out their private sensibilities. Regardless, the same law that prohibited an African American from marrying a white, under pain of a $100 fine, also imposed a $100 fine for anyone who issued a marriage license to a black-white couple.[6]

The three-judge federal court handed down its decision in *Davis* v. *Gately* on June 26, two weeks after the Supreme Court's decision in *Loving* v. *Virginia*. "Any issue as to the violation of the prohibitions of the Fourteenth Amendment" by Delaware's miscegenation provisions, the court ruled, "is settled beyond question and in the plaintiffs' favor by the decision of the Supreme Court" in the *Loving* case. The Virginia miscegenation law that had been successfully challenged in *Loving* was, to all intents and purposes, identical to the Delaware law under review in *Davis* in that it sought "to prohibit marriage and its consummation on the grounds of race alone." The court held: "The ruling of the Supreme Court clears the board of all racial barriers to marriage."[7]

Postscript in Alabama

Authorities in Alabama demonstrated that, notwithstanding *Loving,* legal challenges to interracial marriages might not yet be over in the South. At the time of the Lovings' victory, their lawyer Philip J. Hirschkop had characterized the high court's decision as "very broad" and "reaching all such laws in other states."[8] Nonetheless, on November 10, 1970, Army Sgt. Louis Voyer, a 21-year-old Vietnam veteran and Massachusetts native, went with Phyllis Bett, his Alabama-born 17-year-old fiancée, before G. Clyde Brittain, probate judge of Calhoun County, Alabama, to obtain a marriage license.

Judge Brittain balked. The couple claimed that he refused on the grounds that Alabama law prohibited the issuance of a marriage license when one party was white, as was Sgt. Voyer, and the other black, as was Miss Bett.[9] Alabama law still made it a felony for them to marry and a misdemeanor for any judge to issue a license in such a situation. The judge, declining to take his chances with an indictment for issuing a marriage license, ended up in court for his failure to issue one.

In the interests of American military policy, the Nixon administration sued the state of Alabama and Judge Brittain. Three and a half years after the *Loving* decision had been handed down, U.S. Attorney General John N. Mitchell sought to have those Alabama statutes, as well as the provision of the state constitution outlawing interracial marriages, declared void in light of *Loving* v. *Virginia* and to have the judge and the state blocked from enforcing such laws. A deputy assistant attorney general of Alabama, John Bookout, for his part, claimed that he considered the Alabama laws still valid regardless of *Loving.* "When the U.S. Supreme Court rules in a case," he declared, "it is binding on people in that particular case. The Alabama law is still law until it is stricken down. They don't just wipe these laws off the book all over the United States because of one ruling."[10]

U.S. District Judge Sam C. Pointer obliged both sides by striking down the Alabama laws. And he gave short shrift to a motion filed by the state to dismiss the case on the basis that the couple had already gone to Clarksville, Tennessee, to get married; otherwise, they might still be liable to criminal prosecution when they returned to live as husband and wife in Alabama so that Sgt. Voyer could fulfill his military obligations at Fort McClellan.[11]

Shortly before Louis Voyer and Phyllis Bett sought a court order so that they could be legally married in Alabama, Johnny L. Ford and Frances Baldwin Rainer had succeeded without challenge. But the thought had troubled Ford: "Oh, man—a mixed marriage in the South? In the Alabama Black Belt? I got to be crazy." But then he and she decided to go ahead. Thus in September 1972, when Ford was elected the first black mayor of the town of Tuskegee, his white wife and their infant son joined in the celebration.[12]

Louisiana, Florida, Arkansas, Mississippi, and Georgia

Although the *Loving* decision struck down miscegenation statutes in Virginia and 15 other states, something very much like the Alabama story unfolded elsewhere, too. In many of those 16 states, legal action was required before an interracial couple could get a marriage license.

Louisiana went quickly but not quietly. John Stephen Ziffert, a white man, and Carol Ann Prejean, an African American, were rebuffed in their effort to get a marriage license in Landry Parish. They went to federal district court, and on August 9, 1967, on the basis of the *Loving* decision, the Louisiana miscegenation statute was overturned on equal protection grounds. Landry parish clerk of court Harold J. Sylvester was ordered to issue the license if the applicants met all other Louisiana requirements, and the state attorney general, Jack P. Gremillion, was directed to cease all efforts to enforce the invalidated law.[13]

In Florida, too, an interracial couple had to file suit in court just to obtain a marriage license. James Van Hook, who was black, and Liane Peters, who was white, took their case to the Florida Supreme Court. There a 5–2 decision in 1968—two justices conceded nothing to *Loving*—noted that the U.S. Supreme Court had invalidated laws like Florida's, which could therefore no longer be enforced. The couple returned on February 1 to the Dade County Court in Miami, where they had failed in their quest back in November, and this time their application was accepted.[14]

Later in 1968, Michael Higgins and Susan Lane, he black and she white, had a similar experience in Arkansas. R. S. Peters, the clerk of Pulaski County, refused them a marriage license, citing a state law dating from 1838. The couple took their case to federal district court in Little Rock, where Judge J. Smith Henley declared the law unconstitutional and enjoined the Pulaski County clerk from continuing to act as though the ancient prohibition remained good law.[15]

In the summer of 1970, the Civil Rights Movement spawned an interracial marriage in Mississippi, described at the time as the first in the modern era there and "toppling a legal barrier" that had stood since the nineteenth century. Roger Mills and Berta Linson tried to get a marriage license in Jackson, where both of them worked in a law office for the NAACP Legal Defense and Educational Fund. He, a 24-year-old white man, was a conscientious objector who had taken time away from law school to help the black freedom movement, and she, a 21-year-old black student at Jackson State College, worked as a file clerk.[16]

The county official accepted their application, but, during the three-day waiting period before the license could be issued, a white supremacist group that styled itself the Southern National Party obtained an injunction from a state judge against issuing the license. The couple appealed in state court, to no avail, and then went to U.S. District Judge Harold Cox. Cox balked, but the Fifth Circuit Court of Appeals leaned on him to order that the license be issued. All of this activity took two weeks. A white clergyman, heralding the marriage as "being born in the movement," performed the August 2 ceremony at a black church in Jackson. After the wedding, the groom's father observed, "I'm quite sure they will have a difficult time. . . . But if it is a good marriage, it will take." The bride's father said, "It's something I never expected. I hope it works out," and her mother echoed the thought, "I think it was beautiful. . . . I hope it works out."[17]

In 1971, a white soldier stationed at Fort Benning, Georgia, tried to marry a black woman from Georgia, but the local judge refused to issue a marriage license. The Georgia law was still on the books, and the judge was determined to comply with it. The couple persisted. Just before Valentine's Day in 1972, U.S. District Judge Albert J. Henderson ruled the statute unconstitutional and ordered state officials to stop enforcing it.[18]

In state after state, couples walked through the doorway that, with the crucial assistance of the U.S. Supreme Court, the Lovings had opened. At some point in the late 1960s or early 1970s, interracial couples could go to a county clerk to get a marriage license without having to go to a higher court to override the local official's balkiness—and without having to worry about going to prison later for breaking a law that made their marriage a felony. Generations after the original enactment of miscegenation laws, racial identity had finally lost its power under the law to sort out who could marry whom. As in the case of Ida Nell Waters, money matters were affected, too.

After *Loving*: Race and Inheritance in Oklahoma

Martin Dick died in 1959 and left no will. Curtis Dick, who was named administrator of his father's estate, claimed to be his son and only heir, but others challenged his claim. Twenty years earlier, in January 1939, Martin Dick had married Nicey Noel. Already, he had a son, Curtis, and she had two daughters. By 1959, one of those daughters had died but left a daughter of her own. Nicey

Noel Dick survived Martin Dick and, as his surviving spouse, should have inherited half the estate—but then she died, also without a will. The other daughter survived her, as did the granddaughter. As Nicey Noel Dick's only surviving heirs, they each claimed a quarter share of Martin Dick's estate.[19]

Curtis Dick had no intentions of sharing his father's estate with relatives he had acquired through his father's marriage, and Oklahoma law appeared to be on his side. For the next few years, he jousted with his rivals in court. Curtis Dick declared that—unlike his father, who was Chickasaw Indian—Nicey Noel Dick was "a Negro, . . . a person of African descent."[20] Under Oklahoma's miscegenation statute, according to Curtis Dick, Martin Dick was white, "not of African descent." Since someone "of African descent" could not marry someone who was not, Martin Dick and Nicey Noel Dick had no valid marriage, and she could not have claimed, as his widow, to inherit his property, nor could her children or grandchildren claim to be his heirs unless he had left a will that named them.

Rebuffed in his efforts, Curtis Dick took his case to the Oklahoma Supreme Court, where he insisted, as he had all along, that under Oklahoma law his father was white and could not have contracted a valid marriage with Nicey Noel Dick. His rivals for half the estate insisted instead that, like Nicey Noel Dick, Martin Dick was—by a tiny fraction—"of African descent," and thus the marriage was valid. Moreover, challenging the constitutionality of Oklahoma's law against interracial marriage, they claimed that no valid law could, on grounds of race, prevent Nicey Noel from marrying Martin Dick. Apply the law of racial identity, they were saying, and we have to prevail. Throw that law out, and we have to prevail.

The Oklahoma Supreme Court handed down its decision on July 10, 1967, just four weeks after the U.S. Supreme Court's ruling in the *Loving* case. The state court acknowledged that, in view of *Loving,* "we feel compelled" to "review the long standing view of this Court" that miscegenation statutes were valid. After quoting at length from the *Loving* decision, Justice Ben T. Williams concluded: "In accordance with this clear mandate of the Supreme Court of the United States, we hereby hold" the Oklahoma miscegenation statutes to violate the Fourteenth Amendment's equal protection and due process clauses, and we "expressly overrule all prior decisions of this Court to the contrary." A unanimous Oklahoma Supreme Court ruled that "the marriage of Martin Dick and Nicey Noel Dick was valid, regardless of the racial ancestry of either party to the marriage."[21]

Curtis Dick might have won or lost his case on racial grounds. Oklahoma's law of inheritance was clear enough, but until the *Loving* decision changed the rules, the racial identities of the people involved in the marriage had to be resolved before the law could be applied. Once racial identity lost its bearing on the case, Curtis Dick could only lose. No longer did it matter, for purposes of resolving such conflicts in the courts, whether one partner to a supposed marriage had been "of African descent" and the other partner not. No longer did it matter whether Native Americans were considered under state law to be white, or at least not black. Beginning in 1967, 60 years after Oklahoma became a state, a marriage was valid "regardless of the racial ancestry of either party" to it.

After *Loving:* Race, Marriage, and the Law of Custody

Whatever *Loving* v. *Virginia* appeared to say about race, marriage, and the family, some people—quite aside from those seeking marriage licenses— found that *Loving* did not guarantee that racial considerations would not reach into the law of family affairs. Into the 1970s and 1980s, especially in the South, a white woman, if she was divorced and had been awarded custody of her children, jeopardized that custody arrangement if she subsequently married a black man.[22]

In Florida, Linda Sidoti and Anthony J. Sidoti got a divorce in May 1980, and she gained custody of their three-year old daughter, Melanie. In September 1981, however, the father filed for custody because of "changed conditions"— the mother was living with Clarence Palmore Jr., a black man, whom she married in November that year.[23]

The trial court ruled that the mother had "chosen for herself and for her child, a life-style unacceptable to the father and to society." The court conceded, "The father's evident resentment of the mother's choice of a black partner is not sufficient to wrest custody from the mother," but it went on to say, "It is of some significance, however, that the mother did see fit to bring a man into her home and carry on a sexual relationship with him without being married to him. Such action tended to place gratification of her own desires ahead of her concern for the child's future welfare." Then it veered off to state that, "despite the strides that have been made in bettering relations between the races in this country," Melanie would, when she started school—if she remained in her current situation—suffer from a stigma attached to her mother's choice in a husband.[24] Race ruled.

Linda Sidoti Palmore challenged the decision. The case went to the Second District Court of Appeals, which, without a written opinion, affirmed the lower court decision. She appealed to the U.S. Supreme Court, and the Court heard her case.

Chief Justice Warren Burger wrote for a unanimous Court. "The judgment of a state court determining or reviewing a child custody decision is not ordinarily a likely candidate for review by this Court," he conceded. But this case demanded the Court's attention. Burger dryly noted how the trial court had declared that the "father's evident resentment" was not enough to change the custody arrangement—and then had expressed concern about the very racial environment to which the father objected: "This raises important federal concerns arising from the Constitution's commitment to eradicating discrimination based on race." The lower court, wrote Burger,

> correctly stated that the child's welfare was the controlling factor. But that court was entirely candid and made no effort to place its findings on any ground other than race. Taking the court's findings and rationale at face value, it is clear that the outcome would have been different had petitioner married a Caucasian male of similar respectability.[25]

So the Supreme Court addressed what it saw as the constitutional question at the core of the matter. The Fourteenth Amendment had as one of its central purposes, Burger said, doing "away with all governmentally imposed discrimination based on race," and the Court cited *McLaughlin* v. *Florida* and *Loving* v. *Virginia*. Yes, prejudices persisted, and that meant "a risk that a child living with a stepparent of a different race may be subject to a variety of pressures and stresses not present if the child were living with parents of the same racial or ethnic origin." But that was not the governing question: "The Constitution cannot control such prejudices but neither can it tolerate them," said the Court. "Private biases may be outside the reach of the law, but the law cannot, directly or indirectly, give them effect."[26]

"Whatever problems racially mixed households may pose for children in 1984," declared Burger, such considerations could not govern the case of little Melanie Sidoti: "The effects of racial prejudice, however real, cannot justify a racial classification removing an infant child from the custody of its natural mother found to be an appropriate person to have such custody." The nation's highest court reversed the trial court and awarded custody back to the mother.[27]

Just as the Court had departed in *Loving* from its traditional refusal to deal with matters of marriage, in *Palmore* it found it necessary to depart in a custody dispute. Racial considerations led the Supreme Court to intervene in a matter that was normally—and had long been exclusively—handled by state courts. The decision in *Loving* was extended to overrule a custody decision and give Melanie back to her mother.

By the 1960s, the Supreme Court had come to view race as a particularly suspect category of analysis. Yet the Sidoti case more than a decade later offered dramatic evidence that race had not gone away as a consideration, even a controlling consideration, in the law of marriage. True, Linda Sidoti Palmore regained legal custody of little Melanie. To win, however, she had to engage in a legal battle, and she had to fight it all the way to the Supreme Court.

Loving and Same-Sex Marriage, 1970–2000

The Supreme Court declared in 1967 that racial identity under the law could not prevent people from making a free choice in their marriage partners. In effect, the high court accepted—and applied across the nation—a statement in 1948 by Justice Jesse Carter of the California Supreme Court in *Perez* v. *Sharp:* "If the right to marry is a fundamental right, then it must be conceded that an infringement of that right by means of a racial restriction is an unlawful infringement of one's liberty."[28]

But what about other kinds of laws, other restrictions than racial ones—laws that restricted siblings, for example, from marrying, or laws that limited people to one marriage at a time, or laws that recognized only marriages between a man and a woman but not between two people of the same sex? Where would it end? Where exactly should it end?

Loving v. *Virginia* was about race, privacy, and the right to marry. Could—should—privacy and the right to marry be detached from the racial element? Should the right to privacy and the right of marriage be extended to same-sex sexual and marital relations? In the aftermath of *Loving,* that question was asked with increasing frequency and insistence. To decide *Loving* the way it had, the Supreme Court had to untie racial considerations from other legal barriers to marriage. The proponents of legalizing same-sex marriage wanted to bundle them back together—or, rather, raise gender considerations to the same privileged level that racial identity had achieved in the law of marriage.

In 1941, the South Carolina Supreme Court spoke, with emphatic approval, of "a sound public policy which gives to every person of age and discretion, white or black, male or female, the right of marriage to another of the same race and of the opposite sex." *Loving* terminated the restriction regarding "the same race," but it left in place the one about "the opposite sex." Successful on the racial front, it spawned challenges on the gender front. In 1970, President Richard M. Nixon responded to the notion of same-sex marriage, "I can't go that far—That's the year 2000. Negroes [and whites]—OK; but that's too far."[29]

Into the 1970s—while some courts in the South were still doing mop-up work to see that *Loving* was recognized as the law of the land in matters of race and marriage—people began to call upon *Loving* in same-sex cases. Even as some interracial couples continued to work to secure the benefits of the *Loving* decision in their own lives, so that their racial identities would not prove an obstacle to their forming a family, other Americans went to court to obtain rulings that might apply *Loving* in such a way as to permit same-sex marriages.

In Hennepin County, Minnesota, Richard John Baker and James Michael McConnell applied for a marriage license in 1970 and were turned down by the clerk, Gerald R. Nelson. They went to court, lost at trial, and lost on appeal. *Loving* v. *Virginia,* the Minnesota Supreme Court ruled, could not support the pair's case, for what had been thrown out was a law that embodied "patent racial discrimination." Rather than say that "all state restrictions upon the right to marry are beyond the reach of the Fourteenth Amendment," the court concluded, *Loving* had left room for "a clear distinction between a marital restriction based merely upon race and one based upon the fundamental difference in sex." The doctrine in *Maynard* v. *Hill* (1888) remained in effect, in other words, and a state's traditional authority over marriage remained in place—aside from placing restrictions based on racial identity. Other efforts met the same fate—in Kentucky in 1973, Washington State in 1974, Pennsylvania in 1984.[30]

In the 1990s, although the *Loving* decision was referred to in a great many law review articles and other publications, their authors had, as a rule, little if any interest in race, and addressed instead the legal standing of same-sex marriage.[31] Renewed efforts in the courts took a different path than in the 1970s, relying this time on state constitutional provisions, and those efforts showed promise of succeeding. Hawaii, Alaska, and Vermont all moved, at least briefly, toward validating same-sex marriages. In each case, a court decision construed the state constitution in a manner that required access to marriage, or benefits for same-sex partners, equal to those of their heterosexual counterparts.

Hawaii moved first, in 1993—and attracted enormous attention for several years, by opponents as well as proponents of same-sex marriage—followed by Alaska in 1998 and Vermont in 1999. Most of the change was turned back. On election day 1998, in both Hawaii and Alaska, voters amended their state constitutions to negate the basis on which state courts had ruled in favor of same-sex marriage.[32]

On election day 2000, Alabama voters removed from their state constitution the ancient prohibition against interracial marriage. Alabama was the last state to do so. On the same day, November 7, voters in Nebraska put into their state constitution a ban against recognizing same-sex marriage, and voters in Nevada did the same. Unlike Hawaii and Alaska, which had been responding to developments in their own states, Nebraska and Nevada were taking preventive measures. Meanwhile, moreover, in 1996, a federal Defense of Marriage Act (DOMA) had become law. DOMA defined marriage as a relationship involving a man and a woman, and it assured states that they did not need to recognize out-of-state same-sex marriages. On yet another front, a proposed amendment—shades of Congressman Roddenbery's effort back in 1912—would have placed such language in the U.S. Constitution.[33]

Same-Sex "Civil Unions" in Vermont

Nina Beck and Stacy Jolles were a couple, and as a couple they wished to marry, yet because both of them were female, they could neither get a license to marry in Vermont nor obtain whatever benefits were conferred on married people. They went to state court, where they argued that the Vermont state constitution's common benefits clause required that they be granted the recognition and benefits that they sought. That clause declared that "government is, or ought to be, instituted for the common benefit, protection, and security of the people, nation, or community, and not for the particular . . . advantage of any single person, family, or set of persons, who are a part only of that community."[34]

The trial court was unimpressed with the argument. Vermont's marriage statutes were not intended to cover same-sex couples, it ruled, and they were constitutional in their limited reach because they furthered a legitimate state interest in fostering "the link between procreation and child rearing."[35]

Together with two other Vermont same-sex couples—Lois Farnham and Holly Puterbaugh as well as Stan Baker and Peter Harrigan—Beck and Jolles carried the case to the Vermont Supreme Court. In oral argument on November 18, 1999, their attorney, Beth Robinson, pointed toward the pathbreaking *Perez* v. *Sharp* decision (1948) in the California Supreme Court a half-century earlier, in which California's miscegenation law was overturned. That decision "was controversial, it was courageous and it was correct," she told the Vermont court, which, she argued, should follow California's lead and apply the same reasoning to the matters under dispute.[36]

Also during oral argument, Justice Denise R. Johnson pointed out to Eve Jacobs-Carnahan, the attorney for the state, that, under Vermont law as currently construed, "A man can't marry another man because he's a man." "Why," she wanted to know, "isn't that gender discrimination?" Then, harking back to language in *Perez* v. *Sharp* as well as *Loving* v. *Virginia,* the justice asked, wasn't marriage "a fundamental right"? Jacobs-Carnahan, relying on a more narrow approach consistent with that taken by the U.S. Supreme Court in *Pace* v. *Alabama* (1883), replied, "Yes, but it's a fundamental right between a man and a woman."[37]

The court had read the briefs, heard the arguments. How would it rule? And when? In the meantime, Holly Puterbaugh exclaimed about herself and Lois Farnham that, if the court ruled in their favor, "I guarantee you we'll make a beeline back to the town clerk's office."[38] Scarcely a month passed, and the decision came down.

On December 20, 1999, the court ruled in their favor, quoting the U.S. Supreme Court in *Loving* v. *Virginia* that "the freedom to marry has long been recognized as one of the vital personal rights." The court began its opinion in

Baker v. *State* with a question: "May the State of Vermont exclude same-sex couples from the benefits and protections that its laws provide to opposite-sex married couples?" Given the justices' understanding of the common benefits clause of the state constitution, the answer had to be no: "We hold that the State is constitutionally required to extend to same-sex couples the common benefits and protections that flow from marriage under Vermont law."[39]

The Vermont legislature would have to act in a manner consistent with the court's ruling, though the court left the specifics up to legislative discretion: "Whether this ultimately takes the form of inclusion within the marriage laws themselves or a parallel 'domestic partnership' system . . . rests with the Legislature." Regardless, said the court, all Vermonters must receive the same "benefit, protection, and security" from their state government. The 1857 *Dred Scott* decision had long since been overruled in matters of race and slavery, observed the Vermont court.[40] Perhaps, the court suggested, a similar sea change was overdue in matters of gender and marriage.

Early in the year 2000, the Vermont legislature passed, and the governor signed, a bill to establish a category called "civil union" that would give, under state law, all the benefits of marriage to same-sex couples that heterosexual married couples enjoyed. In Brattleboro, town clerk Annette Cappy opened her office at midnight on July 1, the moment the new law went into effect. Kathleen Peterson and Carolyn Conrad took out a license, handed it to a justice of the peace, and became the first couple to be recognized as civil union partners under the new law. After the ceremony, Conrad exclaimed, "This is more than I ever thought I'd see in my lifetime."[41]

Across the state, the initial signals were mixed. On the same day, in South Burlington, Holly Puterbaugh and Lois Farnham also picked up a license. In Tunbridge, by contrast, Kathleen Welch, refusing to issue such licenses, resigned her post as assistant town clerk rather than go against her conscience. Her boss quit, too. Welch explained, "It's immoral."[42]

The only openly gay member of the Vermont legislature, William Lippert Jr., exulted, "It's exciting to look ahead and realize that young people growing up now will have a new model of what's possible in terms of committed and loving relationships between two members of the same sex." "After July 1, 2000," he went on, "things will never be the same." One of his colleagues in the state legislature, Nancy Shelton, by contrast, had formed a political action committee to defeat legislators who voted for the bill. In a statement that, in reverse, mirrored Carolyn Conrad's celebration of the significance of the day's events, Nancy Shelton vented her disapproval: "I never thought this would happen in my state." She explained, "As a Christian woman, I believe this is really an abomination to God."[43]

From the perspective of either side in the continuing controversy, much had changed. Much, however, had not. Declan Buckley and Kevin Gato knew that, whatever the legal status they obtained in Vermont through their ceremony in Hartland that day, it—and any tangible benefits it conferred—vanished when they crossed the state line on their way back into neighboring New Hampshire. Thomas Lang and Alexander Westerhoff, dealers in antiques in another adjacent state, Massachusetts, recognized the same limits on the civil union they nonetheless celebrated in Brattleboro that first possible day.[44]

Each same-sex couple was celebrating a "civil union," not a marriage. The newly validated relationship carried no benefits under federal law, including any federal tax advantages (or, for that matter, the so-called marriage penalty). Moreover, federal law had already declared that no state had to recognize such relationships, and any number of states had declared their intent to confer no recognition of same-sex marriages, no matter what they were called. The history of miscegenation laws demonstrated that the full faith and credit clause offered no reliable basis for a couple's claim to transport a marriage from one state to another.[45]

Aside from racial identity, marriage law remained largely a matter of state constitutions and state statutes. As for same-sex marriage, an experiment was clearly under way in one state, although Vermont might change its constitution and thereby undo what had been initiated there.[46] Either way, traditional barriers to same-sex marriages had become a matter of public debate.[47]

Race, Law, and Marriage after Loving

Chief Justice Earl Warren and his colleagues on the U.S. Supreme Court in 1967 spoke confidently about equal protection, due process, a right to privacy, and the right to marry. In doing so, they had in mind bringing down the racial barriers to the right of two people who loved each other to enter into a heterosexual marriage.

The decision had great impact, very soon, on countless Americans. William Wesley Davis and Sandra Jean Drummond obtained a marriage license in Delaware, as did Roger Mills and Berta Linson in Mississippi. Ida Nell Waters obtained death benefits regardless of her racial identity or that of her late husband. In Oklahoma, Curtis Dick had to share an inheritance. So decisive was Loving v. Virginia, the complex of questions regarding race and marriage that the decision addressed soon vanished as a significant policy issue.

Loving settled many matters. It established a new racial regime across the nation. Heterosexual couples, regardless of their racial identities, could marry in any state in the Union and move to any other state, impeded by no law of race and marriage. In *Loving*'s wake, however, new questions about the law of marriage arose—and, of course, questions and issues regarding racial identity persisted, though they might take new forms. *Loving* v. *Virginia* closed some chapters in the story of America. It also opened new chapters.

THE COLOR OF LOVE AFTER *LOVING*

"All we ever wanted was to get married, because we loved each other"

—Mildred D. Loving (1994)

In the late 1990s, the state constitutions of Alabama and South Carolina still had provisions banning interracial marriages, and efforts were underway to remove them. South Carolina's fell in 1998, and the last of them, Alabama's, was finally removed by the voters in November 2000. Though no longer enforceable, such fossils served as reminders of a time, not so long ago, when a person could be arrested for marrying someone who had a different racial identity.

When the new Fourteenth Amendment of the 1960s reached marriage, consider what had changed over the century since the 1860s. During the era of Reconstruction, some trial or appellate judges—in Indiana and Alabama, for example—thought that the Civil Rights Act of 1866, followed by the Fourteenth Amendment, had brought an end to the patchwork regime under which states could outlaw marriage between two people on the basis of their racial identities. By the 1880s, particularly after the Supreme Court's decision in *Pace* v. *Alabama* (1883), it became clear that such was not the case. The patchwork continued, and the Supreme Court made it clear in *Maynard* v. *Hill* (1888) that matters of marriage lay outside the purview of federal courts.

The twentieth century brought other possibilities. Congressman Seaborn Anderson Roddenbery's proposed constitutional amendment in 1912 conjured visions of a nation in which federal law banned black-white marriages everywhere. It did not pass in Congress, let alone achieve ratification, however, and mounting evidence revealed that Roddenbery's proposal marked the crest of the antimiscegenation crusade—despite the addition of Filipinos as another group barred from marrying "white" people in four states as late as the 1930s. By 1948, when California's Supreme Court overturned that state's law against interracial marriage, the antimiscegenation regime was in retreat, though only outside the South. The retreat was entirely in terms of state law. There seemed no greater likelihood of a national law of interracial marriage then than at any previous time.

As the Civil Rights Act of 1866 and the Fourteenth Amendment approached their one hundredth birthdays, however, the U.S. Supreme Court turned its attention to matters of race and marriage. After ducking two miscegenation cases in the mid-1950s, the Supreme Court in 1964 overturned a Florida miscegenation law in a criminal case that did not directly address marriage. Three years later, the Court handed down its decision in *Loving* v. *Virginia,* and the antimiscegenation regime had been toppled at last.

Beginning in 1967, for the first time in the nation's history, there was a uniform law of marriage as it related to race. In contrast to Congressman Roddenbery's proposal in 1912, the new uniform law prevented rather than required a ban on interracial marriage. Social and cultural factors would still weigh in as to whether people even met and how they evaluated prospective marriage partners; family preferences and religion would continue to influence people's decisions, as would where one lived, went to school, and worked. But law no longer governed that most personal of choices.

The Lovings may well have been the last couple in the United States to go on trial under a miscegenation law. The Supreme Court decision in their case was designed to guarantee that no subsequent couple would face the ordeal of arrest, conviction, and imprisonment or exile that the Lovings had endured as a consequence of the racial identity of the person each had chosen for a marriage partner. The *Palmore* case (see chapter 16), however, in its trial-level application to matters of child custody, demonstrated that race could still play a key role in the law of marriage. The Supreme Court turned that decision back, to be sure, yet the fact that it had occasion to do so revealed that race had hardly vanished as a consideration in family law, even if nobody could any longer be prosecuted for the crime of contracting an interracial marriage.

Even as the implications of the *Loving* decision worked their way through American life and law, it became increasingly evident that race worked in very different ways in the late twentieth century than it had across the years of the antimiscegenation regime, from the 1660s to the 1960s. The binary world of black and white made less and less sense to most Americans, in part because so many people were neither black nor white. A growing number had immigrated from Asia or were the children or grandchildren of people who had. And a growing number claimed a mixed racial ancestry—they rejected the view of a binary world along with all demands that they be defined within it.

Multiracial America—and Multiracial Americans

Tiger Woods, who at the dawn of the twenty-first century is the planet's best golfer and one of the most famous and wealthy athletes, is black, or Negro, or African American—if the world is binary and if one must be either black or white. He has called himself "Cablinasian." The back half of this term, a word that he contrived, refers to his mother, who, a native of Thailand, is of "Asian" ancestry. The first half of the word contains two letters each to refer to his Caucasian, black, and Indian ancestry. Descended from residents of Asia, Africa, Europe, and Native America, he is clearly black, but only partly black, and mostly not black.

Some people who identify themselves as African Americans object that Tiger Woods rejects those binary terms. Why, they demand to know, when an American of African ancestry achieves great prominence, does he insist on escaping his roots. He might respond, of course, that he is recognizing all of his ancestral past, instead of just one portion—and that he is resisting the authority of anyone else to tell him his racial identity.

The anxiety in black America stems, nonetheless, from a three-fold realization that racial identity has long mattered a great deal, that a black identity has been the object of enormous discrimination, and that—to the extent that some people escape the "one-drop rule" of black racial identity or even the "nonwhite" category entirely—those who remain identified as black face an uncertain future in a largely non-black nation. Surely that has something to do with black opposition to a related phenomenon, the adoption of African American children by parents with other racial identities.

For all the talk about how the United States is in the process of becoming majority-minority, with whites a numerical minority, there are no guarantees. People who are not Caucasian—but also not African American—are as likely to end up taking on an all-purpose white identity as they are a pan-nonwhite one.[1] Oklahoma's racial categories from 1907 to 1967 point the way. There—under the law, whatever the case in the local culture or the wider world—people were either "of African ancestry" or they were "not," and if they were not, then they were "white."

In 1995, a book appeared with the title *How the Irish Became White*. It was soon followed by *How Jews Became White Folks,* and at that point one could readily predict that *How the Italians Became White* would soon appear as well.[2] Moreover, one could anticipate the distinct possibility that, somewhere down the road—and perhaps not so very far—bookstores might stock titles like *How the Chinese Became White* and *How the Japanese Became White*. African Americans, who as a group had supplied "white" Americans with a reference point for three centuries and more, were the group least likely to shed that function in American society and appear in a book with the title *How Black Became White*.

Law in the United States has long grappled with two awkward facts. One is that not all residents have had European ancestry; many, at least for a considerable time, had only African ancestors, and many whites displayed a powerful need to distinguish between the two groups. Another is that it proved challenging to distinguish clearly between any such two groups. Many people had both European and African antecedents, and, no matter what rule was applied to them, some could not be readily classified in either category. Moreover, some saw their classification change or at least come under challenge. As has been demonstrated in many court cases throughout this book, individuals could lose their liberty, or at least much of their property, if the law determined that they were of one racial category rather than another. Much was at stake, for the partners to a marriage and for their children.

In the world of the twenty-first century—a generation and more after *Loving*—less is at stake, but much can still ride on racial identity. Even where no law intrudes to deny a marriage license, or to convict a couple of a felony for entering into an interracial marriage, people's identities are often still at issue, in their own minds and in the minds of others. As long as boundaries remain between one racial identity and another, wherever such a boundary may lie, much remains open to dispute.

This is America. You can be anyone you want to be. At least, that is far more true after *Loving* than it was before. The notion of changeability has come to apply more to race than it long did, so racial identity is more like religion, occupation, and place of residence—more subject to individual choice. Yet it is generally far, of course, from simply a matter of individual choice. And in any case, how to identify oneself when a simple category is demanded and none seems to apply? Finding a solution to this question, many people have come to call themselves "biracial" or "multiracial."[3]

A notable genre of late-twentieth century writing has produced a collection of striking memoirs, autobiographies, and commentaries that address the experiences of mixed-race Americans. These include James McBride's bestselling *The Color of Water: A Black Man's Tribute to His White Mother* (1996). The authors of some of these books are people whose parents have differing racial identities, while others recount how they are the descendants of a long-ago mixed-race marriage or other relationship.[4]

"All We Ever Wanted Was To Get Married": The Lovings after *Loving*

The Lovings' three children, as they entered the twenty-first century, carried within them the genetic ingredients of all three "races" of seventeenth-century Virginia, a world that preceded the Virginia colonial assembly's adoption of language about "abominable mixture" and "spurious issue." They each had one or more of their own children. The descendants of Africa, Europe, and the Americas lived on, even in the same person.

All three children grew up and made their way out into a world that, in some respects, was strikingly different than the one their parents had experienced in the realm of race and law and love. Peggy, the youngest and fairest in feature, has celebrated her parents' successful struggle to achieve for themselves the right to choose a marriage partner. She attributed to that struggle her own ability to marry another mixed-race person. She was certainly right when she said, "Their struggle gave me the opportunity to marry who I wanted." Yet there was an ambiguity, in that, by law (at least in Virginia), she would have been black ("colored") in the world before *Loving,* and so would her husband, so they could have legally married there under the old rules, though the relative indeterminacy of her own racial identity might have left them both ripe for prosecution somewhere, sometime. Her self-designated racial identity, "mixed-race," was a post-*Loving* phenomenon. It was available to her precisely because of the breakthrough court case her parents won.[5]

The middle child, Donald, married a woman to all appearances white, and theirs is an evidently white family, though he brings African ancestry—and Native American, too—to the mix. The oldest child, Sidney—the darkest, the one whose color most approximated their mother's—had the least space to find any racial identity other than black, a definition that itself, however, was different in the post-*Loving* world from what it had been when Mrs. Loving was growing up black or Negro or colored.

Freedom regarding marriage and racial identity narrowed in the second half of the seventeenth century, and it broadened again in the second half of the twentieth. For the Loving children, and for the generation that followed them, the law no longer regulated marriage according to racial identity. The couple who wanted to be Mr. and Mrs. Loving—and to live free and in Virginia—had brought the case that put an end to the antimiscegenation regime. Their daughter has said, "I believe that's what they were put here on earth to do."[6]

As for Mildred Loving, she remained as private as possible and continued to shun the publicity that came with the events stretching from her arrest in 1958 to the Supreme Court decision in 1967. As she told an interviewer in 1994—some years after her husband's death and 36 years after the wedding that had proved so disruptive as well as fulfilling: "We weren't bothering anyone. And if we hurt some people's feelings, that was just too bad. All we ever wanted was to get married, because we loved each other." She observed, "I married the only man I had ever loved, and I'm happy for the time we had together."[7]

PERMANENT REPEAL OF STATE
MISCEGENATION LAWS, 1780–1967

The territory governed by the antimiscegenation regime kept changing. After beginning in the seventeenth century in the Chesapeake colonies, it spread north as well as south and then, in the nineteenth century, west to the Pacific. Over the years, some states peeled away from the regime, either temporarily or permanently. Suspensions of miscegenation laws took place in most of the Deep South during Reconstruction but proved temporary. With restoration there, and repeal in some northern states, the territory took on its twentieth-century contours, and was eventually—very briefly—restricted to the South.

As many as 12 states (or as few as 8) never had laws restricting interracial sex or marriage. Four of these were among the original 13 states: New Hampshire, Connecticut, New Jersey, and New York (although New York, when it was New Amsterdam, a Dutch colony, had a law against interracial sex). Five other states never had such laws: Vermont, Minnesota, and Wisconsin, together with Hawaii and Alaska, both admitted in 1959. Three territories had such laws for a time but repealed them before statehood: Kansas (1859), New Mexico (1866), and Washington (1868); Wyoming did so, too (1882), but then it passed a new miscegenation law in 1913.

Between 1780 and 1887, 8 states (in addition to those 3 territories) permanently repealed their miscegenation laws (and 7 southern states abandoned the antimiscegenation regime for some years after 1867). Then, for many years, no states repealed such measures, while additional states inaugurated miscegenation laws as late as 1913, and 30 states (out of 48) retained those laws at the end of World War II. Repeal by 13 of the 30 by 1965 left 17 holdout states—Maryland (which repealed its law shortly before the Supreme Court handed down the decision in *Loving* v. *Virginia* in June 1967) and 16 other states, from Delaware to Texas. The *Loving* decision brought an end to the enforceability of miscegenation laws in those remaining 16 states: Alabama, Arkansas, Delaware,

Florida, Georgia, Kentucky, Louisiana, Mississippi, Missouri, North Carolina, Oklahoma, South Carolina, Tennessee, Texas, Virginia, and West Virginia.

A list of states with miscegenation laws follows, together with the years in which—through state action, between 1780 and the eve of the *Loving* decision in 1967—they permanently ended their participation in the antimiscegenation regime:[1]

Pennsylvania	1780
Massachusetts	1843
Iowa	1851
Illinois	1874
Rhode Island	1881
Maine and Michigan	1883
Ohio	1887
California (court decision)	1948
Oregon	1951
Montana	1953
North Dakota	1955
South Dakota and Colorado	1957
Idaho and Nevada	1959
Arizona	1962
Utah and Nebraska	1963
Wyoming and Indiana	1965
Maryland	1967

INTERMARRIAGE IN NAZI GERMANY
AND APARTHEID SOUTH AFRICA

The antimiscegenation regime in America endured from a Maryland law in 1664 to the Supreme Court decision in *Loving* v. *Virginia* in 1967; corresponding systems developed in the twentieth century on other continents. In Europe, Germany's was born in 1935, and it died with Allied victory in World War II in 1945. A South African version, in place by 1949, was repealed in 1985; and Protas Madlala and American-born Suzanne Leclerc married that summer.[1]

For ten years, the color line in the law of marriage and the family in the United States had its counterparts in Hitler's Germany. Who had what racial identity? What pool of prospective marriage partners did that identity allow? What was the status, and the identity, of the children of a mixed marriage? What penalties might await violations of the law of race and marriage? A number of the major themes of America's antimiscegenation regime recurred in Hitler's Germany under the Nuremburg Laws of 1935. Though American culture tends to view the term "Jewish" as connoting "religion" rather than "race," race was the more relevant category in Hitler's Germany. There the preferred equivalent for the term "miscegenation" was "Rassenschande," or "race defilement."

Under the Nazi regime, people were classified in terms of their ancestry going back two generations, and that classification could change if a grandparent remarried and this time the spouse was Jewish rather than Aryan. Germans were divided into several categories, chiefly "Jews" (people with either three or four Jewish grandparents) and "Aryans" (who had none), although "mixed blood" people, "Mischlinge," fell in between. The rules governed which group could marry within which other groups. Mixed marriages were viewed as better if the man was "Aryan" than if he was the "Jewish" partner.

Mixed marriages already entered into could cause enough of a problem, but entering new ones could be out of the question. Authorities and informal influences alike pressured people in mixed marriages to separate and divorce. Partners sometimes saw suicide as the best way out. As for new marriages, male offenders against the restrictions, whether "Jewish" or "Aryan," could get penitentiary sentences of four years or worse. Among people committed to entering a mixed marriage, an occasional couple tried to evade German law by marrying in another country, but doing so subjected them to prosecution anyway. If, alternatively, people sought to evade the law by cohabiting, the "Aryan" partner might be imprisoned and the "Jewish" (or part-Jewish) partner sentenced to death.[2]

South Africa imposed its own antimiscegenation regime, particularly from 1949 on. The law had not always criminalized sexual or marital relations across racial lines, and miscegenation—mostly between white men and nonwhite women, whether slaves or servants—had been widespread from the seventeenth century through the nineteenth. Informal sexual relations persisted across the color line, but intermarriage became ever less frequent. The twentieth century brought a series of laws restricting sexual relations, and then marriage, between whites and other South Africans. First was a law (passed in 1902 in the Cape Colony; in 1903 in Natal, Transvaal, and the Orange Free State) that banned sexual relations between black men and white prostitutes. The Immorality Act of 1927 substantially broadened the ban by prohibiting sexual intercourse between whites and "Africans."

In 1949, the Prohibition of Mixed Marriages Act criminalized subsequent marriages between Europeans and all non-Europeans—Coloureds (mixed-race people), Indians, and Africans. The 1949 law was justified with reference to the United States, where 30 states, it was said, "have found it necessary to take legislative steps to keep down this social evil." The Immorality Act of 1927 was amended in 1950 and 1957, banning "immoral or indecent acts" as well as intercourse between whites and Africans and extending the restrictions to relations between whites and all other nonwhites. The maximum imprisonment for "immorality" was seven years, though not all people convicted were incarcerated, and prison terms typically ran between three and six months.[3]

Sometimes a way could be found to evade the full rigors of the apartheid regime. As a white woman, Susan Schoeman could not marry Harry May, a native of China. In the 1960s they nonetheless lived together in a poor Johannesburg suburb for four years and had three children, but then, clearly guilty of having had sexual relations, they were convicted in 1969 under the Immorality Act. Schoeman appealed to the Interior Department for a racial reclassification as Chinese so she could marry May and they could be free from further prosecution. Granted her request, and no longer white, she exclaimed, "This is all I've ever wanted—to be Harry's legal wife. We will be married as soon as possible."[4]

APPENDIX 3

IDENTITY AND AUTHORITY:
AN INTERFAITH COUPLE IN ISRAEL

The trouble was that teenagers Yaffa Ajami and Abdul Rahim Majdaleh loved each other. Obstacles to their love included her Jewish family and Israeli law, as well as his Arab family and Muslim religion. Had Yaffa fallen in love with another Jew, and Abdul with another Muslim, their families (especially Yaffa's) would not have proven so intractable in their opposition to the match, and public authorities would not have stepped into the picture. Israeli law did not permit civil marriages, and the couple could not marry as either Jews or Muslims as long as they did not share the same religion. Opposed by both sets of parents, they tried to run away to be together. Yaffa's parents arranged for her to be a ward of the Ministry of Welfare. Abdul spent 50 days in jail.[1]

Eventually, in September 1960, they got a place of their own in Tel Aviv and moved in together. She became pregnant, and they still could not marry. Although his parents reconciled to the match and helped them furnish their place, her parents continued their adamant opposition. Shortly before she gave birth, her parents pleaded with her to agree to place the child in a local Ministry of Welfare institution for one month so that her older sister, who was about to be married herself, could be free of family scandal during the time of celebration. Yaffa agreed. She also agreed to take a sealed letter to the institution, together with her baby. She did not know that the letter, from the Ministry of Welfare, said something to the effect that "the bearer may want to take her child away after some time. However, she may not do so without our permission."[2]

At the end of the month, the ministry refused to turn the child over to the parents, and the couple went to court to regain custody. Weeks passed, and the baby remained in the institution. Though both parents could visit him and take care of him there, they could not take him home. At trial, ministry representatives testified that, unable to marry, the couple could not provide a suitable home for their child. The court agreed and made the child a ward of the ministry for three years.

Yaffa could not wait three years to provide her son a home. The very next Sunday, when she went to visit him, she did not return home alone. By Wednesday, she had been arrested, and her son was taken away and returned to the institution. On Thursday, she was in Magistrate's Court for arraignment on the charge of kidnapping her own four-month-old baby. The judge was stern, and the ministry unyielding, but many spectators in the courtroom clearly supported her. When the judge set bail for Yaffa, four of them jumped to their feet to offer to put up the money, a little over $1,000. She promised the court that, pending resolution of the case, neither she nor Abdul would visit their child without first getting the court's permission.

Yaffa and Abdul struggled to find a way to get and keep their family together. In their personal lives, their different religious identities caused no insurmountable problems. But they lived in a country where religious law governed marriage and in which a public judge had authority to determine whether their son lived with them or in an institution. When they sought advice from a Cadi (a Muslim religious judge), he told them that Yaffa could marry a Muslim and retain her Jewish faith, but her son would necessarily take the religious identity of his father and thus be a Muslim himself. Under Jewish religious law, however, and under Israeli law as it applied to her, the child of a Jewish mother would be considered a Jew, regardless of whether the mother was married to a Muslim.

Fearing that state authorities would not relinquish custody of a child who, though identified under Jewish law as a Jew, might be raised as a Muslim, she told the Cadi that she planned to convert to Islam. That should make her son a Muslim under both Jewish religious law and Muslim religious law, and, with that issue resolved, perhaps she could regain custody of her child. It seemed the most promising option available to her.

Perhaps in view of the public support for the couple, perhaps in view of their dedication and persistence, the Ministry of Welfare withdrew its objection that they could not provide a proper home for their child, and a court ruling dropped the kidnapping charge against Yaffa Ajami and awarded her custody of her son, though under the ministry's supervision for the first year. As one newspaper reported, "When she heard the decision, the 19-year-old mother cried out with joy, then sank back into her chair, laughing and rubbing away tears."[3] She and Abdul Rahim Majdaleh went straight from the courtroom to the institution to get their child and take him home. With the baby no longer in an Israeli institution, Yaffa could reconsider her stated plans to change her religious identity. Their future remained uncertain, but the turmoil of the previous months—their baby taken away, his mother charged with kidnapping in her effort to get him back—had receded.

Transsexuals, Gender Identity, and the Law of Marriage

Gender identity can be remarkably like racial identity. Each can raise questions of where to draw a dividing line and on which side of it to place various people. As with race under the antimiscegenation regime, individuals and the law generally demand an unambiguous dividing line creating a binary world of male and female. People tend to insist that every individual be clearly placed on one side of the line or the other—and that they stay there, even though states long exercised the power to reclassify people according to racial identity.

What happens when it is not entirely clear what sexual identity should be assigned to a person? Is it a matter of self-identity? If not, who decides? If same-sex marriages are not valid, what about transsexuals? What must the sexual identity of a transsexual's spouse be for the marriage to be heterosexual and valid?

Consider the case of Christie Lee Littleton, who was born in San Antonio, Texas in 1952, and named Lee Cavazos Jr. Lee Cavazos Jr. grew up with male physical features but a female sexual identity, and—in an effort to bring the two identities into greater congruence—his/her parents took the child to a doctor who administered male hormones. As an adult, Lee Cavazos Jr. took a different approach to resolving the conflict, adopted the name Christie Lee Cavazos in 1977, underwent surgery, and received female hormones. As a woman, in 1989 she married Jonathon Mark Littleton in Kentucky and became Christie Lee Littleton. They lived together as husband and wife until his death in Texas in 1996.

Charging medical malpractice in her husband's death, Christie Littleton filed a wrongful death suit against Dr. Mark Prange, who sought to deflect the suit by asserting that Christie Littleton, born a male, could not be the surviving wife of the dead man. When the trial court granted the doctor's motion for a summary judgment, Christie Littleton appealed to the Texas Court of Appeals in San Antonio. There, Chief Justice Phil Hardberger began his opinion with the statement, "This case involves the most basic of questions. When is a man a man, and when is a woman a woman?" More particularly, he went on, "Is Christie a man or a woman? There is no dispute that Christie and Jonathon went through a ceremonial marriage ritual. If Christie is a woman, she may bring this action. If Christie is a man, she may not."[1]

To medical experts, Christie Littleton was "medically a woman." The appeals court, however, ruled differently: "We hold, as a matter of law, that Christie Littleton is a male. As a male, Christie cannot be married to another male. Her marriage to Jonathon was invalid, and she cannot bring a cause of action as his surviving spouse."[2] Christie Lee Littleton therefore lost her case when two judges—Chief Justice Hardberger and Justice Karen Angelini—upheld the trial court's ruling, although a third justice, Alma E. López, argued that a factual question had been raised that ought to be considered on its merits. To the court majority, there was no doubt that the person who claimed to be a surviving wife was legally a man—had started out male and could not change that fact—who therefore had no standing to bring such a case. Her name might be Mrs. Littleton, but she was no female and could not have been married to Mr. Littleton.

In view of the thousands of sex-change operations conducted each year in the United States, Mrs. Littleton's story cannot be assumed to be unique. Take the story of another woman, J'Noel Ball, who was born a male named Jay Ball and then became a woman, both medically and, so it seemed, legally. Unlike Christie Lee Cavazos, J'Noel Ball had her Wisconsin birth certificate changed to show her new gender identity—thereby averting an important defect in Christie Lee Littleton's case. As a woman, she married Marshall Gardiner in Kansas. After he died, his son (from a previous marriage) had her investigated, discovered her birth gender, and sued to prevent her from taking half her deceased husband's considerable wealth. In January 2000, the trial judge ruled—as in Christie Lee Littleton's case—that, once a male, always a male. J'Noel Ball Gardiner, legally a woman in Wisconsin where she was born and in Missouri where she lived, was a man in Kansas.[3]

The two cases raised critical questions for any marriage involving a transsexual. With whom could a transsexual have a marriage that would reliably be construed as valid? Could the couple be sure that they could transport their marriage from one state to another? Might they be unable to inherit from the other without a will? These and other questions, questions of the sort that had long beset people on the basis of their racial identities, could arise in the case of a transsexual.

NOTES

Introduction

1. Robert A. Pratt, "Crossing the Color Line: A Historical Assessment and Personal Narrative of *Loving* v. *Virginia*," *Howard Law Journal* 41 (winter 1998), 236.

2. Davis notes a dual purpose in maintaining caste lines, as in the 30 American states that had miscegenation laws at the time he published—"first as the institutional mechanism through which descent and socialization are regulated, second as the genetic mechanism through which biological identity is maintained." Kingsley Davis, "Intermarriage in Caste Societies," *American Anthropologist*, New Series 43 (1941): 376–95, quotations 389 and 394.

3. *Plessy* v. *Ferguson*, 163 U.S. 537, 545 (1896).

4. Charles W. Chesnutt, "What Is a White Man?" *The Independent* 41 (30 May 1889), reprinted in Werner Sollors, ed., *Interracialism: Black-White Intermarriage in American History, Literature, and Law* (New York: Oxford Univ. Press, 2000), 37–42.

5. Three fine recent studies of the family in American history, particularly as shaped by the law, are Peter W. Bardaglio, *Reconstructing the Household: Families, Sex, and the Law in the Nineteenth-Century South* (Chapel Hill: Univ. of North Carolina Press, 1995); Nancy F. Cott, *Public Vows: A History of Marriage and the Nation* (Cambridge, Mass.: Harvard Univ. Press, 2000); and Hendrik Hartog, *Man and Wife in America: A History* (Cambridge, Mass.: Harvard Univ. Press, 2000).

6. Philip B. Kurland and Gerhard Casper, eds., *Landmark Briefs and Arguments of the Supreme Court of the United States: Constitutional Law* (Arlington, Va.: Univ. Publications of America, 1975), 64: 971.

7. Among the more illuminating writings along these lines are Barbara J. Fields, "Ideology and Race in American History," in J. Morgan Kousser and James M. McPherson, eds., *Region, Race, and Reconstruction: Essays in Honor of C. Vann Woodward* (New York: Oxford Univ. Press, 1982), 143–77; James B. McKee, *Sociology and the Race Problem: The Failure of a Perspective* (Urbana: Univ. of Illinois Press, 1993); Ian F. Haney López, *White by Law: The Legal Construction of Race* (New York: New York Univ. Press, 1996); Lee D. Baker, *From Savage to Negro: Anthropology and the Construction of Race, 1896–1954* (Berkeley: Univ. of California Press, 1998); and Matthew Frye Jacobson, *Whiteness of a Different Color: European Immigrants and the Alchemy of Race* (Cambridge, Mass.: Harvard Univ. Press, 1998).

Cheryl I. Harris, "Whiteness as Property," *Harvard Law Review* 106 (June 1993): 1707–1791, supplies a pathbreaking analysis, and Charles W. Mills, *The Racial Contract* (Ithaca: Cornell Univ. Press, 1997), a work of political philosophy, adopts a global approach to the phenomenon of racial privilege. Other valuable recent explorations are George Lipsitz, *The Possessive Investment in Whiteness: How White People Profit from Identity Politics* (Philadelphia: Temple Univ. Press, 1998); Grace Elizabeth Hale, *Making Whiteness: The Culture of Segregation in the South, 1890–1940* (New York: Pantheon Books, 1998); Birgit Brander Rasmussen et al., eds., *The Making and Unmaking of Whiteness* (Durham: Duke Univ. Press, 2001); and David R. Roediger, *Colored White: Transcending the Racial Past* (Berkeley: Univ. of California Press, 2002).

8. Two recent compendia of such works are Sollors, *Interracialism,* and Martha Hodes, ed., *Sex, Love, Race: Crossing Boundaries in North American History* (New York: New York Univ. Press, 1999).

Among the pioneering studies of various portions of the history of the law of race and marriage are David H. Fowler, *Northern Attitudes towards Interracial Marriage: Legislation and Public Opinion in the Middle Atlantic and the States of the Old Northwest, 1780–1930* (New York: Garland, 1987), a published edition of a 1963 dissertation that reaches well beyond the eight states that are its focus; Chang Moon Sohn, "Principle and Expediency in Judicial Review: Miscegenation Cases in the Supreme Court" (Ph.D. diss., Columbia Univ., 1970); Robert J. Sickels, *Race, Marriage, and the Law* (Albuquerque: Univ. of New Mexico Press, 1972); Byron Curti Martyn's encyclopedic "Racism in the United States: A History of Anti-Miscegenation Legislation and Litigation" (Ph.D. diss., Univ. of Southern California, 1979), covering three centuries of statutes and court cases; and Michael Grossberg, *Governing the Hearth: Law and Family in Nineteenth-Century America* (Chapel Hill: Univ. of North Carolina Press, 1985).

Works that explore related phenomena are Joel Williamson, *New People: Miscegenation and Mulattoes in the United States* (New York: Free Press, 1980); John D'Emilio and Estelle B. Freedman, *Intimate Matters: A History of Sexuality in America* (New York: Harper & Row, 1988); Paul R. Spickard, *Mixed Blood: Intermarriage and Ethnic Identity in Twentieth-Century America* (Madison: Univ. of Wisconsin Press, 1989); and Martha Hodes, *White Women, Black Men: Illicit Sex in the Nineteenth-Century South* (New Haven: Yale Univ. Press, 1997).

Themes of this book can be explored in memoirs and family histories, among them Carrie Allen McCray, *Freedom's Child: The Life of a Confederate General's Black Daughter* (Chapel Hill: Algonquin Books, 1998), and Henry Wiencek, *The Hairstons: An American Family in Black and White* (New York: St. Martin's Press, 1999)—the latter might better be titled *The Hairstons and the Hairstons,* with "hair" pronounced "hair" and then "har" so as to catch what seem to be the characteristic pronunciations by black Hairstons and white Hairstons. These issues are also explored in works of fiction, such as George S. Schuyler, *Black No More* (1931; New York: Modern Library, 1999), and Howard Means, *C.S.A.—Confederate States of America* (New York: Morrow, 1998).

Signaling a new generation of historical explorations of racial identity, sexual relations, and the law of marriage are Rachel F. Moran, *Interracial Intimacy: The Regulation of Race and Romance* (Chicago: Univ. of Chicago Press, 2001), which emphasizes the twentieth century, especially the generation after *Loving* (but is unreliable on the colonial era and the nineteenth century, 18–27); Kirsten Fischer, *Suspect Relations: Sex, Race, and Resistance in Colonial North Carolina* (Ithaca: Cornell Univ. Press, 2002); and works in progress by such scholars as Jane Dailey, Randall Kennedy, Peggy Pascoe, Charles F. Robinson II, Joshua D. Rothman, and Renee Romano.

I. Sex, Marriage, and the Law of Race and Freedom

1. Helen C. Rountree, *Pocahontas's People: The Powhatan Indians of Virginia through Four Centuries* (Norman: Univ. of Oklahoma Press, 1990), 59–60; Robert S. Tilton, *Pocahontas: The Evolution of an American Narrative* (Cambridge: Cambridge Univ. Press, 1994), 1–33; David D. Smits, "'Abominable Mixture': Toward the Repudiation of Anglo-Indian Intermarriage in Seventeenth-Century Virginia," *Virginia Magazine of History and Biography* 95 (April 1987): 157–92; Daniel K. Richter, *Facing East from Indian Country: A Native History of Early America* (Cambridge, Mass.: Harvard Univ. Press, 2001), 69–78.

2. Seventeenth-century Virginia's more significant laws bearing on racial identity and legal status are compiled in Willie Lee Rose, ed., *A Documentary History of Slavery in North America* (New York: Oxford Univ. Press, 1976), 18–22.

3. William Waller Hening, ed., *The Statutes at Large, Being a Collection of All the Laws of Virginia, from the First Session of the Legislature in the Year 1619,* 13 vols. (1809–1823; reprint, Char-

lottesville: Univ. Press of Virginia, 1969), 2: 170. Most of these laws are also published (though often rephrased) in June Purcell Guild, *Black Laws of Virginia: A Summary of the Legislative Acts of Virginia Concerning Negroes from Earliest Times to the Present* (1936; reprint, New York: Negro Universities Press, 1969). Paul Finkelman analyzes them in "The Crime of Color," *Tulane Law Review* 67, no. 6 (1993), 2081–87. See also Peter Wallenstein, "Race, Marriage, and the Law of Freedom: Alabama and Virginia, 1860s–1960s," *Chicago-Kent Law Review* 70, no. 2 (1994), 389 notes 90–91. It is untrue that, as Tilton, *Pocahontas,* says, the 1662 law "expressly prohibited interracial marriage" (14).

4. For examples of black-white marriages in Virginia in the late-seventeenth century, see Edmund S. Morgan, *American Slavery, American Freedom: The Ordeal of Colonial Virginia* (New York: Norton, 1975), 334–35. For Indian-white relations and the "people who refused to vanish," see Rountree, *Pocahontas's People,* 141–42. For a powerful analysis of the origins and consequences of Virginia's early race laws, see George M. Fredrickson, *White Supremacy: A Comparative Study in American and South African History* (New York: Oxford Univ. Press, 1981), ch. 3.

5. Hening, *Statutes,* 3: 86–88. For extended discussion and analysis, see the interlude following chapter 8 in this book; A. Leon Higginbotham Jr. and Barbara K. Kopytoff, "Racial Purity and Interracial Sex in the Law of Colonial and Antebellum Virginia," *Georgetown Law Journal* 77 (1989): 1967–2029; Kathleen M. Brown, *Good Wives, Nasty Wenches, and Anxious Patriarchs: Gender, Race, and Power in Colonial Virginia* (Chapel Hill: Univ. of North Carolina Press, 1996), 187–211; Thomas D. Morris, *Southern Slavery and the Law, 1619–1860* (Chapel Hill: Univ. of North Carolina Press, 1996), 21–25.

6. Perceiving that not all Virginia laws secured the full attention of local authorities, the Burgesses directed that "the justices of each respective countie within this dominion make it their perticular care, that this act be put in effectuall execution." Hening, *Statutes,* 3: 87.

7. Ibid. Hoping to foster enforcement, the legislature provided that one-third of the fine (or proceeds of sale) would go to "the informer."

8. Ibid.

9. Morgan, *American Slavery, American Freedom,* 336.

10. Hening, *Statutes,* 3: 250–52.

11. Ibid., 3: 453–54 (ch. 49, par. 19).

12. Ibid. (pars. 18, 20).

13. Ibid., 4: 133 (sec. 22).

14. Ibid., 4: 132–34 (secs. 17, 23).

15. Ibid., 8: 134 (ch. 24, sec. 3).

16. Ibid., 12: 184 (ch. 78, art. 1). Regarding the law of race and marriage from the Revolution to the Civil War, see Wallenstein, "Race, Marriage, and the Law of Freedom," 394 note 107, and Joshua Daniel Rothman, "'Notorious in the Neighborhood': Interracial Sex and Interracial Families in Early National and Antebellum Virginia" (Ph.D. diss., Univ. of Virginia, 2000). See also Jan Ellen Lewis and Peter S. Onuf, eds., *Sally Hemings and Thomas Jefferson: History, Memory, and Civil Culture* (Charlottesville: Univ. Press of Virginia, 1999).

17. *Gwinn v. Bugg,* Jeff. (1 Va.) 87 (1770). For additional examples, see *Howell v. Netherland,* Jeff. (1 Va.) 90 (1770), and Anita Wills's posts to the VA-HIST listserve, <http://listlva.lib.va.us/archives/va-hist.html>, 10 Feb. 1999 and 20 Feb. 1999.

18. T. O. Madden Jr. with Ann L. Miller, *We Were Always Free: The Maddens of Culpeper County, Virginia, a 200-Year Family History* (New York: Norton, 1992), 2–26, 37.

19. Ibid., 35–39.

20. Hening, *Statutes,* 9: 471 (secs. 1, 3).

21. Ibid., 11: 39 (sec. 2); James Thomas Flexner, *Washington: The Indispensable Man* (Boston: Little, Brown, 1974), 385–94.

22. Samuel Shepherd, comp., *The Statutes at Large of Virginia, From October Session 1792, to December Session 1806, . . . Being a Continuation of Hening,* 3 vols. (1835; reprint, New York: AMS Press, 1970), 3: 252 (sec. 10).

23. Peter Wallenstein, "Indian Foremothers: Race, Sex, Slavery and Freedom in Early Virginia," in Catherine Clinton and Michele Gillespie, eds., *The Devil's Lane: Sex and Race in the Early South* (New York: Oxford Univ. Press, 1997), 61, 70 note 14.

24. *Hook v. Nanny Pagee and Her Children,* 2 Mun. (16 Va.) 379, 385 (1811). (For a guide to the reporters of these early state decisions, see Morris, *Southern Slavery and the Law,* 445–46.) See also Duncan J. MacLeod, *Slavery, Race, and the American Revolution* (New York: Cambridge Univ. Press, 1974), 109–126, and Michael L. Nicholls, "'The Squint of Freedom': African-American Freedom Suits in Post-Revolutionary Virginia," *Slavery and Abolition* 20 (Aug. 1999): 47–62. For a later account of physical inspection, see chapter 10.

25. Jonathan L. Alpert, "The Origins of Slavery in the United States—The Maryland Precedent," *American Journal of Legal History* 14 (1970): 189–221, quotation at 195; *William and Mary Butler v. Richard Boarman,* 1 Har. and McH. 371 (1771); Helen Tunnicliff Catterall and James J. Hayden, eds., *Judicial Cases Concerning American Slavery and the Negro,* 5 vols. (Washington, D.C.: Carnegie Institution of Washington, 1926–37), 4: 1–2; Martha Hodes, *White Women, Black Men: Illicit Sex in the Nineteenth-Century South* (New Haven: Yale Univ. Press, 1997), 19–38 and 224 note 35.

26. *Butler v. Boarman,* 376.

27. Lorena S. Walsh, "Rural African Americans in the Constitutional Era in Maryland, 1776–1810," *Maryland Historical Magazine* 84 (winter 1989): 327–41, quoted passage 335; see also 340 note 13. Indeed, perhaps the Maryland suit helped inspire the Virginia cases that began about that time.

28. *Butler v. Boarman; Toogood v. Scott,* 2 Har. and McH. 26 (1783); *Butler v. Craig,* 2 Har. and McH. 214, 215 (1791). For more on freedom suits in the post-revolutionary era, see Ira Berlin, *Slaves without Masters: The Free Negro in the Antebellum South* (New York: Pantheon, 1974), 33–35, 79–85, and Ira Berlin, *Many Thousands Gone: The First Two Centuries of Slavery in North America* (Cambridge, Mass.: The Belknap Press of Harvard Univ. Press, 1998), 281–82.

29. *Shorter v. Rozier,* 3 Har. and McH. 238 (1794). An extended discussion of these cases is in Peter Wallenstein, "'Most Unjust and Cruel to the Offspring': Racial Lineage, Slavery, and Freedom Suits in Colonial and Revolutionary Maryland," paper presented at an annual meeting of the Association for the Study of African-American Life and History, Washington, D.C., 27 Sept. 2001.

30. Alpert, "The Origins of Slavery," 195. For similar developments elsewhere, see Kirsten Fischer, *Suspect Relations: Sex, Race, and Resistance in Colonial North Carolina* (Ithaca: Cornell Univ. Press, 2002), 122–29, especially the account of the family of Sarah Boe.

31. Carter G. Woodson, "The Beginnings of Miscegenation of the Whites and Blacks," *Journal of Negro History* 3 (Oct. 1918): 335–53; *Higgins v. Allen,* 3 Har. and McH. 504 (1796).

32. *Higgins v. Allen,* 504.

2. Indian Foremothers and Freedom Suits

1. Charles L. Perdue Jr. et al., eds., *Weevils in the Wheat: Interviews with Virginia Ex-Slaves* (Charlottesville: Univ. Press of Virginia, 1976), 91.

2. Stafford County, Register of Free Negroes, 5 (20 July 1790), Central Rappahannock Regional Library, Fredericksburg, Va. My thanks to Michael L. Nicholls of Utah State University for pointing me to this source in 1990.

3. Ibid.

4. *Virginia Gazette,* 26 Nov. 1772, 15 July 1773.

5. *Robin* v. *Hardaway,* Jeff. (1 Va.) 109, 114 (1772); Duncan J. MacLeod, *Slavery, Race, and the American Revolution* (New York: Cambridge Univ. Press, 1974), 109–126.

6. *Jenkins* v. *Tom and Others,* 1 Wash. (2 Va.) 123 (1792); Virginia Supreme Court of Appeals, Order Book 2 (1790–94), 187 (microfilm, Library of Virginia, Richmond).

7. Ibid., 124.

8. Helen Tunnicliff Catterall and James J. Hayden, eds., *Judicial Cases Concerning American Slavery and the Negro,* 5 vols. (Washington, D.C.: Carnegie Institution of Washington, 1926–37). Vol. 1 contains a history and analysis of the Virginia laws and the cases that arose from them (61–71) as well as abstracts of the Virginia cases (76–265). The cases regarding the manumission of Indians are at 91–166 passim; the cases from 1792 through 1811 are at 99–122.

9. *Coleman* v. *Dick and Pat,* 1 Wash. (2 Va.) 233, 239 (1793); Order Book 2, 255. The court divided 2–2 on the case and thus affirmed the outcome in the lower court, where a jury had found for the plaintiffs.

10. For some of the literature, see Peter Wallenstein, "Indian Foremothers: Race, Sex, Slavery and Freedom in Early Virginia," in Catherine Clinton and Michele Gillespie, eds., *The Devil's Lane: Sex and Race in the Early South* (New York: Oxford Univ. Press, 1997), 70–71 note 23.

11. The phrase is from *Pallas* v. *Hill,* 2 Hen. and M. (12 Va.) 149 (1808).

12. Samuel Shepherd, comp., *The Statutes at Large of Virginia, From October Session 1792, to December Session 1806, . . . Being a Continuation of Hening,* 3 vols. (1835; reprint, New York: AMS Press, 1970), 1: 364 (secs. 1–2); *Peter* v. *Hargrave,* 5 Grattan (46 Va.) 12, 17 (1848).

13. *Coleman* v. *Dick and Pat,* 239. Such a right to sue for freedom prevailed throughout the South (Wallenstein, "Indian Foremothers," 71 note 25).

14. Such "true emancipators" also freed their own slaves, if any, and provided the impetus to enactment of the 1782 measure that facilitated such private manumissions. Robert McColley, *Slavery and Jeffersonian Virginia,* 2d ed. (Urbana: Univ. of Illinois Press, 1973), 159–60; John H. Russell, *The Free Negro in Virginia, 1619–1865* (1913; reprint, New York: Dover, 1969), 46–65.

15. Virginia Code (1819), 1: 482; McColley, *Slavery and Jeffersonian Virginia,* 159–61; Wallenstein, "Indian Foremothers," 71 note 27.

16. Morgan, *American Slavery, American Freedom,* 328–30; Catterall, *Judicial Cases,* 1: 91–166 passim; "Indian Foremothers," 71 note 29; A. E. Keir Nash, "Reason of Slavery: Understanding the Judicial Role in the Peculiar Institution," *Vanderbilt Law Review* 32 (Jan. 1979): 7–218. The General Court heard Hannah's case in the 1780s, but, after 1789, such cases—including *Jenkins* v. *Tom*—went to the Supreme Court of Appeals, and the General Court heard only criminal cases until the constitution of 1851 abolished it.

17. St. George Tucker, *A Dissertation on Slavery, with a Proposal for the Gradual Abolition of It, in the State of Virginia* (1796; reprint, Westport, Conn.: Negro Universities Press, 1970), 34–37; Winthrop D. Jordan, *White over Black: American Attitudes toward the Negro, 1550–1812* (Chapel Hill: Univ. of North Carolina Press, 1968), 551–60; Wallenstein, "Indian Foremothers," 72 note 30.

18. Wallenstein, "Indian Foremothers," 72 note 31; MacLeod, *Slavery, Race, and the American Revolution,* 124, 219 note 49.

19. *Hudgins* v. *Wrights,* 1 Hen. and M. (11 Va.) 134 (1806); Order Book 5 (1804–07), 345, 348; Catterall, *Judicial Cases,* 1: 65, 99–100, 112–13.

20. *Hudgins* v. *Wrights,* 134; Robert M. Cover, *Justice Accused: Antislavery and the Judicial Process* (New Haven: Yale Univ. Press, 1975), 50–55.

21. *Hudgins* v. *Wrights,* 134.

22. Ibid., 135, 141, 144.

23. Ibid., 139, 141, 142. In a cluster of six cases from the Petersburg area, 57 slaves—among them Pallas, Bridget, James, Tabb, Hannah, and Sam, all identified as "Indians"—sued for their freedom in 1807. They produced evidence that they were "descendants in the maternal line of a native American Indian named Bess" who had been "brought into Virginia in or about the year

1703." *Pallas* v. *Hill;* Wallenstein, "Indian Foremothers," 66–67; Order Book 6 (1808–11), 24–27; Catterall, *Judicial Cases,* 1: 66, 116–17.

24. *Butt* v. *Rachel and Others,* 4 Munf. (18 Va.) 209, 209–210 (1814); Order Book 8 (1814–17), 49.

25. Ibid., 209. See also *Pegram* v. *Isabell,* 1 Hen. and M. (11 Va.) 387 (1807), and *Pegram* v. *Isabell,* 2 Hen. and M. (12 Va.) 193 (1808), recounted in Wallenstein, "Indian Foremothers," 67, 72 note 38.

26. The phrase is Joel Williamson's: *New People: Miscegenation and Mulattoes in the United States* (New York: Free Press, 1980).

27. Cover, *Justice Accused,* 67–75; Ira Berlin, *Slaves without Masters: The Free Negro in the Antebellum South* (New York: Pantheon, 1974), 15–50.

28. Luther Porter Jackson, *Free Negro Labor and Property Holding in Virginia, 1830–1860* (1942; reprint, New York: Atheneum, 1969); Berlin, *Slaves without Masters,* 381–95.

29. Gary B. Nash, "The Hidden History of Mestizo America," *Journal of American History* 82 (Dec. 1995): 941–62; Wallenstein, "Indian Foremothers," 72–73 note 43.

30. Martha Hodes, in *White Women, Black Men: Illicit Sex in the Nineteenth-Century South* (New Haven: Yale Univ. Press, 1997), 37–38, makes this suggestion.

3. From the Chesapeake Colonies to the State of California

1. *Bryan* v. *Walton,* 14 Ga. 185, 200, 205 (italics removed) (1853).

2. Examples for the West are given in Robert R. Dykstra, *Bright Radical Star: Black Freedom and White Supremacy on the Hawkeye Frontier* (Cambridge, Mass.: Harvard Univ. Press, 1993), 45–46; Thomas C. Cox, *Blacks in Topeka, Kansas, 1865–1915: A Social History* (Baton Rouge: Louisiana State Univ. Press, 1982), 1–2, 21–24; and Lorenzo J. Greene, Gary R. Kremer, and Antonio F. Holland, *Missouri's Black Heritage* (rev. ed.; Columbia: Univ. of Missouri Press, 1993), 13–14. As for the South, the availability of rich materials has permitted reconstructing some families' experiences in considerable detail, as in Martha Hodes, *White Women, Black Men: Illicit Sex in the Nineteenth-Century South* (New Haven: Yale Univ. Press, 1997), and Joshua D. Rothman, "'Notorious in the Neighborhood': An Interracial Family in Early National and Antebellum Virginia," *Journal of Southern History* 67 (Feb. 2001): 73–114.

3. David H. Fowler, *Northern Attitudes towards Interracial Marriage: Legislation and Public Opinion in the Middle Atlantic and the States of the Old Northwest, 1780–1930* (New York: Garland, 1987), 52–55.

4. Ibid., 85 note 5. In New York in 1785, when the legislature considered a gradual emancipation bill, the lower house had wanted to include bans on black suffrage and black-white marriage, but when a gradual emancipation measure finally became law in 1799, it did so with no such restrictions. Ibid., 88–92.

5. Ibid., 84–88, 218–19; Gary B. Nash, *Forging Freedom: The Formation of Philadelphia's Black Community, 1720–1840* (Cambridge, Mass.: Harvard Univ. Press, 1988), 59–99; Louis Ruchames, "Race, Marriage, and Abolition in Massachusetts," *Journal of Negro History* 40 (July 1955): 250–73; Dykstra, *Bright Radical Star,* 26, 109.

6. Fowler, *Northern Attitudes,* 170–76.

7. Ibid., 109, appendix.

8. Ibid., 50, 60.

9. For examples from Virginia, see Thomas E. Buckley, "Unfixing Race: Class, Power, and Identity in an Interracial Family," *Virginia Magazine of History and Biography* 102 (July 1994): 349–80, and Rothman, "'Notorious in the Neighborhood.'"

10. As white Americans moved west, demography in newly settled areas resembled an earlier period on the East Coast, in that more men than women migrated and therefore white men perceived a shortage of white women. Fowler, *Northern Attitudes,* 71–79, 144–45, 219–20.

11. Ibid., 176–82, appendix.

12. Ibid., 134–48.

13. *Inhabitants of Medway* v. *Inhabitants of Needham,* 16 Mass. 157, 157–59 (1819). Any other ruling, the court said, would mean that a marriage "could be dissolved at the will of either of the parties, by stepping over the line of a state, which might prohibit such marriages" (159). See chapter 10 for a contrary ruling about comity and the perils of an "imaginary line."

14. *Inhabitants of Medway* v. *Inhabitants of Natick,* 7 Mass. 88 (1810).

15. Ibid., 88–89.

16. *Bailey* v. *Fiske,* 34 Me. 77 (1852).

17. Ibid., 77–78. See also Joanne Pope Melish, *Disowning Slavery: Gradual Emancipation and "Race" in New England, 1780–1860* (Ithaca: Cornell Univ. Press, 1998), 39–40, 122–26.

18. *Inhabitants of Raymond* v. *Inhabitants of North Berwick,* 60 Me. 114 (1871).

19. *State* v. *Hooper,* 27 N.C. 201 (1844).

20. Manuscript Census of 1850, Free Population Schedule, Rutherford County, N.C., 328–29, Family No. 1453 (microfilm, National Archives).

21. *LeGrand* v. *Darnall,* 2 Peters (27 U.S.) 663 (1829).

22. Ibid., 666.

23. A garbled account appears in Irving Dilliard, "Gabriel Duvall," in Leon Friedman and Fred L. Israel, eds., *The Justices of the United States Supreme Court, 1789–1969,* 4 vols. (New York: Chelsea House, 1969), 1: 425. *LeGrand* v. *Darnall*'s significance was contested in *Dred Scott* v. *Sandford,* 60 U.S. (19 How.) 393 (1857); see Chief Justice Taney's opinion for the Supreme Court and Justice Curtis's dissent.

24. For a sampling of those other stories, see Joel Williamson, *A Rage for Order: Black-White Relations in the American South since Emancipation* (New York: Oxford Univ. Press, 1986), 33–36; Kent Anderson Leslie, *Woman of Color, Daughter of Privilege: Amanda America Dickson, 1849–1893* (Athens: Univ. of Georgia Press, 1995).

25. *Bryan* v. *Walton,* 20 Ga. 480, 496 (1856).

26. Ibid., 491–92, 494, 496.

27. Ibid., 498–99.

28. *Bryan* v. *Walton,* 14 Ga. 185, 198, 201 (1853). See also *Bryan* v. *Walton,* 33 Ga. supp. 11 (1864); Peter Wallenstein, *From Slave South to New South: Public Policy in Nineteenth-Century Georgia* (Chapel Hill: Univ. of North Carolina Press, 1987), 86–96; and Hodes, *White Women, Black Men,* 98–108, 251–53.

29. Gary B. Mills, "Miscegenation and the Free Negro in Antebellum 'Anglo' Alabama: A Reexamination of Southern Race Relations," *Journal of American History* 68 (June 1981): 16–34.

30. Harry Toulmin, *A Digest of the Laws of the State of Alabama* (Catawba, Ala., 1823), 576–79; John G. Aiken, *A Digest of the Laws of the State of Alabama* (Philadelphia, 1833), 305, quoted in Mills, "Miscegenation and the Free Negro," 18; John J. Ormand et al., *The Code of Alabama* (Montgomery, 1852), 376–77 (title 5, ch. 1, arts. 1946, 1956).

31. Thurman, a "free mulatto," had been convicted of the charge of rape of a white woman, a conviction that, in the case of a "slave, free negro, or mulatto," required that the perpetrator "suffer death," according to statute. Thurman, claiming to be the son of a white woman and a mixed-race man, challenged his conviction under this law. *Thurman* v. *State,* 18 Ala. 276, 277 (1850).

32. Adopting a definition that Virginia had originated in 1705 (and had relaxed in 1785), the Alabama Code of 1852 stated: "The term 'negro' within the meaning of this code includes 'mulatto.' The term 'mulatto,' or 'person of color,' within the meaning of this code, is a person of mixed blood, descended on the part of the father or the mother, from negro ancestors, to the third generation inclusive, though one ancestor of each generation may have been a white person." Ormand, *Code of Alabama,* 58 (title 1, ch. 1, art. 2, sec. 4).

33. Fowler, *Northern Attitudes,* 214–19 and appendix. See appendix 1 of this book.

34. The great exception to this long-term trend came during Reconstruction, when most of the Deep South withdrew for a time from the antimiscegenation regime.

4. Race, Marriage, and the Crisis of the Union

1. Sidney Kaplan, "The Miscegenation Issue in the Election of 1864," *Journal of Negro History* 34 (July 1949): 274–343, and J. M. Bloch, *Miscegenation, Melaleukation, and Mr. Lincoln's Dog* (New York: Schaum, 1958), esp. 34–48.

2. Walter Johnson, "The Slave Trader, the White Slave, and the Politics of Racial Determination in the 1850s," *Journal of American History* 87 (June 2000): 13–38.

3. *Morrison v. White*, 16 La. Ann. 100, 102 (1861).

4. *Dred Scott v. Sandford*, 60 U.S. (19 How.) 393, 419–20 (1857); Don E. Fehrenbacher, *The Dred Scott Case: Its Significance in American Law and Politics* (New York: Oxford Univ. Press, 1978), ch. 15.

5. Ibid., 408–409, 413.

6. Ibid., 600. Regarding the couple's marriage and their life together, see Paul Finkelman, ed., *Dred Scott v. Sandford: A Brief History with Documents* (Boston: Bedford Books, 1997), 14–20.

7. Roy P. Basler, ed., *The Collected Works of Abraham Lincoln,* 9 vols. (New Brunswick, N.J.: Rutgers Univ. Press, 1953), 2: 405.

8. Ibid.

9. Ibid., 407–408.

10. Ibid., 408–409.

11. Harold Holzer, ed., *The Lincoln-Douglas Debates* (New York: HarperCollins, 1993), 67, 189; see also 1–32, 245, 283.

12. Ibid., 190; Finkelman, *Dred Scott,* 201.

13. David H. Fowler, *Northern Attitudes towards Interracial Marriage: Legislation and Public Opinion in the Middle Atlantic and the States of the Old Northwest, 1780–1930* (New York: Garland, 1987), 187–89.

14. Ibid., 189.

15. Ibid., 189, 191.

16. Ibid., 188–90.

17. Percy Lee Rainwater, *Mississippi, Storm Center of Secession, 1856–1861* (Baton Rouge, La.: Otto Claitor, 1938), 147–48.

18. Peter Wallenstein, *From Slave South to New South: Public Policy in Nineteenth-Century Georgia* (Chapel Hill: Univ. of North Carolina Press, 1987), chs. 12–14.

19. Eric Foner, *Reconstruction: America's Unfinished Revolution, 1863–1877* (New York: Harper and Row, 1988), 198–210; Mississippi, *Laws* (1865), 82 (ch. IV, sec. 1). For fresh treatments of the power struggle at the heart of which lay matters of black suffrage, black labor and landownership, and interracial marriage, see Martha Hodes, *White Women, Black Men: Illicit Sex in the Nineteenth-Century South* (New Haven: Yale Univ. Press, 1997), ch. 7, and Laura F. Edwards, *Gendered Strife and Confusion: The Political Culture of Reconstruction* (Urbana: Univ. of Illinois Press, 1997).

20. Foner, *Reconstruction,* 242–46; "An Act to protect all Persons in the United States in their Civil Rights, and furnish the Means of their Vindication," U.S., *Statutes at Large,* 14: 27.

21. James D. Richardson, ed., *A Compilation of the Messages and Papers of the Presidents, 1789–1897,* 10 vols. (Washington: Government Printing Office, 1896–97), 6: 407–408. Johnson may have confused himself as he ranted against the bill. He observed that, "as the whites are forbidden to intermarry with the blacks, the blacks can only make such contracts as the whites themselves are allowed to make, and therefore can not under this bill enter into the marriage contract with the whites." One might conclude, rather, as some judges soon did, that blacks could marry whites in making "such contracts as the whites themselves are allowed to make."

22. Foner, *Reconstruction*, 251–57.

23. Quoted in Joseph B. James, *The Framing of the Fourteenth Amendment* (Urbana: Univ. of Illinois Press, 1956), 60.

24. Foner, *Reconstruction*, 261–79.

25. For white residents of Virginia, for example, the U.S. census of 1870 showed as many males as females below the age of 21, and parity again in the age group 45–59. In between those two categories, by contrast, males were in a substantial deficit—only 47 percent of the 21–24 age-group, 46 percent for 35–39 and 40–44, and 45 percent in the 25–29 and 30–34 groups. U.S. Census Bureau, *Ninth Census*, vol. II, *The Vital Statistics of the United States* (Washington: Government Printing Office, 1872), 612–14. Joel Williamson notes this pattern in *New People: Miscegenation and Mulattoes in the United States* (New York: Free Press, 1980), 89–90.

26. *Ninth Census*, II, *Vital Statistics*, 652–55.

27. See the discussions in Kathleen M. Blee, *Women of the Klan: Racism and Gender in the 1920s* (Berkeley: Univ. of California Press, 1991), 12–16; Hodes, *White Women, Black Men*, ch. 7; Edwards, *Gendered Strife and Confusion*.

28. Paul C. Palmer, "Miscegenation as an Issue in the Arkansas Constitutional Convention of 1868," *Arkansas Historical Quarterly* 24 (summer 1965), 101.

29. Ibid., 102.

30. Ibid., 106, 111, 116.

31. Ibid., 117–18.

32. Ibid., 108–109, 113–18. Because the ban was kept out of the constitution, the Code of 1874 was able to drop it (see chapter 5).

33. *State* v. *Gibson*, 36 Ind. 389 (1871). My thanks to Stephen E. Towne at the Indiana State Archives, Indianapolis, for supplying me the *Gibson* case file.

34. *State* v. *Gibson*, 403. For another state court's holding that the reach of federal law remained extremely limited even after 1866, see *Bowlin* v. *Commonwealth*, 2 Bush (65 Ky.) 5 (1867).

35. A fresh examination, together with a review of previous literature, is Steven A. Bank, "Anti-Miscegenation Laws and the Dilemma of Symmetry: The Understanding of Equality in the Civil Rights Act of 1875," *University of Chicago Law School Roundtable* 2 (1995): 303–343.

5. Post–Civil War Alabama

1. Harold Holzer, ed., *The Lincoln-Douglas Debates* (New York: HarperCollins, 1993), 189.

2. Alabama Constitution of 1865, art 4, sec. 31.

3. A. J. Walker, *The Revised Code of Alabama* (Montgomery, 1867), 690 (title 1, ch. 5, arts. 3602, 3603). For evidence relating to interracial sex, marriage, and the law in early post–Civil War Alabama, see Peter Kolchin, *First Freedom: The Responses of Alabama's Blacks to Emancipation and Reconstruction* (Westport, Conn.: Greenwood Press, 1972), 61–62. Because interracial marriages were not criminalized before 1865 (though a penalty had been enacted against officiating at a wedding between a white person and an African American), the statement is misleading that, in the aftermath of the 1865 Alabama convention, "Marriages between whites and blacks remained prohibited," as stated by John B. Myers in "The Freedman and the Law in Post-Bellum Alabama, 1865–1867," *Alabama Review* 23 (Jan. 1970), 59.

4. Joel Williamson observes in *New People: Miscegenation and Mulattoes in the United States* (New York: Free Press, 1980): "It is a tremendous irony that the emancipation of Negroes entailed the emancipation of racism. It had been black versus white within the bounds of slavery before; now there were no bounds" (78).

5. Walter L. Fleming, *Civil War and Reconstruction in Alabama* (New York: Columbia Univ. Press, 1905), chs. 8, 14–15, 24; Sarah Woolfolk Wiggins, *The Scalawag in Alabama Politics, 1865–1881* (Tuscaloosa: Univ. of Alabama Press, 1977).

6. Alabama Constitution of 1868, art. 6, secs. 11–12. Before and after the interlude that followed the 1868 elections, the men who sat on the Alabama Supreme Court were—in postwar terms—Democrats, whatever their prewar affiliations had been. Wiggins, *Scalawag*, 31, 88, 94, 98, 136–37. For sketches of the Republican justices, see Joel D. Kitchens, "E. W. Peck: Alabama's First Scalawag Chief Justice," *Alabama Review* 54 (Jan. 2001): 3–32, and Thomas McAdory Owen, ed., *History of Alabama and Dictionary of Alabama Biography*, 4 vols. (1921), 3: 1349, 1486; see also 3: 214, 951, and 4: 1628–29.

7. *The Slaughter-House Cases*, 83 U.S. 36 (1873). For a good example of the literature, see Richard L. Aynes, "Constricting the Law of Freedom: Justice Miller, the Fourteenth Amendment, and the *Slaughter-House Cases*," *Chicago-Kent Law Review* 70, no. 2 (1994): 627–88.

8. *Ellis* v. *State*, 42 Ala. 525 (1868).

9. Ibid., 526.

10. Ibid.

11. Ibid., 526–27.

12. *Burns* v. *State*, 48 Ala. 195, 197 (1872); D. D. Shelby, "The Thirteenth and Fourteenth Amendments," *Southern Law Review* 3 (1874), 529.

13. *Burns* v. *State*, 197–98; *Dred Scott* v. *Sandford*, 60 U.S. (19 How.) 393, 408 (1857). Steven A. Bank in "Anti-Miscegenation Laws and the Dilemma of Symmetry: The Understanding of Equality in the Civil Rights Act of 1875," *University of Chicago Law School Roundtable* 2 (1995), guesses about this case—related as it was to a white minister, not a black groom—that it was "likely a test case for a friendly court hoping to overrule the law during a less controversial case" (note 224).

14. Shelby (1847–1914), a future state legislator and federal judge, is described as having been "a Republican in politics." Owen, *History of Alabama*, 4: 1541; Shelby, "Amendments," 524–32, quotations at 531.

15. Shelby, "Amendments," 531–32.

16. *Ford* v. *State*, 53 Ala. 150, 151 (1875).

17. Ibid., 151.

18. Ibid.

19. *Green* v. *State*, 58 Ala. 190, 191 (1878). My thanks to Edwin C. Bridges and Norwood A. Kerr at the Alabama Department of Archives and History for supplying me copies of the pages of the Alabama Supreme Court bar docket that confirm the year 1878 as the year of the decision in *Green* (and in *Hoover*, below).

20. *Green* v. *State*, 191.

21. Ibid., 192.

22. *Maguire* v. *Maguire*, 7 Dana (37 Ky.) 181, 184 (1838), quoted (as here, with minor stylistic changes) at *Green* v. *State*, 193.

23. *Green* v. *State*, 194.

24. Ibid., 194–95; U.S. Census Office, *A Compendium of the Ninth Census* (Washington: Government Printing Office, 1872), 24–25.

25. *Green* v. *State*, 195.

26. Ibid., 195–97; *State* v. *Ross*, 76 N.C. 242 (1877); *State* v. *Kennedy*, 76 N.C. 251 (1877).

27. *Hoover* v. *State*, 59 Ala. 57, 58 (1878).

28. Ibid., 58.

29. Ibid., 59.

30. Ibid., 59–60.

31. Ibid., 60.

32. Ibid.

33. Alabama, Board of Inspectors of Convicts, annual report (1877–78), 18, 26.

34. Ibid., biennial report (1882–84), 111, 114; biennial report (1884–86), 200, 202; Alabama, Dept. of Corrections and Institutions, State Convict Record, 1885–1952, Alabama Dept. of Archives and History.

35. Peter W. Bardaglio, *Reconstructing the Household: Families, Sex, and the Law in the Nineteenth-Century South* (Chapel Hill: Univ. of North Carolina Press, 1995), 289 note 19.

6. Reconstruction and the Law of Interracial Marriage

1. Mississippi, *Laws* (1865), 82 (ch. IV, sec. 3); *Laws* (1870), 73 (ch. X, sec. 2); Vernon L. Wharton, *The Negro in Mississippi, 1865–1890* (Chapel Hill: Univ. of North Carolina Press, 1947), 87, 227–28.

2. Noralee Frankel, *Freedom's Women: Black Women and Families in Civil War Era Mississippi* (Bloomington: Indiana Univ. Press, 1999), 113–15.

3. *Dickerson* v. *Brown*, 49 Miss. 357, 367 (1873). Regarding the kinds of questions generated by this case and the others in this chapter, see Adrienne G. Davis, "The Private Law of Race and Sex: An Antebellum Perspective," *Stanford Law Review* 51 (Jan. 1999): 221–88.

4. *Dickerson* v. *Brown*, 363–66.

5. Ibid., 359.

6. Ibid., 360–62.

7. Ibid., 374–75.

8. The case was remanded to the trial court to determine the sole question left open — was the couple "cohabiting as husband and wife,' at the time of the present constitution"?—and report back within 40 days. Ibid., 375–76.

9. *Hart* v. *Hoss and Elder*, 26 La. Ann. 90 (1874). For analyses of laws and cases regarding interracial families in post–Civil War Louisiana, see Virginia R. Domínguez, *White by Definition: Social Classification in Creole Louisiana* (New Brunswick, N.J.: Rutgers Univ. Press, 1986), 23–55, and Charles Frank Robinson II, "The Antimiscegenation Conversation: Love's Legislated Limits (1868–1967)" (Ph.D. diss., Univ. of Houston, 1998), 111–42.

10. *Hart* v. *Hoss and Elder*, 91.

11. Ibid., 92.

12. Ibid.

13. Ibid., 93–94.

14. Ibid., 96.

15. Ibid., 97.

16. Ibid., 99–100.

17. The state supreme court between 1869 and 1877 was "solidly Republican," as Joe Gray Taylor says in *Louisiana Reconstructed, 1863–1877* (Baton Rouge: Louisiana State Univ. Press, 1974), 248. Yet it mustered only the slimmest majority for Chief Justice Ludeling's ruling.

18. *Bonds* v. *Foster*, 36 Tex. 68 (1871–72).

19. Ibid., syllabus, 68.

20. Ibid., 69–70. Summaries of miscegenation as an issue in late-nineteenth century Texas appear in Lawrence D. Rice, *The Negro in Texas, 1874–1900* (Baton Rouge: Louisiana State Univ. Press, 1971), 149–50, and Alwyn Barr, *Black Texans: A History of African Americans in Texas, 1528–1995* (1973; 2nd ed.; Norman: Univ. of Oklahoma Press, 1996), 82–83. For a lengthier and more satisfying examination, see Robinson, "Antimiscegenation Conversation," 38–76. For an account of the Texas Supreme Court during Reconstruction, together with biographical sketches of the judges, see George E. Shelley, "The Semicolon Court of Texas," *Southwestern Historical Quarterly* 48 (April 1945): 449–68.

21. In listing only Alabama and Louisiana, Nancy F. Cott in *Public Vows: A History of Marriage and the Nation* (Cambridge, Mass.: Harvard Univ. Press, 2000), 101 and 259, could be said

to neglect Texas as a state whose supreme court, for a time during Reconstruction, found a mis-cegenation statute unconstitutional. Then again, Peter Wallenstein, "Race, Marriage, and the Law of Freedom: Alabama and Virginia, 1860s–1960s," *Chicago-Kent Law Review* 70, no. 2 (1994), 405 note 170, states that Alabama was unique in doing so, and Rachel F. Moran, *Interracial Intimacy: The Regulation of Race and Romance* (Chicago: Univ. of Chicago Press, 2001), 77, seems to as well. So does Renee Christine Romano, "Crossing the Line: Black-White Interracial Marriage in the United States, 1945–1990" (Ph.D. diss., Stanford Univ., 1996), 142 note 8, relying on Walter Wadlington, "The *Loving* Case: Virginia's Anti-Miscegenation Statute in Historical Perspective," *Virginia Law Review* 52 (Nov. 1966), 1212.

22. *Honey* v. *Clark,* 37 Tex. 686 (1872–73).

23. Ibid., 687.

24. Ibid., 688–89.

25. Ibid., 689, 697.

26. Ibid., 689.

27. Ibid., 706–708.

28. Ibid., 709.

29. *Clements* v. *Crawford,* 42 Tex. 601, 603–604 (1875).

30. *Frasher* v. *State,* 3 Tex. App. 263, 265 (1877).

31. Ibid., 277–78.

32. *François* v. *State,* 9 Tex. App. 144, 145, 147 (1880).

33. Robinson, "Antimiscegenation Conversation," 124–25.

34. Wharton, *Negro in Mississippi,* 229.

35. Statements that point out even one example of judicial invalidation during Reconstruction are a huge improvement over declarations that no nineteenth-century court ever ruled a miscegenation law unconstitutional. That position, voiced by the minority in *Perez* v. *Sharp* in 1948 (see chapter 13), is echoed in Robert J. Sickels, *Race, Marriage, and the Law* (Albuquerque: Univ. of New Mexico Press, 1972): "Until 1948, no state or federal court had found an antimiscegenation law unconstitutional on any ground" (98). Similar assertions appear in such very different law review articles as R. Carter Pittman, "The Fourteenth Amendment: Its Intended Effect on Anti-Miscegenation Laws," *North Carolina Law Review* 43 (1964–65), 108, and James Trosino, "American Wedding: Same-Sex Marriage and the Miscegenation Analogy," *Buffalo University Law Review* 73 (Jan. 1993), 104, as well as in Paul R. Spickard, *Mixed Blood: Intermarriage and Ethnic Identity in Twentieth-Century America* (Madison: Univ. of Wisconsin Press, 1989), 287; Andrew Kull, *The Color-Blind Constitution* (Cambridge, Mass.: Harvard Univ. Press, 1992), 275 note 27; William N. Eskridge Jr., *The Case for Same-Sex Marriage: From Sexual Liberty to Civilized Commitment* (New York: Free Press, 1996), 155; and Benjamin Thomas Field, "Justice Roger Traynor and His Case for Judicial Activism" (Ph.D. diss., Univ. of California, Berkeley, 2000), vi and ch. 2.

Robinson, in "The Antimiscegenation Conversation," errs in stating that Louisiana was "unlike any other southern state" in that it "had several years in its post-civil war . . . history where no antimiscegenation laws existed" (128). Quite aside from Texas and Alabama, where the courts acted, he thereby neglects Mississippi and South Carolina—and Arkansas and Florida, too—where the legislature did. Getting it right about the five states that took some kind of legislative action to drop the ban is Peter W. Bardaglio, *Reconstructing the Household: Families, Sex, and the Law in the Nineteenth-Century South* (Chapel Hill: Univ. of North Carolina Press, 1995), 289 note 19. Getting it wrong is Eskridge, *The Case for Same-Sex Marriage,* where reference is made to "different-race marriages, which had never been allowed in the South" (108) before the *Loving* decision was handed down in 1967. There had been a time in every colony before black-white marriages were banned—although all southern states had miscegenation laws by 1865–66, and, after an interlude in seven of them, all southern states had them again in the twentieth century.

7. Accommodating the Law of Freedom to the Law of Race

1. *Scott* v. *State,* 39 Ga. 321 (1869).

2. Ibid., 323, 326.

3. *Lonas* v. *State,* 3 Heiskell (50 Tenn.) 287 (1871).

4. Ibid., 311–12.

5. *State* v. *Hairston and Williams,* 63 N.C. 451, 452–53 (1869).

6. *State* v. *Reinhardt and Love,* 63 N.C. 547 (1869).

7. Peter Wallenstein, "Cartograms and the Mapping of Virginia History, 1790–1990," *Virginia Social Science Journal* 28 (winter 1993), 92, 96; Virginia, *Code* (1860), 529 (title 31, ch. 109, sec. 1).

8. Virginia, *Code* (1860), 803–804 (title 54, ch. 196, secs. 4, 8–9).

9. Wallenstein, "Cartograms," 97, 103; Virginia, *Acts* (1865–66), 85–86 (ch. 18); *Code* (1873), 850 (ch. 105, art. 1), and 1208 (ch. 192, arts. 7–9); Walter Wadlington, "The *Loving* Case: Virginia's Anti-Miscegenation Statute in Historical Perspective," *Virginia Law Review* 52 (Nov. 1966), 1195 note 48. With regard to the maximum imprisonment of 12 months for a "white person" who married a "negro," and the maximum fine of $100 (art. 8), the Code of 1873 specifically noted (at 1208) that "a similar penalty is not imposed on the negro."

10. *Code* (1860), 804 (title 54, ch. 196, secs. 6–7); *Code* (1873), 1208 (ch. 192, art. 6).

11. *Kinney* v. *Commonwealth,* 30 Gratt. (71 Va.) 858 (1878); Alrutheus Ambush Taylor, *The Negro in the Reconstruction of Virginia* (Washington, D.C.: Association for the Study of Negro Life and History, 1926), 54–62. For other accounts see Charles E. Wynes, *Race Relations in Virginia, 1870–1902* (Charlottesville: Univ. of Virginia Press, 1961), 92–94; Samuel N. Pincus, *The Virginia Supreme Court, Blacks, and the Law, 1870–1902* (New York: Garland, 1990), 63–84.

12. *Code* (1860), 804 (title 54, ch. 196, sec. 8); left unchanged in *Code* (1873), 1208 (title 54, ch. 105, sec. 8); Virginia, *Acts* (1877–78), 302–303 (ch. 7, secs. 4, 8–9).

13. Virginia, *Acts* (1877–78), 302 (ch. 7, sec. 3). Such restrictions had appeared in Virginia law as early as 1818; a version from 1819 had applied language of that sort only to people "within certain degrees of relationship." Virginia, *Acts* (1817–18), 19 (ch. 18); Virginia, *Code* (1819), 1: 399 (ch. 106, sec. 18). Cases from the Virginia Court of Appeals in the 1870s and 1880s, not detailed here, appear in later chapters—a federal case in chapter 8, cohabitation cases in the interlude, and cases regarding racial identity as well as interstate comity (the recognition in one state of a marriage contracted elsewhere) in chapter 10. For a connecting narrative and overall analysis of those cases, see Peter Wallenstein, "Race, Marriage, and the Law of Freedom: Alabama and Virginia, 1860s–1960s," *Chicago-Kent Law Review* 70, no. 2 (1994), 398–406.

14. *State* v. *Jackson,* 80 Mo. 175, 176 (1883).

15. Ibid., 176.

16. Ibid., 177.

17. Like other southern state courts, the Missouri Supreme Court displayed approval, even glee, in citing the Indiana case, *State* v. *Gibson* (see chapter 4), on the constitutionality of laws against interracial marriage in the face of the Fourteenth Amendment. Although it conceded that the Alabama Supreme Court had ruled otherwise in *Burns* v. *State* (see chapter 5), it noted (*State* v. *Jackson,* 178) that "that decision is in conflict not only with the weight of authority on the subject elsewhere, but with a decision of the same court," *Ellis* v. *State.* Either the court was careless in specifying *Ellis,* which predated the Fourteenth Amendment, or it was twisting the knife, insisting again, this time implicitly, that the Fourteenth Amendment had made no difference whatsoever.

18. *State* v. *Jackson,* 179. The court does not specify *Pace* v. *Alabama,* but it cites *Slaughter-House* (which seemed to leave the Fourteenth Amendment with too short a reach to touch laws against interracial marriage) and *Minor* v. *Happersett* (which said that the Fourteenth Amendment

created no new rights, only further safeguards against trespass against those rights that citizens had had all along).

19. Ibid., 179. The Missouri court's reliance on pseudoscience in this manner made it sound as though the policy objection to interracial marriages was, on the one hand, that any children who resulted would be mixed-race or, on the other, that there might be no children.

20. *Dodson v. State,* 61 Ark. 57, 59 (1895).

21. Ibid., 57–58.

22. Ibid., 58, 60; *Green v. State,* 58 Ala. 190 (1878).

23. *Dodson v. State,* 61. Charles F. Robinson, in "'Most Shamefully Common': Arkansas and Miscegenation" (a paper presented at the 67th annual meeting of the Southern Historical Association, New Orleans, Nov. 2001), provides a more extended treatment of late nineteenth-century Arkansas.

24. David H. Fowler, *Northern Attitudes towards Interracial Marriage: Legislation and Public Opinion in the Middle Atlantic and the States of the Old Northwest, 1780–1930* (New York: Garland, 1987), appendix.

25. South Carolina, *Acts* (1879), 3; George Brown Tindall, *South Carolina Negroes, 1877–1900* (Columbia: Univ. of South Carolina Press, 1952), 296–98. South Carolina's temporary tolerance of interracial marriage, when it attracted interracial couples from a more restrictive neighboring state, North Carolina (see chapter 10), helped spur passage of a law that ended the opportunity for residents and non-residents alike.

26. Such prosecutions are discussed in various chapters, as well as in the interlude. The denial of the right to inherit is detailed in chapter 11.

27. W. Fitzhugh Brundage, *Lynching in the New South: Georgia and Virginia, 1880–1930* (Urbana: Univ. of Illinois Press, 1993); Leon F. Litwack, *Trouble in Mind: Black Southerners in the Age of Jim Crow* (New York: Knopf, 1998), ch. 6.

28. Martha Hodes in *White Women, Black Men: Illicit Sex in the Nineteenth-Century South* (New Haven: Yale Univ. Press, 1997), offers a number of examples to support her thesis that black men in the South could more readily, before emancipation than afterward, get away with liaisons with white women. In view, however, of the continued prosecutions—those in Alabama in 1890, for example, or those in Alabama, Mississippi, and Louisiana as well as Virginia in the 1950s, as well as numerous ones in between—one has to be skeptical of the final clause of her statement that, in contrast to the post–Civil War world, such pre–Civil War liaisons were met "with a measure of toleration, tempered by harsh judgment and ostracism, though not yet by inevitable white violence" (37). The prewar and postwar eras may well, in this respect, have been different, but they weren't *that* different.

29. Jim Crow's career was indeed strange, as C. Vann Woodward said many years ago—although Woodward said nothing about marriage; focused on transportation; and did not seek to square his thesis about segregated transportation with developments in education. C. Vann Woodward, *The Strange Career of Jim Crow* (New York: Oxford Univ. Press, 1955); Howard N. Rabinowitz, *Race Relations in the Urban South, 1865–1890* (New York: Oxford Univ. Press, 1978).

8. Interracial Marriage and the Federal Courts, 1857–1917

1. *In re Dobbs,* 12 Fed. Cas. 262 (Circuit Court, N.D. Georgia), 1871 U.S. App. LEXIS 1693.

2. Ibid., 264.

3. *Ex parte Brown,* as referenced in *Ex parte François,* 9 Fed. Cas. 699, 700 (Circuit Court, W. D. Texas), 1879 U.S. Dist. LEXIS 256.

4. *Ex parte François,* 700.

5. Ibid., 700–701.

6. Ibid., 700.

7. Ibid., 701.

8. Ibid.

9. *Ex parte Kinney,* 14 Fed. Cas. 602 (C.C.E.D. Va., 1879).

10. Ibid., 604.

11. Ibid., 607.

12. Ibid., 605.

13. Ibid.; Virginia, *Annual Report of the Penitentiary* (1879), 24, 28; (1880), 41; (1881), 35; (1882), 29.

14. *Pace and Cox v. State,* 69 Ala. 231 (1881); Transcript of Record, *Pace v. Alabama* (Record No. 908), 1–3.

15. Transcript of Record, 5.

16. *Pace and Cox v. State,* 232.

17. Brief for Appellant, 4–6.

18. Brief for Appellee, 2–3. Despite the identical surnames, the two lawyers had no discernible kinship; Thomas McAdory Owen, ed., *History of Alabama and Dictionary of Alabama Biography,* 4 vols. (1921), 4: 1674–75. The attorney general had moved to Alabama from Virginia in 1866; his opponent had moved to Alabama from South Carolina in 1859.

19. Brief for Appellee, 3.

20. Brief for Appellant, 2; Brief for Appellee, 6, 9, 11.

21. Brief for Appellee, 15–16.

22. Ibid., 5, 14.

23. *Pace v. Alabama,* 106 U.S. 583, 585 (1883). For further analysis see David P. Currie, *The Constitution in the Supreme Court: The First Hundred Years, 1789–1888* (Chicago: Univ. of Chicago Press, 1985), 387–90, and John R. Howard, *The Shifting Wind: The Supreme Court and Civil Rights from Reconstruction to Brown* (Albany: State Univ. of New York Press, 1999), 134–35, 138, 187.

24. *Pace v. Alabama,* 585.

25. *Maynard v. Hill,* 125 U.S. 190 (1888).

26. Ibid., 205.

27. Ibid., 209.

28. Ibid., 211.

29. *Tutty v. State,* 41 Fed. Cas. 753 (1890).

30. Ibid., 755.

31. Ibid., 756. See also *Tutty v. State,* 87 Ga. 160 (1891).

32. Charles A. Lofgren, *The Plessy Case: A Legal-Historical Interpretation* (New York: Oxford Univ. Press, 1987); C. Vann Woodward, "The Case of the Louisiana Traveler," in John A. Garraty, ed., *Quarrels That Have Shaped the Constitution* (1962; rev. ed., New York: Harper & Row, 1987), 157–74; Barbara Young Welke, *Recasting American Liberty: Gender, Race, Law, and the Railroad Revolution, 1865–1920* (Cambridge: Cambridge Univ. Press, 2001), ch. 9.

33. Brief by Tourgée, 10, in Philip B. Kurland and Gerhard Casper, eds., *Landmark Briefs and Arguments of the Supreme Court of the United States: Constitutional Law* (Arlington, Va.: Univ. Publications of America, 1975), 13: 37.

34. Ibid., 72; also 70–71.

35. *Plessy v. Ferguson,* 163 U.S. 537, 540, 545 (1896).

36. *Buchanan v. Warley,* 245 U.S. 60 (1917); Roger L. Rice, "Residential Segregation by Law, 1910–1917," *Journal of Southern History* 34 (May 1968): 179–99; David Delaney, *Race, Place, and the Law, 1836–1948* (Austin: Univ. of Texas Press, 1998), ch. 5.

37. Kurland and Casper, *Landmark Briefs and Arguments,* 18: 36, 76–77, 130, 158–60, 272–73, 436, 442.

38. *Buchanan v. Warley,* 79, 81; Howard, *The Shifting Wind,* 184–94.

39. *The Civil Rights Cases,* 109 U.S. 3 (1883). For a valuable discussion, see Linda Przybyszewski, *The Republic according to John Marshall Harlan* (Chapel Hill: Univ. of North Carolina Press, 1999), 86–87, 109–117.

Interlude. Polygamy, Incest, Fornication, Cohabitation

1. Thomas Brown, "The Miscegenation of Richard Mentor Johnson as an Issue in the National Election Campaign of 1835–1836," *Civil War History* 39 (March 1993): 5–30.

2. Mary Frances Berry, *The Pig Farmer's Daughter and Other Tales of American Justice: Episodes of Racism and Sexism in the Courts from 1865 to the Present* (New York: Knopf, 1999), 36–41. For an observer's fascinating report—from shortly before Jack Johnson's marriage—of attitudes toward race mixing, and practices regarding it, in both the North and the South, see Ray Stannard Baker, *Following the Colour Line* (1908; reprint, New York: Harper and Row, 1964), ch. 8.

3. Al-Tony Gilmore, *Bad Nigger! The National Impact of Jack Johnson* (Port Washington, N.Y.: Kennikat Press, 1975), 95; Randy Roberts, *Papa Jack: Jack Johnson and the Era of White Hopes* (New York: Free Press, 1983), 140–61.

4. "Intermarriage," *The Crisis* 5 (Feb. 1913), 180–81, reprinted in Herbert Aptheker, ed., *Writings in Periodicals Edited by W. E. B. Du Bois: Selections from the Crisis,* 2 vols. (Millwood, N.Y.: Kraus-Thomson, 1983), 1 (1911–25): 49–50.

5. Gilmore, *Bad Nigger,* 111.

6. For observations along these lines, see Rachel F. Moran, *Interracial Intimacy: The Regulation of Race and Romance* (Chicago: Univ. of Chicago Press, 2001), 65–68.

7. *Scott* v. *Commonwealth,* 77 Va. 344, 345–46 (1883).

8. *Jones* v. *Commonwealth,* 80 Va. 18, 18–21 (1885); Samuel N. Pincus, *The Virginia Supreme Court, Blacks, and the Law, 1870–1902* (New York: Garland, 1990), 73–74. Unmarried cohabitation in Great Britain is examined in Stephen Parker, *Informal Marriage, Cohabitation, and the Law, 1750–1989* (New York: St. Martin's Press, 1990).

9. *Lewis* v. *State,* 18 Ala. App. 263, 264 (1921).

10. *Jackson* v. *State,* 23 Ala. App. 555, 556 (1930). The court decision spells the woman's first name (perhaps correctly) "Alexander." For a similar case from the 1920s (*Rollins* v. *State,* 18 Ala. App. 354) and an alternative analysis—regarding judicial doubt as to whether all "white" women merited the protection of the miscegenation laws—see Matthew Frye Jacobson, *Whiteness of a Different Color: European Immigrants and the Alchemy of Race* (Cambridge, Mass.: Harvard Univ. Press, 1998), 4 and passim.

11. *State* v. *Bell,* 7 Baxter (66 Tenn.) 9, 11 (Dec. term 1872). This case also appears in chapter 10.

12. *Lonas* v. *State,* 3 Heiskell (50 Tenn.) 287, 312 (Sept. term 1871); Edwin Brown Firmage and Richard Collin Mangrum, *Zion in the Courts: A Legal History of the Church of Jesus Christ of Latter-day Saints, 1830–1900* (Urbana: Univ. of Illinois Press, 1988), 129–32, 151–59; Sarah Barringer Gordon, *The Mormon Question: Polygamy and Constitutional Conflict in Nineteenth-Century America* (Chapel Hill: Univ. of North Carolina Press, 2002), esp. 113–45.

13. *State* v. *Jackson,* 80 Mo. 175, 177 (1883).

14. Nancy F. Cott comments on this problem in *Public Vows: A History of Marriage and the Nation* (Cambridge, Mass.: Harvard Univ. Press, 2000), 98–100. The matter came up in *Loving* when, in oral argument before the Supreme Court, the Virginia assistant attorney general put "the State's prohibition of racial intermarriage . . . on the same footing as the prohibition of polygamous marriage, or incestuous marriage," or such other restrictions as "the prescription of minimum ages at which people may marry." Philip B. Kurland and Gerhard Casper, eds., *Landmark Briefs and Arguments of the Supreme Court of the United States: Constitutional Law* (Arlington, Va.: Univ. Publications of America, 1975), 64: 987.

15. John Brown, a black man convicted in the 1870s in Michigan of bigamy, argued that he ought to be let off because his second marriage—the one that led to his legal problems—was to a white woman, violated Michigan's miscegenation law, and was therefore void. The appeals court rejected the claim. *People* v. *Brown,* 34 Mich. 339 (1876).

16. *Tutty* v. *State,* 41 F. Cas. 753, 756 (1890).

17. See chapters 12 and 15; *Ratcliff* v. *State,* 107 So.2d 728 (Miss., 1958); *Rose* v. *State,* 107 So.2d 730 (Miss., 1958); *State* v. *Brown,* 236 La. 562, 108 So.2d 233 (La., 1959).

9. Drawing and Redrawing the Color Line

1. "Attacks Johnson Marriage," *New York Times,* 12 Dec. 1912: 24.

2. Ibid.

3. Ibid.

4. Ibid.

5. W. E. B. Du Bois, *The Souls of Black Folk: Essays and Sketches* (1903; reprint, Greenwich, Conn.: Fawcett, 1961), 23. For more on Du Bois, see Lee D. Baker, *From Savage to Negro: Anthropology and the Construction of Race, 1896–1954* (Berkeley: Univ. of California Press, 1998), and Matthew Pratt Guterl, *The Color of Race in America, 1900–1940* (Cambridge, Mass.: Harvard Univ. Press, 2001), ch. 3. As for the origins of the southern surge toward a more impassable color line, an account that has regionwide implications is Glenda Elizabeth Gilmore, *Gender and Jim Crow: Women and the Politics of White Supremacy in North Carolina, 1896–1920* (Chapel Hill: Univ. of North Carolina Press, 1996); see 68–73.

6. The NAACP Papers (Library of Congress) reveal the considerable effort that the organization invested in keeping the antimiscegenation regime from spreading. The organization was mounting a containment policy, not a rollback effort; the object was to prevent enactment of new statutes, not obtain repeal of current ones. According to one close student of the subject, "The NAACP and its allies had succeeded in every anti-miscegenation free jurisdiction in preventing the passage of the intermarriage legislation introduced in the 1914–1929 period." Byron Curti Martyn, "Racism in the United States: A History of Anti-Miscegenation Legislation and Litigation" (Ph.D. diss., Univ. of Southern California, 1979), 1078.

7. Appendix 1; David H. Fowler, *Northern Attitudes towards Interracial Marriage: Legislation and Public Opinion in the Middle Atlantic and the States of the Old Northwest, 1780–1930* (New York: Garland, 1987), 247–65, appendix.

8. Georgia, *Acts* (1927), 272–79 (no. 317, secs. 1 and 14).

9. Virginia, *Acts* (1910), 581 (ch. 357, art. 49). On the eve of the Civil War, according to Virginia law, "Every person who has one-fourth part or more of negro blood shall be deemed a mulatto, and the word 'negro' [in any Virginia statute] shall be construed to mean mulatto as well as negro." Immediately after the Civil War and emancipation, an 1866 act offered new language—dropping the term "mulatto"—but left definitions largely intact: "every person having one-fourth or more of negro blood, shall be deemed a colored person, and every person, not a colored person, having one-fourth or more of Indian blood, shall be deemed an Indian." Virginia, *Code* (1860), 510 (title 30, ch. 103, sec. 9); Virginia, *Acts* (1865–66), 84 (ch. 17, sec. 1).

10. Regarding twentieth-century definitions of race for purposes of regulating marriage, see Paul Finkelman, "The Color of Law," *Northwestern University Law Review* 87, no. 3 (1993), 955 note 96, drawn from Pauli Murray, comp., *States' Laws on Race and Color* (1950; reprint, Athens: Univ. of Georgia Press, 1997).

11. *Moon* v. *Children's Home Society of Virginia,* 112 Va. 737, 741 (1911); Linda Cousins, "The Case against the Moons," graduate student research paper, Virginia Tech, HIST 4124, History of Virginia, March 1994.

12. *Moon* v. *Children's Home Society of Virginia,* 742.

13. Note on the *Moon* case, by James F. Minor and Minor Bronaugh, *Virginia Law Review* 17 (Jan. 1911): 692–99, quotation from 698.

14. Ibid., 692.

15. Virginia, *Acts* (1924), 534–35 (ch. 371, art. 5). Regarding the new law and its cultural context, see Richard B. Sherman, "'The Last Stand': The Fight for Racial Integrity in Virginia in the 1920s," *Journal of Southern History* 54 (Feb. 1988): 69–92; Paul A. Lombardo, "Miscegenation, Eugenics, and Racism: Historical Footnotes to *Loving* v. *Virginia*," *U.C. Davis Law Review* 21 (winter 1988): 421–52; John Douglas Smith, "Managing White Supremacy: Politics and Culture in Virginia, 1919–1939" (Ph.D. diss., Univ. of Virginia, 1998), 85–104; Barbara Bair, "Remapping the Black/White Body: Sexuality, Nationalism, and Biracial Antimiscegenation Activism in 1920s Virginia," in Martha Hodes, ed., *Sex, Love, Race: Crossing Boundaries in North American History* (New York: New York Univ. Press, 1999), ch. 19; and, more broadly, Keith E. Sealing, "Blood Will Tell: Scientific Racism and the Legal Prohibitions against Miscegenation," *Michigan Journal of Race & Law* 5 (spring 2000): 559–609.

16. If Virginia was not intentionally targeting Asians in 1924, Congress that year certainly was, in the Immigration Act of 1924, which has also been called the Oriental Exclusion Act; see David M. Reimers, *Still the Golden Door: The Third World Comes to America* (New York: Columbia Univ. Press, 1985), 4–7, and Mae M. Ngai, "The Architecture of Race in American Immigration Law: Reexamination of the Immigration Act of 1924," *Journal of American History* 86 (June 1999): 67–92.

17. In the wake of Virginia's 1924 law on racial purity, the courts faced cases alleging hidden African ancestry; then Plecker went to work to maintain the color line in public schools by propelling some children out of "white" schools. Smith, "Managing White Supremacy," 305–312.

18. Sherman, "'The Last Stand,'" 80–81; Lombardo, "Miscegenation, Eugenics, and Racism," 440–46; J. David Smith, *The Eugenic Assault on America: Scenes in Red, White, and Black* (Fairfax, Va.: George Mason Univ. Press, 1993), 71–77; Smith, "Managing White Supremacy," 104–109.

19. Smith, "Managing White Supremacy," 302–305.

20. Virginia, *Acts* (1932), 68 (ch. 78). The new one-year minimum remained in effect when the Lovings encountered the Virginia statute in 1958.

21. *The Code of Alabama* (1852), 58 (title 1, ch. 1, art. 2, sec. 4).

22. Even after the change in 1907, Alabama's definition of a "negro" for purposes of determining miscegenation remained, as it long had, at one-eighth. *The Code of Alabama,* 3 vols. (1907), vol. 1 (Political): 218 (ch. 1, sec. 2, subsec. 5), and vol. 3 (Criminal): 791 (ch. 256, sec. 7421); Wallenstein, "Race, Marriage, and the Law of Freedom," 406–407; Joel Williamson, *New People: Miscegenation and Mulattoes in the United States* (New York: Free Press, 1980), 94, 103–108.

23. Alabama, *Acts* (1927), 717 (no. 626).

24. Ibid., 219. As the editor of the Alabama *Code* of 1940 noted (at 4: 217 [ch. 60, sec. 360]), "now one drop of negro blood seems to be sufficient to create the offense of miscegenation, when there is marriage, adultery or fornication."

25. *Thurman* v. *State,* 18 Ala. 276, 277 (1850).

26. One outcome of the 1927 redefinition of race in Alabama was a decision that some students, though formerly defined as white, would have to enroll instead at a local black school. Samuel Farmer's two children, an 8-year-old boy and a 12-year-old girl, had been attending white schools in Mobile for some years, but then the parents of some other children challenged the family's racial identity as white. When the children were refused further admission to the white schools, Farmer went to court to obtain an order that the school board readmit them. At trial, some people in the community recognized the family as white, but others pointed toward some African ancestry through the children's mother. Farmer, refused his petition, appealed to the Alabama Supreme Court. That court conceded, "The case presents a regrettable situation," but saw

insufficient grounds to overrule the trial court. *State ex rel. Farmer* v. *Board of School Commissioners of Mobile County et al.,* 226 Ala. 62, 64 (1933). For a similar case, see *Tucker* v. *Blease,* 97 S.C. 303 (1914).

27. In fact, the "one-drop" definition came to permeate the culture as well as the law, as people of all racial backgrounds, in the South and elsewhere, adopted it as a given; see F. James Davis, *Who Is Black? One Nation's Definition* (University Park: Pennsylvania State Univ. Press, 1991). Yet, though a number of southern states had legislated the "one-drop" rule by 1927, not all had, and certainly not all had done so "by the end of the nineteenth century," as stated in Adam Fairclough, *Better Day Coming: Blacks and Equality, 1890–2000* (New York: Viking, 2001), 26.

28. T. Lindsay Baker and Julie P. Baker, eds., *The WPA Oklahoma Slave Narratives* (Norman: Univ. of Oklahoma Press, 1996), 314–16; see also 227. Census figures for 1910 showed 1,657,155 residents: 1,444,531 whites (87.2 percent), 137,612 African Americans (8.3 percent), 74,825 Native Americans (4.5 percent), 139 Chinese, and 48 Japanese. U.S. Census Bureau, *Thirteenth Census of the United States: 1910,* vol. I, *Population* (Washington, D.C.: Government Printing Office, 1913), 141.

29. Phillip Mellinger, "Discrimination and Statehood in Oklahoma," *Chronicles of Oklahoma* 49 (autumn 1971): 340–77; Danney Goble, *Progressive Oklahoma: The Making of a New Kind of State* (Norman: Univ. of Oklahoma Press, 1980); Jimmie Lewis Franklin, *Journey toward Hope: A History of Blacks in Oklahoma* (Norman: Univ. of Oklahoma Press, 1982), 44–49; Murray R. Wickett, *Contested Territory: Whites, Native Americans, and African Americans in Oklahoma, 1865–1907* (Baton Rouge: Louisiana State Univ. Press, 2000), 34–41.

30. Desmond King, *Making Americans: Immigration, Race, and the Origins of the Diverse Democracy* (Cambridge, Mass.: Harvard Univ. Press, 2000), 129–54, quotation from 133.

31. Ibid., 135–36, 153; Frances Janet Hassencahl, "Harry H. Laughlin, 'Expert Eugenics Agent' for the House Committee on Immigration and Naturalization, 1921 to 1931" (Ph.D. diss., Case Western Reserve Univ., 1970). Nancy F. Cott, *Public Vows: A History of Marriage and the Nation* (Cambridge, Mass.: Harvard Univ. Press, 2000), ch. 6, explores the confluence of race, marriage, immigration, and policy. Ian F. Haney López, *White by Law: The Legal Construction of Race* (New York: New York Univ. Press, 1996), analyzes a series of federal court cases on racial identity and immigration and, in appendix A, 203–208, supplies a table summarizing them.

32. Fowler, *Northern Attitudes,* appendix. Widespread though the color line was, it could be a treacherous thing to define. Legislators in Arizona managed in 1901—by imposing two color lines, rather than just one—to produce a law banning "all marriages of persons of Caucasian blood, or their descendants, with negroes, Mongolians or Indians, and their descendants." Here was a law that placed one racial boundary between people with any "Caucasian blood" and everyone else—and drew another racial boundary between people with any African, Mongolian, or Native American ancestry and everyone else. As the law was drawn, a mixed-race person, partly Caucasian, could not marry anyone—not full Caucasian, not full non-Caucasian, and not a mixture of the two. In 1942 the Arizona Supreme Court, sympathetic but unyielding, saw the situation and described it: "Under [the Arizona law] a descendant of mixed blood cannot marry a Caucasian or a part Caucasian, for the reason that he is part Indian. He cannot marry an Indian or a part Indian because he is part Caucasian." The court conceded, "We think the language used by the lawmakers went far beyond what was intended." Nonetheless, the court would not second-guess the legislature, so the statute stood. *State* v. *Pass,* 121 Pac. 882, 883–84 (Ariz., 1942).

33. Ronald Takaki, *Strangers from a Different Shore: A History of Asian Americans* (Boston: Little, Brown, 1989), ch. 9.

34. Barbara M. Posadas, "Crossed Boundaries in Interracial Chicago: Pilipino American Families since 1925," *Amerasia Journal* 8, no. 2 (fall-winter 1981): 31–52, quotation at 41.

35. Takaki, *Strangers from a Different Shore,* 317–30, 341–43; Sucheng Chan, *Asian Americans: An Interpretive History* (Boston: Twayne, 1991), 59–60. For more regarding miscegenation laws

and Asians and Asian Americans, see Rachel F. Moran, *Interracial Intimacy: The Regulation of Race and Romance* (Chicago: Univ. of Chicago Press, 2001), 30–41; Henry Yu, *Thinking Orientals: Migration, Contact, and Exoticism in Modern America* (Oxford: Oxford Univ. Press, 2001), 54–63 (though Washington State did not have a miscegenation law); and Leti Volpp, "Constructing Lat-Crit Theory—Diversity, Commonality, and Identity: American Mestizo—Filipinos and Antimiscegenation Laws in California," *U.C. Davis Law Review* 33 (summer 2000): 795–835.

36. *Roldan* v. *Los Angeles County*, 129 Cal. Apps. 267 (1933); California, *Acts* (1933), 561–62 (chs. 104–105).

37. The Maryland law defined only one of the three groups, "a person of negro descent, to the third generation, inclusive." In much the same way, the Utah statute prohibited marriages between "a Mongolian, member of the malay race or a mulatto, quadroon, or octoroon, and a white person." Arizona, *Acts* (1931), 27 (ch. 17); Maryland, *Acts* (1935), 101–102 (ch. 60); Utah, *Acts* (1939), 66 (ch. 50). In all, 14 states expressly restricted marriages between Caucasians and at least some Asians; in addition, Virginia's 1924 act left Asians on the nonwhite side of the racial boundary.

38. Regarding inheritance, see chapter 11. Regarding education, see above, notes 17 and 26, and Peter Wallenstein, "Black Southerners and Non-Black Universities: Desegregating Higher Education, 1935–1967," *History of Higher Education Annual* 19 (1999): 121–48. Regarding the adoption of miscegenation laws in Nazi Germany and apartheid South Africa, see appendix 2. For a revealing episode from the 1920s in New York (a state that never had a miscegenation law), see Earl Lewis and Heidi Ardizzone, *Love on Trial: An American Scandal in Black and White* (New York: Norton, 2001).

10. Boundaries of Race and Place

1. "Intermarriage of the Races," Charleston (S.C.) *News and Courier,* 31 Oct. 1881. The mysteries—and the critical importance to the parties concerned—of discerning racial identity prevailed before the Civil War as well as afterwards. On this, see Ariela J. Gross, "Litigating Whiteness: Trials of Racial Determination in the Nineteenth Century South," 108 *Yale Law Journal* (Oct. 1998): 109–188, and Eva Saks, "Representing Miscegenation Law," *Raritan* 8 (1988): 39–69. For one appeals court's thorough airing of various state provisions on racial identity, and the problems of assigning racial identity under the law, see *State* v. *Treadaway,* 52 So. 500 (La., 1910).

2. George Brown Tindall, *South Carolina Negroes, 1877–1900* (Columbia: Univ. of South Carolina Press, 1952), 299.

3. For literature on the individual, social, and legal construction of racial identity in America between the Civil War and the end of the twentieth century, see Ian F. Haney López, *White by Law: The Legal Construction of Race* (New York: New York Univ. Press, 1996); Virginia R. Domínguez, *White by Definition: Social Classification in Creole Louisiana* (New Brunswick, N.J.: Rutgers Univ. Press, 1986); Ruth Frankenberg, *White Women, Race Matters: The Social Construction of Whiteness* (Minneapolis: Univ. of Minnesota Press, 1993); Matthew Frye Jacobson, *Whiteness of a Different Color: European Immigrants and the Alchemy of Race* (Cambridge, Mass.: Harvard Univ. Press, 1998); and epilogue, notes 2–3.

4. *McPherson* v. *Commonwealth,* 69 Va. (28 Gratt.) 939 (1877).

5. Ibid., 940–41.

6. Ibid.

7. *Jones* v. *Commonwealth,* 79 Va. 213, 216–17 (1884) (hereafter Jones I); marriage license issued to Isaac Jones and Martha A. Gray, 15 Feb. 1883, Montgomery County Courthouse, Christiansburg, Va. My thanks to Virginia Tech undergraduate Chas Novak for tracking down the license.

8. *Jones* v. *Commonwealth* and *Gray* v. *Commonwealth,* 80 Va. 538, 541 (1885) (hereafter Jones II); Ann S. Swain, "Christiansburg Institute: From Freedmen's Bureau Enterprise to Public High School" (M.A. thesis, Radford Univ., 1975), 25, 66–67.

9. Jones II, 542.

10. Jones I, 216.

11. Jones II, 538, 544.

12. Ibid., 542.

13. Ibid., 544–45. For a provocative analysis of the politics of white identity in late-nineteenth century Virginia (and by extension elsewhere), see Jane Dailey, *Before Jim Crow: The Politics of Race in Postemancipation Virginia* (Chapel Hill: Univ. of North Carolina Press, 2000), chs. 3 and 5.

14. *State* v. *Bell,* 7 Baxter (66 Tenn.) 9 (Dec. term 1872).

15. Ibid. See the interlude for a long quotation from this decision.

16. *Kinney* v. *Commonwealth,* 30 Grattan (71 Va.) 858 (1878).

17. Ibid., 858–60.

18. Ibid., 861–62.

19. Ibid., 866; *Inhabitants of Medway* v. *Inhabitants of Needham,* 16 Mass. 157 (1819).

20. *Kinney* v. *Commonwealth,* 868.

21. Ibid., 869.

22. Ibid., 870; Soundex, Census of 1880, Virginia, microfilm, National Archives (the microfilmed Population Schedule is missing the pages around the Kinney household).

23. Virginia, *Acts* (1877–78), 302 (ch. 7, art. 8).

24. Ibid. (art. 3).

25. *State* v. *Isaac Kennedy and Mag Kennedy,* 76 N.C. 251, 252–53 (1877). Compare this statement with *Inhabitants of Medway* v. *Inhabitants of Needham,* a Massachusetts decision that had ruled the contrary (see chapter 3).

26. *State* v. *Pink Ross and Sarah Ross,* 76 N.C. 242, 243 (1877).

27. Ibid., 245.

28. Ibid., 243–44, 247.

29. Ibid., 245, 249–50.

30. Ibid., 249–50.

31. Ibid., 250.

32. *Jackson* v. *Jackson,* 82 Md. 17, 30 (1895).

33. *Toler* v. *Oakwood Smokeless Coal Corporation,* 173 Va. 425, 430 (1939).

34. "Ruled a Negro, Man Must Quit White Wife," *Richmond Times-Dispatch,* 8 June 1938: 1.

35. Ibid. For another account, with photographs, see J. Robert Smith, "Nazi Virginians Separate Man and Ofay Wife," *Afro American and Richmond Planet,* 18 June 1938: 1–2. For other cases from Virginia, including *Keith* v. *Commonwealth,* 165 Va. 705 (1935), see chapter 9 and Peter Wallenstein, "Race, Marriage, and the Law of Freedom: Alabama and Virginia, 1860s–1960s," *Chicago-Kent Law Review* 70, no. 2 (1994), 411–14. For greater context, see John Douglas Smith, "Managing White Supremacy: Politics and Culture in Virginia, 1919–1939" (Ph.D. diss., Univ. of Virginia, 1998).

36. "Miscegenation Charge Here Is Dismissed," *Richmond Times-Dispatch,* 4 Feb. 1949: 2.

37. Ibid. Resembling Purcell's case, but far more visible at the time, was the case of a mystery man from Mississippi, *Knight* v. *State,* 207 Miss. 564 (1949). Davis Knight, who served in the U.S. Navy as a white man during World War II, married a white woman, Junie Lee Spradley, in 1946. Two years later, he was indicted for miscegenation, a black man with a white wife. He was convicted, but the Mississippi Supreme Court reversed the verdict and remanded the case, and Knight, whether "white" or "black," was never tried again. Victoria E. Bynum, "'White Negroes' in Segregated Mississippi: Miscegenation, Racial Identity, and the Law," *Journal of Southern History* 64 (May 1998): 247–76.

38. *Calma* v. *Calma,* 203 Va. 880 (1962).

39. Ibid., 882.

40. Ibid.

11. Racial Identity and Family Property

1. *In re Walker's Estate,* 5 Ariz. 70, 46 Pac. 67, 69 (1896). For a similar, later case, see *In re Takahashi's Estate,* 113 Mont. 490 (1942). For a complementary assessment, see Peggy Pascoe, "Race, Gender, and the Privileges of Property: On the Significance of Miscegenation Law in the U.S. West," in Valerie Matsumoto and Blake Allmendinger, eds., *Over the Edge: Remapping the American West* (Berkeley: Univ. of California Press, 1999), 215–30. More generally, see Cheryl I. Harris, "Whiteness as Property," *Harvard Law Review* 106 (1993): 1707–91.

2. *Greenhow* v. *James Executor,* 80 Va. 636, 644 (1885).

3. Ibid.

4. Ibid., 641–42.

5. Ibid., 645.

6. Ibid., 645, 649.

7. Ibid., 649–50.

8. *Whittington* v. *McCaskill,* 65 Fla. 162 (1913).

9. Ibid., 165. For a comparable case with a similar outcome, see *Miller* v. *Lucks,* 203 Miss. 824 (1948).

10. *Keen* v. *Keen,* 184 Mo. 358, 369 (1904); Kim Schreck, "Contested Wills: Race, Gender and the Missouri Supreme Court's Renunciation of a Family," paper presented at the Fifth Southern Conference on Women's History, Richmond, Va., 16 June 2000.

11. *Keen* v. *Keen,* 201 U.S. 319 (1906).

12. *Succession of Yoist,* 132 La. 309 (1913).

13. *Succession of Segura,* 134 La. 84, 85 (1913).

14. Ibid., 92–93.

15. *Murdock* v. *Potter,* 99 So. 18 (La., 1924).

16. Ibid.

17. Ibid., 19.

18. Ibid., 22.

19. *Baker* v. *Carter,* 180 Okla. 71 (1937).

20. Ibid., 72.

21. Ibid.

22. *Eggers* v. *Olson,* 104 Okla. 297, 301 (1924).

12. Miscegenation Laws and Federal Courts, 1941–1963

1. Regarding Oklahoma's law of racial identity, see chapter 9.

2. Peter Wallenstein, "Native Americans Are White, African Americans Are Not: Racial Identity, Marriage, Inheritance, and the Law—Oklahoma, 1907–1967," *Journal of the West* 39 (Jan. 2000): 55–63; *Atkins* v. *Rust,* 151 Okla. 294 (1931). A later case, *Dick* v. *Reaves* (1967), appears in chapter 16. For another treatment, see Charles Frank Robinson II, "The Antimiscegenation Conversation: Love's Legislated Limits (1868–1967)" (Ph.D. diss., Univ. of Houston, 1998), ch. 5.

3. *Blake* v. *Sessions,* 94 Okla. 59, 61–62 (1923).

4. The sources for this account of William Stevens and Stella Sands are *Stevens* v. *United States,* 146 F.2d 120 (1944), and a folder on *Stevens* v. *U.S.* in the NAACP Papers, II B 82, Library of Congress. My thanks to Virginia Tech undergraduate Kirsten Carter Davis for her assistance in getting me copies of the NAACP materials.

5. Response to Objections to Probate of Will; Complaint in Intervention of the United States of America, in NAACP Papers.

6. Reply to Response to Objections to Probate of Will.

7. Findings of Fact and Conclusions of Law; Judgment of the U.S. District Court.

8. Emery to Marshall, 5 Jan. 1944.

9. Ibid.

10. Marshall to Emery, 20 Jan. 1944.

11. Emery to Marshall, 25 Jan. 1944.

12. Konvitz to Emery, 12 April 1944.

13. Hastie actually told Konvitz that Oklahoma probably had authority "to invalidate interracial marriages and to invalidate any such inheritance of such property predicated upon such a marriage," though that may have been Hastie's assessment of a likely ruling, not his own considered opinion. Emery to Konvitz, 14 April 1944; Konvitz to Emery, 17 April 1944; Hastie to Konvitz, 18 April 1944; Konvitz to Marshall, 25 July 1944.

14. Marshall to Emery, 4 May 1944.

15. *Stevens v. United States*, 122.

16. Ibid., 123.

17. Ibid., 124.

18. Emery to Marshall, 9 March 1944.

19. Emery to Marshall, 8 March 1945.

20. For example, Emery was told, the NAACP was at that very time trying to figure out what course of action to pursue regarding another matter: "One of the toughest problems facing the Negro today from a legal standpoint is the breaking down of segregation in transportation throughout the South yet there is divided opinion upon whether or not the time is ripe to present to the Supreme Court the question—is segregation per se discrimination?" The white Democratic primary—a primary election from which black voters were excluded—offered an even better example, Emery was told: "I am sure you can appreciate the fact that one bad decision may operate as a precedent which it will take many years to undo. The case of *Grovey* vs. *Townsend* is but one example"—a decision (upholding the white Democratic primary) that was handed down by the Supreme Court in 1935 and not overturned until *Smith* v. *Allwright* in 1944. Edward R. Dudley, assistant special counsel, to Emery, 16 March 1945.

21. *Jackson v. State*, 37 Ala. App. 519, 521 (1954); Chang Moon Sohn, "Principle and Expediency in Judicial Review: Miscegenation Cases in the Supreme Court" (Ph.D. diss., Columbia Univ., 1970), 70–73.

22. *Jackson v. State*, 260 Ala. 698 (1954); *Jackson v. Alabama*, 348 U.S. 888 (1954); *Brown* v. *Board of Education*, 347 U.S. 483 (1954); *Brown* v. *Board of Education*, 349 U.S. 294 (1955).

23. Justice William O. Douglas Papers, Box 1156, Library of Congress; Peter Wallenstein, "Race, Marriage, and the Law of Freedom: Alabama and Virginia, 1860s–1960s," *Chicago-Kent Law Review* 70, no. 2 (1994), 415, 416 note 215.

24. William O. Douglas Papers; *Jackson v. Alabama*, 888.

25. Gregory Michael Dorr, "Principled Expediency: Eugenics, *Naim* v. *Naim*, and the Supreme Court," *American Journal of Legal History* 42 (April 1998): 119–59; *Naim* v. *Virginia*, 350 U.S. 891 (1955); *Naim* v. *Virginia*, 350 U.S. 985 (1956); Sohn, "Principle and Expediency," 73–94; "Racial Intermarriage Case Faces High Court," *Richmond Times-Dispatch*, 7 Oct. 1954: 2; "State's High Court Spurns U.S. Order," *Richmond Times-Dispatch*, 19 Jan. 1956: 1.

26. "Virginia Ban on Racial Intermarriages Is Upheld," *Richmond Times-Dispatch*, 14 June 1955: 5.

27. Sohn, "Principle and Expediency," 74–75.

28. *Naim v. Naim*, 197 Va. 80, 90 (1955).

29. Ibid., 88.

30. Bernard Schwartz, *Super Chief: Earl Warren and His Supreme Court—A Judicial Biography* (New York: New York Univ. Press, 1983), 158–62. The clerks are quoted in Dorr, "Principled Expediency," 149, 149 note 134.

31. The refusal to take the Jackson and Naim cases reflected less an inclination to uphold the antimiscegenation regime than a strong sense that the time was inauspicious for throwing out the ancient laws; see Andrew Kull, *The Color-Blind Constitution* (Cambridge, Mass.: Harvard Univ. Press, 1992), 159–60, 278 note 11.

32. Memorandum from Justice Frankfurter, read at conference 4 Nov. 1955, John Marshall Harlan Papers, Box 11, Mudd Library, Princeton Univ. The memorandum's author is identified in Kull, *Color-Blind Constitution,* 159, and Dorr, "Principled Expediency," 150 note 139.

33. Memorandum from Justice Frankfurter.

34. *Naim v. Naim,* 350 U.S. 891 (1955); *Naim v. Naim,* 197 Va. 734, 735 (1956). See the caustic evaluation of the Supreme Court's actions, Mark Tushnet, "The Warren Court as History: An Interpretation," in Mark Tushnet, ed., *The Warren Court in Historical and Political Perspective* (Charlottesville: Univ. Press of Virginia, 1993), 5.

35. "Virginia's Top Tribunal Rejects Order of U.S. Supreme Court," *Richmond Times-Dispatch,* 19 Jan. 1956: 12.

36. *Naim v. Naim,* 350 U.S. 985 (1956); "High Court Shelves Plea by Seaman," *Richmond Times-Dispatch,* 13 Mar. 1956: 3; Walter Wadlington, "The *Loving* Case: Virginia's Anti-Miscegenation Statute in Historical Perspective," *Virginia Law Review* 52 (Nov. 1966)," 1210–12; Dorr, "Principled Expediency," 155–59; Gerald Gunther, *Learned Hand: The Man and the Judge* (New York: Knopf, 1994), 666–70, 782. Gunther says about miscegenation laws that "most southern states" (666) had them in the 1950s. In fact, all 17 did until 1967.

37. Sohn, "Principle and Expediency," 70, 73–94.

38. "Views of Two Negro Leaders on Integration and Interracial Marriages," *U.S. News & World Report,* 19 Sept. 1958, 90.

39. CBS transcript from 7 Sept. 1958, ibid.

40. "Interracial Marriage and the Race Problem—as Leading Authorities See It," *U.S. News & World Report,* 18 Nov. 1963: 88. Nabrit was a former professor and then dean of the Howard University Law School, where many civil rights lawyers had trained. See also Peter Wallenstein, "Race, Marriage, and the Law of Freedom: Alabama and Virginia, 1860s–1960s," *Chicago-Kent Law Review* 70, no. 2 (1994), 435–36; Gunnar Myrdal, with the assistance of Richard Sterner and Arnold Rose, *An American Dilemma: The Negro Problem and Modern Democracy* (New York: Harper & Brothers, 1944), 60–62; David W. Southern, *Gunnar Myrdal and Black-White Relations: The Use and Abuse of An American Dilemma, 1944–1969* (Baton Rouge: Louisiana State Univ. Press, 1987), 283–87.

41. "Truman Opposes Biracial Marriage," *New York Times,* 12 Sept. 1963: 30.

42. Ibid.

43. Ibid.

44. Benjamin Quarles, "A. Philip Randolph: Labor Leader at Large," in John Hope Franklin and August Meier, eds., *Black Leaders of the Twentieth Century* (Urbana: Univ. of Illinois Press, 1982), ch. 7; Paula Pfeffer, *A. Philip Randolph: Pioneer of the Civil Rights Movement* (Baton Rouge: Louisiana State Univ. Press, 1990).

13. A Breakthrough Case in California

1. For an account and assessment of the Monks case, see Peggy Pascoe, "Miscegenation Law, Court Cases, and Ideologies of 'Race' in Twentieth-Century America," *Journal of American History* 83 (June 1996), 56–60.

2. Darlene Clark Hine, *Black Victory: The Rise and Fall of the White Democratic Primary in Texas* (Millwood, N.Y.: KTO Press, 1979); Clement E. Vose, *Caucasians Only: The Supreme Court,*

the *NAACP, and the Restrictive Covenant Cases* (Berkeley: Univ. of California Press, 1959); Donald G. Nieman, *Promises to Keep: African-Americans and the Constitutional Order, 1776 to the Present* (New York: Oxford Univ. Press, 1991).

3. Catherine A. Barnes, *Journey from Jim Crow: The Desegregation of Southern Transit* (New York: Columbia Univ. Press, 1983); Richard Kluger, *Simple Justice: The History of Brown v. Board of Education and Black America's Struggle for Equality* (New York: Knopf, 1976), chs. 9, 12.

4. *Meyer v. Nebraska*, 262 U.S. 390, 399 (1923); David J. Garrow, *Liberty and Sexuality: The Right to Privacy and the Making of Roe v. Wade* (New York: Macmillan, 1994); William G. Ross, *Forging New Freedoms: Nativism, Education, and the Constitution, 1917–1927* (Lincoln: Univ. of Nebraska Press, 1994).

5. *Perez v. Sharp*, 32 Cal.2d 711, 198 P.2d 171 (1948). The *Perez* case started out much as did that of Salvador Roldan in the 1930s (see chapter 9).

6. *Perez v. Sharp*, 713.

7. Points and Authorities in Opposition to Issuance of Alternative Writ of Mandate, 18 Aug. 1947; Return by Way of Demurrer: Points and Authorities in Support of Demurrer, 6 Oct. 1947, 11, both in the *Perez* case file. I am indebted to Peggy Pascoe, now at the Univ. of Oregon, for supplying me a copy of the *Perez* case file (L.A. 20305) from the California State Archives, located in Roseville.

Regarding the state's arguments on polygamy, see interlude. On sterilization, see *Buck v. Bell*, 274 U.S. 200 (1927); William E. Leuchtenburg, *The Supreme Court Reborn: The Constitutional Revolution in the Age of Roosevelt* (New York: Oxford Univ. Press, 1995), ch. 1; and Philip R. Reilly, *The Surgical Solution: A History of Involuntary Sterilization in the United States* (Baltimore: Johns Hopkins Univ. Press, 1991).

8. One is tempted to guess that the American Civil Liberties Union took a hand in the case partly because of the First Amendment angle (also, perhaps, because individual rights of privacy were at the core of the controversy) but also by default, because no other organization would take on the issue. Benjamin Thomas Field, however, in "Justice Roger Traynor and His Case for Judicial Activism" (Ph.D. diss., Univ. of California, Berkeley, 2000), 36–38, warns that the ACLU's participation in *Perez* can be overstated—that in fact the group took no active role—and Marshall had his own political and religious reasons for playing the role he did. Either way, later cases show the ACLU's deepening involvement in a subsequent California case involving an interracial couple (see below, note 27); in the *Naim* case in the 1950s (see chapter 12); and in the 1960s cases, including its central involvement in *Loving v. Virginia* (see chapter 15). For a contrary view regarding *Perez*, see Chang Moon Sohn, "Principle and Expediency in Judicial Review: Miscegenation Cases in the Supreme Court" (Ph.D. diss., Columbia Univ., 1970), 127–29; for a discussion of the 1950s and 1960s as well, see ibid., 126–47.

9. Oral Argument in Support of Petition, 6 Oct. 1947, 3.

10. Ibid., 8, 13.

11. Ibid., 13; Oral Argument on Behalf of Respondent, 6 Oct. 1947, 6.

12. Petitioners' Reply Brief, 3 Nov. 1947, 27.

13. Ibid., 48.

14. Ibid., 24, 52, 55. For *Burns* and *Green*, see chapter 5.

15. *Perez v. Sharp*, 742, 752.

16. Ibid., 714–15. For assessments of Justice Traynor, see G. Edward White, *The American Judicial Tradition: Profiles of Leading American Judges* (expanded ed.; New York: Oxford Univ. Press, 1988), ch. 13, and Field, "Justice Roger Traynor."

17. *Perez v. Sharp*, 717, 727, 731–32; Pascoe, "Miscegenation Law, Court Cases, and Ideologies of 'Race' in Twentieth-Century America," 61–64.

18. *Perez v. Sharp*, 738–40. The larger Civil Rights Movement was played out in a Cold War context, a theme explored in Mary L. Dudziak, *Cold War Civil Rights: Race and the Image of*

American Democracy (Princeton: Princeton Univ. Press, 2000), and Thomas Borstelmann, *The Cold War and the Color Line: American Race Relations in the Global Arena* (Cambridge, Mass.: Harvard Univ. Press, 2001).

19. *Perez* v. *Sharp*, 733–35.

20. Answer to Petition for Rehearing, 2, 8.

21. Ibid., 11–12.

22. "State High Court Rules out Race as Barrier to Marriage," *Los Angeles Times*, 2 Oct. 1948, Part II: 5.

23. *Perez* v. *Sharp*, 726, 737.

24. Ibid., 748.

25. The minority's error was picked up by subsequent writers (on both sides of the issue) who assumed that the dissenting California judges had the history of miscegenation cases right, no matter how one evaluated their position on the law.

26. Rachel F. Moran, *Interracial Intimacy: The Regulation of Race and Romance* (Chicago: Univ. of California Press, 2001), 84–88.

27. Even in California, even after *Perez*, an interracial marriage could cause difficulties at the hands of public authority, as is recounted in *Race Relations Law Reporter* 3 (1958): 1002–1006.

28. Phillip I. Earl, "Nevada's Miscegenation Laws and the Marriage of Mr. and Mrs. Harry Bridges," *Nevada* 37 (spring 1994): 1–18.

29. Roger D. Hardaway, "Unlawful Love: A History of Arizona's Miscegenation Law," *Journal of Arizona History* 27 (winter 1986): 377–90. The decision in *Oyama* v. *O'Neill* is in *Race Relations Law Reporter* 5 (1960): 136–37.

30. In 1957, on the basis of the Fourteenth Amendment's equal protection clause, a judge in Baltimore overturned a Maryland miscegenation law, dating from 1699, that provided for imprisonment for at least 18 months for "any white woman who shall suffer or permit herself to be got with child by a Negro or mulatto." *Race Relations Law Reporter* 2 (1957): 676–78. The decision hinged on the disparate punishment for the white woman; it did not affect the law against interracial marriage.

14. Contesting the Antimiscegenation Regime

1. A case from Kentucky illustrates how questions of racial identity could jeopardize a divorced mother's retaining custody of her children from a failed marriage. Anna Eilers divorced George Eilers in 1963, and she was granted custody of their five children. That arrangement came into question, however, when she married Marshall C. Anderson in January 1964. All members of the Eilers family were white, but Anderson was black. Kentucky law did not permit Anna Eilers and Marshall Anderson to marry there, so they traveled from Louisville into Illinois, the nearest state without a miscegenation law. (Crossing the Ohio River into Indiana merely took them into another state that, as late as 1964, continued to bar their marriage, and Ohio was even farther away than Illinois.) Having solved one problem, the newlyweds encountered others just as big. He worked in a restaurant and part-time as a musician, and she was a waitress, but when he showed up in their car to pick her up at the end of her work day, she was fired. A custody dispute caused far greater grief, however, as her former husband took her to court to revoke the custody agreement. In September 1964, Judge Lyndon R. Schmid of the Jefferson County Circuit Court, ruling that Mrs. Anderson's marriage to "a colored man" was "detrimental to their best interests," ordered that the children be taken out of the Andersons' home, and they were placed in foster homes and juvenile institutions. A year and a half later, she was still fighting to regain custody. Ben A. Franklin, "Kentucky Facing Race Custody Suit," *New York Times* (hereafter *NYT*), 25 March 1966: 29; Ben A. Franklin, "Judge Bars Case of Miscegenation," *NYT*, 26 March 1966: 30; "N.A.A.C.P. to Fight Ruling on Custody," *NYT*, 8 July 1966: 12. See also chapter 16.

2. "Unitarian Cleric Who Visited Georgia Backs Miscegenation," *NYT*, 17 Sept. 1962: 63.

3. Ibid.

4. For evidence of widespread concern over interfaith marriages in 1960s America—and evidence that some couples sought to overcome all obstacles—see Paul R. Spickard, *Mixed Blood: Intermarriage and Ethnic Identity in Twentieth-Century America* (Madison: Univ. of Wisconsin Press, 1989), 185–99, 364, and 450 note 70, as well as "Rabbi Attacks Intermarriage," *NYT*, 2 Dec. 1963: 47; Paul L. Montgomery, "Orthodox Church Can Use English," *NYT*, 4 July 1964: 36; "Catholic Monk and Episcopalian Officiate Jointly at Wedding Rite," *NYT*, 4 July 1964: 15; "Ecumenical Jaywalking," *The Christian Century* 81 (28 Oct. 1964), 1326 (my thanks to Virginia Tech undergraduate Corinne Burton for bringing this item to my attention); "U.S. Clerics at Council Split on Marriage Laws," *NYT*, 21 Nov. 1964: 8; "Trenton Mayor Wed in Two Ceremonies," *NYT*, 2 Oct. 1966: 80; "George Dugan, "Lutherans Issue a Wedding Curb," *NYT*, 22 Oct. 1966: 33.

5. George Dugan, "Catholics Uphold Biracial Couples," *NYT*, 18 Nov. 1963: 47.

6. Ibid.

7. George Dugan, "Presbyterians Urged to Oppose Bans on Interracial Marriages," *NYT*, 22 May 1965: 20; George Dugan, "Race in Marriage Held Irrelevant," *NYT*, 25 May 1965: 24; George Dugan, "Presbyterians Favor New Doctrine," *NYT*, 26 May 1965: 40.

8. Dugan, "Presbyterians Favor New Doctrine." The 1966 International Convention of Christian Churches (Disciples of Christ) adopted a resolution urging members to "overcome" state miscegenation laws. George Dugan, "Protestant Unity Found Advancing," *NYT*, 29 Sept. 1966: 29.

9. "Panel Votes Race-Law Repeal," *NYT*, 21 Jan. 1965: 39; Austin C. Wehrwein, "Branigin in Quest of a New Indiana," *NYT*, 7 Feb. 1965: 52; Roger D. Hardaway, "Prohibiting Interracial Marriage: Miscegenation Laws in Wyoming," *Annals of Wyoming* 52 (spring 1980): 55–60. In Indiana, modest numbers of black-white marriages—roughly 50 per year, barely one per thousand total marriages—had been taking place even before repeal; Todd H. Pavela, "An Exploratory Study of Negro-White Intermarriage in Indiana," *Journal of Marriage and the Family* 26 (May 1964): 209–211.

10. Peter Wallenstein, "Black Southerners and Non-Black Universities: Desegregating Higher Education, 1935–1967," *History of Higher Education Annual* 19 (1999): 121–48.

11. James T. Patterson, *Brown v. Board of Education: A Civil Rights Milestone and Its Troubled Legacy* (New York: Oxford Univ. Press, 2001), xix (source of quotation), 6. Responses along these lines can be seen in letters at the Library of Virginia, Richmond, written at that time to U.S. District Judge Sterling Hutcheson. See also "What South Really Fears about Mixed Schools," *U.S. News & World Report*, 19 Sept. 1958, 76–90.

12. Evidence can be found in the chancellors' papers (particularly from the period around 1956, when the first two black students were admitted), in the archives of the University of North Carolina at Greensboro, a historically white school that, in the 1950s, was the Woman's College of the University.

13. Calvin Trillin, *An Education in Georgia: Charlayne Hunter, Hamilton Holmes, and the Integration of the University of Georgia* (1964; reprint Athens: Univ. of Georgia Press, 1991); Charlayne Hunter-Gault, *In My Place* (New York: Farrar Strauss Giroux, 1992), 177, 206–207; *Race Relations Law Reporter* 6 (1961–62): 125–26.

14. Martin Arnold, "First Negro Girl at U. of Georgia Wed Fellow Student from South," *NYT*, 3 Sept. 1963: 27; Trillin, *An Education in Georgia*, 175–78; Hunter-Gault, *In My Place*, 232–39, 252–53.

15. "Negro Coed Applied to Marry in Ohio," *NYT*, 5 Sept. 1963: 21; "Negro Coed Is Said to Have Wed Twice," *NYT*, 7 Sept. 1963: 10; Hunter-Gault, *In My Place*, 232–33.

16. "Negro Coed Is Said to Have Wed Twice."

17. "Georgia Calls Negro Coed's Wedding Illegal," *NYT,* 4 Sept. 1963: 27 (with photo); "Georgia Governor Assails Negro Girl's Marriage," *NYT,* 6 Sept. 1963: 13.

18. "Georgia Calls Negro Coed's Wedding Illegal"; "Mrs. Stovall Has Girl," *NYT,* 17 Nov. 1963: 77.

19. "Court in Maryland Avoids a Ruling on Miscegenation," *NYT,* 14 Feb. 1964: 33.

20. "Illinois Allows Wedding Prohibited in Missouri," *NYT,* 11 July 1965: 49.

21. "Samoa Dancer and White Nurse Denied a Marriage in Maryland," *NYT,* 12 Feb. 1966: 46 (with photo); "Samoan Wed in Washington after Baltimore Rejection," *NYT,* 20 Feb. 1966: 51.

22. "Maryland Bars Repeal on Interracial Marriage," *NYT,* 9 March 1966: 8; "Maryland Senate Approves Ending Miscegenation Ban," *NYT,* 23 March 1966: 30; "Miscegenation Ban Voted in Maryland," *NYT,* 29 March 1966: 29.

23. "Maryland Governor Gets a Bill To Abolish Miscegenation Bill," *NYT,* 4 March 1967: 15; *Race Relations Law Reporter* 12 (1967): 1625.

24. *McLaughlin v. State,* 153 So.2d 1 (1963); *McLaughlin v. Florida,* 379 U.S. 184, 187 (1964); Arthur Krock, "A Direct High Court Test of Miscegenation Laws," *NYT,* 1 Nov. 1963: 32; Anthony Lewis, "Race, Sex, and the Supreme Court," *NYT Magazine,* 22 Nov. 1964, VI: 30, 130–34. Regarding the NAACP Legal Defense Fund's leadership in the case, see Chang Moon Sohn, "Principle and Expediency in Judicial Review: Miscegenation Cases in the Supreme Court (Ph.D. diss., Columbia Univ., 1970), 94–107.

25. *McLaughlin v. State,* 2–3.

26. *McLaughlin v. Florida,* 187.

27. Ibid., 186–87, 193–94; Peter Wallenstein, "Race, Marriage, and the Law of Freedom: Alabama and Virginia, 1860s–1960s," *Chicago-Kent Law Review* 70, no. 2 (1994), 421 note 241.

28. *McLaughlin v. Florida,* 188–89.

29. Ibid., 191–92; Del Dickson, ed., *The Supreme Court in Conference (1940–1985): The Private Discussions behind Nearly 300 Supreme Court Decisions* (New York: Oxford Univ. Press, 2001), 693–94.

30. *McLaughlin v. Florida,* 196.

31. Ibid., 195.

32. Ibid., 195–96.

33. Ibid., 198.

34. Tinsley E. Yarbrough, *John Marshall Harlan: Great Dissenter of the Warren Court* (New York: Oxford Univ. Press, 1992), 267–69.

35. For leads on other possible test cases, see Sohn, "Principle and Expediency," 135–36; Melvin L. Wulf to Robert Cohen (7 June 1963, ACLU Papers, 1963, vol. 32), regarding a prosecution that appeared imminent in Norfolk, Virginia; and D. A. Berube Jr. to ACLU (9 Jan. 1966, ACLU Papers, 1966, vol. 13), for a case that looked like it might emerge in Mississippi.

36. Samuel Walker, *In Defense of American Liberties: A History of the ACLU* (New York: Oxford Univ. Press, 1990), ch. 12, focuses on "The Civil Rights Revolution," but Walker neither discusses the ACLU's crusade against miscegenation laws nor mentions the *Loving* case. A single sentence (239) mentions the successful suit in *Perez* v. *Sharp* (see chapter 13).

37. See chapters 9 and 12.

38. *Jones* v. *Shaw,* 441 P.2d 990, 991 (Okla., 1965).

39. "State Miscegenation Laws Challenged," ACLU Weekly Bulletin #2269, 13 June 1966; Sohn, "Principle and Expediency," 136–37.

40. *Jones* v. *Shaw,* 992.

41. *Jones* v. *Lorenzen,* 441 P.2d 986, 987–88 (Okla., 1965).

42. Ibid., 989–90. In 1965, four black members of the Oklahoma legislature sponsored a bill to repeal the miscegenation law. But that effort failed, as did another in 1967, and the law was re-

pealed only after the U.S. Supreme Court's 1967 ruling in the *Loving* case. Gene Aldrich, *Black Heritage of Oklahoma* (Edmond, Okla.: Thompson Book and Supply Co., 1973), 53–65.

43. *Jones* v. *Lorenzen*, 986; "State Miscegenation Laws Challenged," ACLU Weekly Bulletin #2269; "Marriage to Negro Barred; Oklahoman Weds White Girl," *NYT*, 30 Nov. 1965: 11.

15. The Lovings versus Virginia

1. "Transcript of the President's News Conference on Foreign and Domestic Matters," *New York Times* (hereafter *NYT*), 2 Aug. 1963: 10.

2. *Loving* v. *Commonwealth* (Record No. 6163), Supreme Court of Appeals of Virginia, 2–4. The Lovings never knew who complained to authorities in Caroline County about them.

3. Phone interview with Mildred D. Loving, 7 Jan. 1994.

4. Ibid.; Record No. 6163, 2–4.

5. Record No. 6163, 5–6.

6. They lived at 1151 Neal Street Northeast with Mildred Loving's cousin, Alex Byrd, and his wife, Laura. Phone interview with Mildred D. Loving, 7 Jan. 1994; interview with Mildred D. Loving, 12 Aug. 1995; *Polk's Washington City Directory* (1962), 226, 950; "The Crime of Being Married," *Life Magazine* 60 (18 Mar. 1966): 85–91.

7. Mildred D. Loving to Eleanor Rose, 31 Jan. 1996. At the request of her mother, historian Anne Rose, I put Eleanor Rose (a public school student at the time working on a National History Day project) in touch with Mrs. Loving, and I thank her for a copy of the letter she received from Mrs. Loving.

8. "Anti Miscegenation Case Move Rejected," *Richmond News Leader*, 29 Oct. 1964: 21. At the time, no Virginia ACLU affiliate yet existed. The ACLU Archives (Mudd Library, Princeton University) demonstrate the organization's long-term commitment to eradicating the nation's miscegenation laws.

9. Interview with Bernard S. Cohen, 4 Jan. 1994.

10. Ibid.; *Fuller* v. *Commonwealth*, 189 Va. 327, 330, 333 (1949).

11. The Lovings are listed as late as 1967 as living at the home of Alex Byrd. Phone interview with Mildred D. Loving, 7 Jan. 1994; *Polk's Washington City Directory* (1967), 827.

12. Interview with Bernard S. Cohen, 4 Jan. 1994; Motion to Vacate Judgment and Set Aside Sentence, Nov. 6, 1963, *Loving* v. *Commonwealth* (Record No. 6163), 6–7.

13. Interview with Bernard S. Cohen, 4 Jan. 1994; phone interview with Philip J. Hirschkop, 18 Aug. 1994.

14. "Pair Files Suit to End State Ban," *Richmond News Leader*, 28 Oct. 1964: 23; "Anti-Miscegenation Case Move Rejected"; "Couple Begins Legal Attack on Mixed-Marriage Law," *NYT*, 29 Oct. 1964: 26; "Mixed-Marriage Ban Is Fought in Virginia," *NYT*, 29 Dec. 1964: 35.

15. Opinion, *Loving* v. *Commonwealth* (Record No. 6163), 10–12; *Kinney* v. *Commonwealth*, 71 Va. (30 Gratt.) 858 (1878).

16. Opinion, *Loving* v. *Commonwealth* (Record No. 6163), 15. For a biographical sketch of the judge, see John Edward Lane III, "Leon Maurice Bazile" (1890–1967), in W. Hamilton Bryson, ed., *Legal Education in Virginia, 1779–1979* (Charlottesville: Univ. Press of Virginia, 1982), 82–86.

17. "Mixed Couple Case Delayed in Virginia," *NYT*, 28 Jan. 1965: 17; "U.S. Court Defers on Race Question," *NYT*, 13 Feb. 1965: 17; *Perez* v. *Sharp*, 32 Cal. 2d. 711, 734–35 (1948); Petition for Writ of Error, *Loving* v. *Commonwealth* (Record No. 6163), 10.

18. *Loving* v. *Commonwealth*, 206 Va. 924, 929 (1966); "Ban on Interracial Marriages Upheld by Virginia High Court," *NYT*, 8 Mar. 1966: 26.

19. "Virginia Suit Scores Mixed Marriage Ban," *NYT*, 30 July 1966: 9.

20. "The Crime of Being Married," 91.

21. Philip B. Kurland and Gerhard Casper, eds., *Landmark Briefs and Arguments of the Supreme Court of the United States: Constitutional Law* (Arlington, Va.: Univ. Publications of America, 1975), 64: 787–88.

22. Nimetz, 10 Oct. 1966, Harlan Papers, Box 285, Mudd Library, Princeton University.

23. William D. Zabel to Arthur L. Berney, 24 Jan. 1967, ACLU Papers, Mudd Library, Princeton University, 1966, vol. 13; see also William D. Zabel, "Interracial Marriage and the Law," *Atlantic Monthly* (Oct. 1965): 75–79.

24. Kurland and Casper, *Landmark Briefs and Arguments,* 64: 976–1003.

25. Ibid., 763, 895, 918; "Supreme Court Agrees to Rule on State Miscegenation Laws," *NYT,* 13 Dec. 1966: 40.

26. Kurland and Casper, *Landmark Briefs and Arguments,* 64: 960–72, 1003–1007. For the full transcript of the oral argument, see ibid., 960–1007. An abbreviated version is in Peter Irons and Stephanie Guitton, eds., *May It Please the Court: The Most Significant Oral Arguments Made before the Supreme Court since 1955* (New York: New Press, 1993), 279–85. The same work (277–79, 285–86) includes a brief history of the case, but it is flawed. It says the Lovings "were forced to leave the state under threat of criminal prosecution," for example, when in fact they had been prosecuted and convicted and had to leave as the condition of their suspended sentence. Mrs. Loving continues to say that she (not Mr. Loving) wrote the letter to Robert Kennedy. Figures for the number of states with miscegenation laws in either 1945 (it was 30, not 31) or 1959 are inaccurate (16 would be a correct figure for June 1967, when the Supreme Court's decision was handed down, but entirely too low for earlier years).

27. Kurland and Casper, *Landmark Briefs and Arguments,* 64: 971, 1005.

28. Ibid., 971.

29. *Loving* v. *Virginia,* 7–9; Bernard Schwartz, *Super Chief: Earl Warren and His Supreme Court—A Judicial Biography* (New York: New York Univ. Press, 1983), 668–69; Del Dickson, ed., *The Supreme Court in Conference (1940–1985): The Private Discussions behind Nearly 300 Supreme Court Decisions* (New York: Oxford Univ. Press, 2001), 695–97 (as for some of the editor's factual statements, see above, note 26).

30. *Loving* v. *Virginia,* 8–9.

31. Ibid., 10–12.

32. Ibid., 12.

33. Ibid.; "Justices Upset All Bans on Interracial Marriage," *NYT,* 13 June 1967: 1, 28; "Miscegenation Ban Is Ended by High Court," *Richmond Times-Dispatch,* 13 June 1967: 1, 4. An excellent idea—a compelling true tale, told to young readers—goes unfortunately awry, given the factual unreliability, in Karen Alonso, *Loving v. Virginia: Interracial Marriage* (Berkeley Heights, N.J.: Enslow Publishers, 2000).

34. "State Couple 'Overjoyed' by Ruling," *Richmond Times-Dispatch,* 13 June 1967: B1; "Mrs. Loving: 'I Feel Free Now,'" *Richmond Afro American,* 17 June 1967: 1–2; Simeon Booker, "The Couple That Rocked Courts," *Ebony* 22 (Sept. 1967): 78–84.

35. Mildred D. Loving to Eleanor Rose, 31 Jan. 1996.

36. "A Unanimous Court," *Virginian-Pilot,* 13 June 1967: 14.

37. Ibid.

38. "Top Court Junks Marriage Bars," *Norfolk Journal and Guide,* 17 June 1967: 1; "Freedom of Choice at the Altar," ibid., 6.

39. "Freedom of Choice at the Altar."

40. Ibid.

41. Hirschkop to Wulf, 20 June 1967, ACLU Papers, 1966, vol. 13.

42. Ibid.

43. Hirschkop to Wulf, 14 July 1967, ACLU Papers, 1966, vol. 13.

44. Wulf to Hirschkop, 24 July 1967, ibid.

45. Robert Y. Button to William R. Durland, 2 Aug. 1967, ACLU Papers, 1967, vol. 7.

46. Ibid.; *Race Relations Law Reporter* 12 (1967): 2302.

47. "Caucasian, Negro Wed in Norfolk," *Richmond Times-Dispatch,* 13 Aug. 1967: B2.

48. "Aides to Robert Kennedy and Dr. King Are Married in Virginia Ceremony," *NYT,* 15 July 1968: 23; Marian Wright Edelman, *The Measure of Our Success: A Letter to My Children and Yours* (New York: HarperCollins, 1992), and *Lanterns: A Memoir of Mentors* (Boston: Beacon Press, 1999), 69.

49. *Loving* v. *Virginia,* 13 (J. Stewart concurring).

50. *NYT,* 13 June 1967: 1, 28; Norfolk *Virginian-Pilot,* 13 June 1967: 4.

51. *Loving* v. *Virginia,* 2; Peter Wallenstein, "Race, Marriage, and the Law of Freedom: Alabama and Virginia, 1860s–1960s," *Chicago-Kent Law Review* 70, no. 2 (1994), 435–36; Robert Mann, *The Walls of Jericho: Lyndon Johnson, Hubert Humphrey, Richard Russell, and the Struggle for Civil Rights* (New York: Harcourt Brace, 1996), chs. 19–20.

16. America after the *Loving* Decision

1. "Miss Rusk Weds Negro," *Richmond Times-Dispatch,* 22 Sept. 1967: 1; "A Marriage of Enlightenment," *Time,* 29 Sept. 1967: 28–31; Deborah L. Kitchen, "Interracial Marriage in the United States, 1900–1980" (Ph.D. diss., Univ. of Minnesota, 1993), 140–44; "Mixed Couple Ends Honeymoon," *Richmond News Leader,* 24 June 1968: 2.

2. "Federal Agency Reverses on Denial of Widow Benefits in Inter-Racial Marriage," ACLU Papers, 1967, vol. 7.

3. Ibid.

4. Ibid.

5. *Davis* v. *Gately,* 269 F. Supp. 996, 997 (Del., 1967).

6. Ibid., 997.

7. Ibid., 999.

8. "State Couple 'Overjoyed' by Ruling," *Richmond Times-Dispatch,* 13 June 1967: B1.

9. "Alabama Marriage Law Contested," *Richmond Times-Dispatch,* 4 Dec. 1970: A13; "Alabama Marriage Law Ruled Unconstitutional," *Richmond Times-Dispatch,* 9 Dec. 1970: A8.

10. "Alabama Marriage Law Contested."

11. Ibid.; "Alabama Marriage Law Ruled Unconstitutional"; *United States* v. *Brittain,* 319 F. Supp. 1058 (N.D. Ala., 1970).

12. Marshall Frady, "An Alabama Marriage," in *Southerners: A Journalist's Odyssey* (New York: New American Library, 1980), 261–78 (originally published in *New York Times* (hereafter *NYT),* 8 March 1974); Robert J. Norrell, *Reaping the Whirlwind: The Civil Rights Movement in Tuskegee* (New York: Knopf, 1985), 201.

13. *Ziffert* v. *Sylvester,* in *Race Relations Law Reporter* 12 (1967), 1445.

14. "Biracial Marriage Ban Overturned in Florida," *NYT,* 25 Jan. 1968: 5; "Mixed Marriage Approved," *NYT,* 2 Feb. 1968: 4; *Van Hook and Peters* v. *Blanton,* in *Race Relations Law Reporter* 12 (1967), 2079–80.

15. "Judge in Arkansas Rules against Miscegenation Law," *NYT,* 26 Sept. 1968: 31.

16. "Mississippi Allows a Mixed Marriage," *NYT,* 3 Aug. 1970: 1, 12. The news story described the Mississippi statute, which in fact dated from 1880, as having been "on the books for more than 100 years."

17. Ibid. For an earlier episode, see "White Advisor to Evers Loses Job after Her Marriage to a Black Man," *NYT,* 7 Dec. 1969: 82; Charles Evers and Andrew Szanton, *Have No Fear: The Charles Evers Story* (New York: Wiley, 1997), 255–58.

18. "Judge Voids Georgia Law Banning Mixed Marriages," *NYT,* 13 Feb. 1972: 63.

19. *Dick* v. *Reaves,* 434 P.2d 295 (Okla., 1967).

20. Ibid., 296.

21. Ibid., 297–98.

22. Renee Romano, "'Immoral Conduct': White Women, Racial Transgressions, and Custody Disputes," in Molly Ladd-Taylor and Lauri Umansky, eds., *"Bad Mothers": The Politics of Blame in Twentieth-Century America* (New York: New York Univ. Press, 1998), ch. 12.

23. *Palmore* v. *Sidoti*, 466 U.S. 429, 430 (1984).

24. Ibid., 431.

25. Ibid., 431–32. Of course, Burger might have noted, the case would not likely have arisen had Palmore been white, so the court would not have had occasion to rule on the matter in the first place.

26. Ibid., 432–33.

27. Ibid., 434; Eileen M. Blackwood, "Race as a Factor in Custody and Adoption Disputes: *Palmore* v. *Sidoti*," *Cornell Law Review* 71 (1985–86): 209–226; Rachel F. Moran, *Interracial Intimacy: The Regulation of Race and Romance* (Chicago: Univ. of Chicago Press, 2001), 129–30.

28. *Perez* v. *Sharp*, 32 Cal.2d 711 (1948), 734–35 (J. Carter concurring).

29. *Grant* v. *Butt*, 198 S.C. 298 (1941); Dean J. Kotlowski, *Nixon's Civil Rights: Politics, Principle, and Policy* (Cambridge, Mass.: Harvard Univ. Press, 2001), 247. Contrary to what is stated in Peter Irons and Stephanie Guitton, eds., *May It Please the Court: The Most Significant Oral Arguments Made before the Supreme Court since 1955* (New York: New Press, 1993), the *Loving* decision did not rule, as they paraphrase it, that "the freedom to marry is an essential personal right which cannot be infringed by the state" (277). What *Loving* did was to remove racial identity as a condition that a state might impose. The decision did nothing to diminish states' authority to regulate incest, bigamy, age of consent, or same-sex marriages. In fact, the first black-white marriage in post-*Loving* Tennessee came to grief when the groom was charged with bigamy. Aside from race, the *Maynard* doctrine lived on; see the Rev. Robert F. Drinan, S.J., "The *Loving* Decision and the Freedom to Marry," *Ohio State Law Journal* 29 (1968): 358–98.

30. *Baker* v. *Nelson*, 291 Minn. 310, 314–15 (1971), recounted in Kay Tobin and Randy Wicker, *The Gay Crusaders* (New York: Arno Press, 1975), 135–55; *Jones* v. *Hallahan*, 501 S.W.2d 588 (Ky., 1973); *Singer* v. *Hara*, 11 Wn. App. 230, 523 P.2d 211 (1974); *DeSanto* v. *Barnsley*, 328 Pa. Superior Ct. 181, 476 A.2d 952 (1984). For background to the 1970s, see John D'Emilio, *Sexual Politics, Sexual Communities: The Making of a Homosexual Minority in the United States, 1940–1970* (Chicago: Univ. of Chicago Press, 1983).

31. Examples are James Trosino, "American Wedding: Same-Sex Marriage and the Miscegenation Analogy," *Boston University Law Review* 73 (1993): 93–119; William N. Eskridge Jr., *The Case for Same-Sex Marriage: From Sexual Liberty to Civilized Commitment* (New York: Free Press, 1996), chs. 5–6; Mark Strasser, *Legally Wed: Same-Sex Marriage and the Constitution* (Ithaca: Cornell Univ. Press, 1997); Cass R. Sunstein, "Homosexuality and the Constitution," in David M. Estlund and Martha C. Nussbaum, eds., *Sex, Preference, and Family: Essays on Law and Nature* (New York: Oxford Univ. Press, 1997), ch. 10. Predominating in this discourse are authors arguing in favor of change, among them Mark Strasser and William N. Eskridge Jr. Very much in evidence, too, however, are people arguing against recognition of same-sex marriage, among them David Orgon Coolidge and Lynn D. Wardle.

32. David L. Chambers, "Couples: Marriage, Civil Union, and Domestic Partnership," in John D'Emilio, William B. Turner, and Urvashi Vaid, eds., *Creating Change: Sexuality, Public Policy, and Civil Rights* (New York: St. Martin's Press, 2000), 281–304; Kevin G. Clarkson, David Orgon Coolidge, and William C. Duncan, "The Alaska Marriage Amendment: The People's Choice on the Last Frontier," *Alaska Law Review* 16 (Dec. 1999): 213–68.

33. Carey Goldberg, "The Ballot Initiatives," *NYT,* 9 Nov. 2000: B10; "Nebraska," *NYT,* 9 Nov. 2000: B16; Robert Bork, "Stop Courts from Imposing Gay Marriage," *Wall Street Journal,* 7 Aug. 2001: A14.

34. *Baker* v. *State of Vermont,* 744 A.2d 864 (Vt., 1999).

35. Ibid., 868.

36. Carey Goldberg, "Vermont Supreme Court Takes up Gay Marriage," *NYT,* 19 Nov. 1998: A20.

37. Ibid.

38. Ibid.

39. *Baker* v. *State of Vermont,* 867, 883.

40. Ibid., 867, 889.

41. Pamela Ferdinand, "Same-Sex Couples Take Vows as Law Takes Effect," *Washington Post,* 2 July 2000: A3; Chambers, "Couples," 296–99.

42. Ferdinand, "Same-Sex Couples Take Vows."

43. Ibid.

44. Ibid.

45. Ken I. Kersch, "Full Faith and Credit for Same-Sex Marriages?" *Political Science Quarterly* 112 (spring 1997), 118, 121, 131.

46. Under Vermont's constitution, an amendment of the sort that Hawaii and Alaska voters approved would be several years away, so the Vermont law would have time to grow roots. Gil Kujovich, "A Essay on the Passive Virtue of *Baker* v. *State,*" *Vermont Law Review* 25 (fall 2000): 93–112, notes 83–84. The entire issue took the title "Vermont Civil Unions." Opposing the decision and looking to roll it back—as Hawaii and Alaska already had—was an essay by David Orgon Coolidge and William C. Duncan, "Beyond *Baker:* The Case for a Vermont Marriage Amendment," ibid., 61–92.

47. For another emerging question of the right to marry, and whom one might marry, see appendix 4 regarding people who had changed their sexual identities.

Epilogue. The Color of Love after *Loving*

1. For one suggestive analysis, see Susan Koshy, "Morphing Race into Ethnicity: Asian Americans and Critical Transformations of Whiteness," *Boundary 2* 28 (spring 2001): 153–94.

2. Noel Ignatiev, *How the Irish Became White* (New York: Routledge, 1995); Karen Brodkin, *How Jews Became White Folks and What That Says about Race in America* (New Brunswick, N.J.: Rutgers Univ. Press, 1998). A caller to a radio talk show in Boston in the late 1960s, contributing to a discussion of interracial marriage in which U.S. Senator Edward W. Brooke had been highlighted, objected that Brooke's wife, whom he had met during World War II in Italy, was not white, she was Italian.

3. See such works as Paul R. Spickard, *Mixed Blood: Intermarriage and Ethnic Identity in Twentieth-Century America* (Madison: Univ. of Wisconsin Press, 1989), ch. 12; Maria P. P. Root, ed., *Racially Mixed People in America* (Newbury Park, Cal.: Sage Publications, 1992); Lise Funderburg, ed., *Black, White, Other: Biracial Americans Talk about Race and Identity* (New York: William Morrow, 1994); Michael Lind, *The Next American Nation: The New Nationalism and the Fourth American Revolution* (New York: Free Press, 1995), ch. 3; Paul E. Peterson, ed., *Classifying by Race* (Princeton: Princeton Univ. Press, 1995); Paul C. Rosenblatt, Terri A. Karis, and Richard D. Powell, *Multiracial Couples: Black and White Voices* (Thousand Oaks, Cal.: Sage Publications, 1995); Ishmael Reed, ed., *MultiAmerica: Essays on Cultural Wars and Cultural Peace* (New York: Viking, 1997); Orlando Patterson, *The Ordeal of Integration: Progress and Resentment in America's "Racial" Crisis* (Washington, D.C.: Civitas/Counterpoint, 1997), 193–98; David K. Shipler, *A Country of Strangers: Blacks and Whites in America* (New York: Knopf, 1997), ch. 2; Jon Michael Spencer, *The New Colored People: The Mixed-Race Movement in America* (New York: New York Univ. Press, 1997); *Of Many Colors: Portraits of Multiracial Families,* with photos by Gigi Kaeser, interviews by Peggy Gillespie, and an introduction by Glenda Valentine (Amherst: Univ. of Massachusetts Press,

1997); Rainier Spencer, *Spurious Issues: Race and Multiracial Identity Politics in the United States* (Boulder, Colo.: Westview Press, 1999); *Love in Black and White*, with photographs and interviews by Mary Motley Kalergis and a foreword by Julius Lester (New York: Kensington, 2002); and Frank H. Wu, *Yellow: Race in America beyond Black and White* (New York: Basic Books, 2002), ch. 7.

4. Among these are Naomi Zack, *Race and Mixed Race* (Philadelphia: Temple Univ. Press, 1993); Brent Staples, *Parallel Time: Growing up in Black and White* (New York: Pantheon Books, 1994); Shirlee Taylor Haizlip, *The Sweeter the Juice* (New York: Simon & Schuster, 1994); Gregory Howard Williams, *Life on the Color Line: The True Story of a White Boy Who Discovered He Was Black* (New York: Dutton, 1995); Patricia Penn Hilden, *When Nickels Were Indians: An Urban, Mixed-Blood Story* (Washington, D.C.: Smithsonian Institution Press, 1995); James McBride, *The Color of Water: A Black Man's Tribute to His White Mother* (New York: Riverhead Books, 1996); Scott Minerbrook, *Divided to the Vein: A Journey into Race and Family* (New York: Harcourt Brace, 1996); Jane Lazarre, *Beyond the Whiteness of Whiteness: Memoir of a White Mother of Black Sons* (Durham: Duke Univ. Press, 1996); Katya Gibel Azoulay, *Black, Jewish, and Interracial: It's Not the Color of Your Skin, but the Race of Your Kin, and Other Myths of Identity* (Durham: Duke Univ. Press, 1997); Kevin R. Johnson, *How Did You Get to Be Mexican? A White/Brown Man's Search for Identity* (Philadelphia: Temple University Press, 1999); Rebecca Walker, *Black, White, Jewish: Autobiography of a Shifting Self* (New York: Riverhead Books, 2001); and Neil Henry, *Pearl's Secret: A Black Man's Search for His White Family* (Berkeley: Univ. of California Press, 2001).

5. Yvette Walker, "The Loving Law," *Detroit News*, 9 Sept. 1991: E1, E4.

6. Ibid., E4.

7. Robert A. Pratt, "Crossing the Color Line: A Historical Assessment and Personal Narrative of *Loving* v. *Virginia*," *Howard Law Journal* 41 (winter 1998), 244.

Appendix 1. Permanent Repeal of State Miscegenation Laws, 1780–1967

1. Lists provided elsewhere often vary from appendix 1. For example, as regards Illinois, Iowa, Kansas, and New Mexico, the compilation here differs from that in Paul R. Spickard, *Mixed Blood: Intermarriage and Ethnic Identity in Twentieth-Century America* (Madison: Univ. of Wisconsin Press, 1989), 374. Many writers follow Robert J. Sickels, *Race, Marriage, and the Law* (Albuquerque: Univ. of New Mexico Press, 1972), 64 and 155 note 2, in giving a figure (31) for states with miscegenation laws as late as World War II that includes Michigan.

Appendix 2. Nazi Germany and Apartheid South Africa

1. George M. Fredrickson, *Racism: A Short History* (Princeton: Princeton Univ. Press, 2002), 86, 99–138; Richard Bernstein, "South Africa Drops a Barrier to Relations between Races," *New York Times*, 21 April 1985: IV, 2; Montgomery Brower, "Suzanne and Protas Madlala Cross South Africa's Color Line by Walking down the Aisle," *People Weekly* 24 (9 Sept. 1985): 32–33.

2. Marion A. Kaplan, *Between Dignity and Despair: Jewish Life in Nazi Germany* (New York: Oxford Univ. Press, 1998), 74–93. See also Kingsley Davis, "Intermarriage in Caste Societies," *American Anthropologist*, New Series 43 (1941), 392–93, and Stefan Kuhl, *The Nazi Connection: Eugenics, American Racism, and German National Socialism* (New York: Oxford Univ. Press, 1994).

3. Pierre L. van den Berghe, *Race and Ethnicity: Essays in Comparative Sociology* (New York: Basic Books, 1970), chs. 3, 13; A. Leon Higginbotham Jr. and Barbara K. Kopytoff, "Racial Purity and Interracial Sex in the Law of Colonial and Antebellum Virginia," *Georgetown Law Journal* 77 (1989), 2027–28 note 245. See also Edward Callan, *Alan Paton* (rev. ed.; Boston: Twayne, 1982), ch. 4.

4. "White Becomes Chinese to Wed in South Africa," *New York Times*, 15 Oct. 1969: 8.

Appendix 3. Identity and Authority: An Interfaith Couple in Israel

1. Lawrence Fellows, "A Harried Couple Gain Support of Israelis in Their Fight to Wed," *New York Times,* 29 Oct. 1961: 27. See also Sharon Waxman, "West Bank Story," *Washington Post,* 5 Nov. 2000: A1.

2. Lawrence Fellows, "Israeli Mother to Change Faith," *New York Times,* 5 Nov. 1961: 6.

3. Lawrence Fellows, "Israeli Mother Wins back Son; Kidnapping Charge Dropped," *New York Times,* 10 Nov. 1961: 21.

Appendix 4. Transsexuals, Gender Identity, and the Law of Marriage

1. *Littleton* v. *Prange,* 9 S.W.3d 223, 225 (Tex. App. 1999).

2. Ibid., 225, 231; see Julie A. Greenberg, "When Is a Man a Man, and When Is a Woman a Woman?" *Florida Law Review* 52 (Sept. 2000): 745–68, and Katrina C. Rose, "The Transsexual and the Damage Done: The Fourth Court of Appeals Opens PanDOMA's Box by Closing the Door on Transsexuals' Right to Marry," *Law and Sexuality: A Review of Lesbian, Gay, Bisexual, and Transgender Legal Issues* 9 (1999/2000): 1–134.

3. Devon Spurgeon, "Double Bind: Woman in Missouri Is a Man in Kansas, and Why," *Wall Street Journal,* 7 July 2000: A1.

INDEX

Aderhold, O. C. (university president), 206
age of consent, 49, 276n14, 292n29
Agnew, Spiro (governor), 208
Alabama, 48–9, 70–80, 110–14, 126, 141–2, 234–5, 241
  court of appeals, 127, 179–80
  supreme court, 49, 72–9, 111–12, 141, 180, 278 9n26
Alaska, 191, 241
alimony, 171–2
Allen, Hannah, and descendants, 25
"amalgamation," 51, 54–5, 56, 63, 119
American Civil Liberties Union (ACLU), 288n36, 289n8
  in the 1940s, 193, 289n8
  in the 1950s, 183
  in the 1960s, 208, 211–14, 217–23, 232–3, 288n35
American Revolution, 12–14, 23, 36–7, 42, 196
  and freedom suits, 21–5, 28–34, 37, 54
  and slave trade, 20
  and manumission, 20–1, 28
  and emancipation, 40, 54, 266n4
"antimiscegenation regime"
  definition of, 7, 9
  territory of, 253–4, 284n36, 294n1, figs. 6–10
  see also Germany, South Africa
Arizona, 144, 161–2, 189, 199–200, 279n32
Arkansas, 62–3, 102–3, 172, 235, 269n32
Asian Americans, 9, 143–5, 199–200, 207–8, 249, 278n16, 280n37
  see also Chinese; Japanese; Malay; Mongolian

Bailey v. Fiske (Me.; 1852), 44–5
Baker v. Carter (Okla.; 1937), 171–2

Baker v. Nelson (Minn.; 1971), 240–1
Baker v. State (Vt.; 1999), 242–3
Bazile, Leon F. (judge), 217, 218–19, 227, fig. 12
bigamy, 129, 156, 203, 276n14, 277n15, 292n29
  see also polygamy
Black Codes, 58–9
Blake v. Sessions (Okla.; 1923), 174
Boe, Sara, and family, 264n30
Bowlin v. Commonwealth (Ky.; 1867), 269n34
Branigin, Roger D. (governor), 204
Branham, Samuel Christian, 157
Breckinridge, John C., 58
Bridges, Harry (labor leader), and Noriko Sawada, 199
Brooke, Edward W. (U.S. senator), 232, 293n2
Brooke, Remi, 232
Brooks, R. Garnett (sheriff), 1, 216
Brown, Albert Gallatin (U.S. senator), 58
Brown, Henry Billings (justice), 118–19, 168
Brown, Joseph E. (governor; judge), 96–7
Brown v. Board of Education (1954, 1955), 180–4, 205, 210–11, 213, 221, 223, 228
Bryan v. Walton (Ga.; 1853), 39, 48
Buchanan, Archibald Chapman (judge), 181
Buchanan, John Alexander (judge), 138
Buchanan v. Warley (Mo.; 1917), 3, 119, 190
Buck v. Bell (Va.; 1927), 193, 194
Bugg, Betty, 19
Burger, Warren (chief justice), 238–9
Burns v. State (Ala.; 1872), 73–80
  lost and found, 102–3, 112, 113, 120, 270n13, 273n17, 286n25
Burton, Harold M. (justice), 180, 182
Butler, Eleanor, and descendants, 23–4, 37

Butler v. *Boarman* (Md.; 1771), 23, 24
Butler v. *Craig* (Md.; 1791), 24
Button, Robert Y. (attorney general), 226–7
Butt v. *Rachel* (Va.; 1814), 34
Butzner, John D. Jr. (judge), 218–19
Byrd, Alex, 289n6, 289n11
Byrd, Susie (writer), 27

California, 42, 144, 145, 189, 192, 232
    supreme court, 145, 192–8
Calma v. *Calma* (Va.; 1962), 58–9
Cameron, Lucille, 124–5
Carliner, David (lawyer), 181, 183
Caroline County (Va.), 1, 216, 224, fig. 12
Carter, Jesse (judge), 196–7, 198, 199, 240
Catholics, 23, 85, 192, 193, 194, 203
Chesnutt, Charles W. (writer), 3–4
Chinese, 137, 144, 225, 256, 279n28
Christian, Joseph (judge), 153
Civil Rights Act of 1866
    enactment of, 58–61
    in post–Civil War law, 63–4, 69, 73, 76,
        79–80, 84–5, 97–8, 108
    in the twentieth century, 177–8
Civil Rights Act of 1875, 65
Civil Rights Act of 1964, 215, 217, 228
Civil Rights Cases (1883), 120
Civil Rights Movement, 5, 184–6, 201–6,
    228–9, 235–6
"civil unions," 243–4
Civil War, 51–2, 57–62, 196
Clark, John C., and Sobrina, 88–90
Coffee, Ishmael, 43–4
cohabitation, 40, 83–4, 87, 91, 96, 102, 108,
    116, 126–7, 129–30, 208–11, 276n8
Cohen, Bernard S. (lawyer), 212–14, 217–23,
    226, 227–8
Cold War, 185–6, 196
Coleman v. *Dick and Pat* (Va.; 1793), 30–1,
    265n9
comity, 232, 234
    denied, 100–1, 109–10, 115–17, 128,
        151–6, 158–9, 163–6, 171–2, 205–6,
        216, 244
    recognized, 43–4, 87, 154–5, 193
Confederate States of America, 57–8, 60–1,
    69–70, 71, 93, 228
Cook, Eugene (attorney general), 206
Croly, David Goodman (writer), 51–2, 63, 65
Curtis, Benjamin R. (justice), 54, 267n23

custody, 138–9, 238–9, 286n1

Darnall, Nicholas, 46–7, 52
Davis, Kingsley (anthropologist), 3, 261n2
Davis, Sylvester S., 192, 203
Davis v. *Gately* (Del.; 1967), 233–4
Declaration of Independence, 55, 194, 196
Defense of Marriage Act (1996), 241
Delaware, 233–4
Democratic Party, 51, 54–7, 59–60, 133,
    185–6, 204, 215
    and Reconstruction, 59–60, 62–3, 70–1,
        79, 91, 93, 104, 270n6
demography, *see* population
Dick v. *Reaves* (Okla.; 1967), 236–8
Disciples of Christ, 287n8
divorce, 158–9
    and alimony, 171–2, 232
    and custody, 238–9, 286n1
In re Dobbs (Ga.; 1871), 108
Douglas, Stephen A. (U.S. senator), 54–5, 56,
    59
Douglas, William O. (justice), 180, 211,
    223–4
Dred Scott v. *Sandford* (Mo.; 1857), 53–4
    mentioned, 56, 57, 59, 107, 120, 134,
        243, 267n23
Du Bois, W. E. B., 124, 130, 135, 136
Dudley, Edward R. (NAACP), 179, 283n20
Durland, William R. (legislator), 226
Duryea, Etta, 124
Duvall, Gabriel (justice), 47
DuVal, Thomas Howard (judge), 108–9

Edelman, Marian Wright, and Peter Edelman,
    227
education, 146, 185, 201, 204, 248
    elementary and secondary, 105, 180–3,
        205, 228, 278n17, 278–9n26
    higher, 191, 204–6, 280n38
Eggers v. *Olson* (Okla.; 1924), 172
electoral college, 60
Ellis v. *State* (Ala.; 1868), 72–3, 74, 75–6,
    273n17
emancipation, 40–1, 57–8, 266n4
    see also manumission
Emancipation Proclamation, 58
Emery, A. L. (lawyer), 175–9
Erskine, John (judge), 108
eugenics, 139, 143–4, 193–4, 196

Fauntleroy, Thomas T. (judge), 126, 151
Featherstone, Octavia, 27, 34, 35
Field, Stephen J. (justice), 114, 115
Filipinos, 3, 144–5, 158, 207, 225, 247
fines, 40, 42, 64, 101, 102, 103, 104, 208–9
  in Alabama, 49, 72
  in Virginia, 16, 18, 19, 99–101, 126, 152,
    273n9
First Amendment, 192–3, 214
Florida, 80, 103, 165–6, 208–11, 235
Ford, Johnny L. (mayor), 235
Ford v. *State* (Ala.; 1878), 74–6
Foster, A. H., and Leah, 86–88
Fourteenth Amendment, 84–5, 96–9, 103,
    104, 107–21, 135, 158, 173, 175–7,
    181–2, 273–4n18
  approved and ratified, 59–61, 69
  due process clause, 158, 207, 213, 222–3,
    224
  equal protection clause, 101–2, 107–21,
    213
  privileges and immunities clause, 71, 108,
    110, 113, 155–6
  Section One, 60, 63
  Section Two, 60
  supports segregation, 71, 79–80, 101–4,
    107–21, 191
  undermines discrimination, 73, 79, 191,
    196–7, 209–11, 286n30
  and *Loving* v. *Virginia*, 218, 221, 222–4
  see also Reconstruction
Ex parte François (Tex.; 1879), 92, 108–9

Frankfurter, Felix (justice), 180, 182, 227
freedom, nonwhite, 39, 47–8, 53–4, 58–9,
    119–20
  mother's relation to, 15–19, 23–5, 37
  father's relation to, 15–19, 23–5, 46–7,
    82–8
  freedom suits, 21–2, 28–35, 52–4,
    265n13
  manumission, 20–1, 28, 46, 265n14
  emancipation, 40–1, 57–8, 266n4
  see also voting rights
Fuller v. *Commonwealth* (Va.; 1949), 218
full faith and credit clause, 115–17, 158, 244

Georgia, 47–8, 108, 116–17, 137, 201–2,
    205–6, 236
  supreme court, 39, 48, 96–7

Germany, 176, 255
Grant v. *Butt* (S.C.; 1941), 240
Great Depression, 144, 186
Greenhow v. *James Executor* (Va.; 1885), 163–5
Green v. *State* (Ala.; 1878), 75–7, 78, 103
Grey, William H. (delegate), 62–3
Grossman, Harvey M. (clerk), 180
Guinn v. *Bugg* (Va.; 1770), 19

Haden, Benjamin (judge), 157
Haltom, E. B. Jr. (lawyer), 179, 183
Harlan, John Marshall (justice, 1877–1911),
    120, fig. 5
Harlan, John Marshall (justice, 1955–71),
    182, 211, 221
Hasler, Donald, 232
Hastie, William H. (lawyer), 176, 283n13
Hawaii, 199, 241
Higgins v. *Allen* (Md.; 1796), 25
Hinton, Drury A. (judge), 151, 164
Hirschkop, Philip J. (lawyer), 212–14,
    218–23, 226, 227–8, 234
Hodes, Martha (historian), 104–5, 266n30,
    274n28
Holmes, Hamilton, 205
Holt, Henry (judge), 140
Hook v. *Nanny Pagee* (Va.; 1811), 22
Hooper, Alfred, and family, 45–6
housing, 185, 248
  segregation ordinances, 119
  restrictive covenants, 190–1
Howard University, 185
Howarth, James, 28
Howell v. *Netherland* (Va.; 1770), 263n17
Hudgins v. *Wrights* (Va.; 1806), 32–3
Hughes, Robert W. (judge), 110, 116
Hunter, Charlayne, 205–6
Hutcheson, C. Sterling (judge), 287n11

Idaho, 144
Illinois, 54–5, 56, 134, 136, 207, 286n1
immigration, 143–4, 146
  restrictions on, 143–4, 278n16
incest, 49, 101, 108, 110, 128–9, 155, 203,
    276n14, 292n29
Indiana, 42, 63–4, 204, 286n1, 287n9
Indians (from South Asia), 137
Indians (Native Americans), 45, 47–8, 171,
    193
  in early Virginia, 13–19

and access to freedom through maternal descent, 27–37
and marriage restrictions, 13–19, 139, 142–3, 171–2, 279n32
defined as "white" in Oklahoma, 142–3, 171–2, 249, fig. 11
and inheritance, 172, 174–9, 236–8
see also Pocahontas
Inhabitants of Medway v. *Inhabitants of Natick* (Mass.; 1810), *see Medway* v. *Natick*
inheritance, *see* property
interfaith marriage, 108, 113, 194, 196, 201–3, 287n4
interracial images
  black men, white women, 51, 53, 63, 133–4, 185, fig. 4
  black women, white men, 53, 55–6, 123
"interracial marriage"
  variable and changing definitions, 137–42
  see also racial identity
Iowa, 41
Israel, 257–8

Jackson, Floyd L. (judge), 213, 214
Jackson, Linnie, 179–80
Jackson v. *Alabama* (1954), 179–80, 182, 228
Jackson v. *Jackson* (Md.; 1895), 156
Jackson v. *State* (Ala.; 1930), 127
Japanese, 137, 176, 199–200, 279n28, 282n1
Japanese American Citizens League, 222, 223
Jenkins v. *Tom* (Va.; 1792), 30
Jeter, Mildred D., *see* Loving, Mildred D.
Jews, 108, 194, 255–6, 257–8
Johnson, Andrew (president), 58, 59, 268n21
Johnson, John Arthur "Jack" (boxer), 124–5, 133–6, 190, 203
Johnson, Richard M. (vice-president), 123–4
Jones, Frances Aline, 212–14
Jones (D'Orsay) v. *Commonwealth* (Va.; 1885), 126
Jones (Isaac) v. *Commonwealth* (Va.; 1884, 1885), 150–1
Jones v. *Lorenzen* (Okla.; 1965), 213–14
Jones v. *Shaw* (Okla.; 1965), 212–13
Jordan, Mary Ann, 200, 203

Kansas, 165–6, 171, 174, 253
Keen v. *Keen* (Mo.; 1904, 1906), 166–8
Keith v. *Commonwealth* (Va.; 1935), 281n35
Kellam, Floyd E. (judge), 181

Kennedy, John F. (president), 215
Kennedy, Robert F. (attorney general), 217, 227, 290n26
Kentucky, 76, 214, 269n34, 286n1
King, Martin Luther Jr., 186, 227
Ex parte Kinney (Va.; 1879), 109–10, 116
Kinney, Andrew, and family, 100, 152–4
Kinney, Edmund, 109–10, 116
Kinney v. *Commonwealth* (Va.; 1878), 152–4, 219
Knight v. *State* (Miss.; 1949), 281n37
Konvitz, Milton R. (lawyer), 176, 177
Krucker, Herbert F. (judge), 200

Lacy, Benjamin Watkins (judge), 151
Laughlin, Harry, 143–4
Lewis v. *State* (Ala.; 1921), 127
Lincoln, Abraham, 51, 54–5, 56, 57–8, fig. 3
Lincoln-Douglas debates, 56
Littleton v. *Prange* (Tex.; 1999), 259–60
Lonas v. *State* (Tenn.; 1871), 97, 128
Louisiana, 80, 86, 92, 93, 117–18, 235
  supreme court, 52–3, 84–6, 168–71, 277n17
Loving, 120, 222–3, 227–8, 248, 289n2, 289n6, 289n11
  Mildred D., 1–2, 216–18, 224, 251, 290n26
  Richard P., 1–2, 6, 216–18, 220, 223, 224, 251
  Sidney, Donald, and Peggy, 217, 250–1, fig. 13
Loving v. *Virginia* (1967)
  trial, 216–17, 290n26
  appeals, 217–20
  at the Supreme Court, 220–3, 276n14
  decision, 223–4, 292n29
  aftermath in Virginia, 224–7
  aftermath elsewhere, 224–5, 231–45, 250, 251
Lumpkin, Joseph Henry (judge), 39, 48
lynchings, 104–5

Madden, Sarah, and descendants, 19–20, 35–6
Madalala, Protas, and Suzanne Leclerc, 255
Maine, 41, 44–5, 136
Malay (race), 145, 146, 207
manumission, 20–1, 28, 46, 265n14
Marquez, Jesse, 212–14

marriage license, 2, 77, 150, 157, 224, 242–4
  denied, 130, 140, 145, 192, 199–200,
    212–14, 233–6, 240–2
Marshall, Daniel G. (lawyer), 193–4, 197,
    285n8
Marshall, Thurgood (NAACP), 175–8
Maryland, 22–5, 46–7, 156
  colonial laws, 22–5, 286n30
  Revolutionary era litigation, 24–5
  whites, blacks, and Malays, 145, 207,
    280n37
  a miscegenation law is overturned, 286n30
  efforts to obtain marriage licenses in,
    207–8
  repeal of miscegenation law, 208
Massachusetts, 41–2, 43–4, 54, 232
Maurice, Harold C. (judge), 157
Maynard v. *Hill* (Ore.; 1888), 114–17
  mentioned, 120, 135, 158, 177, 189, 195,
    221–3, 241, 247
McBride, James (writer), 250
McColley, Robert (historian), 31
McLaughlin v. *Florida* (1964), 208–11, 213,
    221–3, 228, 239
McPherson v. *Commonwealth* (Va.; 1877),
    149–50
Medway v. *Natick* (Mass.; 1810), 44–5
Medway v. *Needham* (Mass.; 1819), 43–4,
    263n13, 281n25
Mein Kampf, 193–4
Menchine, W. Albert (judge), 207
Mexico, 89, 193
Meyer v. *Nebraska* (1923), 191–2, 194, 195,
    213
Michigan, 136, 206, 277n15, 294n1
Miller v. *Lucks* (Miss.; 1948), 282n9
"miscegenation"
  definition, 9, 51
  origins of term, 51–2
  diffusion of term, 63, 65, 79, 97
Miscegenation (1864), 51–2
Minnesota, 240–1
Mississippi, 58, 59, 81–4, 93, 152, 184,
    235–6, 288n35, 291nn16–17
  supreme court, 82–4, 277n17, 281n37
Missouri, 101, 144, 166–8, 207
  supreme court, 101–2, 128, 167–8,
    273–4nn17–19
Mitchell, John N. (attorney general), 234
"mixed-race," 248–51, 279n32

Mongolian (race), 137, 144–5, 146, 207,
    279n32
Monks, Allan, 189
Montana, 144, 198, 281n1
Moon v. *Children's Home Society* (Va.; 1911),
    138–9
Morrison, Alexina, 52–3
Morrison v. *White* (La.; 1861), 52–3
"mulatto," 15–18, 24–5, 89, 90, 193, 225,
    267n31
  definitions of, 17, 44–5, 49, 277n9,
    267n32, 280n37
  see also "one-drop" rule
Murdock v. *Potter* (La.; 1924), 170–1
Muslims, 257–8

Nabrit, James M. Jr. (university president),
    185, 284n40
Naim v. *Naim* (Va.; 1955, 1956), 180–3
  as precedent, 219, 220, 221–2, 223,
    228
National Association for the Advancement of
    Colored People (NAACP), 136,
    183–5, 202, 277n6, 283n20
  Legal Defense and Educational Fund,
    175–9, 208, 221–2, 236, 288n24
National Catholic Conference for Interracial
    Justice, 203
Native Americans, *see* Indians
Nazism, 196, 255, 281n35
Nebraska, 144, 241
Nevada, 144, 199, 241
New York, 253, 266n4, 280n38
New York Times, 228
Nixon, Richard M. (president), 240
Norfolk Journal and Guide, 225
Norfolk Virginian-Pilot, 225
North Carolina, 42, 45–6, 77, 180
  supreme court, 45–6, 98–9, 154–6
Nunez, Joseph, xi, 47–8, 52

Ohio, 86, 136
Oklahoma
  alimony, 171–2
  attempt to repeal miscegenation law,
    288–9n42
  inheritance, 172, 174–9, 236–8
  marriage licenses, 212–14
  racial definitions, 142–3, 249, fig. 11
  supreme court, 171–2, 212–14, 237

"one-drop" rule, 4, 7, 49, 134, 139–43, 216, 249, 278n24, 279n27
Oregon, 144, 198
Oyama, Henry, 200, 203

Pace, Tony, 111
Pace v. Alabama (1883), 110–14, 119–21
    mentioned, 173, 177, 180, 189, 195, 198, 209–11, 222, 242, 247
Pagee, Nanny, and children, 22
Pallas v. Hill (Va.; 1808), 265n11, 265–6n23
Palmore v. Sidoti (Fla.; 1984), 238–9, 248
Pegram v. Isabell (Va.; 1807, 1808), 266n25
Pendleton, Edmund (judge), 31
Pennsylvania, 40–1, 241
People v. Brown (Mich.; 1876), 277n15
Perez, Andrea D., 192, 203
Perez v. Sharp (Cal.; 1948), 192–9, 213, 219, 240, 242
Perryman, Patsy, 142–3
Philippines, *see* Filipinos
Pierce v. Society of Sisters (Ore.; 1925), 191–2, 195
Plecker, Walter, 139, 140, 278n17
Plessy v. Ferguson (La.; 1896), 3, 117–19, 120–1, 168, 191
Pocahontas, 13, 139, 203, fig. 1
polygamy, 110, 128–9, 155, 192, 276n14
population
    numbers of free nonwhites, 21
    race percentages, 13–14, 21, 76, 99
    sex ratios at settlement, 17, 61, 266n10
    sex ratios following the Civil War, 61–2, 269n25
Posadas, Barbara (historian), 144
Powell, John, 139
prison terms, 42, 91–2, 97, 101, 103, 104, 108, 208–9
    Alabama, 72, 74–9, 111, 127, 141, 179
    Indiana, 42, 63–4
    Mississippi, life sentence in, 81–2
    Virginia, 1–2, 18, 100–1, 110, 140, 150–1, 153–4, 157, 216–17, 273n9
privacy, 191–2, 194, 195, 218, 221, 224, 240
property
    alimony, 171–2
    death benefits, 232–3
    homestead rights, 90–1

inheritance, 44–5, 46–7, 81–90, 146, 161–79, 236–8
social security, 222–3
Purcell, Willie E., 157–8

Rabinowitz, Howard N. (historian), 105
racial identity, 7, 101, 134–5, 137, 280n1
    determined by physical inspection, 22, 33, 148
    in Alabama, 141–2
    in Georgia, 137
    in Mississippi, 93
    in Oklahoma, 142–3
    in South Carolina, 148–9
    in Virginia, 137–41
    see also Indians; Malay; Mongolian; "mulatto"; "one-drop" rule
Randolph, A. Philip, 186
Ratcliff v. State (Miss.; 1958), 277n17
Raymond v. North Berwick (Me.; 1871), 45
Reconstruction
    national politics and policies of, 58–61
    and miscegenation laws and litigation, 62–121, 268n34
    and judicial recruitment in southern states, 71, 90–1, 270n6, 271n17, 271n20
religion, 14–15, 23, 192, 207, 243
    and support for miscegenation laws, 153, 186, 219
    and opposition to miscegenation laws, 201–4
    see also Catholics; interfaith marriage; Jews; Muslims
Republican Party, 51–2, 54–7, 128–9
    and Reconstruction, 58–61, 62–3, 69–71, 79, 84, 92, 93, 104, 271n17
Reynolds v. United States (Utah, 1879), 192–3
Rhode Island, 41, 43, 136
Rice, Eugene (judge), 175
Richardson, Robert A. (judge), 164–5
Richmond News Leader, 232
Richmond Times-Dispatch, 157, 183, 231–2
Roane, Spencer (judge), 32, 33
Robin v. Hardaway (Va.; 1772), 29
Roddenbery, Seaborn Anderson (congressman), 133–6, 137, 200, 247–8
Rodman, William R. (judge), 154–5
Roldan v. Los Angeles County (Cal.; 1933), 145, 195, 197, 285n5

Rolfe, John, 13, 139
Rollins v. State (Ala, 1922), 276n10
Roosevelt, Franklin D. (president), 186
Rose v. State (Miss.; 1958), 277n17
Rountree, Helen C. (anthropologist), 14, 263n4
Rusk, Margaret Elizabeth, 231–2, fig. 14

Saffold, Benjamin F. (judge), 73
same-sex marriage, 6, 240–4, 292n29, 292n31
Samoa, 207
Sanders, Carl (governor), 206
Sanford, John W. A. (attorney general), 74–5, 78, 79–80
Scott, Dred, and family, 54, 55
Scott v. Commonwealth (Va.; 1883), 126
secession, 52, 57
segregation
    emergence of, 3–4, 105
    litigation against, 117–20, 190–1
    dismantlement of, 5, 185, 220, 228
    see also education
servitude, 13
    indentured, 14, 16–20, 23
    for 30 or 31 years, 17–20, 24–5, 35–6, 40
    see also freedom; slavery
sex ratios, see population
Shaw, Virgil M. (judge), 212
Shelby, David Davie (lawyer), 73–4, 270n14
Shelley v. Kraemer (Mo.; 1948), 190–1, 197
Shorter, Elizabeth, and descendants, 24
Shorter v. Rozier (Md.; 1794), 24
Sickels, Robert J. (historian), 272n35, 294n1
Skinner v. Oklahoma (Okla.; 1942), 192, 194, 195, 213
Slaughter-House Cases (La.; 1873), 71, 74, 113, 273n18
slavery, 13–15, 20–1, 25, 52
    as a political issue, 40–1, 53–6, 57–61
    as related to family formation, 22–4, 30, 36–7, 42, 54
    as related to miscegenation, 47, 55, 82, 84, 89, 184–5
    end of, as related to representation, 60–1
Smith, Guy Gibson, 231–2, fig. 14
Smith v. Allwright (Tex.; 1944), 190, 283n20
South Africa, 255–6
South Carolina, 80, 103–4, 147–9, 154–6, 184, 247, 274n25
    supreme court, 240, 279n26

Spanish-American War, 144
Stanley, Charles C. Jr. (lawyer), 193–4
State ex rel. Farmer v. Board of School Commissioners of Mobile County (Ala.; 1933), 279n26
State v. Bell (Tenn.; 1872), 128, 152
State v. Brown (La.; 1959), 277n17
State v. Gibson (Ind.; 1871), 63–4, 74, 77, 92, 273n17
State v. Jackson (Mo.; 1883), 101–2, 128, 273–4nn17–19
State v. Kennedy (N.C.; 1877), 154
State v. Pass (Ariz.; 1942), 279n32
State v. Reinhardt (N.C.; 1869), 98
State v. Ross (N.C.; 1877), 154–6
State v. Treadaway (La.; 1910), 280n1
sterilization, 192, 193, 194, 285n7
Stevens v. United States (Okla.; 1944), 174–9, 192, 198, 221
Stevens, William, 174–8
Stewart, Potter (justice), 211, 223–4, 228
Stovall, Walter, 205–6
Succession of Segura (La.; 1913), 169
Succession of Yoist (La.; 1913), 168–9
suffrage, see voting rights

In re Takahashi's Estate (Mont.; 1942), 282n1
Talmadge, Herman (governor), 205
Taney, Roger B. (chief justice), 7, 53–4, 267n23, fig. 2
Taylor, George Keith (lawyer), 32, 33, 34, 43
Tennessee, 60, 123, 292n29
    supreme court, 97, 128, 152
Texas, 86–92, 108–9, 232–3, 259–60, 271n20
Thailand, 249
Thirteenth Amendment, 58, 59, 69
Thurman v. State (Ala.; 1850), 49, 141, 267n31
Toler v. Oakwood Smokeless Coal Corp. (Va.; 1939), 156
Tompkins, Henry Clay (attorney general), 112–14, 275n18
Tompkins, John R. (lawyer), 112, 275n18
Toogood v. Scott (Md.; 1783), 24
Tourgée, Albion W. (lawyer), 118
transsexuals, 259–60
Traynor, Roger (judge), 193–6, 197–8
Trezise, Jack P. (lawyer), 212–13
Truman, Harry S. (president), 185–6

Trumbull, Lyman (U.S. senator), 59
Tucker, St. George (judge), 32, 33
Tucker v. *Blease* (S.C.; 1914), 279n26
Tutty v. *State* (Ga.; 1890), 116–17, 193–4
Tydings-McDuffie Act (1934), 144

United Nations, charter of, 196
United Presbyterian Church, 203–4
U.S. Congress, 190, 215
    politics and policies of Reconstruction,
      58–61
    amendment to ban interracial marriage,
      134–6
    immigration restriction, 143–4, 278n16
    Defense of Marriage Act (1996), 241
U.S. Constitution
    First Amendment, 192–3, 214
    full faith and credit clause, 115–17, 158,
      244
    supremacy clause, 175, 176
    Tenth Amendment, 135, 181–2, 222
    three-fifths clause, 60
    see also Fourteenth Amendment
U.S. Supreme Court, 46–7, 190–4
    Dred Scott v. *Sandford*, 53–54
    Pace v. *Alabama*, 112–14, 209–11
    Maynard v. *Hill*, 114–16
    Plessy v. *Ferguson*, 117–19
    Keen v. *Keen*, 168
    Buchanan v. *Warley*, 119
    Jackson v. *Alabama*, 180, 284n31
    Naim v. *Naim*, 182–3, 284n31
    McLaughlin v. *Florida*, 209–11
    Loving v. *Virginia*, 220–4
    Palmore v. *Sidoti*, 238–9
    see also Fourteenth Amendment; privacy
University of Georgia, 205–6
University of North Carolina at Greensboro,
    287n12
Utah, 144, 145
    see also polygamy

Vermont, 242–4, 293n46
Virginia
    colonial and revolutionary, 13–22,
      27–37
    post–Civil War, 99–101, 109–10, 126,
      149–51, 152–4, 163–5
    twentieth-century, 137–41, 156–9, 180–3,
      215–29, 285n35

Virginia appellate courts, 265n16
    cohabitation, 126
    comity, 152–3
    custody, 138
    freedom suits, 22, 29–34
    inheritance, 164–5
    racial identity, 138, 149–51
    Naim v. *Naim*, 181–3
    Loving v. *Commonwealth*, 219–20
Virginia statutes on sex, marriage, freedom,
    and racial identity
    law of 1662, 15, 21, 36
    law of 1691, 2, 15–17, 32, 36, 41–2,
      263nn6–7
    law of 1705, 17–18, 32
    law of 1723, 18
    law of 1765, 18–19
    law of 1778, 20, 22
    law of 1782, 20–1, 28
    law of 1795, 31
    law of 1806, 21
    law of 1878, 2, 100–1, 153–4
    law of 1910, 137–9
    law of 1924, 139–41, 216, 221–2
    law of 1932, 140, 216
    see also servitude
voting rights (African American), 7–8
    before the Civil War, 18, 41, 42–3, 55,
      56, 266n4
    and Reconstruction, 58–61, 62, 69, 70
    restoration of, 8, 185, 190, 283n20
Voting Rights Act (1965), 8

Wakeman, George (writer), 51–2, 63, 65
Walker, James C. (lawyer), 118
In re Walker's Estate (Ariz.; 1896), 161–2
Walsh, Lorena S. (historian), 24
Warren Earl (chief justice), 119, 180, 223–4,
    228–9, 244
Washington (state), 241, 253, 280n35
Washington, D.C., 1, 97, 109, 136, 152,
    153, 163–5, 216–18
Washington, George (president), 21, 22
Waters, Ida Nell, 232–3
Watts, A. B. (sheriff), 157
Welcome, Verda (legislator), 208
West Virginia, 99, 167
What Miscegenation Is! (1865), fig. 4
Wheelwright, Farley W. (minister), 201–2
White, Byron R. (justice), 209–11

white Democratic primary, 190, 283n20
White, Walter F. (NAACP), 184
Whittington v. *McCaskill* (Fla.; 1913), 165–6
Wilkins, Roy (NAACP), 184–5
will, *see* property
Williams, Ben T. (judge), 237
Williams, John Sharp (U.S. senator), 144
Williamson, Joel (historian), 34, 269n4, 266n26
Wilson, Woodrow (president), 133
Wines, Taylor H. (judge), 199
Wisconsin, 56–7

Woods, Tiger, 249
Woodward, C. Vann (historian), 105, 274n29
Works Progress Administration, 27
World War II, 176, 186, 196, 293n2
Wright, Jacky, and descendants, 32–3, 35–6
Wulf, Melvin (ACLU), 226
Wyoming, 144, 146, 204, 253
Wythe, George (judge), 32–3

Zabel, William D. (ACLU), 221
Ziffert v. *Sylvester* (La.; 1967), 235